Software Merging and Slicing

Software Merging and Slicing

Valdis Berzins

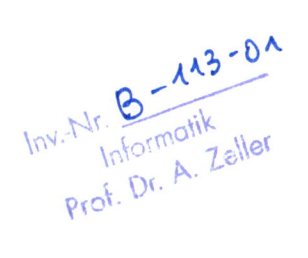

IEEE Computer Society Press
Los Alamitos, California

Washington • Brussels • Tokyo

> **Library of Congress Cataloging-in-Publication Data**
>
> Software merging and slicing / [collected by] Valdis Berzins.
>   p.   cm.
>   Includes bibliographical references.
>   ISBN 0-8186-6792-3
>   1. Software maintenance.   I. Berzins, Valdis Andris.
>   QA76.76.S64S65   1995
>   005.1 ' 6—dc20   95-7313
>   CIP

Published by the
IEEE Computer Society Press
10662 Los Vaqueros Circle
P.O. Box 3014
Los Alamitos, CA 90720-1264

© 1995 by The Institute of Electrical and Electronics Engineers, Inc. All rights reserved.

Copyright and Reprint Permissions: Abstracting is permitted with credit to the source. Libraries are permitted to photocopy beyond the limits of US copyright law, for private use of patrons, those articles in this volume that carry a code at the bottom of the first page, provided that the per-copy fee indicated in the code is paid through the Copyright Clearance Center, 222 Rosewood Drive, Danvers, MA 01923. For other copying, reprint, or republication permission, write to IEEE Copyrights Manager, IEEE Service Center, 445 Hoes Lane, P.O. Box 1331, Piscataway, NJ 08855-1331.

IEEE Computer Society Press Order Number BP06792
IEEE Catalog Number EH0424-2
Library of Congress Number 95-7313
ISBN 0-8186-6792-3

Additional copies can be ordered from

IEEE Computer Society Press	IEEE Service Center	IEEE Computer Society	IEEE Computer Society
Customer Service Center	445 Hoes Lane	13, avenue de l'Aquilon	Ooshima Building
10662 Los Vaqueros Circle	P.O. Box 1331	B-1200 Brussels	2-19-1 Minami-Aoyama
P.O. Box 3014	Piscataway, NJ 08855-1331	BELGIUM	Minato-ku, Tokyo 107
Los Alamitos, CA 90720-1264	Tel: (908) 981-1393	Tel: +32-2-770-2198	JAPAN
Tel: (714) 821-8380	Fax: (908) 981-9667	Fax: +32-2-770-8505	Tel: +81-3-3408-3118
Fax: (714) 821-4641			Fax: +81-3-3408-3553
Email: cs.books@computer.org			

Technical Editor: Carl K. Chang
Copy Editor: David Sims
Production Editor: Lisa O'Conner
Cover Art: Joe Daigle
Printed in the United States of America by KNI, Incorporated

The Institute of Electrical and Electronics Engineers, Inc.

Contents

Preface vii

I. Background: Program Slicing 1

Program Slicing 4
      M. Weiser
      IEEE Transactions on Software Engineering, July 1984

Interprocedural Slicing Using Dependence Graphs 10
      S. Horwitz, T. Reps, and D. Binkley
      ACM Transactions on Programming Languages and Systems, January 1990

Program Slicing for C—The Problems in Implementation 45
      J. Jiang, X. Zhou, and D.J. Robson
      Proceedings 1991 IEEE Conference on Software Maintenance

Dynamic Program Slicing 54
      B. Korel and J. Laski
      Information Processing Letters, October 1988

Dynamic Program Slicing 63
      H. Agrawal and J.R. Horgan
      Proceedings ACM SIGPLAN '90 Conference on Programming Language Design and Implementation, 1990

II. Foundations of Software Merging 75

On Merging Software Extensions 77
      V. Berzins
      Acta Informatica, November 1986

A Theory of Program Modifications 90
      G. Ramalingam and T. Reps
      Proceedings Colloquium on Combining Paradigms for Software Development, LNCS 494, 1991

Software Merge: Semantics of Combining Changes to Programs 106
      V. Berzins
      ACM Transactions on Programming Languages and Systems, November 1994

III. Merging Imperative Programs 135

Integrating Noninterfering Versions of Programs 137
      S. Horwitz, J. Prins, and T. Reps
      ACM Transactions on Programming Languages and Systems, July 1989

Software Merge: Models and Methods for Combining Changes to Programs 180
    V. Berzins
    Journal of Systems Integration, August 1991

IV. Merging for Other Languages 201

A Graph Model for Software Evolution 202
    Luqi
    IEEE Transactions on Software Engineering, August 1990

Automated Merging of Software Prototypes 213
    D.A. Dampier, Luqi, and V. Berzins
    Journal of Systems Integration, February 1994

Bibliography 231

About the Author 233

Preface

Most software development effort is spent on maintaining and enhancing existing software components, rather than developing entirely new systems. Real software systems comprise many related versions that are constantly being updated. As society's reliance on computers matures, we can expect the emphasis on software updates to increase. Despite this trend, much software engineering research and most software development texts have concentrated on methods for building systems from scratch.

This volume collects and organizes a set of papers that describe methods for effectively combining several people's work on updating a software system. It also introduces some theoretical underpinnings of software updates and maintenance. We focus on results from software engineering and programming languages that contribute to two closely related aspects of software development and maintenance: change merging and slicing.

- Merging combines two independent enhancements to the same version of a software system into a new system that includes the semantics of both enhancements. Merging methods provide computer aid for combining the results of several people's separate efforts. Merging also includes applying an enhancement to many related versions of a system, and undoing the effects of a faulty change while preserving effects of later, desirable changes.
- Slicing extracts all the parts of a software system that can affect a variable or output value. Our focus includes slicing because it provides a simple way to certify semantic integrity in software merging. Slicing technology was originally developed to support debugging tools that reduce apparent complexity by showing only the program statements that can affect a faulty output value. Later applications of slicing include reengineering, coordinating concurrent updates to software systems, and software testing.

The papers in this collection describe emerging models and methods to guarantee the semantic integrity of change merging in a variety of contexts. We also address some related issues of controlling software evolution and coordinating teamwork. The common technical basis for this work is a rich set of representations for programs and their meanings, including program dependence graphs (Horwitz, Reps, and Binkley, 1990, reprinted in section I), meaning functions (Linger, Mills, and Witt, 1979, see the Bibliography), semantic lattices (Scott, 1976, see the Bibliography), Boolean algebras (Berzins, 1994, reprinted in section II), Browerian algebras (Ramalingam and Reps, 1991, reprinted in section II), configuration graphs (Luqi, 1990, reprinted in section IV), and others. We describe or cite existing applications of the models and methods surveyed, where approaches are old enough for applications to exist.

This collection shows how formal methods from a broad range of areas could help software maintenance by providing reliable computer aid. It surveys and organizes current results in this new area and assesses the potential for putting the promise of this approach into practice.

Audience

This volume provides an overview of current results and directions in this relatively new area of software engineering. It should be useful to software engineers who want to track emerging trends or who are concerned with developing new and improved computer-aided software engineering tools. Researchers should find it useful as a guide to known results and current problems in the area, and it can be used as a basis for a seminar or graduate course on the subject.

Overview

Program slicing is a supporting technology for change merging. A program slice is a subset of a program whose execution trace is independent of the rest of the program. Weiser (1984) developed the idea of program slicing for debugging and parallel execution. Subsequent applications have included reengineering, pro-active concurrency control for software updates, and regression testing. Several approaches to change merging described in this volume (Horwitz, Prins, Reps, 1989 and Dampier, Luqi, and Berzins, 1994) are based on variations of slicing. We include material on interprocedural slicing and the issues to face when implementing slicing for a commercial language like C, to address scaling up to systems of practical size. We also address dynamic slicing, which uses input data to produce more selective slices and can help reduce intellectual overhead when debugging.

The foundations for software merging are mathematical models of the problem. Berzins (1986) describes the first semantic model of program merging and provides some early methods for merging functional programs. This model combines two programs via least upper bounds in a semantic lattice and covers extensions but not modifications. Ramalingam and Reps (1991) model modifications as transformations on programs and explore some properties of functional modification algebras. Ramalingam formulates the problem of reversing bad changes as the solution of certain equations in these algebras. Berzins (1994) models modifications using Boolean algebras, formalizes and models the idea of semantic conflicts, shows how semantic domains for programming languages can be embedded in such algebras, and explores the relation to Browerian algebra models. This model shows that modifications to different modules of a system can interfere, and it finds conditions under which such modifications can be independently combined.

Change merging for imperative programs is interesting because many practical systems are written in that style. Horwitz, Prins, and Reps (1989) introduce the idea of merging changes to *while-programs* using slicing. Slicing has the advantages of simplicity, safety, and efficiency and the disadvantages of being unable to combine changes that reach the same output or that use different algorithms to compute the same function. Berzins (1991) presents a high-resolution change-merging method based on the program meaning functions, originally introduced by Harlan Mills to simplify program verification. This approach can successfully merge changes to the same output if both changes cannot take effect for the same initial state, and it can accommodate algorithm changes, such as speedup transformations. However, it can also require large amounts of computation and can fail to terminate if not suitably constrained.

Others have explored change merging for other computing paradigms. Luqi (1990) presents a graph model of software evolution that shows how a change-merging facility can be integrated with other kinds of decision support for software evolution, including configuration management, project planning, project scheduling, and teamwork coordination. Dampier, Luqi, and Berzins (1994) introduces a change-merging method for PSDL, a prototyping language with hard real-time constraints and concurrent execution semantics, based on a variant of program slices.

Vision

Since software maintenance accounts for the lion's share of software cost, potential advances in computer-aided software evolution have high leverage. Recombining parts of existing designs and implementations should be much easier than unrestricted program synthesis or modification, making this a relatively tractable part of automated program construction. Consequently, we expect to see growing interest in change merging and the development and practical application of greatly improved methods in the years to come. Merging methods of the future are likely to impact many other subjects, including configuration management, software reuse and customization, inheritance in object-oriented programming languages, and the evolution of database schemas and other data representations.

Acknowledgments

My special thanks go to Professor Luqi for her vision of slicing and merging in software engineering research for the past decade, her persistence that the results must have a practical impact, her effort to communicate to researchers and sponsors, and her initiative on the workshop and technology series on the subject. I would like to thank the participants of the 1993 Army Research Office/Air Force Office of Scientific Research/Office of Naval Research Workshop on Increasing the Practical Impact of Formal Methods for Computer-Aided Software Development: Software Slicing, Merging, and Integration for helping to connect the various advances in this area into a coherent whole. Although it is not possible to mention all the workshop participants individually here, I would like to thank Professor Tom Reps for his strong support to this research area and the workshop, Dr. David Dampier for organizing the workshop, and Dr. David Hislop and the Army Research Office for providing support that made the research and workshop possible.

Valdis Berzins
May 1995

I. Background: Program Slicing

Behavioral projections and slicing

We can get a simplified projection of a program's behavior by ignoring some of its outputs. We can use behavioral projections to decompose a program's semantics into independent parts. A behavioral projection is the part of the behavior of a program visible from a particular vantage point, such as an output variable or output stream. Such projections help us understand complex systems, and Weiser (1982) offers experimental evidence that programmers use them when debugging. Program slicing is a way to materialize behavioral projections: a slice contains all parts of a program that can affect the variables or outputs specified by a given slicing criterion. Slices are concrete syntactic structures that correspond to behavioral projections.

Software updates and merging

Projections and slices are relevant to software updates because slices are semantically self-contained units. A slice can be moved from one context to another without changing the associated behavioral projection, provided that it is still a slice in the new context. We can model software updates as a sequence of steps:

- decompose into disjoint behavioral projection,
- replace some projections with new versions, and
- recombine the new versions with the unaffected components.

We can merge several updates without interference if the affected behavioral projections are disjoint and the affected program parts are slices of the new (as well as previous) versions of the system. Gallagher and Lyle (1991) applied this idea to prevent interactions between concurrent updates.

Reengineering and restructuring

Slices can be useful for extracting modules from monolithic programs because they trace back the computational dependencies for a given output. More sophisticated reengineering applications depend on slicing to detect behavioral equivalences between program fragments: if two programs have the same slice with respect to a slicing criterion, then the corresponding behavioral projections are the same. Griswold (1993) used a similar idea in a code-restructuring tool to ensure that the restructuring transformations do not affect the program's behavior. This tool uses constant-time incremental algorithms for maintaining program dependence graphs that are fast enough for interactive use.

Software reuse

Because a slice's behavior does not vary in contexts where its boundaries are unaffected, we can use slices in software reuse, particularly when we employ mature capabilities for software merging. Eventually, we may be able to customize software by merging slices that represent different aspects of system behavior, choosing from among several alternatives for each aspect.

Software testing

Detecting behavioral equivalences through slicing may also improve regression testing. If a software update does not affect a slice with respect to a given output, then tests to check that output need not be repeated, because the results are guaranteed not to change (Gupta, Harrold, and Soffa, 1992).

Overview of the papers

The first three papers discuss static slicing, the earliest version of the problem to be investigated. Static slicing is relevant to merging and most aspects of software maintenance. The last two papers discuss dynamic slicing, which is primarily relevant to debugging.

In the first paper of this section, Weiser develops the idea of static program slicing for debugging and parallel execution. This seminal paper defines the idea, gives methods for computing both intraprocedural and interprocedural slices, and gives timing figures for a rough implementation of the initial method. In the second paper, Horwitz, Reps, and Binkley improve the accuracy of the interprocedural slicing method by producing smaller slices, explain methods for dealing with recursion and aliasing introduced by reference parameters, and include a careful complexity analysis. A significant result is that slices can be computed within a number of steps that is proportional to the size of the system dependence graph, indicating that slicing is practical even for large systems. In the third paper, Jiang, Zhou, and Robson examine some practical issues in implementing slicing for programming languages such as C, which include arrays, pointers, and unstructured control constructs. These results show that slicing applications are not limited to the simplified languages used in the initial research studies.

The criteria for dynamic slicing includes the initial values of the input variables as well as the result variables at given points in the program. This is useful when a test case revealing a fault is known. Dynamic slices are smaller than static slices because they include only statements actually executed for the given test case. In the fourth paper, Korel and Laski first introduce the idea of a dynamic slice and explain how to construct one. In the last paper, Agrawal and Horgan give a more accurate method for dynamic slicing and explain a refinement that requires less memory space. Experimental evaluation is not available for this method, but in a private communication Agrawal indicates that experiments have been run on nine programs varying in size from 50 to 7,500 lines of C code for another dynamic slicer (Venkatesh 1995). The experiments indicate the execution time overhead imposed by the instrumentation ranges from a factor of 2 to a factor of 25. Ball and Larus (1992) and Choi, Miller, and Netzer (1991) use several optimizations to significantly reduce overhead in earlier studies.

Remaining challenges

Slicing is fairly well developed for classical sequential programs. Current efforts aim at tuning some finer points, such as finding more efficient and more accurate algorithms for handling pointers and aliasing. Researchers have yet to adequately explore the treatment of generic programs, procedural parameters, data structures, persistent storage, abstract data types, inheritance, and parallel programs.

References

Ball, T., and J. Larus, "Optimally profiling and Tracing Programs," *Conf. Record 19th ACM Symp. Principles of Programming Languages,* ACM Press, New York, N.Y., 1992, pp. 59–70.

Choi, J., B. Miller, and R. Netzer, "Techniques for Debugging Parallel Programs with Flowback Analysis," *ACM Trans. Programming Languages and Systems*, Vol. 13, No. 4, Oct. 1991, pp. 491–530.

Gallagher, K., and J. Lyle, "Using Program Slicing in Software Maintenance," *IEEE Trans. Software Eng.,* Vol. 17, No. 8, Aug. 1991, pp. 751–761.

Griswold, W., "Direct Update of Data Flow Representations for a Meaning-Preserving Program Restructuring Tool," *Proc. First ACM SIGSOFT Symp. Foundations of Software Eng.*, Software Eng. Notes, Vol. 18, No. 5, Dec. 1993, pp. 42–55.

Gupta, R., M. Harrold, and M. Soffa, "An Approach to Regression Testing using Slicing," *Proc. 1992 IEEE Conf. Software Maintenance*, IEEE CS Press, Los Alamitos, Calif., 1992, pp. 299–308.

Venkatesh, G., "Experimental Results from Slicing C Programs," to appear in *ACM Trans. Programming Languages and Systems*, Vol. 17, No. 2, Mar. 1995.

Weiser, M., "Programmers Use Slices When Debugging," *Comm. ACM,* Vol. 25, Vol. 7, July 1982, pp. 446–452.

Program Slicing

MARK WEISER

Abstract—Program slicing is a method for automatically decomposing programs by analyzing their data flow and control flow. Starting from a subset of a program's behavior, slicing reduces that program to a minimal form which still produces that behavior. The reduced program, called a "slice," is an independent program guaranteed to represent faithfully the original program within the domain of the specified subset of behavior.

Some properties of slices are presented. In particular, finding *statement-minimal* slices is in general unsolvable, but using data flow analysis is sufficient to find approximate slices. Potential applications include automatic slicing tools for debugging and parallel processing of slices.

Index Terms—Data flow analysis, debugging, human factors, parallel processing, program maintenance, program metrics, slicing, software tools.

INTRODUCTION

LARGE computer programs must be decomposed for understanding and manipulation by people. Not just any decomposition is useful to people, but some—such as decomposition into procedures and abstract data types—are very useful. Program slicing is a decomposition based on data flow and control flow analysis.

A useful program decomposition must provide pieces with predictable properties. For instance, block-structured languages [17] are powerful in part because their scope and control flow rules permit understanding procedures independent of context. Similarly, abstract data type languages [12], [15], [25] make further control and scope restrictions for even greater context independence. Therefore, the pieces of a program decomposed by dataflow, i.e., the "slices," should be related to one another and the original program in well defined and predictable ways.

As we will see, slices have a very clear semantics based on projections of behavior from the program being decomposed. Unlike procedures and data abstractions, slices are designed to be found automatically after a program is coded. Their usefulness shows up in testing, parallel processor distribution, maintenance, and especially debugging. A previous study showed experienced programmers mentally slicing while debugging, based on an informal definition of slice [22]. Our concern here is with 1) a formal definition of slices and their abstract properties, 2) a practical algorithm for slicing, and 3) some experience slicing real programs.

Manuscript received August 27, 1982; revised June 28, 1983. This work was supported in part by the National Science Foundation under Grant MCS-80-18294 and by the U.S. Air Force Office of Scientific Research under Grant F49620-80-C-001. A previous version of this paper was presented at the 5th International Conference on Software Engineering, San Diego, CA, 1981.

The author is with the Department of Computer Science, University of Maryland, College Park, MD 20742.

DEFINITIONS

This section considers programs without procedure calls. Procedures are discussed later. The first few definitions review the standard definitions of digraph, flowgraph, and computation in terms of state trajectory. Finally, a slice is defined as preserving certain projections from state trajectories.

The next few definitions simply establish a terminology for graphs, and restrict attention to programs whose control structure is single-entry single-exit ("hammock graphs").

Definition: A *digraph* is a structure $\langle N, E \rangle$, where N is a set of nodes and E is a set of edges in $N \times N$. If (n, m) is in E, then n is an *immediate predecessor* of m and m is an *immediate successor* of n. A *path* from n to m of length k is a list of nodes $p_0, p_1, \cdots, p_k$ such that $p_0 = n$, $p_k = m$, and for all i, $1 \leq i \leq k - 1$, (p_i, p_{i+1}) is in E.

Definition: A *flowgraph* is a structure $\langle N, E, n_0 \rangle$, where $\langle N, E \rangle$ is a digraph and n_0 is a member of N such that there is a path from n_0 to all other nodes in N. n_0 is sometimes called the initial node. If m and n are two nodes in N, m *dominates* n if m is on every path from n_0 to n.

Definition: A *hammock graph* is a structure $\langle N, E, n_0, n_e \rangle$ with the property that $\langle N, E, n_0 \rangle$ and $\langle N, E^{-1}, n_e \rangle$ are both flowgraphs. Note that, as usual, $E^{-1} = \{(a, b) | (b, a) \text{ is in } E\}$. If m and n are two nodes in N, m *inverse dominates* n if m is on every path from n to n_e.

In the remainder of the paper, all flowgraphs will be assumed to be hammock graphs. In addition to its flowgraph, every program is assumed to provide the following information.

Definition: Let V be the set of variable names which appear in a program P. Then for each statement n in P (i.e., node in the flowgraph of P) we have the following two sets, each a subset of V: $REF(n)$ is the set of variables whose values are used at n, and $DEF(n)$ is the set of variables whose values are changed at n.

A state trajectory of a program is just a trace of its execution which snapshots all the variable values just before executing each statement.

Definition: A *state trajectory* of length k of a program P is a finite list of ordered pairs

$$(n_1, s_1)(n_2, s_2) \cdots (n_k, s_k)$$

where each n is in N (the set of nodes in P) and each s is a function mapping the variables in V to their values. Each (n, s) gives the values of V immediately before the execution of n. Our attention will be on programs which halt, so infinite state trajectories are specifically excluded.

Slices reproduce a projection from the behavior of the original program. This projection must be the values of certain variables as seen at certain statements.

```
The original program:
  1     BEGIN
  2       READ(X,Y)
  3       TOTAL := 0.0
  4       SUM := 0.0
  5       IF X <= 1
  6         THEN SUM := Y
  7         ELSE BEGIN
  8           READ(Z)
  9           TOTAL := X*Y
 10           END
 11       WRITE(TOTAL,SUM)
 12     END.
Slice on criterion <12,{Z}>.
        BEGIN
          READ(X,Y)
          IF X <= 1
            THEN
            ELSE READ(Z)
          END.
Slice on criterion <9,{X}>.
        BEGIN
          READ(X,Y)
          END.
Slice on criterion <12,{TOTAL}>.
        BEGIN
          READ(X,Y)
          TOTAL := 0.0
          IF X <= 1
            THEN
            ELSE TOTAL := X*Y
          END.
```

Fig. 1. Examples of slices.

Definition: A *slicing criterion* of a program P is a tuple $\langle i, V \rangle$, where i is a statement in P and V is a subset of the variables in P.

A slicing criterion $C = \langle i, V \rangle$ determines a projection function Proj_C which throws out of the state trajectory all ordered pairs except those starting with i, and from the remaining pairs throws out everything except values of variables in V.

Definition: Let $T = (t_1, t_2, \cdots, t_n)$ be a state trajectory, n any node in N and s any function from variable names to values. Then

$$\text{Proj}'_{\langle i, V \rangle}((n,s)) = \begin{cases} \lambda & \text{if } n \neq i \\ (n, s|V) & \text{if } n = i \end{cases}$$

where $s|V$ is s restricted to domain V, and λ is the empty string. Proj' is now extended to entire trajectories:

$$\text{Proj}_{\langle i, V \rangle}(T) = \text{Proj}'_{\langle i, V \rangle}(t_1) \cdots \text{Proj}'_{\langle i, V \rangle}(t_n).$$

A slice is now defined behaviorally as any subset of a program which preserves a specified projection of its behavior.

Definition: A slice S of a program P on a slicing criterion $C = \langle i, V \rangle$ is any executable program with the following two properties.

1) S can be obtained from P by deleting zero or more statements from P.

2) Whenever P halts[1] on an input I with state trajectory T, then S also halts on input I with state trajectory T', and $\text{Proj}_C(T) = \text{Proj}_{C'}(T')$, where $C' = \langle \text{succ}(i), V \rangle$, and $\text{succ}(i)$ is the nearest successor to i in the original program which is also in the slice, or i itself if i is in the slice.

There can be many different slices for a given program and slicing criterion. There is always at least one slice for a given slicing criterion—the program itself. Fig. 1 gives some examples of slices.

Finding Slices

The above definition of a slice does not say how to find one. The smaller the slice the better, but the following argument shows that finding minimal slices is equivalent to solving the halting problem—it is impossible.

Definition: Let C be a slicing criterion on a program P. A slice S of P on C is *statement-minimal* if no other slice of P on C has fewer statements than S.

Theorem: There does not exist an algorithm to find statement-minimal slices for arbitrary programs.

Informal Proof: Consider the following program fragment:

```
1 read (X)
2 if (X)
      then
        ...
      perform any function not involving x here
        ...
3     X := 1
4 else X := 2 endif
5 write (X)
```

Imagine slicing on the value of x at line 5. An algorithm to find a statement-minimal slice would include line 3 if and only if the function before line 3 did halt. Thus such an algorithm could determine if an arbitrary program could halt, which is impossible.

A similar argument demonstrates that statement-minimal slices are not unique.

More interesting are slices that *can* be found. Data flow analysis can be used to construct conservative slices, guaranteed to have the slice properties but with possibly too many statements. The remainder of this section outlines how this is done. To avoid repetition, an arbitrary program P with nodes N and variables V is assumed.

In general, for each statement in P there will be some set of variables whose values can affect a variable observable at the slicing criterion. For instance, if the statement

$$Y := X$$

is followed by the statement

$$Z := Y$$

then the value of X before the first statement can affect the value of Z after the second statement. X is said to be directly "relevant" to the slice at statement n. (See Fig. 2.) The set of all such relevant variables is denoted R_C^0, and defined below.

---

[1] Extending this definition of slice to inputs on which the original program does not halt causes many new problems. For example, the proof of Theorem 1 below demonstrates that there is no way to guarantee that a slice will fail to halt whenever the original program fails to halt.

```
(from definition of $R_C^0$):
    1       Y := X
    2       A := B
    3       Z := Y
```

$R_{\langle 3,\{Y\}\rangle}^0(3) = \{Y\}$ by rule 1.

$R_{\langle 3,\{Y\}\rangle}^0(2) = \{Y\}$ by rule 2b.

$R_{\langle 3,\{Y\}\rangle}^0(1) = \{X\}$ by rule 2a.

Fig. 2. Definition of direct influence.

The superscript 0 indicates how indirect the relevance is; higher valued superscripts are defined later.

Definition: Let $C = \langle i, V \rangle$ be a slicing criterion. Then

$R_C^0(n)$ = all variables v such that either:
1. $n = i$ and v is in V,

or
2. n is an immediate predecessor of a node m such that either:
   a) v is in REF(n) and there is a w in both DEF(n) and $R_C^0(m)$,
   or
   b) v is not in DEF(n) and v is in $R_C^0(m)$.

The reader can check that the recursion is over the length of paths to reach node i, where (1) is the base case. Case (2a) says that if w is a relevant variable at the node following n and w is given a new value at n, then w is no longer relevant and all the variables used to define w's value are relevant. Case (2b) says that if a relevant variable at the next node is not given a value at node n, then it is still relevant at node n. This is a simplification of the usual data flow information which would use a PRE set to represent preservation of variable values.

The author has previously proved [20] that the computation of R_C^0 can be imbedded in a fast monotone information propagation space [11], and so can be computed in time $O(e \log e)$ for arbitrary programs and time $O(e)$ for structured programs where e is the number of edges in the flowgraph.

The statements included in the slice by R_C^0 are denoted S_C^0. S_C^0 is defined by

S_C^0 = all nodes n s.t. $R_C^0(n+1) \cap \text{DEF}(n) \neq \phi$.

Note that R_C^0 is a function mapping statements to sets of variables, but S_C^0 is just a set of statements.

S_C^0 does not include indirect effects on the slicing criterion, and therefore is a sufficient but not necessary condition for including statements in the slice. For instance, in the following program statement 2 obviously has an affect on the value of Z at statement 5, yet 2 is not in $S_{\langle 5,\{Z\}\rangle}^0$.

```
1    READ (X)
2    IF X < 1
3         THEN Z := 1
4         ELSE Z := 2
5    WRITE (Z).
```

Generally any branch statement which can choose to execute or not execute some statement in S_C^0 should also be in the slice. Denning and Denning [8] use the nearest inverse dominator of a branch to define its range of influence.

Definition: INFL(b) is the set of statements which are on a path P from b to its nearest inverse dominator d, excluding the endpoints of P.

INFL(b) will be empty unless b has more than one immediate successor (i.e., is a branch statement).

INFL allows the following definition of branch statements with indirect relevance to a slice.

Definition:

$$B_C^0 = \bigcup_{n \in S_C^0} \text{INFL}(n).$$

To include *all* indirect influences, the statements with direct influence on B_C^0 must now be considered, and then the branch statements influencing those new statements, etc. The full definition of the influence at level n is the following.

Definition: For all $i \geq 0$:

$$R_C^{i+1}(n) = R_C^i(n) \bigcup_{b \in B_C^i} R_{BC(b)}^0(n)$$

$$B_C^{i+1} = \bigcup_{n \in S_C^{i+1}} \text{INFL}(n)$$

S_C^{i+1} = all nodes n s.t.
$\quad n \in B_C^i$
or $R_C^{i+1}(n+1) \cap \text{DEF}(n) \neq \phi$

where $BC(b)$ is the branch statement criterion, defined as $\langle b, \text{REF}(b) \rangle$.

Considered as a function of i for fixed n and C, R_C^i and S_C^i define nondecreasing subsets and are bounded above by the set of program variables and set of program statements, respectively. Therefore, each has a least fixed point denoted R_C and S_C, respectively.

It is easy to see that S_C and R_C have the following combining property:

$S_{\langle i,A\rangle} \cup S_{\langle i,B\rangle} = S_{\langle i,A \cup B\rangle}$

$R_{\langle i,A\rangle} \cup R_{\langle i,B\rangle} = R_{\langle i,A \cup B\rangle}$.

An upper bound on the complexity of computing S is estimated as follows: each computation of S_C^{i+1} from S_C^i requires an initial $O(e \log e)$ step to compute R. Followed by a computation of B_C^{i+1}. Finding B_C^{i+1} is primarily finding dominators, an almost linear task [14]. Hence each step takes $O(e \log e)$ time. Since one statement must be added each iteration, the total number of steps is at most n. Hence the total complexity is $O(n\, e \log e)$. This bound is probably not tight, since practical times seem much faster.

S_C is not always the "smallest" slice which can found using only dataflow analysis. Fig. 3 gives a counter example. However, the author has proven that only anomalous cases like Fig. 3 will make S give a less than data flow smallest slice [20].

```
1    A := constant
2    WHILE P(k) DO
3       IF Q(C) THEN BEGIN
4          B := A
5          X := 1
           END
        ELSE BEGIN
6          C := B
7          Y := 2
           END
8       K := K + 1
        END
9    Z := X + Y
10   WRITE(Z)

Slicing criterion C = <10,{Z}>.
```

Fig. 3. A special case for data flow slicing. Statement 1 will be in S_C, but cannot affect the values of Z at statement 10. It cannot because any path by which A at 1 can influence C at 3 will also execute both statements 5 and 7, resulting in a constant value for Z at line 10. Hence, statement 1 can have no effect on the value of Z at 10, and should not be in the slice. Note that this argument is not semantic, but requires knowledge only of the flowgraph, REF, and DEF sets for each statement.

INTERPROCEDURAL SLICING

If a slice originates in a procedure which calls or is called by other procedures, then the slice may need to preserve statements in the calling or called procedures. Our method of slicing across procedure boundaries requires two steps. First, a single slice is made of the procedure P containing the slicing criterion. Summary data flow information about calls to other procedures is used [5], but no attempt is made to slice the other procedures. In the second step slicing criteria are generated for each procedure calling or called by P. Steps one and two are then repeated for each of these new slicing criteria. The process stops when no new slicing criteria are seen, and this must happen eventually since a program has only a finite number of slicing criteria.

The generation of new criteria is straightforward. In each case (caller or callee) the hard work is translating the set of variables computed by R_C into the scope of the new procedure. Suppose procedure P is being sliced, and P has a call at statement i to procedure Q. The criterion for extending the slice to Q is

$$\langle n_e^Q, \text{ROUT}(i)_{F \to A} \cap \text{SCOPE}_Q \rangle$$

where n_e^Q is the last statement in Q, $F \to A$ means substitute formal for actual parameters, SCOPE_Q is the set of variables accessible from the scope of Q, and

$$\text{ROUT}(i) = \bigcup_{j \in \text{Succ}(i)} R_C(j).$$

Alternatively, again suppose P is being sliced, and now suppose P is called at statement i from procedure Q. The new criterion is then

$$\langle i, R_C(f_P)_{A \to F} \cap \text{SCOPE}_Q \rangle$$

where f_P is the first statement in P, $A \to F$ means substitute actual for formal parameters, and SCOPE_Q is as before.

For each criterion C for a procedure P, there is a set of criteria

```
1    READ(A,B)
2    CALL Q(A,B)
3    Z := A + B

     PROCEDURE Q(VAR X,Y : INTEGER)
4    X := 0
5    Y := X + 3
6    RETURN

DOWN(<3,{Z}>) = {<6,{X,Y}>}
UP(<4,{Y}>) = {<2,{B}>}
```
Fig. 4. Extending slices to called and calling routines.

$\text{UP}_0(C)$ which are those needed to slice callers of P, and a set of criteria $\text{DOWN}_0(C)$ which are those needed to slice procedures called by P. $\text{UP}_0(C)$ and $\text{DOWN}_0(C)$ are computed by the methods outlined above (see Fig. 4). UP_0 and DOWN_0 can be extended to functions UP and DOWN which map sets of criteria into sets of criteria. Let CC be any set of criteria. Then

$$\text{UP}(CC) = \bigcup_{C \in CC} \text{UP}_0(C)$$

$$\text{DOWN}(CC) = \bigcup_{C \in CC} \text{DOWN}_0(C).$$

The union and transitive closure of UP and DOWN are defined in the usual way for relations. $(\text{UP} \cup \text{DOWN})^*$ will map any set of criteria into all those criteria necessary to complete the corresponding slices through all calling and called routines. The complete interprocedural slice for a criterion C is then just the union of the intraprocedural slices for each criterion in $(\text{UP} \cup \text{DOWN})^*(C)$.

This algorithm could possibly be improved by using the properties of slices mentioned above. For instance, before slicing on a criterion $\langle a, v \rangle$, the list of criteria could be checked to see if there were already criteria $\langle a, v1 \rangle$, $\langle a, v2 \rangle$ such that $v1$ union $v2 = v$. Other improvements in speed at the expense of accuracy and memory might make use of the value of R from previous slices to avoid recomputing slices. This seems to have the potential for eliminating quite a bit of slicing work, at the expense of remembering the value of R for all slices.

No speed-up tricks have been implemented in a current slicer. It remains to be seen if slow slicing speeds will compel the use of speed-up heuristics.

SEPARATE COMPILATION

Slicing a program which calls external procedures or which can be called externally creates special problems for computing slices. Assuming the actual external code is unavailable, worst case assumptions must be made. First, calls on external routines must be assumed to both reference and change any external variable. This worst case assumption ensures that slices are at least as large as necessary.

The worst case assumption for procedures called externally (sometimes called "entry" procedures) is that the calling program calls them in every possible order, and between each call references and changes all variables used as parameters and all external variables. The worst case assumption therefore implies a certain data flow between entry procedures. As with called and calling procedures, this data flow causes a slice for one entry procedure to generate slicing criteria for other entry procedures.

Let ENT_0 be a function which maps a criterion into the set of criteria possible under the above worst case assumption. Specifically, $\text{ENT}_0(C)$ is empty unless C is a criterion for an entry procedure P, in which case ENT_0 is computed as follows: let n_0 be the unique initial statement in P, let EE be the set of all entry procedures, let OUT be the set of all external variables, and for each E in EE let n_e^E be the unique final statement in E and F^E be the set of ref parameters to E. Then

$$\text{ENT}_0(C) = \{\langle n_e^E, R_C(i) \cup OUT \cup F^E \rangle | \text{for all } E \text{ in } EE\}.$$

ENT_0 can be extended to a function ENT which maps sets of criteria into sets of criteria in the same manner as UP and DOWN.

Of course, it is now a simple matter to include the entry criteria in the interprocedural slicing algorithm. $(\text{UP} \cup \text{DOWN} \cup \text{ENT})^*(C)$ is the total set of criteria needed to slice from an initial criterion C. Notice that computing this set requires slicing the program.

A Sampling of Slices

Program slicers have been built at the University of Maryland for several different languages, including Fortran and the abstract data type language Simpl-D [9]. To look at typical slices of programs larger than toy examples, slices were made of the 19 load-and-go compilers used in the Basili and Reiter study [6]. These compilers were student projects, written by both individuals and teams, between 500 and 900 executable statements long, with between 20 and 80 subroutines.

The compilers were sliced as follows. For each write statement i which output the values of a set of variables V, a slice was taken on the criterion $\langle i, V \rangle$. Slices that differed by less than 30 statements were then merged into a new slightly larger slice. Merging continued until all slices differed by at least 30 statements.

Slicing was done automatically by a system using an abstract data type for flow analysis [23]. Finding all the output related slices for all compilers took approximately 36 hours of CPU time on a VAX-11/780.[2]

Some basic statistics about the slices are shown in Table I.

Useless:	Number of statements not in any slice.
Common:	Number of statements in all slices.
Slices:	Number of slices per program (this is also the number of output statements).
Clusters:	Number of slices after merging slices with less than 30 statements difference.
Contig:	Length of a run of contiguous statements in a cluster which were contiguous in the original program.
% Size:	Size of cluster as a percentage of total program size, as measured by counting statements.
% Unique:	Number of cluster statements which are in *no* other cluster, expressed as a percentage of cluster size.
% Overlap:	Pairwise sharing of statements between clusters, expressed as a percentage of cluster size.

[2]The slicer was compiled by an early compiler which generated particularly bad object code. A better compiler could probably cut the slicing time by a factor of 10.

TABLE I
STATISTICS ON SLICES

Measure	Mean	Median	Min	Max
Per program measures $N = 19$				
Useless	9.16	6	1	23
Common	14.32	0	0	86
Slices	37.26	32	7	74
Clusters	9.74	7	3	25
Per cluster measures $N = 185$				
Contig	11.78	9.10	0	65.4
% Size	44	40	0	97
% Unique	6	1	0	100
% Overlap	52	51	0	93

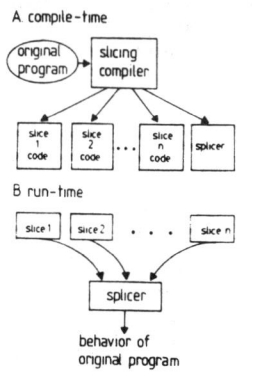

Fig. 5. Parallel execution of slices.

The useless statements were usually either subroutine stubs which immediately returned or loops which computed statistics never written out. The number of statements in a contiguous run is a measure of the scattering of slices through the code. The average of 11.8 shows that components of the original program show up fairly often in slices. The low uniqueness of slices reflects the high degree of interrelatedness of compilers, as does the pairwise overlap.

Parallel Execution of Slices

Because slices execute independently they are suitable for parallel execution on multiprocessors without synchronization or shared memory. Each slice will produce its projection of the final behavior, and one or more "splicing" programs will fit these projections back together into the original program's total behavior (see Fig. 5).

Splicers work in real time (i.e., produce immediate output for every input without delay), so introduce only communications overhead. Splicers require occasional additional output from each slice, and use knowledge of the path expressions corresponding to each slice to properly piece together the slices' output. Splicers can be cascaded, with a few splicers merging the slice output and then a splicer merging splicer output. Details on splicers are described elsewhere [24].

Slices avoid the need for shared memory or synchronization by duplicating in each slice any computation needed by that slice. Although total CPU cycles among all processors are wasted this way, the time to receive an answer is not delayed.

If no computation was duplicated, processors could not proceed until some other processor produced needed immediate results.

Parallel execution of slices might be particularly appropriate for distributed systems, where shared memory is impossible and synchronization requires excessive handshaking. The one way flow of data from slices to splicers mean interprocessor communication is a tree, simplifying VLSI multiprocessor design for parallel execution of slices.

Previous Work

Isolating portions of programs according to their behavior has has been discussed previously. Schwartz [18] hints at such a possibility for a debugging system. Brown and Johnson [7] describe a database for Fortran programs which, through a succession of questions, could be made to reveal the slices of a program although very slowly. Several on-line debuggers permit a limited traceback of the location of variable references (e.g., Aygun [37]), and this information is a kind of "dynamic slice."

Slicing is a source-to-source transformation of a program. Previous work in program transformation has concentrated on preserving program correctness while improving some desirable property of programs. Baker [4] and Ashcroft and Manna [2] try to add "good structure" to programs. Wegbreit [19], Arsac [1], Gerhart [10], and Loveman [16] try to improve program performance. King [13] suggests using input domain restrictions to eliminate statements from a program. This is close in spirit to slicing, which uses projections from the output domain to eliminate statements.

Future Directions

The power of slices comes from four facts: 1) they can be found *automatically*, 2) slices are generally *smaller* than the program from which they originated, 3) they execute *independently* of one another, and 4) each *reproduces exactly* a projection of the original program's behavior. The independence of slices suggests their use in loosely coupled multiprocessors. The simple relationship between a slice's semantics and the original program's semantics makes slices useful for decomposing any semantical operation, such as program verification or testing. The automatic nature of slicing and its data flow origin suggest basing program complexity metrics on slices. Finally, the small size of slices means people may find them directly understandable and useful.

The problems with slices are: 1) they can be expensive to find, 2) a program may have no significant slices, and 3) their total independence may cause additional complexity in each slice that could be cleaned up if simple dependencies could be represented. However, large classes of programs have significant, easy to find, and revealing slices.

Acknowledgment

B. Rounds encouraged the initial formalization of these ideas. B. Riddle guided the initial application of slicing to real problems.

References

[1] J. J. Arsac, "Syntactic source to source transformations and program manipulation," *Commun. ACM*, vol. 22, pp. 43-53, Jan. 1979.

[2] E. A. Ashcroft and Z. Manna, *The Translation of Goto Programs into While Programs*. Amsterdam, The Netherlands: North-Holland, 1973. Information Processing 71.

[3] B. O. Aygun, "Dynamic analysis of execution–possibilities, techniques, and problems," Ph.D. dissertation, Comput. Sci., Dep. Carnegie-Mellon Univ., Tech Rep. CMU-083, Sept. 1973.

[4] B. Baker, "An algorithm for structuring flowgraphs," *J. Ass. Comput. Mach.*, vol. 24, pp. 98-120, Jan. 1977.

[5] J. M. Barth, "A practical interprocedural dataflow analysis algorithm," *Commun. Ass. Comput. Mach.*, vol. 21, pp. 724-736, Sept. 1978.

[6] V. R. Basili and R. W. Reiter, "An investigation of human factors in software development," *Comput.*, vol. 12, pp. 21-38, Dec. 1979.

[7] J. C. Browne and D. B. Johnson, "FAST: A second generation program analysis system," in *Proc. Third Int. Conf. Software Eng.*, pp. 142-148, May 1978. IEEE Catalog 78CH1317-7C.

[8] D. E. Denning and P. J. Denning, "Certification of programs for secure information flow," *Commun. Ass. Comput. Mach.*, vol. 20, pp. 504-513, July 1977.

[9] J. D. Gannon and J. Rosenberg, "Implementing data abstraction features in a stack-based language," *Software-Practice and Experience 9*, pp. 547-560, 1979.

[10] S. Gerhart, "Correctness preserving program transformations," in *Proc. ACM Second Conf. Principles of Programming Languages*, pp. 54-66, Jan. 1975.

[11] S. L. Graham and M. Wegman, "A fast and usually linear algorithm for global flow analysis," *J. Ass. Comput. Mach.*, vol. 23, pp. 172-202, Jan. 1976.

[12] J. D. Ichbiah *et al.*, "Preliminary Ada reference manual and rationale," *Sigplan Notices*, vol. 14, no. 6, 1979.

[13] J. King, "Program reduction using symbolic evaluation," *ACM SIGSOFT, Software Engineering Notes 6*, Jan. 1, 1981.

[14] T. Lengauer and R. E. Tarjan, "A fast algorithm for finding dominators in a flowgraph," *ACM Trans. Programming Languages and Systems*, vol. 1, pp. 121-141, July 1979.

[15] B. Liskov, A. Snyder, R. Atkinson, and C. Schaffert, "Abstraction mechanisms in CLU," *Commun. ACM*, vol. 20, pp. 564-576, Aug. 1977.

[16] D. B. Loveman, "Program improvement by source to source transformation," *J. Ass. Comput. Mach.*, vol. 24, pp. 121-145, Jan. 1977.

[17] T. W. Pratt, *Programming Languages: Design and Implementation*. Englewood Cliffs, NJ: Prentice-Hall, 1975.

[18] J. T. Schwartz, "An overview of bugs," in *Debugging Techniques in Large Systems*, R. Rustin, Ed. Englewood Cliffs, NJ: Prentice-Hall, 1971.

[19] B. Wegbreit, "Goal-directed program transformation," *IEEE Trans. Software Eng.*, vol. SE-2, pp. 69-80, June 1976.

[20] M. Weiser, "Program slices: Formal, psychological, and practical investigations of an automatic program abstraction method," Ph.D. dissertation, Univ. Michigan, Ann Arbor, MI, 1979.

[21] —, "Program slicing," in *Proc. Fifth Int. Conf. Software Eng.*, San Diego, CA, Mar. 1981.

[22] —, "Programmers use slices when debugging," *Commun. ACM*, vol. 25, pp. 446-452, July, 1982.

[23] —, "Experience with a data flow datatype," *J. Comput. Languages*, to be published, 1983.

[24] —, "Reconstructing sequential behavior from parallel behavior projections," *Inform. Processing Lett.*, vol. 17, pp. 129-135, Oct. 5, 1983.

[25] W. A. Wulf, R. L. London, and M. Shaw, "An introduction to the construction and verification of Alphard programs," *IEEE Trans. Software Eng.*, vol. 2, no. 4, pp. 253-265, 1976.

Interprocedural Slicing Using Dependence Graphs

SUSAN HORWITZ, THOMAS REPS, and DAVID BINKLEY
University of Wisconsin–Madison

The notion of a *program slice*, originally introduced by Mark Weiser, is useful in program debugging, automatic parallelization, and program integration. A slice of a program is taken with respect to a program point p and a variable x; the slice consists of all statements of the program that might affect the value of x at point p. This paper concerns the problem of interprocedural slicing—generating a slice of an entire program, where the slice crosses the boundaries of procedure calls. To solve this problem, we introduce a new kind of graph to represent programs, called a *system dependence graph*, which extends previous dependence representations to incorporate collections of procedures (with procedure calls) rather than just monolithic programs. Our main result is an algorithm for interprocedural slicing that uses the new representation. (It should be noted that our work concerns a somewhat restricted kind of slice: rather than permitting a program to be sliced with respect to program point p and an *arbitrary* variable, a slice must be taken with respect to a variable that is *defined* or *used* at p.)

The chief difficulty in interprocedural slicing is correctly accounting for the calling context of a called procedure. To handle this problem, system dependence graphs include some data dependence edges that represent *transitive* dependences due to the effects of procedure calls, in addition to the conventional direct-dependence edges. These edges are constructed with the aid of an auxiliary structure that represents calling and parameter-linkage relationships. This structure takes the form of an attribute grammar. The step of computing the required transitive-dependence edges is reduced to the construction of the subordinate characteristic graphs for the grammar's nonterminals.

Categories and Subject Descriptors: D.3.3 [**Programming Languages**]: Language Constructs—*control structures, procedures, functions, and subroutines*; D.3.4 [**Programming Languages**]: Processors—*compilers, optimization*

General Terms: Algorithms, Design

Additional Key Words and Phrases: Attribute grammar, control dependence, data dependence, data-flow analysis, flow-insensitive summary information, program debugging, program dependence graph, program integration, program slicing, subordinate characteristic graph

---

An earlier version of this paper appeared in abridged form in the *Proceedings of the ACM SIGPLAN 88 Conference on Programming Language Design and Implementation*, (Atlanta, Ga., June 22–24, 1988), *ACM SIGPLAN Not. 23*, 7 (July 1988) [10].
This work was supported in part by a David and Lucile Packard Fellowship for Science and Engineering, by the National Science Foundation under grants DCR-8552602, DCR-8603356, and CCR-8958530, by the Defense Advanced Research Projects Agency, monitored by the Office of Naval Research under contract N00014-88-K-0590, as well as by grants from IBM, DEC, and Xerox.
Authors' address: Computer Sciences Department, University of Wisconsin–Madison, 1210 W. Dayton St., Madison, WI 53706.
Permission to copy without fee all or part of this material is granted provided that the copies are not made or distributed for direct commercial advantage, the ACM copyright notice and the title of the publication and its date appear, and notice is given that copying is by permission of the Association for Computing Machinery. To copy otherwise, or to republish, requires a fee and/or specific permission.

"Interprocedural Slicing Using Dependence Graphs" by S. Horwitz, T. Reps, and D. Binkley from *ACM Trans. Programming Languages and Systems*, Vol. 12, No. 1, Jan. 1990, pp. 26–60. Copyright 1990, Association for Computing Machinery, Inc., reprinted with permission.

1. INTRODUCTION

The *slice* of a program with respect to program point p and variable x consists of all statements and predicates of the program that might affect the value of x at point p. This concept, originally discussed by Mark Weiser in [22], can be used to isolate individual computation threads within a program. Slicing can help a programmer understand complicated code, can aid in debugging [17], and can be used for automatic parallelization [3, 21]. Program slicing is also used by the algorithm for automatically integrating program variants described in [11]; slices are used to compute a safe approximation to the change in behavior between a program P and a modified version of P, and to help determine whether two different modifications to P interfere.

In Weiser's terminology, a *slicing criterion* is a pair $\langle p, V \rangle$, where p is a program point and V is a subset of the program's variables. In his work, a slice consists of all statements and predicates of the program that might affect the values of variables in V at point p. This is a more general kind of slice than is often needed: rather than a slice taken with respect to program point p and an *arbitrary* variable, one is often interested in a slice taken with respect to a variable x that is *defined* or *used* at p. The value of a variable x defined at p is directly affected by the values of the variables used at p and by the loops and conditionals that enclose p. The value of a variable y *used* at p is directly affected by assignments to y that reach p and by the loops and conditionals that enclose p. When slicing a program that consists of a single monolithic procedure (which we will call in*tra*procedural slicing), a slice can be determined from the closure of the directly-affects relation. Ottenstein and Ottenstein pointed out how well suited *program dependence graphs* are for this kind of slicing [19]; once a program is represented by its program dependence graph, the slicing problem is simply a vertex-reachability problem, and thus slices may be computed in linear time.

This paper concerns the problem of in*ter*procedural slicing—generating a slice of an entire program, where the slice crosses the boundaries of procedure calls. Our algorithm for interprocedural slicing produces a more precise answer than that produced by the algorithm given by Weiser in [22]. Our work follows the example of Ottenstein and Ottenstein by defining the slicing algorithm in terms of operations on a dependence graph representation of programs [19]; however, in [19] Ottenstein and Ottenstein only discuss the case of programs that consist of a single monolithic procedure, and do not discuss the more general case where slices cross procedure boundaries.

To solve the interprocedural-slicing problem, we introduce a new kind of graph to represent programs, called a *system dependence graph*, which extends previous dependence representations to incorporate collections of procedures (with procedure calls) rather than just monolithic programs. Our main result is an algorithm for interprocedural slicing that uses the new representation.

It is important to understand the distinction between two different but related "slicing problems:"

Version 1. The slice of a program with respect to program point p and variable x consists of all statements and predicates of the program that might affect the value of x at point p.

Version 2. The slice of a program with respect to program point p and variable x consists of a reduced program that computes the same sequence of values for x at p. That is, at point p the behavior of the reduced program with respect to variable x is indistinguishable from that of the original program.

For in*tra*procedural slicing, a solution to Version 1 provides a solution to Version 2, since the "reduced program" required in Version 2 can be obtained by restricting the original program to just the statements and predicates found in the solution for Version 1 [20].

For in*ter*procedural slicing, restricting the original program to just the statements and predicates found for Version 1 may yield a program that is syntactically incorrect (and thus certainly not a solution to Version 2). The reason behind this phenomenon has to do with multiple calls to the same procedure: it is possible that the program elements found by an algorithm for Version 1 will include more than one such call, each passing a different subset of the procedure's parameters. (It should be noted that, although it is imprecise, Weiser's algorithm produces a solution to Version 2.)

In this paper we address Version 1 of the interprocedural slicing problem (with the further restriction, mentioned earlier, that a slice can only be taken with respect to program point p and variable x if x is defined or used at p). The algorithm given in the paper identifies a subgraph of the system dependence graph whose components might affect the sequence of values for x at p. A solution to Version 2 requires either that the slice be extended or that it be transformed by duplicating code to specialize procedure bodies for particular parameter-usage patterns.

Weiser's method for interprocedural slicing is described in [22] as follows:

> For each criterion C for a procedure P, there is a set of criteria $UP_0(C)$ which are those needed to slice callers of P, and a set of criteria $DOWN_0(C)$ which are those needed to slice procedures called by P. ... $UP_0(C)$ and $DOWN_0(C)$ can be extended to functions UP and DOWN which map sets of criteria into sets of criteria. Let CC be any set of criteria. Then
>
> $$UP(CC) = \bigcup_{C \in CC} UP_0(C)$$
> $$DOWN(CC) = \bigcup_{C \in CC} DOWN_0(C)$$
>
> The union and transitive closure of UP and DOWN are defined in the usual way for relations. $(UP \cup DOWN)^*$ will map any set of criteria into all those criteria necessary to complete the corresponding slices through all calling and called routines. The complete interprocedural slice for a criterion C is then just the union of the intraprocedural slices for each criterion in $(UP \cup DOWN)^*(C)$.

However, this method does not produce as precise a slice as possible because the transitive-closure operation fails to account for the calling context of a called procedure.[1]

---

[1] For example, the relation $(UP \cup DOWN)^*(\langle p, V \rangle)$ includes the relation $UP(DOWN(\langle p, V \rangle))$. $UP(DOWN(\langle p, V \rangle))$ includes all call sites that call procedures containing the program points in $DOWN(\langle p, V \rangle)$, not just the procedure that contains p. This fails to account for the calling context, namely the procedure that contains p.

Example. To illustrate this problem, and the shortcomings of Weiser's algorithm, consider the following example program, which sums the integers from 1 to 10. (Except in Section 4.3, where call-by-reference parameter passing is discussed, parameters are passed by value-result.)

```
program Main          procedure A(x, y)      procedure Add(a, b)   procedure Increment(z)
    sum := 0;             call Add(x, y);        a := a + b            call Add(z, 1)
    i := 1;               call Increment(y)      return                return
    while i < 11 do       return
        call A(sum, i)
    od
end
```

Using Weiser's algorithm to slice this program with respect to variable z and the **return** statement of procedure *Increment*, we obtain everything from the original program. However, a closer inspection reveals that computations involving the variable *sum* do not contribute to the value of z at the end of procedure *Increment*; in particular, neither the initialization of *sum*, nor the first actual parameter of the call on procedure A in *Main*, nor the call on *Add* in A (which adds the current value of i to *sum*) should be included in the slice. The reason these components are included in the slice computed by Weiser's algorithm is as follows: the initial slicing criterion "⟨end of procedure *Increment*, z⟩", is mapped by the DOWN relation to a slicing criterion "⟨end of procedure *Add*, a⟩". The latter criterion is then mapped by the UP relation to *two* slicing criteria—corresponding to *all* sites that call *Add*—the criterion "⟨call on *Add* in *Increment*, z⟩" and the (irrelevant) criterion "⟨call on *Add* in A, x⟩". Weiser's algorithm does not produce as precise a slice as possible because transitive closure fails to account for the calling context (*Increment*) of a called procedure (*Add*), and thus generates a spurious criterion (⟨call on *Add* in A, x⟩).

A more precise slice consists of the following elements:

```
program Main          procedure A(y)         procedure Add(a, b)   procedure Increment(z)
    i := 1;               call Increment(y)      a := a + b            call Add(z, 1)
    while i < 11 do       return                 return                return
        call A(i)
    od
end
```

This set of program elements is computed by the slicing algorithm described in this paper.

The chief difficulty in interprocedural slicing is correctly accounting for the calling context of a called procedure. To address the calling-context problem, system dependence graphs include some data dependence edges that represent *transitive* dependences due to the effects of procedure calls, in addition to the conventional edges for direct dependences. The presence of transitive-dependence edges permits interprocedural slices to be computed in two passes, each of which is cast as a reachability problem.

The cornerstone of the construction of the system dependence graph is the use of an attribute grammar to represent calling and parameter-linkage relationships among procedures. The step of computing the required transitive-dependence edges is reduced to the construction of the subordinate characteristic graphs for the grammar's nonterminals. The need to express this step in this fashion (rather than, for example, with transitive closure) is discussed further in Section 3.2.

The remainder of the paper is organized as follows: Section 2 defines the dependence graphs used to represent programs in a language without procedure calls. Section 2 also defines the operation of intraprocedural slicing on these dependence graphs. Section 3 extends the definition of dependence graphs to handle a language that includes procedures and procedure calls. The new graphs are called *system dependence graphs*. Section 4 presents our slicing algorithm, which operates on system dependence graphs and correctly accounts for the calling context of a called procedure. It then describes how to improve the precision of interprocedural slicing by using interprocedural summary information in the construction of system dependence graphs, how to handle programs with aliasing, how to slice incomplete programs, and how to compute *forward slices* (i.e., the program elements potentially *affected by* a given variable at a given point). Section 5 discusses the complexity of the slicing algorithm. We have not yet implemented this algorithm in its entirety; thus, Section 5 provides an analysis of the costs of building system dependence graphs and of taking interprocedural slices rather than presenting empirical results. Section 6 discusses related work.

With the exception of the material on interprocedural data-flow analysis employed in Section 4.2, the paper is self-contained; an introduction to the terminology and concepts from attribute-grammar theory that are used in Section 3.2 may be found in the Appendix.

2. PROGRAM-DEPENDENCE GRAPHS AND PROGRAM SLICES

Different definitions of program dependence representations have been given, depending on the intended application; they are all variations on a theme introduced in [16], and share the common feature of having an explicit representation of data dependences (see below). The "program dependence graphs" defined in [7] introduced the additional feature of an explicit representation for control dependences (see below). The definition of program dependence graph given below differs from [7] in two ways. First, our definition covers only a restricted language with scalar variables, assignment statements, conditional statements, while loops, and a restricted kind of "output statement" called an *end statement*,[2] and hence is less general than the one given in [7]. Second, we omit certain classes of data dependence edges and make use of a class introduced in [8, 11]. Despite these differences, the structures we define and those defined in [7] share the feature of explicitly representing both control and data dependences; therefore, we refer to our graphs as "program dependence graphs," borrowing the term from [7].

---

[2] An end statement, which can only appear at the end of a program, names one or more of the variables used in the program; when execution terminates, only those variables will have values in the final state; the variables named by the end statement are those whose final values are of interest to the programmer.

2.1 The Program Dependence Graph

The program dependence graph for program P, denoted by G_P, is a directed graph whose vertices are connected by several kinds of edges.[3] The vertices of G_P represent the assignment statements and control predicates that occur in program P. In addition, G_P includes three other categories of vertices:

(1) There is a distinguished vertex called the *entry vertex*.
(2) For each variable x for which there is a path in the standard control-flow graph for P on which x is used before being defined (see [1]), there is a vertex called the *initial definition of x*. This vertex represents an assignment to x from the initial state. The vertex is labeled "$x := \text{InitialState}(x)$".
(3) For each variable x named in P's end statement, there is a vertex called the *final use of x*. It represents an access to the final value of x computed by P, and is labeled "$\text{FinalUse}(x)$".

The edges of G_P represent *dependences* among program components. An edge represents either a *control dependence* or a *data dependence*. Control dependence edges are labeled either **true** or **false**, and the source of a control dependence edge is always the entry vertex or a predicate vertex. A control dependence edge from vertex v_1 to vertex v_2, denoted by $v_1 \rightarrow_c v_2$, means that, during execution, whenever the predicate represented by v_1 is evaluated and its value matches the label on the edge to v_2, then the program component represented by v_2 will eventually be executed if the program terminates. A method for determining control dependence edges for arbitrary programs is given in [7]; however, because we are assuming that programs include only assignment, conditional, and while statements, the control dependence edges of G_P can be determined in a much simpler fashion. For the language under construction here, the control dependences reflect a program's nesting structure; program dependence graph G_P contains a *control dependence edge* from vertex v_1 to vertex v_2 of G_P iff one of the following holds:

(1) v_1 is the entry vertex and v_2 represents a component of P that is not nested within any loop or conditional; these edges are labeled **true**.
(2) v_1 represents a control predicate and v_2 represents a component of P immediately nested within the loop or conditional whose predicate is represented by v_1. If v_1 is the predicate of a while-loop, the edge $v_1 \rightarrow_c v_2$ is labeled **true**; if v_1 is the predicate of a conditional statement, the edge $v_1 \rightarrow_c v_2$ is labeled **true** or **false** according to whether v_2 occurs in the **then** branch or the **else** branch, respectively.[4]

---

[3] A *directed graph* G consists of a set of *vertices* $V(G)$ and a set of *edges* $E(G)$, where $E(G) \subseteq V(G) \times V(G)$. Each edge $(b, c) \in E(G)$ is directed from b to c; we say that b is the *source* and c the *target* of the edge.

[4] In other definitions that have been given for control dependence edges, there is an additional edge from each predicate of a **while** statement to itself, labeled **true**. This kind of edge is left out of our definition because it is not necessary for our purposes.

A data dependence edge from vertex v_1 to vertex v_2 means that the program's computation might be changed if the relative order of the components represented by v_1 and v_2 were reversed. In this paper, program dependence graphs contain two kinds of data dependence edges, representing *flow dependences* and *def-order dependences*.[5] The data dependence edges of a program dependence graph are computed using data-flow analysis. For the restricted language considered in this section, the necessary computations can be defined in a syntax-directed manner.

A program dependence graph contains a flow dependence edge from vertex v_1 to vertex v_2 iff all of the following hold:

(1) v_1 is a vertex that defines variable x.

(2) v_2 is a vertex that uses x.

(3) Control can reach v_2 after v_1 via an execution path along which there is no intervening definition of x. That is, there is a path in the standard control-flow graph for the program by which the definition of x at v_1 reaches the use of x at v_2. (Initial definitions of variables are considered to occur at the beginning of the control-flow graph; final uses of variables are considered to occur at the end of the control-flow graph.)

A flow dependence that exists from vertex v_1 to vertex v_2 is denoted by $v_1 \rightarrow_f v_2$.

Flow dependences can be further classified as *loop carried* or *loop independent*. A flow dependence $v_1 \rightarrow_f v_2$ is carried by loop L, denoted by $v_1 \rightarrow_{lc(L)} v_2$, if in addition to (1), (2), and (3) above, the following also hold:

(4) There is an execution path that both satisfies the conditions of (3) above and includes a backedge to the predicate of loop L.

(5) Both v_1 and v_2 are enclosed in loop L.

A flow dependence $v_1 \rightarrow_f v_2$ is loop-independent, denoted by $v_1 \rightarrow_{li} v_2$, if in addition to (1), (2), and (3) above, there is an execution path that satisfies (3) above and includes *no* backedge to the predicate of a loop that encloses both v_1 and v_2. It is possible to have both $v_1 \rightarrow_{lc(L)} v_2$ and $v_1 \rightarrow_{li} v_2$.

A program dependence graph contains a def-order dependence edge from vertex v_1 to vertex v_2 iff all of the following hold:

(1) v_1 and v_2 both define the same variable.

(2) v_1 and v_2 are in the same branch of any conditional statement that encloses both of them.

(3) There exists a program component v_3 such that $v_1 \rightarrow_f v_3$ and $v_2 \rightarrow_f v_3$.

(4) v_1 occurs to the left of v_2 in the program's abstract syntax tree.

A def-order dependence from v_1 to v_2 with "witness" v_3 is denoted by $v_1 \rightarrow_{do(v_3)} v_2$.

Note that a program dependence graph is a multigraph (i.e., it may have more than one edge of a given kind between two vertices). When there is more than one loop-carried flow dependence edge between two vertices, each is labeled by a

---

[5] For a complete discussion of the need for these edges and a comparison of def-order dependences with anti- and output dependences see [9].

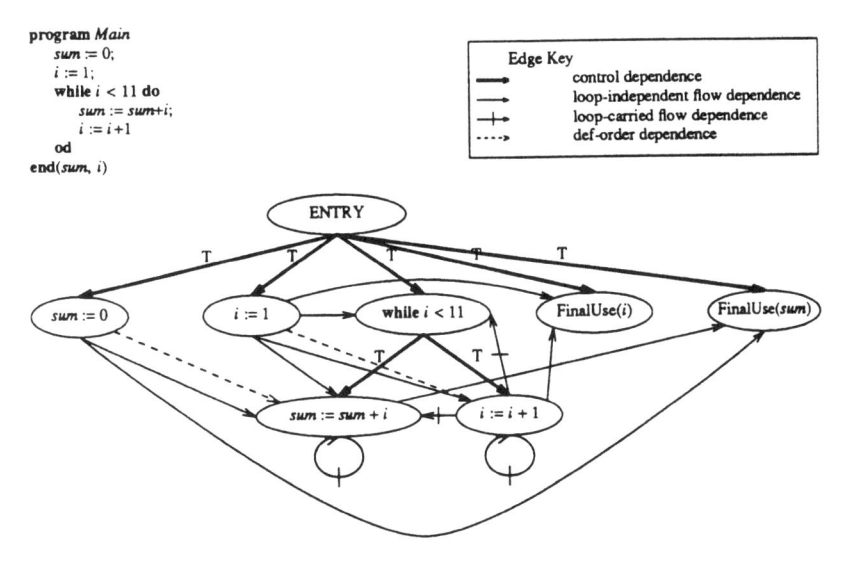

```
program Main
    sum := 0;
    i := 1;
    while i < 11 do
        sum := sum+i;
        i := i+1
    od
end(sum, i)
```

Fig. 1. An example program, which sums the integers from 1 to 10 and leaves the result in the variable *sum*, and its program dependence graph. The boldface arrows represent control dependence edges, solid arrows represent loop-independent flow dependence edges, solid arrows with a hash mark represent loop-carried flow dependence edges, and dashed arrows represent def-order dependence edges.

different loop that carries the dependence. When there is more than one def-order edge between two vertices, each is labeled by a vertex that is flow-dependent on both the definition that occurs at the edge's source and the definition that occurs at the edge's target.

Example. Figure 1 shows an example program and its program dependence graph.

The boldface arrows represent control dependence edges; solid arrows represent loop-independent flow dependence edges; solid arrows with a hash mark represent loop-carried flow dependence edges; dashed arrows represent def-order dependence edges.

2.2 Program Slices (of Single-Procedure Programs)

For vertex s of program dependence graph G, the *slice* of G with respect to s, denoted by G/s, is a graph containing all vertices on which s has a transitive flow or control dependence (i.e., all vertices that can reach s via flow and/or control edges): $V(G/s) = \{w \mid w \in V(G) \land w \rightarrow^*_{c,f} s\}$. We extend the definition to a set of vertices $S = \bigcup_i s_i$ as follows: $V(G/S) = V(G/(\bigcup_i s_i)) = \bigcup_i V(G/s_i)$. Figure 2 gives a simple worklist algorithm for computing the vertices of a slice using a program dependence graph.

The edges in the graph G/S are essentially those in the subgraph of G induced by $V(G/S)$, with the exception that a def-order edge $v \rightarrow_{do(u)} w$ is included only if G/S contains the vertex u that is directly flow-dependent on the definitions at

```
procedure MarkVerticesOfSlice(G, S)
declare
    G: a program dependence graph
    S: a set of vertices in G
    WorkList: a set of vertices in G
    v, w: vertices in G
begin
    WorkList := S
    while WorkList ≠ ∅ do
        Select and remove vertex v from WorkList
        Mark v
        for each unmarked vertex w such that edge w →_f v or edge w →_c v is in E(G) do
            Insert w into WorkList
        od
    od
end
```

Fig. 2. A worklist algorithm that marks the vertices in G/S. Vertex v is in G/S if there is a path along flow and/or control edges from v to some vertex in S.

v and w. In terms of the three types of edges in a program dependence graph, we define

$$\begin{aligned}E(G/S) = \ & \{(v \to_f w) \,|\, (v \to_f w) \in E(G) \land v, w \in V(G/S)\} \\ \cup \ & \{(v \to_c w) \,|\, (v \to_c w) \in E(G) \land v, w \in V(G/S)\} \\ \cup \ & \{(v \to_{do(u)} w) \,|\, (v \to_{do(u)} w) \in E(G) \land u, v, w \in V(G/S)\}.\end{aligned}$$

The relationship between a program's dependence graph and a slice of the graph has been addressed in [20]. We say that G is a *feasible* program dependence graph iff G is the program dependence graph of some program P. For any $S \subseteq V(G)$, if G is a feasible program dependence graph, the slice G/S is also a feasible program dependence graph; it corresponds to the program P' obtained by restricting the syntax tree of P to just the statements and predicates in $V(G/S)$ [20].

Example. Figure 3 shows the graph that results from taking a slice of the program dependence graph from Figure 1 with respect to the final-use vertex for i, together with the one program to which it corresponds.

The significance of an intraprocedural slice is that it captures a portion of a program's behavior in the sense that, for any initial state on which the program halts, the program and the slice compute the same sequence of values for each element of the slice [20]. In our case, a program point may be (1) an assignment statement, (2) a control predicate, or (3) a final use of a variable in an end statement. Because a statement or control predicate may be reached repeatedly in a program by "computing the same sequence of values for each element of the slice," we mean: (1) for any assignment statement the same *sequence* of values are assigned to the target variable; (2) for the predicate the same *sequence* of Boolean values are produced; and (3) for each final use the same value for the variable is produced.

```
program Main
    i := 1;
    while i < 11 do
        i := i + 1
    od
end(i)
```

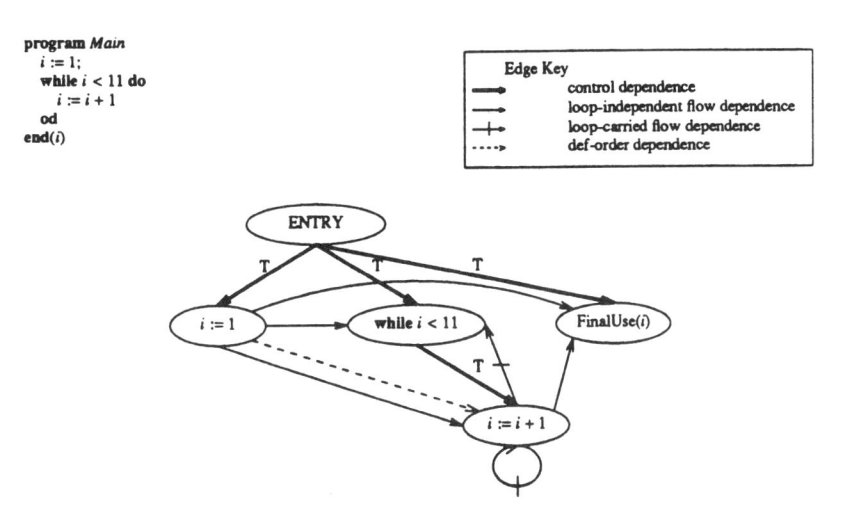

Fig. 3. The graph and the corresponding program that result from slicing the program dependence graph from Figure 1 with respect to the final-use vertex for i.

3. THE SYSTEM DEPENDENCE GRAPH: AN INTERPROCEDURAL DEPENDENCE GRAPH REPRESENTATION

We now turn to the definition of the *system dependence graph*. The system dependence graph, an extension of the dependence graphs defined in Section 2.1, represents programs in a language that includes procedures and procedure calls.

Our definition of the system dependence graph models a language with the following properties:

(1) A complete system consists of a single (main) program and a collection of auxiliary procedures.
(2) Procedures end with **return** statements instead of **end** statements (as defined in Section 2). A **return** statement does not include a list of variables.
(3) Parameters are passed by value-result.

We make the further assumption that there are no call sites of the form $P(x, x)$ or of the form $P(g)$, where g is a global variable. The former restriction sidesteps potential copy-back conflicts. The latter restriction permits global variables to be treated as additional parameters to each procedure; thus, we do not discuss global variables explicitly in this paper.

It should become clear that our approach is not tied to the particular language features enumerated above. Modeling different features will require some adaptation; however, the basic approach is applicable to languages that allow nested scopes and languages that use different parameter-passing mechanisms. Section 4.3 discusses how to deal with systems that use call-by-reference parameter passing and contain aliasing.

A system dependence graph includes a *program dependence graph*, which represents the system's main program, *procedure dependence graphs*, which represent the system's auxiliary procedures, and some additional edges. These additional edges are of two sorts: (1) edges that represent direct dependences between a call site and the called procedure, and (2) edges that represent transitive dependences due to calls.

Section 3.1 discusses how procedure calls and procedure entry are represented in procedure dependence graphs and how edges representing dependences between a call site and the called procedure are added to connect these graphs together. Section 3.2 defines the *linkage grammar*, an attribute grammar used to represent the call structure of a system. Transitive dependences due to procedure calls are computed using the linkage grammar and are added as the final step of building a system dependence graph.

In the sections below, we use "procedure" as a generic term referring to both the main program and the auxiliary procedures when the distinction between the two is irrelevant.

3.1 Procedure Calls and Parameter Passing

Extending the definition of dependence graphs to handle procedure calls requires representing the passing of values between procedures. In designing the representation of parameter passing, we have three goals:

(1) It should be possible to build an individual procedure's procedure dependence graph (including the computation of data dependences) with minimal knowledge of other system components.
(2) The system dependence graph should consist of a straightforward connection of the program dependence graph and procedure dependence graphs.
(3) It should be possible to extract a precise interprocedural slice efficiently by traversing the graph via a procedure analogous to the procedure MarkVerticesOfSlice given in Figure 2.

Goal (3) is the subject of Section 4.1, which presents our algorithm for slicing a system dependence graph.

To meet the goals outlined above, our graphs model the following slightly nonstandard, two-stage mechanism for runtime parameter passing: when procedure P calls procedure Q, values are transferred from P to Q by means of intermediate temporary variables, one for each parameter. A different set of temporary variables is used when Q returns to transfer values back to P. Before the call, P copies the values of the actual parameters into the call temporaries; Q then initializes local variables from these temporaries. Before returning, Q copies return values into the return temporaries, from which P retrieves them.

This model of parameter passing is represented in procedure dependence graphs through the use of five new kinds of vertices. A call site is represented using a *call-site* vertex; information transfer is represented using four kinds of *parameter* vertices. On the calling side, information transfer is represented by a set of vertices called *actual-in* and *actual-out* vertices. These vertices, which are control dependent on the call-site vertex, represent assignment statements that copy the values of the actual parameters to the call temporaries and from the return temporaries, respectively. Similarly, information transfer in the called procedure is represented by a set of vertices called *formal-in* and *formal-out* vertices. These vertices, which are control dependent on the procedure's entry vertex, represent assignment statements that copy the values of the formal parameters from the call temporaries and to the return temporaries, respectively.

Using this model, data dependences between procedures are limited to dependences from actual-in vertices to formal-in vertices and from formal-out vertices to actual-out vertices. Connecting procedure dependence graphs to form a system dependence graph is straightforward, involving the addition of three new kinds of edges: (1) a *call* edge is added from each call-site vertex to the corresponding procedure-entry vertex; (2) a *parameter-in* edge is added from each actual-in vertex at a call site to the corresponding formal-in vertex in the called procedure; (3) a *parameter-out* edge is added from each formal-out vertex in the called procedure to the corresponding actual-out vertex at the call site. (Call edges are a new kind of control dependence edge; parameter-in and parameter-out edges are new kinds of data dependence edges.)

Another advantage of this model is that flow dependences can be computed in the usual way, using data-flow analysis on the procedure's control-flow graph. The control-flow graph for a procedure includes nodes analogous to the actual-in, actual-out, formal-in and formal-out vertices of the procedure dependence graph. A procedure's control-flow graph starts with a sequence of assignments that copy values from call temporaries to formal parameters and ends with a sequence of assignments that copy values from formal parameters to return temporaries. Each call statement within the procedure is represented in the procedure's control-flow graph by a sequence of assignments that copy values from actual parameters to call temporaries, followed by a sequence of assignments that copy values from return temporaries to actual parameters.

An important question is *which* values are transferred from a call site to the called procedure and back again. This point is discussed further in Section 4.2, which presents a strategy in which the results of interprocedural data-flow analysis are used to omit some parameter vertices from procedure dependence graphs. For now, we assume that all actual parameters are copied into the call temporaries and retrieved from the return temporaries. Thus, the parameter vertices associated with a call from procedure P to procedure Q are defined as follows (G_P denotes the procedure dependence graph for P):

> In G_P, subordinate to the call-site vertex that represents the call to Q, there is an actual-in vertex for each actual parameter e of the call to Q. The actual-in vertices are labeled $r\_in := e$, where r is the formal parameter name.
>
> For each actual parameter a that is a variable (rather than an expression), there is an actual-out vertex. These are labeled $a := r\_out$ for actual parameter a and corresponding formal parameter r.

The parameter vertices associated with the entry to procedure Q and the return from procedure Q are defined as follows (G_Q denotes the procedure dependence graph for Q):

> For each formal parameter r of Q, G_Q contains a formal-in vertex and a formal-out vertex. These vertices are labeled $r := r\_in$ and $r\_out := r$, respectively.

Example. Figure 4 repeats the example system from the Introduction and shows the corresponding program and procedure dependence graphs connected with parameter-in edges, parameter-out edges, and call edges.

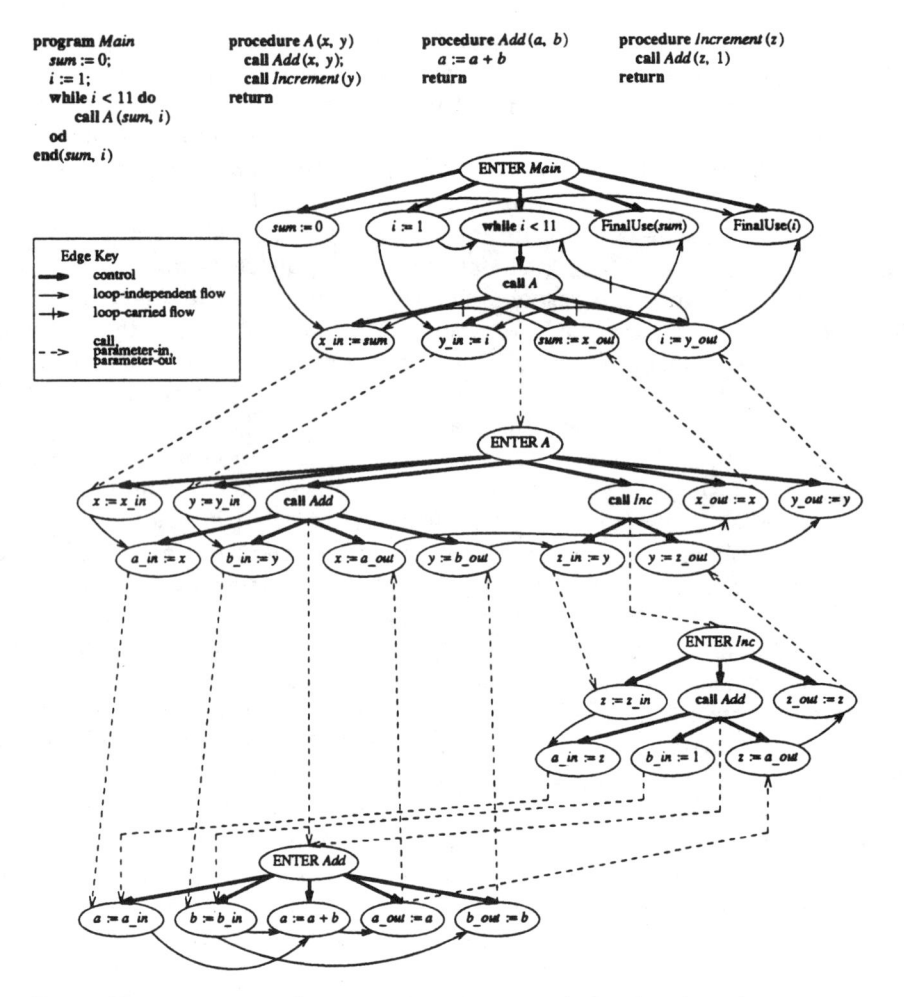

Fig. 4. Example system and corresponding program and procedure dependence graphs connected with parameter-in, parameter-out, and call edges. Edges representing control dependences are shown (unlabeled) in boldface; edges representing intraprocedural flow dependences are shown using arcs; parameter-in edges, parameter-out edges, and call edges are shown using dashed lines.

(In Figure 4, as well as in the remaining figures of the paper, def-order edges are not shown. Edges representing control dependences are shown unlabeled; all such edges in this example would be labeled **true**.)

3.2 The Linkage Grammar: An Attribute Grammar that Models Procedure-Call Structure

Using the graph structure defined in the previous section, interprocedural slicing could be defined as a graph-reachability problem, and the slices obtained would be the same as those obtained using Weiser's slicing method. As explained in the Introduction, Weiser's method does not produce as precise a slice as possible because it fails to account for the calling context of a called procedure.

Example. The problem with Weiser's method can be illustrated using the graph shown in Figure 4. In the graph-reachability vocabulary, the problem is that there is a path from the vertex of procedure *Main* labeled "$x\_in := sum$" to the vertex of *Main* labeled "$i := y\_out$", even though the value of i after the call to procedure A is independent of the value of *sum* before the call. The path is as follows:

$$Main: "x\_in := sum" \rightarrow A: "x := x\_in" \rightarrow A: "a\_in := x" \rightarrow Add: "a := a\_in"$$
$$\rightarrow Add: "a := a+b" \rightarrow Add: "a\_out := a" \rightarrow Inc: "z := a\_out"$$
$$\rightarrow Inc: "z\_out := z" \rightarrow A: "y := z\_out" \rightarrow A: "y\_out := y"$$
$$\rightarrow Main: "i := y\_out"$$

The source of this problem is that not all paths in the graph correspond to possible execution paths (e.g., the path from vertex "$x\_in := sum$" of *Main* to vertex "$i := y\_out$" of *Main* corresponds to procedure *Add* being called by procedure A, but returning to procedure *Increment*).

To overcome this problem, we add an additional kind of edge to the system dependence graph to represent transitive dependences due to the effects of procedure calls. The presence of transitive-dependence edges permits interprocedural slices to be computed in two passes, each of which is cast as a reachability problem. Thus, the next step in the construction of the system dependence graph is to determine such transitive dependences. For example, for the graph shown in Figure 4, we need an algorithm that can discover the transitive dependence from vertex "$x\_in := sum$" of *Main* to vertex "$sum := x\_out$" of *Main*. This dependence exists because the value of *sum* after the call to A depends on the value of *sum* before the call to A.

One's first impulse might be to compute transitive dependences due to calls by taking the transitive closure of the graph's control, flow, parameter, and call edges. However, this technique is imprecise for the same reason that transitive closure (or, equivalently, reachability) is imprecise for interprocedural slicing, namely that not all paths in the system dependence graph correspond to possible execution paths. Using transitive closure to compute the dependence edges that represent the effects of procedure calls would put in a (spurious) edge from vertex "$x\_in := sum$" of *Main* to vertex "$i := y\_out$" of *Main*.

For a language without recursion, this problem could be eliminated by using a separate copy of a procedure dependence graph for each call site; however, to handle a language *with* recursion, a more powerful technique is required. The technique we use involves defining an attribute grammar, called the *linkage grammar*, to model the call structure of each procedure as well as the in*tra*procedural transitive flow dependences among the procedure's parameter vertices. *Inter*procedural transitive flow dependences among a system dependence graph's parameter vertices are determined from the linkage grammar using a standard attribute-grammar construction: the computation of the *subordinate characteristic graphs* of the linkage grammar's nonterminals.[6]

In this section we describe the construction of the linkage grammar and the computation of its subordinate characteristic graphs. It should be understood that the linkage grammar is used *only* to compute transitive dependences due to

---

[6] A summary of attribute-grammar terminology can be found in the Appendix.

calls; we are not interested in the language defined by the grammar, nor in actual attribute values.

The context-free part of the linkage grammar models the system's procedure-call structure. The grammar includes one nonterminal and one production for each procedure in the system. If procedure P contains no calls, the right-hand side of the production for P is ϵ; otherwise, there is one right-hand side nonterminal for each call site in P.

Example. For the example system shown in Figure 4, the productions of the linkage grammar are as follows:

$Main \rightarrow A \quad A \rightarrow Add\ Increment \quad Add \rightarrow \epsilon \quad Increment \rightarrow Add$

The attributes in the linkage grammar correspond to the parameters of the procedures. Procedure inputs are modeled as inherited attributes, procedure outputs as synthesized attributes. For example, the productions shown above are repeated in Figure 5, this time in tree form.

In Figure 5, each nonterminal is annotated with its attributes; a nonterminal's inherited attributes are placed to its left; its synthesized attributes are placed to its right.

More formally, the program's linkage grammar has the following elements:

(1) For each procedure P, the linkage grammar contains a nonterminal P.
(2) For each procedure P, there is a production $p: P \rightarrow \beta$, where for each site of a call on procedure Q in P there is a distinct occurrence of Q in β.
(3) For each actual-in vertex of P, there is an inherited attribute of nonterminal P.
(4) For each actual-out vertex of P, there is a synthesized attribute of nonterminal P.

Attribute a of nonterminal X is denoted by "$X.a$".

Dependences among the attributes of a linkage-grammar production are used to model the (possibly transitive) intraprocedural dependences among the parameter vertices of the corresponding procedure. These dependences are computed using (intraprocedural) slices of the procedure's procedure dependence graph as described in Section 2.2. For each grammar production, attribute equations are introduced to represent the intraprocedural dependences among the parameter vertices of the corresponding procedure dependence graph. For each attribute occurrence a, the procedure dependence graph is sliced with respect to the vertex that corresponds to a. An attribute equation is introduced for a so that a depends on the attribute occurrences that correspond to the parameter vertices identified by the slice. More formally:

> For each attribute occurrence of $X.a$ of a production p, let v be the vertex of the procedure dependence graph G_P that corresponds to $X.a$. Associate with p an attribute equation of the form $X.a = f(\ldots, Y.b, \ldots)$ where the arguments $Y.b$ to the equation consist of the attribute occurrences of p that correspond to the parameter vertices in G_P/v.

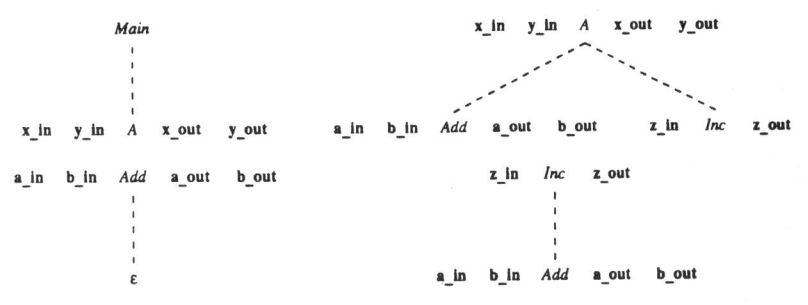

Fig. 5. The productions of the example linkage grammar shown in tree form. Each nonterminal is annotated with its attributes; a nonterminal's inherited attributes are placed to its left; its synthesized attributes are placed to its right.

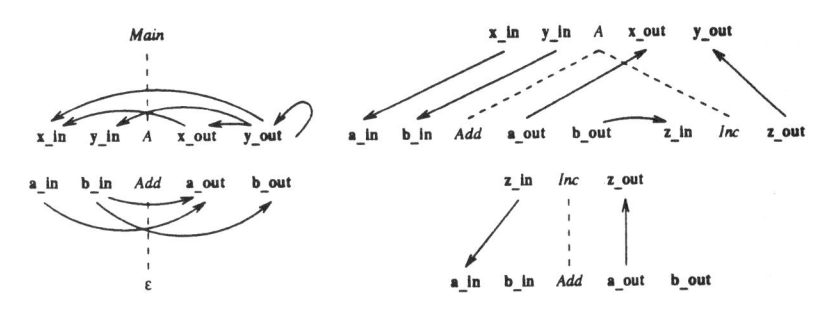

Fig. 6. The productions of Figure 5, augmented with attribute dependences.

Note that the actual function f on the right-hand side of the equation is completely irrelevant because the attribute grammar is *never* used for evaluation; all we need is that the equation induce the dependences described above.

Example. Figure 6 shows the productions of the grammar from Figure 5, augmented with attribute dependences.

The dependences for production $Main \rightarrow A$, for instance, correspond to the attribute-definition equations

$A.x\_in = f1(A.x\_out, A.y\_out)$
$A.y\_in = f2(A.y\_out)$
$A.x\_out = f3(A.y\_out)$
$A.y\_out = f4(A.y\_out)$

It is entirely possible that a linkage grammar will be a circular attribute grammar (i.e., there may be attributes in some derivation tree of the grammar that depend on themselves); additionally, the grammar may not be well formed (e.g., a production may have equations for synthesized attribute occurrences of right-hand side symbols). This does not create any difficulties as the linkage grammar is used *only* to compute transitive dependences and *not* for attribute evaluation.

Example. The equation $A.y\_out = f4(A.y\_out)$ makes the example attribute grammar both circular and not well formed. This equation is added to the attribute grammar because of the following (cyclic) path in the graph shown in Figure 4:

Main: "$i := y\_out$" → *Main*: "**while** $i < 11$"
→ *Main*: "**call** A" → *Main*: "$i := y\_out$"

Transitive dependences from a call site's actual-in vertices to its actual-out vertices are computed from the linkage grammar by constructing the subordinate characteristic graphs for the grammar's nonterminals. The algorithm we give exploits the special structure of linkage grammars to compute these graphs more efficiently than can be done for attribute grammars in general. For general attribute grammars, computing the sets of possible subordinate characteristic graphs for the grammar's nonterminals may require time exponential in the number of attributes attached to some nonterminal. However, a linkage grammar is an attribute grammar of a restricted nature. For each nonterminal X in the linkage grammar, there is only one production with X on the left-hand side. Because linkage grammars are restricted in this fashion, for each nonterminal of a linkage grammar there is one subordinate characteristic graph that covers all of the nonterminal's other possible subordinate characteristic graphs. For such grammars it is possible to give a polynomial-time algorithm for constructing the (covering) subordinate characteristic graphs.

The computation is performed by an algorithm, called ConstructSubCGraphs, which is a slight modification of an algorithm originally developed by Kastens to construct approximations to a grammar's transitive dependence relations [13]. The covering subordinate characteristic graph of a nonterminal X of the linkage grammar is captured in the graph $TDS(X)$ (standing for "Transitive Dependences among a Symbol's attributes"). Initially, all the TDS graphs are empty. The construction that builds them up involves the auxiliary graph $TDP(p)$ (standing for "Transitive Dependences in a Production"), which expresses dependences among the attributes of a production's nonterminal occurrences.

The basic operation used in ConstructSubCGraphs is the procedure "AddEdgeAndInduce($TDP(p)$, (a, b))", whose first argument is the TDP graph of some production p and whose second argument is a pair of attribute occurrences in p. AddEdgeAndInduce carries out three actions:

(1) The edge (a, b) is inserted into the graph $TDP(p)$.
(2) Any additional edges needed to transitively close $TDP(p)$ are inserted into $TDP(p)$.
(3) In addition, for each edge added to $TDP(p)$ by (1) or (2), (i.e., either the edge (a, b) itself or some other edge (c, d) added to reclose $TDP(p)$), AddEdgeAndInduce may add an edge to one of the TDS graphs. In particular, for each edge added to $TDP(p)$ of the form $(X_0.m, X_0.n)$, where X_0 is the left-hand side occurrence of nonterminal X in production p and $(X.m, X.n) \notin TDS(X)$, an edge $(X.m, X.n)$ is added to $TDS(X)$.

An edge in one of the TDS graphs can be *marked* or *unmarked*; the edges that AddEdgeAndInduce adds to the TDS graphs are unmarked.

```
procedure ConstructSubCGraphs(L)
declare
    L: a linkage grammar
    p: a production in L
    X_i, X_j, X: nonterminal occurrences in L
    a, b: attributes of nonterminals in L
    X: a nonterminal in L
begin
    /* Step 1: Initialize the TDS and TDP graphs */
        for each nonterminal X in L do
            TDS(X) := the graph containing a vertex for each attribute X.b but no edges
        od
        for each production p in L do
            TDP(p) := the graph containing a vertex for each attribute occurrence X_j.b of p but no edges
            for each attribute occurrence X_j.b of p do
                for each argument X_i.a of the equation that defines X_j.b do
                    Insert edge (X_i.a, X_j.b) into TDP(p)
                    let X be the nonterminal corresponding to nonterminal occurrence X_j in
                        if i = 0 and j = 0 and (X.a, X.b) ∉ TDS (X) then Insert an unmarked edge (X.a, X.b) into TDS(X) fi
                    ni
                od
            od
        od
    /* Step 2: Determine the sets of induced transitive dependences */
        while there is an unmarked edge (X.a, X.b) in one of the TDS graphs do
            Mark (X.a, X.b)
            for each occurrence X̂ of X in any production p do
                if (X̂.a, X̂.b) ∉ TDP (p) then AddEdgeAndInduce(TDP (p), (X̂.a, X̂.b)) fi
            od
        od
end
```

Fig. 7. Computation of a linkage grammar's sets of TDP and TDS graphs.

The TDS graphs are generated by the procedure ConstructSubCGraphs, given in Figure 7, which is a slight modification of the first two steps of Kasten's algorithm for constructing a set of evaluation plans for an attribute grammar [13].

ConstructSubCGraphs performs a kind of closure operation on the TDP and TDS graphs. Step 1 of the algorithm—the first two for-loops of Construct-SubCGraphs—initializes the grammar's TDP and TDS graphs; when these loops terminate, the TDP graphs contain edges representing all direct dependences that exist between the grammar's attribute occurrences, and the TDS graphs contain unmarked edges corresponding to direct left-hand-side-to-left-hand-side dependences in the linkage grammar's productions. Our construction of attribute equations for the linkage grammar ensures that the graph of direct attribute dependences is transitively closed; thus, at the end of Step 1, $TDP(p)$ is a transitively closed graph. In Step 2 of ConstructSubCGraphs, the invariant for the **while**-loop is

> If a graph $TDP(p)$ contains an edge e' that corresponds to a marked edge e in one of the TDS graphs, then e has been induced in all of the other graphs $TDP(q)$.

When all edges in all TDS graphs have received marks, the effects of all dependences have been induced in the TDP and TDS graphs. Thus, the $TDS(X)$ graphs computed by ConstructSubCGraphs are guaranteed to cover the transitive dependences among the attributes of X that exist at any occurrence of X in any derivation tree.

Put more simply, because for each nonterminal X in a linkage grammar there is only a single production that has X on the left-hand side, the grammar only derives one tree. (For a recursive grammar it will be an infinite tree.) All marked edges in TDS represent transitive dependences in this tree, and thus the TDS(X) graph computed by ConstructSubCGraphs represents a subordinate characteristic graph of X that covers the subordinate characteristic graph of any partial derivation tree derived from X, as desired.

Example. The nonterminals of our example grammar are shown below annotated with their attributes and their subordinate characteristic graphs.

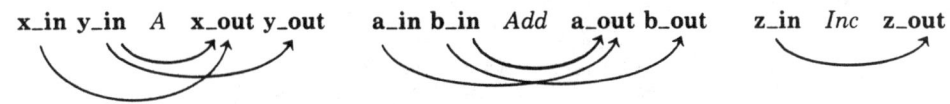

x_in y_in *A* x_out y_out   a_in b_in *Add* a_out b_out   z_in *Inc* z_out

3.3 Recap of the Construction of the System Dependence Graph

The system dependence graph is constructed by the following steps:

(1) For each procedure of the system, construct its procedure dependence graph.
(2) For each call site, introduce a call edge from the call-site vertex to the corresponding procedure-entry vertex.
(3) For each actual-in vertex v at a call site, introduce a parameter-in edge from v to the corresponding formal-in vertex in the called procedure.
(4) For each actual-out vertex v at a call site, introduce a parameter-out edge to v from the corresponding formal-out vertex in the called procedure.
(5) Construct the linkage grammar corresponding to the system.
(6) Compute the subordinate characteristic graphs of the linkage grammar's nonterminals.
(7) At all call sites that call procedure P, introduce flow dependence edges corresponding to the edges in the subordinate characteristic graph for P.

Example. Figure 8 shows the complete system dependence graph for our example system.

4. INTERPROCEDURAL SLICING

In this section we describe how to perform an interprocedural slice using the system dependence graph defined in Section 3. We then discuss modifications to the definition of the system dependence graph to permit more precise slicing and to extend the slicing algorithm's range of applicability.

4.1 An Algorithm for Interprocedural Slicing

As discussed in the Introduction, the algorithm presented in [22], while safe, is not as precise as possible. The difficult aspect of interprocedural slicing is keeping track of the calling context when a slice "descends" into a called procedure.

The key element of our approach is the use of the linkage grammar's characteristic graph edges in the system dependence graph. These edges represent transitive data dependences from actual-in vertices to actual-out vertices due to

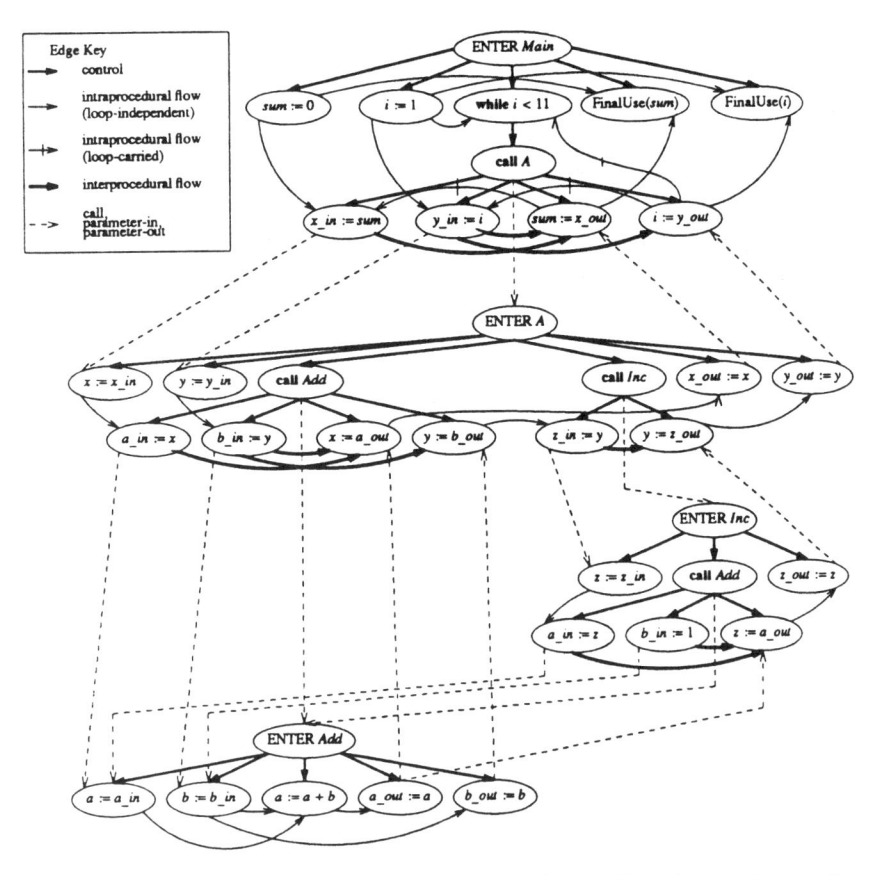

Fig. 8. Example system's system dependence graph. Control dependences, shown unlabeled, are represented using medium-bold arrows; intraprocedural flow dependences are represented using arcs; transitive interprocedural flow dependences (corresponding to subordinate characteristic graph edges) are represented using heavy, bold arcs; call edges, parameter-in edges, and parameter-out edges (which connect program and procedure dependence graphs together) are represented using dashed arrows.

procedure calls. The presence of such edges permits us to sidestep the "calling context" problem; the slicing operation can move "across" a call without having to descend into it.

Our algorithm for interprocedural slicing is given in Figure 9.

In Figure 9, the computation of the slice of system dependence graph G with respect to vertex set S is performed in two phases. Both Phases 1 and 2 operate on the system dependence graph using essentially the method presented in Section 2.2 for performing an in*tra*procedural slice—the graph is traversed to find the set of vertices that can reach a given set of vertices along certain kinds of edges. The traversal in Phase 1 follows flow edges, control edges, call edges, and parameter-in edges, but does *not* follow def-order edges or parameter-out edges. The traversal in Phase 2 that follows flow edges, control edges, and parameter-out edges, but does *not* follow def-order edges, call edges, or parameter-in edges.

```
procedure MarkVerticesOfSlice(G, S)
declare
   G: a system dependence graph
   S, S': sets of vertices in G
begin
   /* Phase 1: Slice without descending into called procedures */
      MarkReachingVertices(G, S, {def-order, parameter-out})

   /* Phase 2: Slice called procedures without ascending to call sites */
      S' := all marked vertices in G
      MarkReachingVertices(G, S', {def-order, parameter-in, call})
end

procedure MarkReachingVertices(G, V, Kinds)
declare
   G: a system dependence graph
   V: a set of vertices in G
   Kinds: a set of kinds of edges
   v, w: vertices in G
   WorkList: a set of vertices in G
begin
   WorkList := V
   while WorkList ≠ ∅ do
      Select and remove a vertex v from WorkList
      Mark v
      for each unmarked vertex w such that there is an edge w → v whose kind is not in Kinds do
         Insert w into WorkList
      od
   od
end
```

Fig. 9. The procedure MarkVerticesOfSlice marks the vertices of the interprocedural slice G/S. The auxiliary procedure MarkReachingVertices marks all vertices in G from which there is a path to a vertex in V along edges of kinds other than those in the set Kinds.

Suppose the goal is to slice system dependence graph G with respect to some vertex s in procedure P; Phases 1 and 2 can be characterized as follows:

Phase 1. Phase 1 identifies vertices that can reach s, and are either in P itself or in a procedure that calls P (either directly or transitively). Because parameter-out edges are not followed, the traversal in Phase 1 does not "descend" into procedures called by P. The effects of such procedures are not ignored, however; the presence of *transitive flow dependence edges* from actual-in to actual-out vertices (subordinate-characteristic-graph edges) permits the discovery of vertices that can reach s only through a procedure call, although the graph traversal does not actually descend into the called procedure.

Phase 2. Phase 2 identifies vertices that can reach s from procedures (transitively) called by P or from procedures called by procedures that (transitively) call P. Because call edges and parameter-in edges are not followed, the traversal in Phase 2 does not "ascend" into calling procedures; the transitive flow dependence edges from actual-in to actual-out vertices make such "ascents" unnecessary.

Figures 10 and 11 illustrate the two phases of the interprocedural slicing algorithm. Figure 10 shows the vertices of the example system dependence graph that are marked during Phase 1 of the interprocedural slicing algorithm when the system is sliced with respect to the formal-out vertex for parameter z in

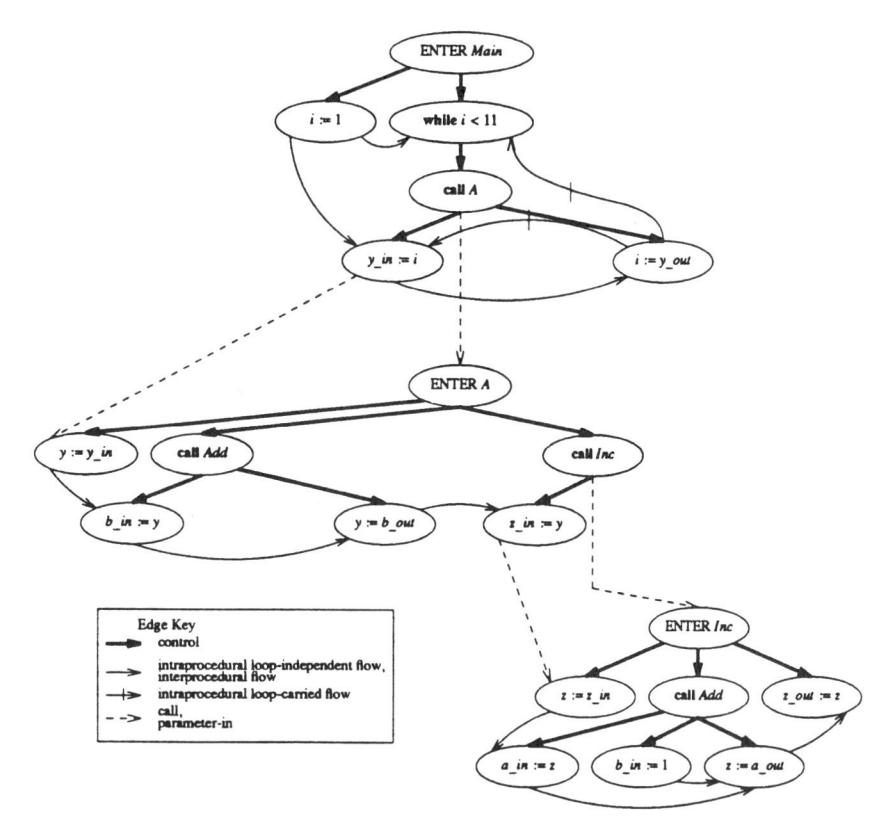

Fig. 10. The example program's system dependence graph is sliced with respect to the formal-out vertex for parameter z in procedure *Increment*. The vertices marked by Phase 1 of the slicing algorithm as well as the edges traversed during this phase are shown above.

procedure *Increment*. Edges "traversed" during Phase 1 are also included in Figure 10.

Figure 11 adds (in boldface) the vertices that are marked and the edges that are traversed during Phase 2 of the slice.

The result of an interprocedural slice consists of the sets of vertices identified by Phase 1 and Phase 2 and the set of edges induced by this vertex set. Figure 12 shows the completed example slice (excluding def-order edges.)

4.2 Using Interprocedural Summary Information to Build Procedure Dependence Graphs

The slice shown in Figure 12 illustrates a shortcoming of the method for constructing procedure dependence graphs described in Section 3. The problem is that including both an actual-in and an actual-out vertex for *every* argument in a procedure call can affect the precision of an interprocedural slice. The slice shown in Figure 12 includes the call vertex that represents the call to *Add* from *A*; however, this call does not in fact affect the value of z in *Increment*. The problem is that an actual-out vertex for argument y in the call to *Add* from *A* is

Fig. 11. The example program's system dependence graph is sliced with respect to the formal-out vertex for parameter z in procedure *Increment*. The vertices marked by Phase 2 of the slicing algorithm as well as the edges traversed during this phase are shown above in boldface.

included in A's procedure dependence graph even though *Add* does not change the value of y.

To achieve a more precise interprocedural slice, we use the results of interprocedural data-flow analysis when constructing procedure dependence graphs, in order to exclude vertices like the actual-out vertex for argument y.

The appropriate interprocedural summary information consists of the following sets, which are computed for each procedure P [4]:

GMOD(P): The set of variables that might be *modified* by P itself or by a procedure (transitively) called from P.

GREF(P): The set of variables that might be *referenced* by P itself or by a procedure (transitively) called from P.

GMOD and GREF sets are used to determine which parameter vertices are included in procedure dependence graphs as follows: for each procedure P, the parameter vertices subordinate to P's entry vertex include one formal-in vertex

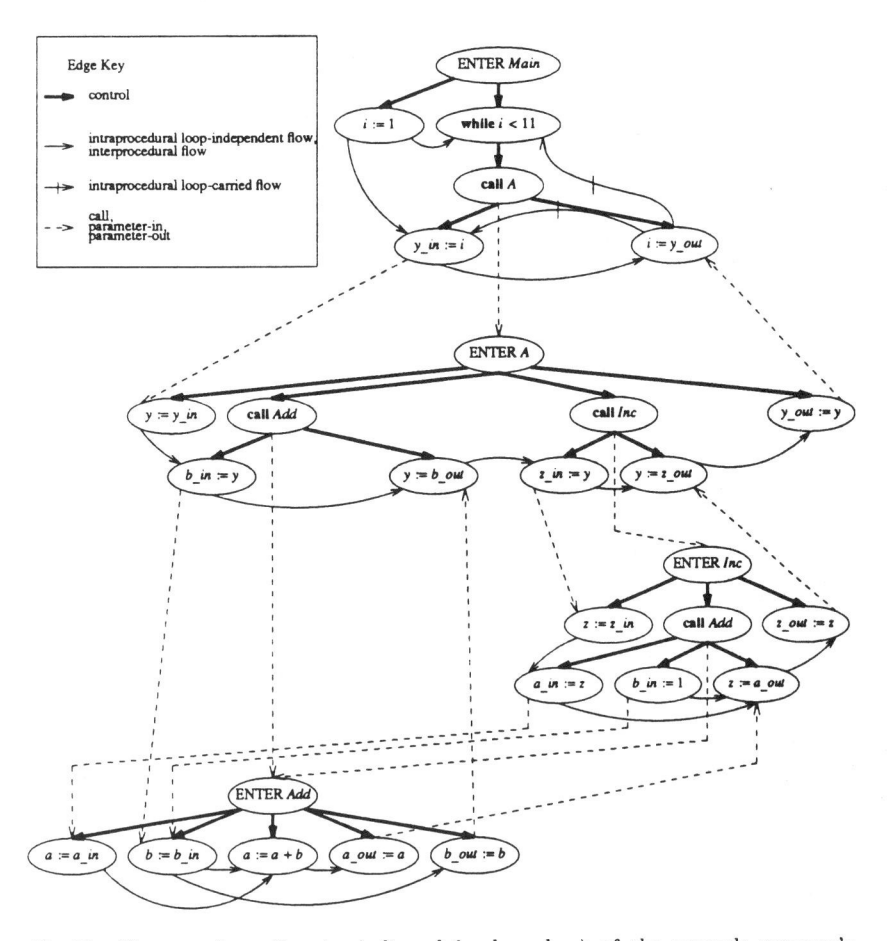

Fig. 12. The complete slice (excluding def-order edges) of the example program's system dependence graph sliced with respect to the formal-out vertex for parameter z in procedure *Increment*.

for each variable in GMOD(P) ∪ GREF(P) and one formal-out vertex for each variable in GMOD(P). Similarly, for each site at which P is called, the parameter vertices subordinate to the call-site vertex include one actual-in vertex for each variable in GMOD(P) ∪ GREF(P) and one actual-out vertex for each variable in GMOD(P). (It is necessary to include an actual-in and a formal-in vertex for a variable x that is in GMOD(P) and is not in GREF(P) because there may be an execution path through P on which x is *not* modified. In this case, a slice of P with respect to the final value of x must include the initial value of x; thus, there must be a formal-in vertex for x in P and a corresponding actual-in vertex at the call to P.)

Example. The GMOD and GREF sets for our example system are:

Procedure	GMOD	GREF
A	x, y	x, y
Add	a	a, b
Inc	z	z

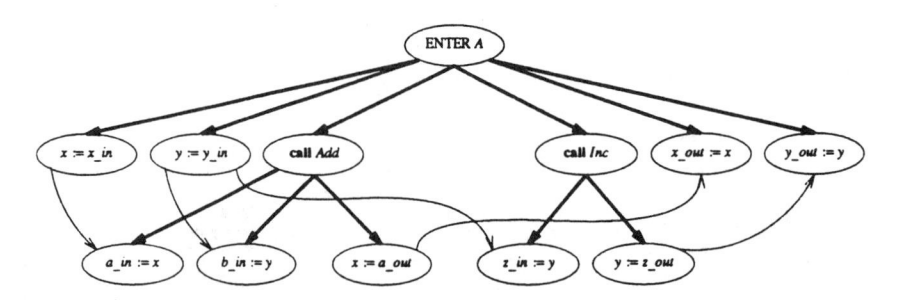

Fig. 13. Procedure A's procedure dependence graph built using interprocedural summary information. The actual-out vertex for argument y of the call to Add has been omitted, and the flow edge from that vertex to the vertex "$z\_in := y$" has been replaced by an edge from the vertex "$y := y\_in$" to the vertex "$z\_in := y$".

Because parameter b is not in GMOD(Add), Add's procedure dependence graph should not include a formal-out vertex for b, and the call to Add from A should not include the corresponding actual-out vertex.

Figure 13 shows A's procedure dependence graph as it would be built using GMOD and GREF information.

The actual-out vertex for argument y of the call to Add is omitted, and the flow edge from that vertex to the actual-in vertex "$z\_in := y$" is replaced by an edge from the formal-in vertex "$y := y\_in$" to the actual-in vertex "$z\_in := y$". The new edge is traversed during Phase 1 of the interprocedural slice instead of the (now omitted) flow edge from "$y := a\_out$" to "$z\_in := y$", thus (correctly) bypassing the call to Add in procedure A.

4.3 Interprocedural Slicing in the Presence of Call-By-Reference Parameter Passing and Aliasing

Our definitions of system dependence graphs and interprocedural slicing have assumed that parameters are passed by value-result. The same definitions hold for call-by-reference parameter passing in the absence of aliasing; however, in the presence of aliasing, some modifications are required. This section presents two approaches for dealing with systems that use call-by-reference parameter passing and contain aliasing. The first approach provides a more precise slice than the second, at the expense of the time and space needed to convert the original system into one that is alias-free. (These costs may, in the worst case, be exponential in the maximum number of parameters passed to a procedure.) The second approach avoids this expense by making use of a generalized notion of flow dependence that includes flow dependences that exist under the possible aliasing patterns.

Our first approach to the problem of interprocedural slicing in the presence of aliasing is to reduce the problem to that of interprocedural slicing in the *absence* of aliasing. The conversion is performed by simulating the calling behavior of the system (using the usual activation-tree model of procedure calls [4]) to discover, for each instance of a procedure call, exactly how variables are aliased at that instance. (Although a recursive system's activation tree is infinite, the number of different alias configurations is finite; thus, only a finite portion of the activation tree is needed to compute aliasing information.) A new copy of the procedure (with a new procedure name) is created for each different alias configuration; the procedure names used at call sites are similarly adjusted. Within each procedure, variables are renamed so that each set of aliased variables is replaced by a single variable.

This process may generate multiple copies of the vertex v, with respect to which we are to perform a slice. If this happens, it is necessary to slice the transformed system with respect to *all* occurrences of v. The slice of the original system is obtained from the slice of the transformed system by projecting elements in the slice of the transformed system back into the original system; a vertex is in the slice of the original system if any of its copies are in the slice of the transformed system.

Example. Figure 14 shows a system with aliasing, and the portion of the system's activation tree that is used to compute alias information for each call instance.

We use the notation of [4], in which each node of the activation tree is labeled with the mapping from variable names to memory locations. The transformed, alias-free version of the system is shown below.

```
program Main          procedure P1(x, y)      procedure P2(xy)
    a := 1;               if y = 0 then           if xy = 0 then
    b := 0;                  call P2(x)              call P2(xy)
    call P1(a, b);        fi;                      fi;
    z := b                y := y + 1              xy := xy + 1
end                       return                   return
```

If our original goal had been to slice with respect to the statement "$y := y + 1$" in procedure P, we must now slice with respect to the set of statements $\{$"$y := y + 1$", "$xy := xy + 1$"$\}$.

Our second approach to the problem of interprocedural slicing in the presence of aliasing is to generalize the definition of a flow dependence to include dependences that arise under the possible aliasing patterns. A procedure dependence graph has a flow dependence edge from vertex v_1 to vertex v_2 iff all of the following hold:

(1) v_1 is a vertex that defines variable x.
(2) v_2 is a vertex that uses variable y.
(3) x and y are potential aliases.
(4) Control can reach v_2 after v_1 via a path in the control-flow graph along which there is no intervening definition of x or y.

Note that clause (4) does not exclude there being definitions of other variables that are potential aliases of x or y along the path from v_1 to v_2. An assignment to a variable z along the path from v_1 to v_2 only overwrites the contents of the memory location written by v_1 if x and z refer to the same memory location. If z is a potential alias of x, then there is only a *possibility* that x and z refer to the same memory location; thus, an assignment to z does not necessarily overwrite the memory location written by v_1, and it may be possible for v_2 to read a value written by v_1.

```
program Main          procedure P(x, y)
  a := 1;               if y = 0 then
  b := 0;                 call P(x, x)
  call P(a, b);         fi;
  z := b                y := y + 1
end                   return
```

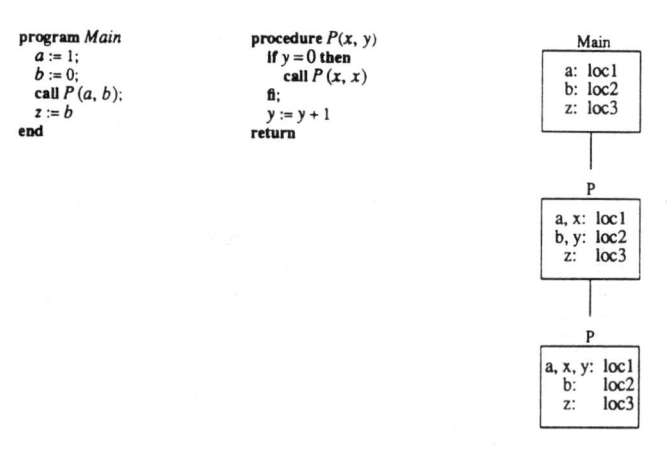

```
Main
a: loc1
b: loc2
z: loc3

P
a, x: loc1
b, y: loc2
z:    loc3

P
a, x, y: loc1
b:       loc2
z:       loc3
```

Fig. 14. A program with aliasing and the portion of its activation tree needed to compute all alias configurations.

The notion of a def-order edge must also be generalized in the presence of aliasing. A procedure dependence graph has a def-order dependence edge from vertex v_1 to vertex v_2 iff all of the following hold:

(1) v_1 and v_2 define variables x_1 and x_2, respectively.
(2) x_1 and x_2 are potential aliases.
(3) v_1 and v_2 are in the same branch of any conditional statement that encloses both of them.
(4) There exists a program component v_3 such that $v_1 \rightarrow_f v_3$ and $v_2 \rightarrow_f v_3$.
(5) v_1 occurs to the left of v_2 in the procedure's abstract syntax tree.

The interprocedural slice of a system dependence graph containing dependence edges as defined above is computed by the same two-phase algorithm used to compute the interprocedural slice of a system in the absence of aliasing. The data dependences in a procedure provide a safe approximation to the true dependences required for each alias configuration. Because these edges cover all possible alias configurations, the resulting slice may contain unnecessary program elements.

Example. Consider again the system shown in Figure 14. The possibility of aliasing between formal parameters x and y of procedure P gives rise to flow dependences from the actual-out vertices "$x := x\_out$" and "$x := y\_out$" of the call $P(x, x)$ to the vertex "$y := y + 1$". Because of these dependences, the slice with respect to the statement "$z := b$" in the main program yields the entire system, even though the statement "$a := 1$" in Main and the conditional statement in P have no effect on the value computed for z. The approach based on replicating procedures determines a more precise slice that does not include the statement "$a := 1$" or the conditional statement, as shown below:

```
program Main       procedure P1(y)
  b := 0;            y := y + 1
  call P1(b);      return
  z := b
end
```

4.4 Slicing Partial System Dependence Graphs

The interprocedural slicing algorithm presented above is designed to be applied to a complete system dependence graph. In this section we discuss how to slice *incomplete* system dependence graphs.

The need to handle incomplete systems arises, for example, when slicing a program that calls a library procedure that is not itself available, or when slicing programs under development. In the first case, the missing components are procedures that are called by the incomplete system; in the second case, the missing components can either be not-yet-written procedures called by the incomplete system (when the program is developed top-down), or possible calling contexts (when the program is developed bottom-up).

In either case, information about the possible effects of missing calls and missing calling contexts is needed to permit slicing. This information takes the form of (safe approximations to) the subordinate characteristic graphs for missing called procedures and the superior characteristic graphs for missing calling contexts.

When no information about missing program components is available, subordinate characteristic graphs in which there is an edge from each inherited attribute to each synthesized attribute, and superior characteristic graphs in which there is an edge from each synthesized attribute to each other attribute (including the other synthesized attributes), must be used. This is because the slice of the incomplete system should include all vertices that could be included in the slice of some "completed" system, and it is always possible to provide a call or a calling context that corresponds to the graphs described above.

For library procedures, it is possible to provide precise subordinate characteristic graphs even when the procedures themselves are not provided. For programs under development, it might be possible to compute characteristic graphs, or at least better approximations to them than the worst-case graphs, given specifications for the missing program components.

4.5 Forward Slicing

Whereas the *slice* of a program with respect to a program point p and variable x consists of all statements and predicates of the program that might affect the value of x at point p, the *forward slice* of a program with respect to a program point p and variable x consists of all statements and predicates of the program that might be affected by the value of x at point p. An algorithm for *forward* interprocedural slicing can be defined on system dependence graphs, using the same concepts employed for (backward) interprocedural slicing. As before, the key element is the use of the linkage grammar's characteristic graph edges in the system dependence graph to represent transitive dependences from actual-in vertices to actual-out vertices due to the effects of procedure calls.

An algorithm for forward interprocedural slicing is given as procedure MarkVerticesOfForwardSlice of Figure 15.

In Figure 15, the computation of the forward slice of system dependence graph G with respect to vertex set S is performed in two phases. The traversal in Phase 1 follows flow edges, control edges, and parameter-out edges, but does *not* follow call edges, def-order edges, or parameter-in edges. Because call edges

```
procedure MarkVerticesOfForwardSlice(G, S)
declare
    G: a system dependence graph
    S, S': sets of vertices in G
begin
    /* Phase 1: Slice forward without descending into called procedures */
        MarkVerticesReached(G, S, {def-order, parameter-in, call})

    /* Phase 2: Slice forward into called procedures without ascending to call sites */
        S' := all marked vertices in G
        MarkVerticesReached(G, S', {def-order, parameter-out})
end

procedure MarkVerticesReached(G, V, Kinds)
declare
    G: a system dependence graph
    V: a set of vertices in G
    Kinds: a set of kinds of edges
    v, w: vertices in G
    WorkList: a set of vertices in G
begin
    WorkList := V
    while WorkList ≠ ∅ do
        Select and remove a vertex v from WorkList
        Mark v
        for each unmarked vertex w such that there is an edge v → w whose kind is not in Kinds do
            Insert w into WorkList
        od
    od
end
```

Fig. 15. The procedure MarkVerticesOfForwardSlice marks the vertices of the forward interprocedural slice G/S. The auxiliary procedure MarkVerticesReached marks all vertices in G to which there is a path from a vertex in V along edges of kinds other than those in the set Kinds.

and parameter-in edges are not followed, the traversal in Phase 1 does not descend into called procedures. The traversal in Phase 2 follows flow edges, control edges, call edges, and parameter-in edges, but does *not* follow def-order edges or parameter-out edges. Because parameter-out edges are not followed, the traversal in Phase 2 does not ascend into calling procedures.

5. THE COMPLEXITY OF THE SLICING ALGORITHM

This section discusses the complexity of the interprocedural slicing algorithm presented in Section 4.1. In the absence of aliasing, the cost is polynomial in (various) parameters of the system. In the presence of aliasing, the cost remains polynomial if we use the generalized definitions of data dependences given in Section 4.3 (at the price of somewhat less precision in taking slices). Alternatively, if we follow the approach of transforming the system to one that is alias-free, more precise slices can be obtained, but the cost can increase by an exponential factor that reflects the blow-up in size that can occur due to the number of aliasing patterns in the program. The measures of system size used below are those associated with the system dependence graph created according to one or the other of these approaches. In particular, if the approach of transforming to an alias-free system is used, the measures of system size used below are those associated with the alias-free system.

5.1 Cost of Constructing the System Dependence Graph

The cost of constructing the system dependence graph can be expressed in terms of the parameters given in the following tables:

	Parameters that measure the size of an individual procedure
V	The larest number of predicates and assignments in a single procedure
E	The largest number of edges in a single procedure dependence graph
$Params$	The largest number of formal parameters in any procedure
$Sites$	The largest number of call sites in any procedure

	Parameters that measure the size of the entire system
P	The number of procedures in the system (= the number of productions in the linkage grammar)
$Globals$	The number of global variables in the system
$TotalSites \leq P \cdot Sites$	The total number of call sites in the system

Interprocedural data-flow analysis is used to compute summary information about side effects. Flow-insensitive interprocedural summary information (e.g., GMOD and GREF) can be determined particularly efficiently. In particular, in the absence of nested scopes, GMOD and GREF can be determined in time $O(P^2 + P \cdot TotalSites)$ steps by the algorithm described in [6].

Intraprocedural data-flow analysis is used to determine the data dependences of procedure dependence graphs. For the structured language under consideration here, this analysis can be performed in a syntax-directed fashion (for example, using an attribute grammar) [8]. This involves propagating sets of program points, where each set consists of program points in a single procedure. This computation has total cost $O(V^2)$.

The cost of constructing the linkage grammar and computing its subordinate characteristic graphs can be expressed in terms of the following parameters:

	Parameters that measure the size of the linkage grammar
$R = Sites + 1$	The largest number of nonterminal occurrences in a single production
$G = P + TotalSites$	The number of nonterminal occurrences in the linkage grammar
$\leq P \cdot R$	
$= P \cdot (Sites + 1)$	
$X = Globals + Params$	The largest number of attributes of a single nonterminal
$D \leq R \cdot X$	The largest number of attribute occurrences in a single production
$= (Sites + 1)$ $\cdot (Global + Params)$	

To determine the dependences among the attribute occurrences in each production, its corresponding procedure is sliced with respect to the linkage vertices that correspond to the attribute occurrences of the production. The cost of each slice is linear in the size of the procedure dependence graph; that is, the cost is bounded by $O(V + E)$. Consequently, the total cost of constructing the linkage grammar is bounded by $O(G \cdot X \cdot (V + E))$.

It remains for us to analyze the cost of computing the linkage grammar's subordinate characteristic graphs. Because there are at most D^2 edges in each TDP(p) relation, the cost of AddEdgeAndInduce, which recloses a single TDP(p) relation, is $O(D^2)$. The cost of initializing the TDP relations with all direct dependences in ConstructSubCGraphs is bounded by $O(P \cdot D^2)$.

In the inner loop of Step 2 of procedure ConstructSubCGraphs, AddEdgeAndInduce is called once for each occurrence of nonterminal N. There are at most X^2 edges in each graph TDS(N) and G nonterminal occurrences where an edge may be induced. No edge is induced more than once because of the marks on TDS edges; thus, the total cost of procedure ConstructSubCGraphs is bounded by $O(G \cdot X^2 \cdot D^2)$ [13].

5.2 Slicing Costs

An interprocedural slice is performed by two traversals of the system dependence graph, starting from some initial set of vertices. The cost of each traversal is linear in the size of the system dependence graph, which is bounded by $O(P \cdot (V + E) + TotalSites \cdot X)$.

6. RELATED WORK

In recasting the interprocedural slicing problem as a reachability problem in a graph, we are following the example of [19], which does the same for intraprocedural slicing. The reachability approach is conceptually simpler than the dataflow equation approach used in [22], and is also much more efficient when more than one slice is desired.

The recasting of the problem as a reachability problem does involve some loss of generality; rather than permitting a program to be sliced with respect to program point p and an *arbitrary* variable, a slice can only be taken with respect to a variable that is defined or used at p. For such slicing problems the interprocedural slicing algorithm presented in this paper is an improvement over Weiser's algorithm because our algorithm is able to produce a more precise slice than the one produced by Weiser's algorithm. However, the extra generality is not the source of the imprecision of Weiser's method; as explained in the Introduction and in Section 3.2, the imprecision of Weiser's method is due to the lack of a mechanism to keep track of the calling context of a called procedure.

After the initial publication of our interprocedural-slicing algorithm [10], a different technique for computing interprocedural slices was presented by Hwang et al. [12]. The slicing algorithm presented in [12] computes an answer that is as precise as our algorithm, but differs significantly in how it handles the calling-context problem. The algorithm from [12] constructs a *sequence* of slices of the system—where each slice of the sequence essentially permits there to be one additional level of recursion—until a fixed-point is reached (i.e., until no further elements appear in a slice that uses one additional level of recursion). Thus, each slice of the sequence represents an approximation to the final answer. During each of these slice approximations, the algorithm uses a stack to keep track of the calling context of a called procedure. In contrast, our algorithm for interprocedural slicing is based on a two-phase process for propagating marks on the system dependence graph. In Phase 1 of the algorithm, the presence of the linkage grammar's subordinate-characteristic-graph edges (representing transitive dependences due to the effects of procedure calls) permits the entire effect of a call to be accounted for by a single backward step over the call site's subordinate-characteristic-graph edges.

Hwang et al. do not include an analysis of their algorithm's complexity in [12], which makes a direct comparison with our algorithm difficult; however, there are several reasons why our algorithm may be more efficient. First, the algorithm from [12] computes a sequence of slices, each of which may involve reslicing a procedure multiple times; in contrast, through its use of marks on system-dependence-graph vertices, our algorithm processes no vertex more than once during the computation of a slice. Second, if one wishes to compute multiple slices of the same system, our approach has a significant advantage. The system dependence graph (with its subordinate-characteristic-graph edges) need be computed only once; each slicing operation can use this graph, and the cost of each such slice is linear in the size of the system dependence graph. In contrast, the approach of [12] would involve finding a new fixed point (a problem that appears to have complexity comparable to the computation of the subordinate characteristic graphs) for each new slice.

In [18], Myers presents algorithms for a specific set of interprocedural data-flow problems, all of which require keeping track of calling context; however, Myers's approach to handling this problem differs from ours. Myers performs data-flow analysis on a graph representation of the program, called a *super graph*, which is a collection of control-flow graphs (one for each procedure in the program), connected by call and return edges. The information maintained at each vertex of the super graph includes a *memory component*, which keeps track of calling context (essentially by using the name of the call site). Our use of the system dependence graph permits keeping track of calling context while propagating simple marks rather than requiring the propagation of sets of names.

It is no doubt possible to formulate interprocedural slicing as a data-flow analysis problem on a super graph and to solve the problem using an algorithm akin to those described by Myers to account correctly for the calling context of a called procedure. As in the comparison with [12], our algorithm has a significant advantage when one wishes to compute multiple slices of the same system. Whereas the system dependence graph can be computed once and then used for each slicing operation, the approach postulated above would involve solving a new data-flow analysis problem from scratch for each slice.

The vertex-reachability approach we have used here has some similarities to a technique used in [5], [6], and [15] to transform data-flow analysis problems to vertex-reachability problems. In each case, a data-flow analysis problem is solved by first building a graph representation of the program and then performing a reachability analysis on the graph, propagating simple marks rather than, for example, sets of variable names. One difference between the interprocedural slicing problem and the problems addressed by the work cited above, is that interprocedural slicing is a "demand problem" [2] whose goal is to determine information concerning a specific set of program points rather than an "exhaustive problem" in which the goal is to determine information for all program points.

APPENDIX: ATTRIBUTE GRAMMARS AND ATTRIBUTE DEPENDENCES

An attribute grammar is a context-free grammar extended by attaching *attributes* to the terminal and nonterminal symbols of the grammar and by supplying *attribute equations* to define attribute values [14]. In every production $p: X_0 \rightarrow X_1, \ldots, X_k$, each X_i denotes an *occurrence* of one of the grammar symbols; associated with each such symbol occurrence is a set of *attribute occurrences* corresponding to the symbol's attributes.

Each production has a set of attribute equations; each equation defines one of the production's attribute occurrences as the value of an *attribute-definition function* applied to other attribute occurrences in the production. The attributes of a symbol X are divided into two disjoint classes: *synthesized* attributes and *inherited* attributes.

An attribute grammar is *well formed* when the terminal symbols of the grammar have no synthesized attributes, the root nonterminal of the grammar has no inherited attributes, and each production has exactly one attribute equation for each of the left-hand side nonterminal's synthesized attribute occurrences and for each of the right-hand side symbols' inherited attribute occurrences. (The grammars that arise in this paper are potentially *not* well formed, in that a production may have equations for synthesized attribute occurrences of right-hand side symbols. The reason that this does not cause problems is that the "linkage grammar" of the interprocedural slicing algorithm is used *only* to compute transitive dependences due to calls; we are not interested in the language defined by the grammar, nor in actual attribute values.)

A derivation tree node that is an instance of symbol X has an associated set of *attribute instances* corresponding to the attributes of X. An *attributed tree* is a derivation tree together with an assignment of either a value or the special token **null** to each attribute instance of the tree.

Ordinarily, although not in this paper, one is interested in analyzing a string according to its attribute-grammar specification. To do this, one first constructs the string's derivation tree with an assignment of **null** to each attribute instance and then evaluates as many attribute instances as possible, using the appropriate attribute equation as an assignment statement. The latter process is termed *attribute evaluation*.

Functional dependences among attribute occurrences in a production p (or attribute instances in a tree T) can be represented by a directed graph, called a *dependence graph*, denoted by $D(p)$ (respectively, $D(T)$), and defined as follows:

(1) For each attribute occurrence (instance) b, the graph contains a vertex b'.
(2) If attribute occurrence (instance) b appears on the right-hand side of the attribute equation that defines attribute occurrence (instance) c, the graph contains the edge $b' \rightarrow c'$.

An attribute grammar that has a derivation tree whose dependence graph contains a cycle is called a *circular* attribute grammar. (The grammars that arise in this paper can be circular grammars.)

A node's *subordinate* and *superior characteristic graphs* provide a convenient representation of transitive dependences among the node's attributes. (A *transitive dependence* exists between attributes that are related in the transitive closure of the tree's attribute dependence relation, or, equivalently, that are connected by a direct path in the tree's dependence graph.) The vertices of the characteristic graphs at node r correspond to the attributes of r; the edges of the characteristic graphs at r correspond to transitive dependences among r's attributes.

The subordinate characteristic graph at r is the projection of the dependences of the subtree rooted at r onto the attributes of r. To form the superior characteristic graph at node r, we imagine that the subtree rooted at r has been pruned from the derivation tree, and project the dependence graph of the remaining tree onto the attributes of r. To define the characteristic graphs precisely, we make the following definitions:

(1) Given a directed graph $G = (V, E)$, a *path* from vertex a to vertex b is a sequence of vertices, $[v_1, v_2, \ldots, v_k]$, such that $a = v_1, b = v_k$, and $\{(v_i, v_{i+1}) \mid i = 1, \ldots, k - 1\} \subseteq E$.

(2) Given a directed graph $G = (V, E)$ and a set of vertices $V' \subseteq V$, the *projection* of G onto V' is defined as

$$G//V' = (V', E')$$

where $E' = \{(v, w) \mid v, w \in V'$, and there exists a path $[v = v_1, v_2, \ldots, v_k = w]$ in G such that $v_2, \ldots, v_{k-1} \notin V'\}$. (That is, $G//V'$ has an edge from $v \in V'$ to $w \in V'$ when there exists a path from v to w in G that does not pass through any other elements of V'.)

The subordinate and superior characteristic graphs of a node r, denoted $r.C$ and $r.\bar{C}$, respectively, are defined formally as follows. Let r be a node in tree T, let the subtree rooted at r be denoted T_r, and let the attribute instances at r be denoted $A(r)$, then the subordinate and superior characteristic graphs at r satisfy:

$$r.C = D(T_r)//A(r)$$
$$r.\bar{C} = (D(T) - D(T_r))//A(r).$$

A characteristic graph represents the projection of attribute dependences onto the attributes of a single tree node; consequently, for a given grammar, each graph is bounded in size by some constant.

REFERENCES

1. AHO, A. V., SETHI, R., AND ULLMAN, J. D. *Compilers: Principles, Techniques, and Tools*, Addison-Wesley, Reading, Mass., 1986.
2. BABICH, W. A., AND JAZAYERI, M. The method of attributes for data flow analysis: Part II. Demand analysis. *Acta Inf. 10*, 3 (Oct. 1978), 265–272.
3. BADGER, L., AND WEISER, M. Minimizing communication for synchronizing parallel dataflow programs. In *Proceedings of the 1988 International Conference on Parallel Processing* (St. Charles, IL, Aug. 15-19, 1988). Pennsylvania State University Press, University Park, PA, 1988.
4. BANNING, J. P. An efficient way to find the side effects of procedure calls and the aliases of variables. In *Conference Record of the Sixth ACM Symposium on Principles of Programming Languages* (San Antonio, Tex., Jan. 29-31, 1979). ACM, New York, 1979, pp. 29–41.
5. CALLAHAN, D. The program summary graph and flow-sensitive interprocedural data flow analysis. In *Proceedings of the ACM SIGPLAN 88 Conference on Programming Language Design and Implementation* (Atlanta, Ga., June 22-24, 1988). *ACM SIGPLAN Not. 23*, 7 (July 1988), 47–56.

6. COOPER, K. D., AND KENNEDY, K. Interprocedural side-effect analysis in linear time. In *Proceedings of the ACM SIGPLAN 88 Conference on Programming Language Design and Implementation* (Atlanta, Ga., June 22-24, 1988). *ACM SIGPLAN Not. 23*, 7 (July 1988), 57-66.
7. FERRANTE, J., OTTENSTEIN, K., AND WARREN, J. The program dependence graph and its use in optimization. *ACM Trans. Program. Lang. Syst. 9*, 3 (July 1987), 319-349.
8. HORWITZ, S., PRINS, J., AND REPS, T. Integrating non-interfering versions of programs. TR-690, Computer Sciences Dept., Univ. of Wisconsin, Madison, March 1987.
9. HORWITZ, S., PRINS, J., AND REPS, T. On the adequacy of program dependence graphs for representing programs. In *Conference Record of the Fifteenth ACM Symposium on Principles of Programming Languages* (San Diego, Calif., Jan. 13-15, 1988). ACM, New York, 1988, pp. 146-157.
10. HORWITZ, S., REPS, T., AND BINKLEY, D. Interprocedural slicing using dependence graphs. In *Proceedings of the ACM SIGPLAN 88 Conference on Programming Language Design and Implementation* (Atlanta, Ga., June 22-24, 1988). *ACM SIGPLAN Not. 23*, 7 (July 1988), 35-46.
11. HORWITZ, S., PRINS, J., AND REPS, T. Integrating non-interfering versions of programs. *ACM Trans. Program. Lang. Syst. 11*, 3 (July 1989), 345-387.
12. HWANG, J. C., DU, M. W., AND CHOU, C. R. Finding program slices for recursive procedures. In *Proceedings of the IEEE COMPSAC 88* (Chicago, Oct. 3-7, 1988). IEEE Computer Society, Washington, D.C., 1988.
13. KASTENS, U. Ordered attribute grammars. *Acta Inf. 13*, 3 (1980), 229-256.
14. KNUTH, D. E. Semantics of context-free languages. *Math. Syst. Theor. 2*, 2 (June 1968), 127-145.
15. KOU, L. T. On live-dead analysis for global data flow problems. *J. ACM 24*, 3 (July 1977), 473-483.
16. KUCK, D. J., MURAOKA, Y., AND CHEN, S. C. On the number of operations simultaneously executable in FORTRAN-like programs and their resulting speed-up. *IEEE Trans. Comput. C-21*, 12 (Dec. 1972), 1293-1310.
17. LYLE, J., AND WEISER, M. Experiments on slicing-based debugging tools. In *Proceedings of the First Conference on Empirical Studies of Programming* (June 1986).
18. MYERS, E. A precise inter-procedural data flow algorithm. In *Conference Record of the Eighth ACM Symposium on Principles of Programming Languages* (Williamsburg, Va., Jan. 26-28, 1981). ACM, New York, 1981, pp. 219-230.
19. OTTENSTEIN, K. J., AND OTTENSTEIN, L. M. The program dependence graph in a software development environment. In *Proceedings of the ACM SIGSOFT/SIGPLAN Software Engineering Symposium on Practical Software Development Environments* (Pittsburgh, Pa., April 23-25, 1984). *ACM SIGPLAN Not. 19*, 5 (May 1984), 177-184.
20. REPS, T., AND YANG, W. The semantics of program slicing. TR-777, Computer Sciences Dept., Univ. of Wisconsin, Madison, June 1988.
21. WEISER, M. Reconstructing sequential behavior from parallel behavior projections. *Inf. Process. Lett. 17* (Oct. 1983), 129-135.
22. WEISER, M. Program slicing. *IEEE Trans. Softw. Eng. SE-10*, 4 (July 1984), 352-357.

Received April 1988; revised August 1989; accepted August 1989

Program Slicing For C - The Problems In Implementation

Jingyue Jiang[*]   Xiling Zhou[‡]   David J. Robson[*]

[*]Centre for Software Maintenance
School of Engineering and Applied Science
University of Durham
Durham, DH1 3LE, England

[‡]Software Engineering Research Centre
Beijing Information Technology Institute,
Beijing, P.R.China

Abstract

Program slicing is a method of finding all statements that might directly or indirectly affect the values of variables. It is implemented by analysing the program's data flow and control flow. The concept was first proposed by Weiser [14,16] and since then its use has been suggested in many applications, such as debugging, testing and maintenance. Standard slicing techniques described in [16] have some problems when applied to the language C. For instance, how to find the correct slice in the presence of array and pointer variables and how to find break, continue and goto statements that have effects on the slice. In this paper such problems and their solutions are discussed.

1 Introduction

Program slicing is a method for automatic program decomposition, originally defined by Weiser [14,16]. In Weiser's terminology, a slicing criterion is a pair <p, V>, where p is a program point and V is a subset of the program's variables. A slice S of a program P with respect to a slicing criterion C=<p, V> is a reduced program that computes the same sequence of values for variables in V at point p. That is, at point p the behaviour of the reduced program is not distinguishable from that of the original program with respect to variables in V. Program slicing can be used to isolate individual computation threads within a program, which can help the maintainer understand complicated programs. In recent years program slicing techniques have been applied to software maintenance [9,10], especially bug location [1,11,12,15].

A static C program slicer (or CPS in short) has been implemented at BITI (Beijing Information Technology Institute). CPS is based on the algorithms described in [16] and uses the data flow and control flow information provided by a C program analyser (or CPA in short) which has also been developed at BITI. On applying the standard techniques given in [16] to the C language, some problems arise. For example:

i) How to find the correct slice in the presence of array and pointer variables.

ii) How to adapt the standard algorithm to cope with goto, break and continue statements which cannot be included in the slice by the algorithm described in [16]. However, these statements do have effects on the behaviour of the slice.

In this paper, some of the problems and possible solutions of program slicing within the C language will be discussed. This paper is organised as follows. In the first part of the paper (section 2) some basic notations and the Weiser's original algorithm are presented. Then slicing problems and solutions are described (section 3). In the last part of the paper (section 4), an algorithm to find the branch statements is introduced.

2 Notations And Weiser's Algorithm

2.1 Definition And Notation

It is convenient to introduce some notational conventions which will be used in this paper.

A *flowgraph* G is a 3-tuple $G = <N, E, n_0>$, where N is the set of nodes, E is the set of edges, n_0 is the initial node. If m and n are two nodes in N, m *dominates* n, indicated by m DOM n or DOM(n)=m, if and only if m is on every path from n_0 to n [16].

A *hammock* graph, HG, is a quadruple $HG = <N, E, n_0, n_1>$ with the property that $<N, E, n_0>$ and $<N, E^{-1}, n_1>$ are both flowgraphs. Note that, as usual, $E^{-1} = \{<a,b> \mid <b,a> \in E\}$. If m and n are two nodes in N, m *reversely dominates* n, indicated by m RDOM n or RDOM(n)=m, if and only if m is on every path from n_1 to n [16].

The terms "node" and "statement" will be interchangeably used in this paper. Additionally, we will

---

Most of the work described here was done when the first author worked at Beijing Information Technology Institute.

assume that the flow graph representing the function's control flow is a hammock graph.

Let $G = <N, E, n_0>$, $n \in N$ and assume

d_i DOM n $1 \leq i \leq s$,
r_j RDOM n $1 \leq j \leq t$, where d_i and $r_j \in N$

If there exists d_j and r_l satisfying the following conditions, then d_j is called the *immediate dominator* of n and r_l is called the *reverse immediate* (or nearest reverse) *dominator* of n, indicated as ID(n) and RID(n) separately.

d_i DOM d_j,   where i =1, 2, ... j-1, j+1, ...s,
r_j RDOM r_l,   where j =1, 2, ... l-1, l+1, ...t,

For an arbitrary statement n and a slicing criterion $C = <p, V>$, let

IMS(n)   represent the set of immediate successors of n.
USE(n)   represent all the variables whose values might be used at n.
MOD(n)   represent all the variables whose values might be modified at n.
ND(n)   represent all the statements which are on a path from n to RID(n) excluding the endpoint n and RID(n). ND(n) will be empty unless n has more than one immediate successor.
$RIN_c(n)$ be a set of variables related to the position of statement n. Each variable in $RIN_c(n)$ has potential effects on the values of variable in V. That is, if the value for some variable x in $RIN_c(n)$ is changed at n during the execution of program then the behaviour of the variables in V will be different from that of original program's execution without interference.
POS(C)   represent the statement position specified in the slicing criterion C, i.e. POS(C) = p.
VAR(C)   represent the variable set of slicing criterion C, i.e. VAR(C) = V.

To clarify these definitions, the example appeared in [16] will be used here again. The program and its control flow graph is shown on this page. Note the numbers in nodes represent the executable statement positions.

$N = \{2, 3, 4, 5, 6, 8, 9, 11\}$,
$E = \{<2,3>,<3,4>,<4,5>,<5,6>,<5,8>,<8,9>, <6,11>,<9,11>\}$
$E^{-1} = \{<11,6>,<11,9>,<9,8>,<8,5>,<6,5>,<5,4>, <4,3>,<3,2>\}$
$n_0 = 2$, $n_1 = 11$

```
Program:
  1.  BEGIN
  2.     read(x,y)
  3.     total := 0.0
  4.     sum := 0.0
  5.     IF  x <= 1
  6.        THEN    sum := y
  7.        ELSE    BEGIN
  8.            read(z)
  9.            total := x*y
 10.        END
 11.     write(total,sum)
 12. END
```

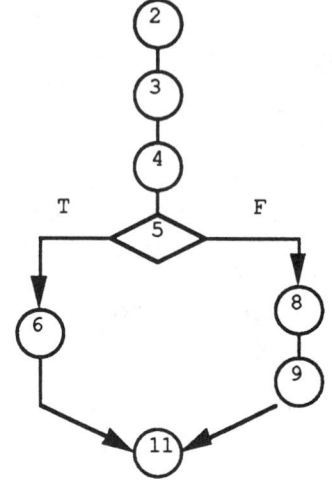

Figure 1:   Program control flow graph

DOM(2) = ∅,   DOM(3) = {2}
DOM(4) = {2,3},   DOM(5) = {2,3,4}
DOM(6) = DOM(8) = {2,3,4,5}
DOM(9) = {2,3,4,5,8}, DOM(11) = {2,3,4,5}
RDOM(11) = ∅,   RDOM(9) = {11}
RDOM(8) = {11,9},   RDOM(6) = {11}
RDOM(5) = {11},   RDOM(4) = {11,5}
RDOM(3) = {11,5,4},   RDOM(2) = {11,5,4,3}

ID(2) = ∅,   RID(2) = 3   IMS(2) = {3}
ID(3) = 2,   RID(3) = 4   IMS(3) = {4}
ID(4) = 3,   RID(4) = 5   IMS(4) = {5}
ID(5) = 4,   RID(5) = 11   IMS(5) = {6,8}
ID(6) = 5,   RID(6) = 11   IMS(6) = {11}
ID(8) = 5,   RID(8) = 9   IMS(8) = {9}
ID(9) = 8,   RID(9) = 11   IMS(9) = {11}
ID(11) = 5,   RID(11) = ∅   IMS(11) = ∅

ND(2) = ND(3) = ND(4 = ND(6) = ND(8) = ND(9) = ND(11) = ∅
ND(5) = {6,8,9}

Given the slicing criterion $C = <12, \{total\}>$, the $RIN_c(n)$ for each statement is:

```
1.    BEGIN
2.    read(x,y)           RIN_c(2)={}
      USE=(2)={},
      MOD(n)={x,y}
3.    total:=0.0          RIN_c(3)={x,y}
      USE(3)={},
      MOD(3)={total}
4.    sum:=0.0            RIN_c(4)={total,x,y}
      USE(4)={},
      MOD(4)={sum}
5.    IF x<=1             RIN_c(5)={total,x,y}
      USE(5)={x},
      MOD(5)={}
6.      THEN sum:=y       RIN_c(6)={total}
             USE(6)={y},
             MOD(6)={sum}
7.      ELSE BEGIN
8.        read(z)         RIN_c(8)={x,y}
          USE(8)={},
          MOD(8)={z}
9.        total:=x*y      RIN_c(9)={x,y}
          USE(9)={x,y},
          MOD(9)={total}
10.       END
11.   write(total,sum)    RIN_c(11)={total}
      USE(11)={total,sum},
      MOD(11)={}
12.   END                 RIN_c(12)={total}
```

2.2 An Intraprocedural Slicing Algorithm

We will assume that the data flow information MOD(n) and USE(n) for each statement is available. Some of the interprocedural data flow analysis techniques can be found in [2,3,4,5,6,13].

Given a slicing criterion C = <p, V> and an arbitrary statement n, then if $RIN_c(IMS(n)) \cap MOD(n) \neq \emptyset$ then the execution of statement n will influence the values of variables in the set $RIN_c(IMS(n))$. According to the definition of $RIN_c(n)$, this influence will be propagated to the variables in VAR(C). Therefore statement n should be included in the slice S_c. For a given slicing criterion C = <p, V>, the formal definition of $RIN_c(n)$ is defined as:

$$RIN_c^0(n) = \{V \mid n = p\} \cup \{USE(n) \mid MOD(n) \cap RIN_c^0(IMS(n)) \neq \emptyset\} \cup \{RIN_c^0(IMS(n)) - MOD(n)\}$$

$$S_c^0 = \{n \mid MOD(n) \cap RIN_c^0(IMS(n)) \neq \emptyset\}$$

$$B_c^0 = \{b \mid ND(b) \cap S_c^0 \neq \emptyset\}^*$$

---
* In [16] $B_c^0 = \cup ND(n)$
             $n \in S_c^0$

Here the superscript 0 represents the first level of $RIN_c(n)$ and S_c. That is, $RIN_c^0(n)$ is composed of the variables whose values can directly influence the behaviour of variables in VAR(C) by propagation. S_c^0 is composed of the statements whose executions can directly influence the values of variables in some $RIN_c^0(n)$.

To include all the statements which have either direct or indirect influence on VAR(C), the author of [16] gives the following iterative equations:

$$RIN_c^{i+1}(n) = RIN_c^i(n) \cup RIN_{BC(b)}^0(n)$$
$$b \in B_c^i$$

$$S_c^{i+1} = \{n \mid MOD(n) \cap RIN_c^{i+1}(IMS(n)) \neq \emptyset \text{ or } n \in B_c^i\}$$

$$B_c^{i+1} = \{b \mid ND(b) \cap S_c^i \neq \emptyset\}^{**}$$

Where BC(b) is the branch statement criterion, defined as <b, USE(b)>. The iteration will stop when the computation satisfies the following conditions.

$$\forall n \in N \Rightarrow RIN_c^{i+1}(n) = RIN_c^i(n)$$

or $S_c^{i+1} = S_c^i$

Finally, the whole slice of the program for a slicing criterion C is $S_c = S_c^i$, where $i \geq 0$.

2.3 An Interprocedural Slicing Algorithm

An interprocedural slicing algorithm was previously presented in [16]. The algorithm can be described as follows:

Assume that P is a procedure being sliced and Q is a procedure which is called at statement i in P. Then the new slicing criterion C′ extended from P to Q is defined as:

$$C' = <n_l^Q, ROUT(i)_{F \rightarrow A} \cap SCOPE_Q>$$

Where n_l^Q is the last statement of Q, F→A means that the actual parameters will be replaced by formal parameters. $SCOPE_Q$ represents all variables which are accessible in procedure Q.

$$ROUT(i) = \cup RIN_c(j), \text{ where } j \in IMS(i).$$

Alternatively, assume that P is a procedure being sliced and it is called at statement i in Q. Then the new criterion C′ extended from P to Q is defined as:

$$C' = <i, RIN_c(f_P)_{A \rightarrow F} \cap SCOPE_Q>$$

** In [16] $B_c^i = \cup ND(n)$ [8]
              $n \in S_c^{i+1}$

Where f_p is the first statement of P. A→F means that formal parameters will be replaced by actual parameters. $SCOPE_Q$ is as above.

3 Slicing Problems For C

3.1 Slicing In The Presence Of Pointer And Array Variables

A major problem in static data flow analysis is that the elements of an array or specified by a pointer cannot be distinguished. All the elements are treated as one object. Modification and reference to different elements are considered as references to the whole object.

To handle pointers and the transition of values via assignments to storage accessible through pointers, some "dummy" variables for each pointer variable are introduced in [13]. This concept is adopted by CPA [17]. For example, (see Figure 2) dummy variables (1)p, (2)p will be introduced for pointer variable **p in C. Annotation (i) represents the number of levels of indirect access through pointer variables. To propagate aliasing information correctly based on the assignment of the address of a variable to another variable, a dummy literal for each variable whose address is copied, such as p=&x, is introduced in [13]. This literal will be denoted by (-1)x and represents the address of x. The value of a dummy variable (i)p is either modified or used by a statement, whereas the values of pointer variable p and dummy variables (1)p, (2)p, ... (i-1)p will always be used.

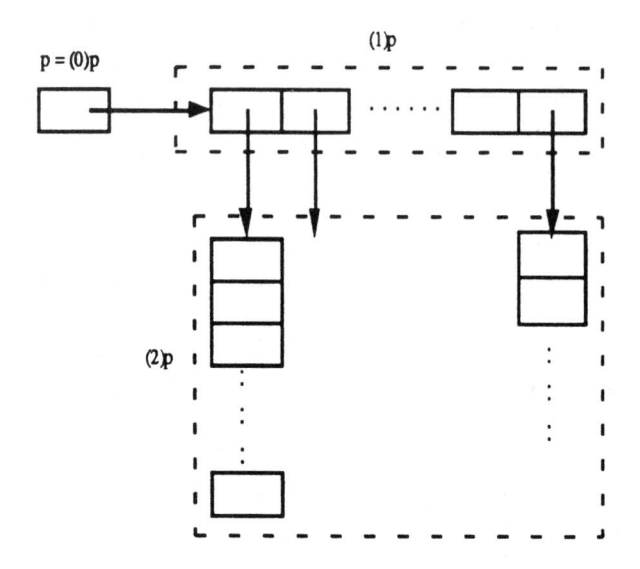

Figure 2: Relationships between Pointer and Dummy Variables

Let us consider a program fragment:

```
1   *(p+i)=c1;  USE(1)={i,p},   MOD(1)={(1)p}
2   *(p+j)=c2;  USE(2)={j,p},   MOD(2)={(1)p}
3   if (e)      USE(3)={e},     MOD(3)=Ø
4      k = i;   USE(4)={i},     MOD(4)={k}
5   else k = j; USE(5)={j},     MOD(5)={k}
6   x = *(p+k);
                USE(6)={p,(1)p,k},
                MOD(6)={x}
7   printf("%d",x); USE(7)={x}, MOD(7)=Ø
```

Using the algorithm described in [16] to slice this fragment with slicing criterion C=<7, {x}>, we obtain statement set {2,3,4,5,6}. However, further inspection reveals that statement "1" should also be included in the slice. The reason that statement "1" is not picked out is that the algorithm does not distinguish the direct-affect propagations between pointer, array variables and simple variables. (In the implementation of CPS, the array variable is considered as pointer variable). In fact, the direct-affect propagations of pointers and simple variables are different.

To produce correct slices for C programs in the presence of pointer and array variables, a modification is made to the definition of $RIN_c(n)$ by considering the dummy variables. Given a slicing criterion C, the modified $RIN_c(n)$ is defined as:

$RIN_c(n)$ = all variables v such that either:

1. n = POS(C) and v ∈ VAR(C),

or 2. a) v ∈ USE(n) ⇒

MOD(n) ∩ RIN_c(IMS(n)) ≠ Ø,

b) v ∈ MOD(n) ∩ RIN_c(IMS(n)) ⇒

DUMMY(v) or ARRAY(v),

c) v ∈ RIN_c(IMS(n)) - MOD(n)

DUMMY and ARRAY are defined as:

$$DUMMY(v) = \begin{cases} true & \text{if v is a dummy variable} \\ false & \text{otherwise} \end{cases}$$

$$ARRAY(v) = \begin{cases} true & \text{if v is an array variable} \\ false & \text{otherwise} \end{cases}$$

Using the modified $RIN_c(n)$ and the algorithm presented in [16] to slice the fragment again with C=<7,{x}>, the slice is {1,2,3,4,5,6}.

3.2 Interprocedural Slicing

3.2.1 Slicing Extension

The interprocedural slicing algorithm introduced in [16] is inaccurate. The method does not generate a precise slice because it fails to account for the calling context of a called procedure [7]. The improved algorithm is introduced in [7]. The example used in [7] is given in the following. In this example, using the original algorithm given in [16], when Add finishes the slicing in its body with the descended slicing criterion from Increment, Add ascends the slice to its caller again (the callers are procedure A and Increment). Here the authors point out that the ascended extension to A is irrelevant. However, after carefully inspecting the interprocedural data flow analysis information for calling statement [3,4,5], we can deduce that the ascended extension from Add to Increment is also irrelevant, although this extension will not increase the size of slice.

```
Program Main              Procedure A(x,y)
  sum := 0;                 call Add(x,y);
  i := 1;                   call Increment(y);
  While i < 11 do           return
    call A(sum, i)
  od
end

Procedure Add(a,b)        Procedure Increment(z)
  a := a+b;                 call Add(z);
return                    return
```

It is not necessary for every procedure being sliced to make the slice ascend to its callers. Two facts about the descended and ascended extensions can be noted:

1) Let P be the procedure containing the initial slicing criterion. For each procedure Q being sliced, only when there exists the relation Q CALL* P between Q and P, is it necessary for Q to ascend the slice to its callers.

2) Let Q be a procedure being sliced. If the calling statement i in Q is included into the slice, then it is always necessary to descend the slice to the procedures called at i.

Figure 3 is a diagram showing the interprocedural slicing extension. In this diagram, the solid line represents the procedure call relationships and the dotted line represents the slicing extension relationships between procedures. P is the procedure containing the initial slicing criterion.

Note that:

i) It is not necessary for procedure S to ascend the slice to T.

ii) The descended extensions from P to Q, P to R, R to S, main to T and T to S, will be done only when the calling statements in the caller are included into the slice.

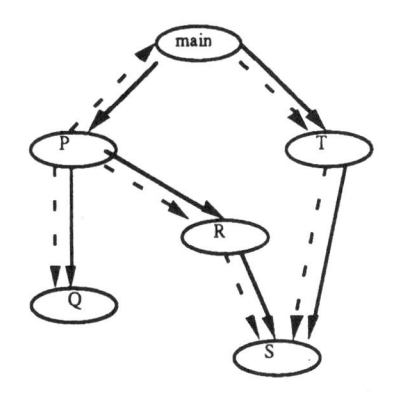

Figure 3: Slicing Extension Diagram

3.2.2 Problems for the C Language

Consider the example.

```
1    main()
2    {int a,b,sum;
3      scanf("%d%d",&a,&b); USE={(-1)a,(-1)b},
                            MOD={a,b}
4      sum=swapsum(&a,&b);
                            USE={(-1)a,a,(-1)b,b},
                            MOD={sum,a,b}
5      printf("%d%d%d",a,b,sum);
                            USE={a,b,sum},
                            MOD=∅
6    }
7    swapsum(x,y)
8    int *x,*y;
9    { int z;
10     z = *x;        USE={x,(1)x},  MOD={z}
11     *x = *y;       USE={x,y,(1)y},
                      MOD={(1)x}
12     *y = z;        USE={y,z},
                      MOD={(1)y}
13     z = (*x) + (*y);
                      USE={x,(1)x,y,(1)y},
                      MOD={z}
14     return(z);     USE={z},       MOD=∅
15   }
```

Using the interprocedural slicing algorithm described in [16] to slice the example with slicing criterion C = <5,{sum}>, we obtain {3,4}. After careful inspection, it should be noticed that statements {10,11,12,13,14} should also be included in the slice. The reason for not selecting statements {10,11,12,13,14} is that the C language allows return statements with expressions. In order to cope with this special case, an improvement is made to the standard algorithm.

3.2.3 Interprocedural Slicing Algorithm For C

Firstly, let us introduce some notations which will be

used. Assume that VV represents the set of all variables and F is an arbitrary function.

GMOD - GMOD(F) contains all the variables that might be modified by F itself or by a function (transitively) called from F.

LOCAL - LOCAL(F) represents the set of all the variables (including dummy variables) declared in F.

PARA - PARA(F) represents the set of all the formal parameter variables of F.

INIT - INIT(P) represents the initial statement of F.

$$ACT(v) = \begin{cases} true & \text{if v is an actual parameter} \\ false & \text{otherwise} \end{cases}$$

MATCH: MATCH is a relation defined on $VV \times VV$. $\forall v \in VV$, if $ACT(v) = true$ and $\exists\ v', f_1, f_2 \in VV$ and the statement s satisfying the following conditions, then $<v,v'>$ is said to be in MATCH.

    1) f_1 CALL f_2
and 2) $v' \in PARA(f_2)$
and 3) f_2 is called by s in f_1
and 4) the ordinal number of v in the actual list to f_2 is the same as that of v' in formal list of f_2.

In the example of 3.2.2, pairs $<(-1)a,x>$, $<a, (1)x>$, $<(-1)b,y>$, $<b,(1)y>$ are in the relation MATCH.

<u>Descended Extended Criterion Algorithm</u>

Let F be a function being sliced and function G is called by s in F. If s is included in the slice, then the new slicing criterion C′ descended extended to G from F, is defined as:

1. POS(C′) is an exit statement of G
2. VAR(C′) is composed of v such that
    a) $v \in ROUT_c(s)$ and $v \in GMOD(G)$
  or b) $v \in PARA(G) \Rightarrow (\exists w): [w \in ROUT_c(s)$ and $ACT(w)$ and $<w, v> \in MATCH]$ and $v \in GMOD(G)$
  or c) $v \in USE(POS(C'))$ if POS(C′) is a return statement of G.

<u>Ascended Extending Criterion Algorithm</u>

Let F be a function being sliced and it is called by i in function G. Then the new slicing criterion C′ ascended extended to G from F is defined as:

1. POS(C′) = i
2. VAR(C′) is composed of v such that
    a) $v \in RIN_c(INIT(F))$ and $v \notin PARA(F)$ and $v \notin LOCAL(F)$
  or b) $v \in USE(i) \cup MOD(i)$ and $ACT(v)$ and $(\exists w): [w \in RIN_c(INIT(F))$ and $w \in PARA(F)$ and $<v, w> \in MATCH]$

4 Slicing Break, Continue, Goto Statements

4.1 Problems

Branch statements, such as break, continue and goto in C (and in other languages), cannot be picked up owing to the fact that sets USE and MOD for these statements are empty. However, sometimes, the omission of these branch statements have important effects on the behaviour of the slice.

A. Goto Statement
Example:
```
1       if (p1)
2       {   s1;
3           if (p2)    {
4               s2;
5               goto l; }
6           }
7       else s3;
8       s4;
9   l:  s5;
```

For this fragment, suppose that the set {1,3,4,7,8} is the result of slicing. Obviously, the behaviour of the slice is not correct if the goto is not included in the slice.

```
if (p1)                 if (p1)
{ if (p2)               { if (p2)    {
    s2;                     s2;
}                           goto l; }
else s3;                }
s4;                     else s3;
                        s4;
                    l:
```

Let us see another example:
```
1       s1;
2   l:
3       s2;
4       if (p)
5           goto l;
6       s3;
```

This time, suppose the set {1,6} is the result of slicing. If the goto statement is included in the slice, then the behaviour of the slice is incorrect.

```
            s1;                 s1;
l:                              s3;
        goto l;
        s3;
```

B. Break And Continue Statements

Break and continue are two special statements. Their occurrences can cause the execution of loop and switch statements to be changed. Unfortunately, they cannot be sliced out as well. Just like a goto statement, inappropriate inclusion or exclusion can both lead to incorrect results. As the break statement is symmetrical with the continue statement, only the break statement will be discussed here.

Example:
```
1           switch(a) {
2    case '1':
3               b='b';
4               c='c';
5               break;
6    case '2':
7               d='d';
8               e='e';
9               break;
10   case '3':
11              f='f';
12              break;
13   default:
14              h='h';
15              break;
16
17              s;
```

Using the slicing algorithm to slice this fragment with slicing criterion C = <17, {b,d}>, the slice is {1,2,3,6,7}. If the slice is organised into a reduced fragment then it is similar to:

```
        switch (a) {
case '1':
        b='b';
case '2':
        d='d'; }
```

Note that the delimiters "{", "}" and label "case" have been put into the slice. According to the semantics of the switch statement in C, we know that when the value of a is 1, the statement d='d' will not be executed in the original fragment, but it will be executed in the reduced fragment. Here we see that break statements sometimes do influence the behaviour of the slice from the control flow aspect rather than the data flow aspect.

Let us see another example. In this example, like the goto, the break statement is included blindly, which also leads to an incorrect slice.

```
1    for (i=1; i<=n; i++)
2    { if (p1)
3       { for (j=1; j<=m; j++)
4           if (p2)
5               break;
6           else
7               s1;
8       }
9       else
10          s2;
11      s3;
12   }
```

Suppose the set {1,2,10,11} is the result of slicing.

```
for (i=1; i<=n; i++)    for (i=1; i<=n; i++)
{ if (p1)               { if (p1)
    break;                  ;
  else                    else
      s2;                     s2;
  s3;                     s3;
}                       }
```

Thus it can be seen that the selection of goto and break requires further rules.

4.2 Collecting Rules of Goto and Break

A. Rules for Goto

Let F be a function and HG(F) be a hammock graph representing the control flow of F. Let n_0 be the initial node of HG(F). We now present an algorithm to collect the goto statements. The algorithm moves on the HG(F) from n_0 to n_1 along all the sliced nodes. Any goto statements passed by the algorithm will be included into the slice. Any other statement will not be included.

Algorithm MOVE(n)
Begin
    <u>if</u>   n is the n_1 node
    <u>then</u>   return
    <u>if</u>   n is goto statement
    <u>then</u>   put the n into the slice
    <u>if</u> $d^{-1}(n) = 1$
    <u>then</u>   call MOVE(IMS(n))
    <u>else if</u>   n ∈ S
        <u>then</u>   <u>for</u> each n' ∈ IMS(n)
                 call MOVE(n')
        <u>else</u> MOVE(RID(n));
End

Note: $d^{-1}(n)$ stands for the output degree of node n. S is the set of statements which belong to the slice.

B. Rules for Break and Continue

Let "For", "While" and "Do-While" be the loops controlled by break and continue statements. The rules for collecting break and continue in loops can be described as follows:

Rule1: If the initial statements of "For" and "While" or the *tail* statement of "Do-While" are included in the slice, then the break and continue statements in these loops should be included in the slice.

Rule1 is based on the definitions of ND(n) and B_c^i. For the break statement that controls a "Switch", the control flow of the Switch statement is represented by the following structure (see Figure 4). In this structure each "case" or "default" label is considered as an immediate successor of the Switch statement head, so the rule is defined as:

Rule2: If a) the innermost "Switch" statement head (e.g. switch(e)) that break belongs to is included in the slice, and b) there is a path from the sliced "case" or "default" label (which is the immediate successor of switch(e) and easy to be picked out) to the RID(switch(e)) that passes the break, then the break should be included in the slice.

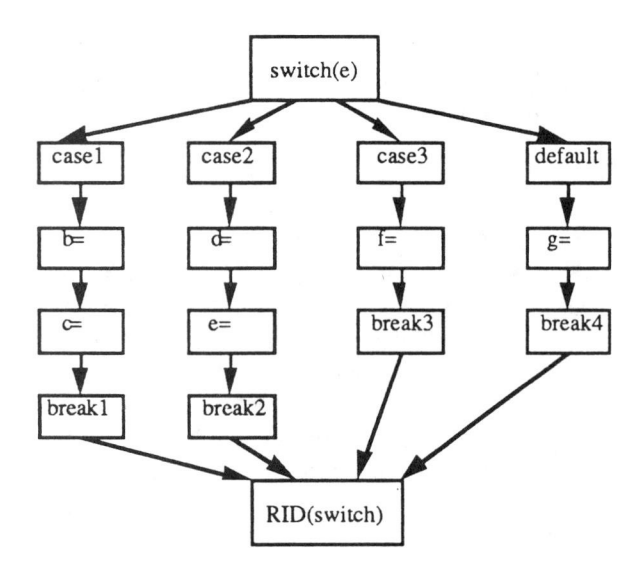

Figure 4: The Control Flow Structure of Switch Statement

In the example in 4.1(B), because "case '1'" and "case '2'" are sliced out and the paths through them to RID(switch) do not pass break3 and break4, only break1 and break2 are included in the slice.

5 Conclusions and Future Work

This paper has described some problems with program slicing for the C language that we met when implementing a C slicer and the solutions that we used to cope with them. There is much work to be done to organise slices into compilable programs, especially for C programs composed of many modules and files. For example, how to collect the declarative statements only related to those variables appearing in the sliced statements is a difficult problem. Also how to collect the include statements which combine many modules, how to deal with labels (cases, default), key words (do, else) and delimiters, and how to insert an empty statement for the empty branch part of the sliced "if" statement in order to produce a correct reduced program. Finally, it should be pointed out that we still face the problem of how to get a smallest slice. For example, if we slice the example in 3.2.2 with the criterion C = <5, {a,b}> by the modified extended criterion algorithm, the result will be {3,4,10,11,12,13,14}. However, statements {13,14} actually are not necessary. At present, the efficiency including the slicing method and the interactive capability of the tool are being improved and also some experiments are presently underway using this tool.

Acknowledgement

The authors would like to acknowledge Mr Biao Xu for his help in developing the CPA (C Program Analyser) and the members of Software Engineering Research and Development Centre of Beijing Information Technology Institute. We also wish to acknowledge all the useful comments given by the referees.

References

[1] H. Agrawal and J. R. Horgan, "Dynamic Program Slicing", *Proc. of ACM SIGPLAN'90 Conf. on Prog. Lan. Des. and Imp.*, New York, pp.246-256, June 20-22 1990

[2] J. Banning, "An efficient way to find the side effects of procedure calls and the aliases of variables", *Proc. of Sixth Ann. ACM Sym. on Prin. of Prog. Lan.*, pp.29-41, Jan. 1979

[3] J. M. Barth, "A practical interprocedural data flow analysis algorithm", *CACM*, 21(9), pp.724-736, 1978

[4] K. Cooper and K. Kennedy, "Efficient computation of flow insensitive interprocedural summary information", *Proc. of ACM SIGPLAN Sym. Compiler Construction*, pp.247-258, June 1984, SIGPLAN Notices, Vol. 19, No. 6,

[5] K. Cooper and K. Kennedy, "Efficient computation of flow insensitive interprocedural summary information -- A correction", *SIGPLAN Notices*, Vol. 23, No. 4, pp.35-42, 1988

[6] M. S. Hecht *Flow Analysis of Computer Programs*, Elsevice North-Holland, 1977

[7] S. Horwitz, T. Reps and D. Binkley, "Interprocedural slicing using dependence graphs", Proceedings of the SIGPLAN'88 Conference on Programming Language Design and Implementation, Atlanta Georgia, pp.35-46, June 22-24, 1988

[8] H. K. N. Leung and H. K. Reghbati, "Comments on program slicing", *IEEE Trans. Soft. Eng.*, Vol. SE-13, No. 12, pp.1370-1371, Dec. 1987

[9] H. K. N. Lueng and L. White, "A study of regression testing", *Technical Report, TR-88-15, Dept. of Comp. Sc., Univ. of Alberta*, Canada, Sept. 1988

[10] J. R. Lyle and K. B. Gallagher, "Using program decomposition to guide modifications", *Proceedings of Conference on Software Maintenance-1988*, Phoenix, Arizona pp.265-269, Oct. 1988

[11] J. R. Lyle and M. Weiser, "Automatic program bug location by program slicing", *In. 2:nd IEEE Symp. on Computers and Applications*, Peking, pp.877-883, June 1987

[12] N. Shahmehri, M. Kamkar, P. Fritzson, "Semi-automatic Bug Localisation in Software Maintenance", *Proceedings of Conference on Software Maintenance-1990*, San Diego, California, pp.30-36, Nov. 1990

[13] W. E. Weihl "Interprocedural Data Flow Analysis in the Presence of Pointers, Procedure Variables and Label Variables", *In Conference Record of the Seventh Annual ACM Symposium on Principles of Programming Languages*, pp.83-94, January 1980

[14] M. Weiser, "Program Slicing", *Proceedings of Fifth International Conference on Software Engineering*, San Diego, CA, pp.439-449, Mar. 1981

[15] M. Weiser, "Programmers Use Slices When Debugging", *Communications of ACM*, Vol.25, No.7, pp.446-452, 1982

[16] M. Weiser, "Program Slicing", *IEEE Trans. Soft. Eng.*, Vol. SE-10, No. 4, pp.352-357, July 1984

[17] Biao Xie "A C Program Analysis Tool: CPAT", Software Engineering Research Centre, Technical Report, Beijing Information Technology Institute, 1989

DYNAMIC PROGRAM SLICING *

Bogdan KOREL

Department of Computer Science, Wayne State University, Detroit, MI 48202, U.S.A.

Janusz LASKI

Department of Computer Science and Engineering, Oakland University, Rochester, MI 48063, U.S.A.

Communicated by W.L. Van der Poel
Received 11 September 1987

A dynamic program slice is an executable subset of the original program that produces the same computations on a subset of selected variables and inputs. It differs from the static slice (Weiser, 1982, 1984) in that it is entirely defined on the basis of a computation. The two main advantages are the following: Arrays and dynamic data structures can be handled more precisely and the size of slice can be significantly reduced, leading to a finer localization of the fault. The approach is being investigated as a possible extension of the debugging capabilities of STAD, a recently developed System for Testing and Debugging (Korel and Laski, 1987; Laski, 1987).

Keywords: Slicing, dynamic slice, trajectory, data dependence, control dependence, debugging

1. Introduction

A slice S of a program P is an executable subset of P that computes the same function as P does in a subset of variables, at some selected point of interest [19,23,24]. Slicing has been shown useful in program debugging by narrowing the size of the suspected piece of incorrect code. As originally introduced [23,24], it is a static concept: it involves all potential terminating program executions, including those which are infeasible. In debugging practice, however, we typically deal with a particular incorrect execution and, consequently, are interested in locating the cause of incorrectness (programming fault) of *that* execution. For this reason we are interested in a slice that preserves the program's behavior for a specific input, rather than that for the set of all inputs for which the program terminates. This type of program slice, which we call a *dynamic* one, is introduced in this paper.

It is shown that dynamic slicing provides a finer localization information. A static slice very often contains statements which have no influence on the values of variables of interest. A dynamic slice can be considered a refinement of the static one: By applying dynamic analysis it is easier to identify those statements in the static slice which do not have influence on the variables of interest. By reducing the searching space for the fault in the program, one can more efficiently localize it.

In this paper we also investigate the dynamic handling of arrays in slicing. In the static approach, an entire array is treated as a single variable, i.e., each definition or use of any array element is treated as a definition or use of the entire array. While this method is easy to implement, it fails to take into account any information about particular array elements. This can lead to the inclusion of statements which do not have any influence on the values of certain array elements.

---

* This research was partly supported by the National Science Foundation under Grant No. ECS-82-18072.

As a result, the slice can be unnecessarily large. In our approach, every array element is treated as a separate variable. This is due to the fact that, during program execution, it is possible to determine the value of an array subscript and, therefore, to determine which array elements are used or modified at every point of program execution. In the concluding Section 5 we also comment on a possible application of the method to other structured data.

The reader is assumed to be familiar with the original static concept of program slicing [23,24]. In what follows, + stands for set union.

2. Background

A *flowgraph* of a program P is a directed graph $C = (N, A, en, ex)$, where N is a set of *nodes*, A is a binary relation on N (a subset of $N \times N$) referred to as the set of *arcs*, and en and ex are, respectively, a unique entry and a unique exit node, $en, ex \in N$.

For the sake of simplicity we restrict our analysis to a subset of structured PASCAL-like programming language constructs, namely: sequencing, **if–then–else**, and **while**-loop. A node in N corresponds to a smallest, not further decomposable, single-entry single-exit executable part of a statement in P, referred to as an *instruction*. It can be, for example, an assignment statement, an input or an output statement, or the ⟨expression⟩ part of an **if–then–else** or **while** statement, in which case it is called a test instruction.

An arc $(n, m) \in A$ corresponds to a possible transfer of control from instruction n to instruction m. A *path* from the entry node en to some node l, $l \in N$, is a *finite* sequence $\langle n_1, n_2, \ldots, n_q \rangle$ of instructions, such that $n_1 = en$, $n_q = l$, and (n_i, n_{i+1}) is in A for all n_i, $1 \leq i < q$. If $n_q = ex$, then the path is a *program path*. A path is *feasible* if there exists input data which causes the path to

---

var n, i, j, p : integer; a : **array**[1..10] **of** integer;

1	input(n, a);
2	$i := 1$;
3	**while** $i < n$ **do begin**
4	min := $a[i]$;
5	$p := i$;
6	$j := i + 1$;
7	**while** $j <= n$ **do begin**
8	**if** $a[j] <$ min **then begin**
9	min := $a[j]$;
10	$p := j$;
	end;
11	$j := j + 1$;
	end;
12	$a[p] := a[i]$;
13	$a[i] :=$ min;
14	$i := i + 1$;
	end;
15	output(a);

Fig. 1. A sorting program.

Instruction number	Instruction text
1^1	$input(n, a)$
2^2	$i := 1$
3^3	$i < n$
4^4	$min := a[i]$ /* $min := a[1]$ */
5^5	$p := i$
6^6	$j := i + 1$
7^7	$j <= n$
8^8	$a[j] < min$ /* $a[2] < min$ */
11^9	$j := j + 1$
7^{10}	$j <= n$
12^{11}	$a[p] := a[i]$ /* $a[1] := a[1]$ */
13^{12}	$a[i] := min$ /* $a[1] := min$ */
14^{13}	$i := i + 1$
3^{14}	$i < n$
15^{15}	$output(a)$

Trajectory $T = \langle 1, 2, 3, 4, 5, 6, 7, 8, 11, 7, 12, 13, 14, 3, 15 \rangle$

Fig. 2. A trajectory of the program from Fig. 1 on input data $n = 2$, $a = (2, 4)$.

be traversed during program execution. A feasible path that has actually been executed for some input will be referred to as a *trajectory*. For example, if the program in Fig. 1 is executed on the input $i = (n, a) = (2, (2, 4))$, the trajectory T in Fig. 2 is traversed. An executed program path is a *program trajectory*. Observe that a trajectory can be an initial (finite) segment of an 'infinite' path if the execution involved does not terminate.

In the deterministic case, the trajectory is uniquely determined by the input while in the nondeterministic case (e.g., referencing an uninitialized variable) there might be many trajectories for the same input. In either case, however, there are many inputs that give rise to the same trajectory. In what follows we assume the deterministic case.

Notationally, T is an abstract list [9] whose elements are accessed by position, for example, for T in Fig. 2 we have $T(5) = 5$, $T(9) = 11$, and $T(14) = 3$. To handle multiple occurrences of the same instructions in the trajectory (for instance, instruction 3 appears twice in T in Fig. 2), every instruction is characterized by its position in the sequence. Let $N(T)$ be the set of pairs (instruction in T, its position in T) defined as follows:

$$N(T) = \{ (X, p) : X \in N, T(p) = X \}.$$

An (X, p) will be written down as X^p and interpreted as "an instruction X at the execution position p". For instance, 3^3 and 3^{14} are two occurrences of instruction 3 in the trajectory T shown in Fig. 2.

The following dataflow concepts are of dynamic nature because they are defined with respect to the trajectory T, rather than to the flowgraph itself.

A *use* of variable v is an instruction X^p in which this variable is referenced. A *definition* of variable v is an instruction X^p which assigns a value to that variable.

In the framework of static program analysis, an assignment to an array element is treated as a definition of the entire array. This does not seem a real obstacle in program optimization, the first area of application of data flow analysis [1,2,3,7,10]. It does cause serious problems, however, in

```
1   i := 1;
2   j := 2;
3   read(k);
4   while i < 3 do begin
5       a[i] := a[j] * a[k];
6       i := i + 1;
7       j := j + 2;
8       k := k + 3;
    end;
```

$T = \langle 1, 2, 3, 4, 5, 6, 7, 8, 4, 5, 6, 7, 8, 4 \rangle$

Fig. 3. A sample program and a trajectory for $k = 2$.

data flow testing and debugging, where it is highly desirable to identify the particular array entries manipulated by the program [11–17]. It is precisely what the dynamic approach makes possible. In it, every array element is treated as a separate variable. For example, the following is the set of all variables in the program in Fig. 1,

$\{ n, i, j, p, \min, a[1], a[2], \ldots, a[10] \}$.

Let $U(X^p)$ be the set of variables whose values are used in X^p and $D(X^p)$ be the set of variables whose values are defined in X^p. It is essential to observe that, unlike their static counterparts, these sets are dynamic. Clearly, given two occurrences X^p and X^q of the same instruction X, these sets might be different in each case. If X handles an array, and every array element is treated as a separate variable, then at each execution of X different entries in the array might be used or defined. For example, during the first execution of instruction 5 of the program of Fig. 3 the following variables are used and defined:

$U(5^5) = \{ i, j, k, a[2] \}, \qquad D(5^5) = \{ a[1] \}$.

However, during the second execution of the same instruction, we have

$U(5^{10}) = \{ i, j, k, a[4], a[5] \}$,
$D(5^{10}) = \{ a[2] \}$.

The dynamic nature of the sets U and D is in contrast with their counterparts in static analysis. In the case of our simple language it is due to the dynamic treatment of arrays. For example, the static analysis of the program in Fig. 3 would render

$U(5) = \{ a, i, j, k \}, \qquad D(5) = \{ a \}$.

It is worth noting, however, that if nodes in the graph correspond to procedure calls or some single-entry single-exit compound statements rather than instructions, the dynamic parts of the sets U and D might also involve scalar variables.

It is assumed that the sets U and D for each instruction in the trajectory can be identified through program instrumentation.

2.1. Definition. Given a trajectory T, an instruction X^p is the *last definition* of variable v at execution position q in T iff $v \in D(X^p)$ and, for all k, $p < k < q$, $v \notin D(Y^k)$.

The last definition X^p of v at q is then the unique instruction which has last assigned a value to variable v when q is reached on T. For instance, in the execution trace of Fig. 2, 2^2 is the last definition of variable i at execution position 6.

The last definition is also a *reaching* one in the static sense [8]. The opposite, however, is not necessarily true. A reaching definition is defined in terms of the flowgraph only, rather than in those of a trajectory. Therefore, it is only potentially last and, moreover, it might also be infeasible.

3. Dynamic slice

Intuitively, a dynamic slice is an executable part of the program whose behavior is identical to that of the original program with respect to a subset of variables of interest and at execution position q. Such a 'view of interest' is captured by the following definition.

3.1. Definition. Let T be the trajectory of program P on input x. A *slicing criterion* of program P

executed on input x is a triple $C = (x, I^q, V)$, where I is an instruction at position q on T and V is a subset of variables in P.

Observe that the corresponding static slicing criterion [24] is just a pair (I, V). Clearly, our slicing criterion is defined w.r.t. a given trajectory on a specific input x rather than w.r.t. the set of all possible paths in the flowgraph. Yet another difference is in the interpretation of the 'position of interest'. In the static case, this is instruction I in P; in our case, this is instruction I at execution position q in trajectory T.

Typically, the set V contains those variables in the program that have been found incorrect at q. The slice is then used to locate the cause of the incorrectness. V might be, however, a set of variables that are correct at q, too; the slice might then be used for verification purposes.

To formally define the dynamic slice we need some definitions of list operations.

Let $T = \langle X_1, X_2, \ldots, X_m \rangle$ be a trajectory of length m and let q be a position in T, $1 \leq q \leq m$. By $F(T, q)$ we denote the *front* of T w.r.t. q, i.e., a sublist $\langle X_1, X_2, \ldots, X_q \rangle$, containing the first q elements of T [9]. Correspondingly, $B(T, q)$, the *back* of T w.r.t. q, is the sublist $\langle X_{q+1}, \ldots, X_m \rangle$, containing elements that follow $T(q)$. We have, of course, $T = F(T, q) \| B(T, q)$, where $\|$ stands for the concatenation of lists. By $DEL(T, r)$, where r is a predicate on the set of instructions in T, we mean a *subtrajectory* obtained from T by deleting from it all elements $T(i)$ that satisfy r. In other words, $DEL(T, r)$ is the result of an exhaustive application of the delete operation to elements $T(i)$ that satisfy $r(T(i))$.

3.2. Definition. Let $C = (x, I^q, V)$ be a slicing criterion of program P and T a trajectory of P on input x. A *dynamic slice* of P on C is any executable program P' that is obtained from P by deleting zero or more statements from it and, when executed on input x, produces a trajectory T' for which there exists an execution position q' such that:

(1) $F(T', q') = DEL(F(T, q), T(i) \notin N'$ and $1 \leq i \leq q)$,

(2) for all $v \in V$, the value of v before the execution of instruction $T(q)$ in T equals the value of v before the execution of instruction $T'(q')$ in T',

(3) $T'(q') = T(q) = I$,

where N' is a set of instructions in P'.

The following observations clarify some salient properties of the dynamic slice.

First, a dynamic slice partially replicates the front of T (w.r.t. q). Clearly, we are interested in the partial reproduction of the behavior of program P up to the execution position q. Moreover, dynamic slice preserves the number of occurrences of instructions in the trajectories T and T'. For instance, if a loop in P iterates five times, then we require that the same loop, if included in P', also iterates five times. But, these requirements do not necessarily hold for the back of T and T' (past the execution positions q and q', respectively). Indeed, the absence of some instructions in P' might cause unpredictable control flow patterns in T' when the execution continues past q'.

Second, it is required that instruction I^q appear in the slice. This is in contrast to the static definition of slice in which that instruction does not necessarily appear [24]. Our experience with static slices shows that the programmer can be lost if statement I is not included in the slice, particularly if I is in a loop. We feel therefore that including it into the slice is more realistic for debugging purposes.

Third, the fact that all variables in V have the same values at q in T and at q' in T' does not necessarily guarantee that variables not in V will have the same values at those positions nor that those in V itself will have the same values along T and T' (except at q and q').

There can be many different dynamic slices for a given program and a slicing criterion, and there is always at least one such a slice: The entire program itself.

3.3. Definition. Let C be a slicing criterion of program P executed on input x. A dynamic slice DS of P on C is *statement-minimal* if no other dynamic slice of P on C has fewer statements than DS.

As in the case of static slices, the problem of finding statement-minimal dynamic slice is undecidable [24]. However, data flow analysis can be used to construct conservative slices, guaranteed to have the slice properties but with, perhaps, too many statements.

4. Finding dynamic slice

Intuitively, given a slicing criterion $C = (x, I^q, V)$, a dynamic slice contains only those instructions from N that (i) influence the variables in V at q, and (ii) appear in T. Data flow analysis along T can help in finding them by tracing backwards some well-defined dependencies between instructions in T. This can be done in two steps. First, find a subtrajectory T' of T that meets the criteria of Definition 3.2 and then reconstruct a P' from T'.

The identification of T' is equivalent to finding a subset of $N(T)$ that contains all instructions in the trajectory T which have influence on V at q and guarantee that I^q is reached in the first place. Such a subset will be referred to as the *slicing set*, denoted S_C.

To capture the intuitive notion of influence we introduce two types of dependence relations between program instructions in the trajectory T. These relations formally define the properties that instructions in $N(T)$ must meet to be in a slice. The relations are constructive in the sense that they can be used to formulate an algorithm, however inefficient it might be [11].

Let $C = (x, I^q, V)$ be a slicing criterion. In what follows we introduce two types of influences (dependences) between instructions in the front of T w.r.t. q. Those are the Data–Data and Test–Control binary relations on $N_C(T)$, where

$$N_C(T) = \{ X^p : X^p \in N(T) \text{ and } 1 \leq p \leq q \}.$$

Clearly, we are only interested in the instructions in the front of the trajectory T, up to the execution position q.

The DD (Data–Data) Relation. The DD relation models a situation where one instruction assigns a

$DD(1^1) = \{3^3, 4^4, 7^7, 8^8, 7^{10}, 12^{11}, 3^{14}, 15^{15}\}$
$DD(2^2) = \{3^3, 4^4, 5^5, 6^6, 12^{11}, 13^{12}, 14^{13}\}$
$DD(4^4) = \{8^8, 13^{12}\}$
$DD(5^5) = \{12^{11}\}$
$DD(6^6) = \{7^7, 8^8, 11^9\}$
$DD(11^9) = \{7^{10}\}$
$DD(13^{12}) = \{15^{15}\}$
$DD(14^{13}) = \{3^{14}\}$

Fig. 4. The DD relation for the trajectory of Fig. 2 and the slicing criterion $C = (x, 15^{15}, \{a[2]\})$, where $x = (n, a) = (2, (2, 4))$. *Notation*: $DD(k) = \{l : k \text{ DD } l\}$.

value to an item of data and the other instruction uses that value. For instance, in the execution trace of Fig. 2, instruction 2^2 assigns a value to variable i and instruction 6^6 uses that value.

DD is a binary relation on $N_C(T)$ defined as follows:

X^p DD y^t, $1 \leq p < t \leq q$, iff there exists a variable v such that: (1) $v \in U(y^t)$, and (2) X^p is the last definition of v at t.

Fig. 4 shows the DD relation for the trajectory in Fig. 2 and the slicing criterion $C = (x, 15^{15}, \{a[2]\})$.

Observe that, appearances to the contrary, the DD relation is *not* a subset of the set of static definition-use chains [7].

The TC (Test–Control) Relation. The TC relation captures the dependence between test instructions and the instructions which can be chosen to execute or not execute by these test instructions. For instance, test instruction 8 in the program of Fig. 1 has 'influence' on the execution of instruction 9, but it has no influence on the execution of instruction 11. To define the TC relation, we need the following notion of the *scope of influence* for the **if** and **while** statements [11].

(a) **if** X **then** B1 **else** B2; instruction Y is in the scope of influence of X iff Y appears in B1 or B2,

$$TC(3^3) = \{4^4, 5^5, 6^6, 7^7, 8^8, 11^9, 7^{10}, 12^{11}, 13^{12}, 14^{13}, 3^{14}\}$$
$$TC(7^7) = \{8^8, 11^9, 7^{10}\}$$
$$TC(3^{14}) = TC(7^{10}) = \{\ \}$$

Fig. 5. TC relation for the program of Fig. 1 and the slicing criterion $C = (x, 15^{15}, \{a[2]\})$, $x = (n, a) = (2, (2, 4))$.

(b) **while** X **do** B; instruction Y is in the scope of influence of X iff Y is in B or $X = Y$.

In the program of Fig. 1, instruction 6 is in the scope of influence of test instruction 3, but instruction 15 is not in the scope of influence of instruction 3. Observe that the test instruction X of a **while**-loop is in the scope of influence of itself because every execution of X has influence on the next execution of X. For instance, in the trajectory of Fig. 2 the outcome of the test instruction 3^3 influences the execution of 3^{14}.

TC is a binary relation on $N_C(T)$ defined as follows:

X^p TC y^t, $1 \leq p < t \leq q$, iff (1) Y is in the scope of influence of X, and (2) for all k, $p < k < t$, $T(k)$ is in the scope of influence of X.

The TC relation for the trajectory in Fig. 2 is shown in Fig. 5.

The relations DD and TC capture the influences that exist between instructions in the trajectory. They fail, however, to guarantee that the number of occurrences of an instruction in T (between 1 and q) and T' (between 1 and q') are the same, a property that follows from condition (1) of Definition 3.2. Towards that goal we define the *Identity Relation* IR on $N_C(T)$ as follows:

X^p IR y^t, $1 \leq p, t \leq q$, iff $X = Y$.

For example, for the trajectory of Fig. 2 we have 3^3 IR 3^{14} and 7^7 IR 7^{10}; observe that IR is symmetric, for example 3^{14} IR 3^3 holds, too.

To find S_C we first find a set A^0 of all instructions that have a direct influence on V at q and on the execution of instruction I^q. We have

$$A^0 = LD(q, V) + LT(I^q),$$

where $LD(q, V)$ is the set of last definitions of variables in V at execution position q, and $LT(I^q)$ is the set of test instructions which have control influence on the execution of I^q. More formally, we can state

$LD(q, V) = \{X^p \in N_C(T) :$ there exists a $v \in V$

such that x^p is the last definition of v at $q\}$

and

$$LT(I^q) = \{X^p \in N_C(T) : X^p \text{ TC } I^q\}.$$

We will find S_C iteratively, as a limit of the sequence $S^0, S^1, \ldots, S^n$, $0 \leq n < q$, defined as follows:

$$S^0 = A^0,$$
$$S^{i+1} = S^i + A^{i+1},$$

where

$A^{i+1} = \{X^p \in N_C(T):$

    (1) $X^p \notin S^i$, and

    (2) there exists a $Y^t \in A^i$, $p, t \leq q$,

    X^p (DD + TC + IR) $y^t\}$.

The sets S^i, $i = 0, 1, \ldots, k$, can be thought of as an increasing sequence of successive approximations of S_C. Each S^i is bounded from above by $N_C(T)$. Eventually, because T is finite, there is an $A^{k+1} = \{\ \}$, for some k. If the above recursive definition is the basis for a corresponding search process, that process will always terminate. According to the postulated properties of a dynamic slice in Section 3, instruction I^q must also be included in S_C. The following will guarantee its inclusion in the slice:

$$S_C = S^k + \{I^q\},$$

where S^k is the limit of sequence $\{S^i\}$.

The (disjoint) sets A^i, $i = 0, 1, \ldots, n$, contain those instructions that have i-level influence on V at q. Clearly, instructions in A^0 have direct influence on V at q. Instructions in A^i, $i > 0$, have indirect influence on V at q by directly influencing those in A^{i-1}. Intuitively, the slicing set contains instructions that have direct or indirect influence on V at q and the execution of I^q.

Given S_C, the slice is found in a straightforward way: Inspect instructions in P and select only those which appear at least once in the slicing set. Needless to say, to ensure syntactical correctness all necessary declarations are to be selected, too.

Example. Consider again the trajectory T in Fig. 2. For the criterion

$$C1 = (x, 15^{15}, \{a[2]\}),$$
$$x = (n, a) = (2, (2, 4))$$

we have

$$LD(15, \{a[2]\}) = \{1^1\}, \qquad LT(15^{15}) = \{\},$$
$$A^0 = \{1^1\}, \qquad S^0 = \{1^1\}, \qquad A^1 = \{\},$$
$$S_{C1} = S^0 + \{15^{15}\} = \{1^1, 15^{15}\},$$

and, finally, the dynamic slice

 1 input(n, a);
15 output(a);

For the slicing criterion

$$C2 = (x, 15^{15}, \{a[1]\})$$

we have

$$LD(15, \{a[1]\}) = \{13^{12}\}, \qquad LT(15^{15}) = \{\},$$
$$A^0 = \{13^{12}\}, \qquad S^0 = \{13^{12}\},$$
$$A^1 = \{2^2, 3^3, 4^4\},$$

$$S^1 = \{2^2, 3^3, 4^4, 13^{12}\},$$
$$A^2 = \{1^1, 3^{14}\},$$
$$S^2 = \{1^1, 2^2, 3^3, 4^4, 13^{12}, 3^{14}\},$$
$$A^3 = \{14^{13}\},$$
$$S^3 = \{1^1, 2^2, 3^3, 4^4, 13^{12}, 14^{13}, 3^{14}\},$$
$$A^4 = \{\},$$
$$S_{C2} = S^3 + \{15^{15}\}$$
$$= \{1^1, 2^2, 3^3, 4^4, 13^{12}, 14^{13}, 3^{14}, 15^{15}\},$$

and the slice

 1 input(n, a);
 2 $i := 1$;
 3 **while** $i < n$ **do begin**
 4   min := $a[i]$;
13     $a[i] :=$ min;
14     $i := i + 1$;
    end;
15 output(a);

In contrast to the above example, a static slice [24] derived for a similar slicing criterion $C = (15, \{a\})$ for the program of Fig. 1 is the entire program itself. This illustrates the fact that dynamic slices are, in general, smaller than static ones. There is, however, a price for this advantage: dynamic slice cannot be used to support reasoning about all possible computations w.r.t. a selected set of variables in the program.

5. Conclusions

Although the idea of dynamic program analysis is not new [4,8,11,25], that of dynamic slicing is: It originated during experiments with a recently implemented System for Testing and Debugging (STAD) [14,16]. The main advantage of dynamic slicing is that the size of a slice can be significantly reduced by the identification of those statements in the program that do not have influence on the variables of interest. This is achieved by dynamic analysis based on the program execution trajectory.

Some related works in the area of dependence-based modeling have been reported in the literature. Most of them deal with dependencies between data items [6]. Additionally, control influence is introduced for constructing program slices [24], for optimization [21], and for static program testing [12]. However, all these models are static, derived from a control flowgraph. The model presented in this paper is dynamic [11] because it is derived mainly from the program execution trajectory.

In the case of arbitrary control flow, the scope of influence can be derived by using the concept of the nearest inverse dominator of test instructions [5,18]. However, for structured programs, the scope of influence can be determined during syntax analysis, as was done in STAD [14].

A promising area of research involves dynamic slicing for pointer variables. Pointers create unique problems since the pointer variable actually represents two variables: the pointer itself and the object pointed to by it. Nameless variables (objects) of a given type are created by calling the standard procedure *new(p)* which is, in fact, a dynamic declaration of the object involved: A storage is reserved for an object but no value is assigned to it. It is impossible to identify dynamic objects by means of static analysis. In contrast, by applying a dynamic analysis, a list of dynamic variables might be created and manipulated during program execution. In this manner, it is possible to determine which dynamic objects are pointed to be pointer variables at every point of program execution. It is also possible to determine which objects (dynamic variables) are used or modified at every point of program execution.

References

[1] A.V. Aho and J.D. Ullman, *Principles of Compiler Design* (Addison-Wesley, Reading, MA, 1977).

[2] J.M. Barth, A practical interprocedural data flow analysis algorithm, *Comm. ACM* **21** (9) (1978) 724–736.

[3] J.F. Bergeretti and B.A. Carre, Information-flow and data-flow analysis of **while**-programs, *ACM Trans. Programming Languages & Systems* **7** (1) (1985) 37–61.

[4] F.T. Chan and T.Y. Chen, AIDA—A dynamic data flow anomaly detection system for PASCAL programs, *Software – Practice & Experience* **17** (3) (1987) 227–239.

[5] D.E. Denning and P.J. Denning, Certification of programs for secure information flow, *Comm. ACM* **20** (7) (1977) 504–513.

[6] L.D. Fosdick and L.J. Osterweil, Data flow analysis in software reliability, *Comput. Surveys* **8** (1976) 305–330.

[7] M.S. Hecht, *Flow Analysis of Computer Programs* (North-Holland, Amsterdam, 1977).

[8] J.C. Huang, Detection of data flow anomaly through program instrumentation, *IEEE Trans. Software Engrg.* **SE-5** (3) (1979) 226–236.

[9] C.B. Jones, *Software Development, A Rigorous Approach* (Prentice-Hall, Englewood Cliffs, NJ, 1980).

[10] K. Kennedy, A comparison of two algorithms for global data flow analysis, *SIAM J. Comput.* **5** (1976) 158–180.

[11] B. Korel, *Dependence-Based Modelling in the Automation of the Error Localization in Computer Programs*, Ph.D. Thesis, School of Engineering and Computer Science, Oakland Univ., Rochester, MI, August 1986.

[12] B. Korel, The program dependence graph in static program testing, *Inform. Process. Lett.* **24** (2) (1987) 103–108.

[13] B. Korel and J. Laski, A tool for data flow oriented program testing, *Softfair II, 2nd Conf. on Software Development, Tools, Techniques, and Alternatives*, San Francisco, CA (December 1985) 34–38.

[14] B. Korel and J. Laski, *STAD—A System for Testing and Debugging*, Tech. Rept. TR-CSE-87-08, School of Engineering and Computer Science, Oakland Univ., Rochester, MI, August 1987.

[15] J.W. Laski, A hierarchical approach to program testing, *SIGPLAN Notices* **15** (1980) 77–85.

[16] J. Laski, *Data Flow Testing of Computer Programs*, Tech. Rept. TR-CSE-87-06, School of Engineering and Computer Science, Oakland Univ., Rochester, MI, June 1987.

[17] J.W. Laski and B. Korel, A data flow oriented program testing strategy, *IEEE Trans. Software Engrg.* **SE-9** (3) (1983) 347–354.

[18] T. Lengauer and R.E. Tarjan, A fast algorithm for finding dominators in a flowgraph, *ACM Trans. Programming Languages & Systems* **1** (1979) 121–141.

[19] H.D. Longworth, L.M. Ottenstein and M.R. Smith, The relationship between program complexity and slice complexity during debugging tasks, *10th Internat. Computer Software & Applications Conf. (COMSAQ-86)*, Chicago, IL (October 1986) 383–389.

[20] S.S. Muchnick and N.D. Jones, *Program Flow Analysis: Theory and Applications* (Prentice-Hall, Englewood Cliffs, NJ, 1981).

[21] K.J. Ottenstein and L.M. Ottenstein, The program dependence graph in a software development environment, *ACM SIGPLAN Notices* **19** (5) (1984) 177–184.

[22] B.K. Rosen, Data flow analysis for procedural languages, *J. ACM* **26** (2) (1979) 322–344.

[23] M. Weiser, Programmers use slices when debugging, *Comm. ACM* **25** (1982) 446–452.

[24] M. Weiser, Program slicing, *IEEE Trans. Software Engrg.* **SE-10** (4) (1984) 352–357.

[25] N.H. White and K.H. Bennett, Run-time diagnostic in PASCAL, *Software — Practice & Experience* **15** (4) (1985) 359–367.

Dynamic Program Slicing

Hiralal Agrawal
Department of Computer Sciences
Purdue University
West Lafayette, IN 47907-2004

Joseph R. Horgan
Bell Communications Research
Morristown, NJ 07960-1910

Abstract

Program slices are useful in debugging, testing, maintenance, and understanding of programs. The conventional notion of a program slice, the *static slice*, is the set of all statements that *might* affect the value of a given variable occurrence. In this paper, we investigate the concept of the *dynamic slice* consisting of all statements that *actually* affect the value of a variable occurrence for a given program input. The sensitivity of dynamic slicing to particular program inputs makes it more useful in program debugging and testing than static slicing. Several approaches for computing dynamic slices are examined. The notion of a Dynamic Dependence Graph and its use in computing dynamic slices is discussed. The Dynamic Dependence Graph may be unbounded in length; therefore, we introduce the economical concept of a Reduced Dynamic Dependence Graph, which is proportional in size to the number of dynamic slices arising during the program execution.

1 Introduction

Finding all statements in a program that directly or indirectly affect the value of a variable occurrence is referred to as Program Slicing [Wei84]. The statements selected constitute a *slice* of the program with respect to the variable occurrence. A slice has a simple meaning: it should evaluate the variable occurrence identically to the original program for *all* testcases.

Uses of program slicing have been suggested in many applications, e.g., program verification, testing, maintenance, automatic parallelization of program execution, automatic integration of program versions, etc. (see, e.g., [Wei84, HPR89]). In this paper we are primarily concerned with its use in program debugging [Wei82]. Often during debugging the value of a variable, *var*, at some program statement, S, is observed to be incorrect. Program slicing with respect to *var* and S gives that relevant subset of the program where one should look for the possible cause of the error. But the above notion of program slicing does not make any use of the particular inputs that revealed the error. It is concerned with finding all statements that *could* influence the value of the variable occurrence for *any* inputs, not all statements that *did* affect its value for the *current* inputs. Unfortunately, the size of a slice so defined may approach that of the original program, and the usefulness of a slice in debugging tends to diminish as the size of the slice increases. Therefore, in this paper we examine a narrower notion of "slice," consisting only of statements that influence the value of a variable occurrence for specific program inputs.[1] We refer to this problem as *Dynamic Program Slicing* to distinguish it from the original problem of *Static Program Slicing*.

Conceptually a program may be thought of as a collection of *threads*, each computing a value of a program variable. Several threads may compute values of the same variable. Portions of these threads may overlap one-another. The more complex the control structure of the program, the more complex the intermingling of these threads. Static program slicing isolates all possible threads computing a particular variable. Dynamic slicing, on the other hand, iso-

---

Part of the work described here was done while the first author worked at Bell Communications Research, Morristown, New Jersey, during the summer of 1989. Other support was provided by a grant from the Purdue University/University of Florida Software Engineering Research Center, and by the National Science Foundation grant 8910306-CCR.

Permission to copy without fee all or part of this material is granted provided that the copies are not made or distributed for direct commercial advantage, the ACM copyright notice and the title of the publication and its date appear, and notice is given that copying is by permission of the Association for Computing Machinery. To copy otherwise, or to republish, requires a fee and/or specific permission.

[1] A slice with respect to a set of variables may be obtained by taking the union of slices with respect to individual variables in the set.

lates the unique thread computing the variable for the given inputs.

During debugging programmers generally analyze the program behavior under the test-case that revealed the error, not under any generic test-case. Consider, for example, the following scenario: A friend while using a program discovers an error. He finds that the value of a variable printed by a statement in the program is incorrect. After spending some time trying to find the cause without luck, he comes to you for help. Probably the first thing you would request from him is the test-case that revealed the bug. If he only tells you the variable with the incorrect value and the statement where the erroneous value is observed, and doesn't disclose the particular inputs that triggered the error, your debugging task would clearly be much more difficult. This suggests that while debugging a program we probably try to find the *dynamic* slice of the program in our minds. The concrete test-case that exercises the bug helps us focus our attention to the "cross-section" of the program that contains the bug.[2] This simple observation also highlights the value of automatically determining dynamic program slices. The distinction between static and dynamic slicing and the advantages of the latter over the former are further illustrated in Section 3.

In this paper we sketch several approaches to computing dynamic program slices. A more detailed discussion with precise algorithmic definitions of these approaches may be found in [AH89]. In Section 2 we briefly review the program representation called the Program Dependence Graph and the static slicing algorithm. Then we present two simple extensions to the static slicing algorithm to compute dynamic slices in Sections 3.1 and 3.2. But these algorithms may compute overlarge slices: they may include extra statements in the dynamic slice that shouldn't be there. In Section 3.3 we present a data-structure called the Dynamic Dependence Graph and an algorithm that uses it to compute accurate dynamic slices. Size of a Dynamic Dependence Graph depends on the length of the program execution, and thus, in general, it is unbounded. In Section 3.4, we introduce a mechanism to construct what we call a Reduced Dynamic Dependence Graph which requires limited space that is proportional to the number of distinct dynamic slices arising during the current program ex-

```
           begin
S1:           read(X);
S2:           if (X < 0)
              then
S3:              Y := f_1(X);
S4:              Z := g_1(X);
              else
S5:              if (X = 0)
                 then
S6:                 Y := f_2(X);
S7:                 Z := g_2(X);
                 else
S8:                 Y := f_3(X);
S9:                 Z := g_3(X);
                 end_if;
              end_if;
S10:          write(Y);
S11:          write(Z);
           end.
```

Figure 1: Example Program 1

ecution, not to the length of the execution. The four approaches to dynamic slicing presented here span a range of solutions with varying space-time-accuracy trade-offs.

2 Program Dependence Graph and Static Slicing

The program dependence graph of a program [FOW87, OO84, HRB88] has one node for each simple statement (assignment, read, write etc., as opposed to compound-statements like if-then-else, while-do etc.) and one node for each control predicate expression (the condition expression in if-then-else, while-do etc.). It has two types of directed edges—data-dependence edges and control-dependence edges.[3] A data-dependence edge from vertex v_i to vertex v_j implies that the computation performed at vertex v_i directly depends on the value computed at vertex v_j.[4] Or more precisely, it means that the computation at vertex v_i uses a variable, *var*, that is defined at vertex v_j, and there is an execution path from v_j to v_i along which *var* is never redefined. A control-dependence

---

[2]When we say the slice contains the bug, we do not necessarily mean that the bug is textually contained in the slice; the bug could correspond to the absence of something from the slice—a missing if statement, a statement outside the slice that should have been inside it, etc. We can discover that something is missing from the slice only after we have found the slice. In this sense, the bug still "lies in the slice."

[3]In other applications like vectorizing compilers program dependence graphs may include other types of edges besides data and control dependence, e.g., anti-dependence, output-dependence etc., but for the purposes of program slicing, the former two suffice.

[4]At other places in the literature, particularly that related to vectorizing compilers, e.g., [KKL+81, FOW87], direction of edges in Data Dependence Graphs is reversed, but for the purposes of program slicing our definition is more suitable.

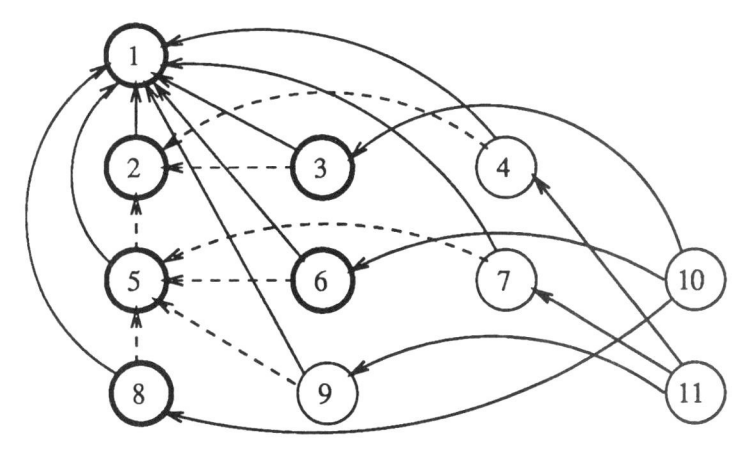

Figure 2: Program Dependence Graph of the Program in Figure 1. The solid edges denote data dependencies and the dashed edges denote control dependencies. Nodes in bold denote the Static Slice with respect to variable Y at statement 10 in the program.

edge from v_i to v_j means that node v_i may or may not be executed depending on the boolean outcome of the predicate expression at node v_j.[5] Consider, for example, the program in Figure 1. Symbols f_i and g_i in the assignment statements are used to denote some unspecified side-effect-free functions with which we are not presently concerned. Figure 2 shows the Program Dependence Graph of this program. Solid edges denote data dependencies and dashed edges denote control dependencies. We do not distinguish between the two types of edges from now on; both are drawn as solid edges.

The static slice of a program with respect to a variable, *var*, at a node, *n*, consists of all nodes whose execution could possibly *affect* the value of *var* at *n*. The static slice can be easily constructed by finding all reaching definitions of *var* at node *n* [ASU86], and traversing the Program Dependence Graph beginning at these nodes. The nodes visited during the traversal constitute the desired slice [OO84, HRB88]. For example, to find the static slice of the program in Figure 1 with respect to variable Y at statement 10, we first find all reaching definitions of Y at node 10. These are nodes 3, 6, and 8. Then we find the set of all reachable nodes from these three nodes in the Program Dependence Graph of the program shown in Figure 2. This set, {1, 2, 3, 5, 6, 8}, gives us the desired slice. These nodes are shown in bold in the figure.

---

[5] This definition of control-dependence is for programs with structured control flow. For such programs, the control-dependence subgraph essentially reflects the nesting structure of statements in the program. In programs with arbitrary control flow, a control-dependence edge from vertex v_i to vertex v_j implies that v_j is the nearest inverse dominator of v_i in the control flow graph of the program (see [FOW87] for details).

3 Dynamic Slicing

As we saw above the static slice for the program in Figure 1 with respect to variable Y at statement 10 contains all three assignment statements, namely, 3, 6 and 8, that assign a value to Y. We know that for any input value of X only one of these three statements may be executed. Consider the test-case when X is -1. In this case only the assignment at statement 3 is executed. So the dynamic slice, with respect to variable Y at statement 10, will contain only statements 1, 2, and 3, as opposed to the static slice which contains statements 1, 2, 3, 5, 6, and 8. If the value of Y at statement 10 is observed to be wrong for the above test-case, we know that either there is an error in f_1 at statement 3 or the if predicate at statement 2 is wrong. Clearly, the dynamic slice, {1, 2, 3}, would help localize the bug much more quickly than the static slice, {1, 2, 3, 5, 6, 8}.

In the next few sections, we examine some approaches to computing dynamic slices. We denote the execution history of the program under the given test-case by the sequence $<v_1, v_2, ..., v_n>$ of vertices in the program dependence graph appended in the order in which they are visited during execution. We use superscripts 1, 2, etc. to distinguish between multiple occurrences of the same node in the execution history. For example, the program in Figure 3 has the execution history $<1, 2, 3, 4, 5^1, 6^1, 7^1, 8^1, 5^2, 6^2, 7^2, 8^2, 5^3, 9>$ when N is 2.

Given an execution history *hist* of a program P for a test-case *test*, and a variable *var*, the dynamic slice of P with respect to *hist* and *var* is the set of all statements in *hist* whose execution had some *effect* on the value of *var* as observed at the end of the execution. Note that unlike static slicing where a slice is defined

```
        begin
S1:         read(N);
S2:         Z := 0;
S3:         Y := 0;
S4:         I := 1;
S5:         while (I <= N)
            do
S6:             Z := f_1(Z, Y);
S7:             Y := f_2(Y);
S8:             I := I + 1;
            end_while;
S9:         write(Z);
        end.
```

Figure 3: Example Program 2

with respect to a given location in the program, we define dynamic slicing with respect to the end of execution history. If a dynamic slice with respect to some intermediate point in the execution is desired, then we simply need to consider the partial execution history up to that point.

3.1 Dynamic Slicing: Approach 1

We saw above that the static slice with respect to variable Y at statement 10 for the program in Figure 1 contains all three assignment statements—3, 6, and 8; although for any given test-case, only one of these statements is executed. If we mark the nodes in the Program Dependence Graph that get executed for the current test-case, and traverse only the marked nodes in the graph, the slice obtained will contain only nodes executed for the current test-case. So our first simple approach to determining dynamic slices is informally stated as follows:

> To obtain the dynamic slice with respect to a variable for a given execution history, first take the "projection" of the Program Dependence Graph with respect to the nodes that occur in the execution history, and then use the static slicing algorithm on the projected Dependence Graph to find the desired dynamic slice.

Figure 4 shows the application of this approach for the program in Figure 1 for test-case X = −1, which yields the execution history <1, 2, 3, 4, 10, 11>. All nodes in the graph are drawn dotted in the beginning. As statements are executed, corresponding nodes in the graph are made solid. Then the graph is traversed only for solid nodes, beginning at node 3, the last definition of Y in the execution history. All nodes reached during the traversal are made bold. The set of all bold nodes, {1, 2, 3} in this case, gives the desired slice.

Unfortunately, the above naive approach does not always yield precise dynamic slices: It may sometimes include extra statements in the slice that did not affect the value of the variable in question for the given execution history. To see why, consider the program in Figure 3 and the test-case N = 1, which yields the execution history <1, 2, 3, 4, 5^1, 6, 7, 8, 5^2, 9>. Figure 5 shows the the result of using the above approach to obtain the dynamic slice of this program with respect to the variable Z at the end of the execution. Looking at the execution history we find that statement 7 assigns a value to Y which is never used later, for none of the statements that appear after 7 in the execution history, namely, 8, 5, and 9, uses variable Y. So statement 7 should not be in the dynamic slice. It is included in the slice because statement 9 depends on statement 6 which has a data dependence edge to statement 7 in the Program Dependence Graph. In the next section we present a refinement to the above approach that avoids this problem.

3.2 Dynamic Slicing: Approach 2

The problem with Approach 1 lies in the fact that a statement may have multiple reaching definitions of the same variable in the program flow-graph, and hence it may have multiple out-going data dependence edges for the same variable in the Program Dependence Graph. Selection of such a node in the dynamic slice, according to that approach, implies that all nodes to which it has out-going data-dependence edges also be selected if the nodes have been executed, even though the corresponding data-definitions may not have affected the current node. In the example above (Figure 3), statement 6 has multiple reaching definitions of the same variables: two definitions of variable Y from statements 3 and 7, and two of variable Z from statements 2 and 6 itself. So it has two outgoing data dependence edges for each of variables Y and Z: to statements 3 and 7, and 2 and 6 respectively (besides a control dependence edge to node 5). For the test-case N = 1, each of these four statements is executed, so inclusion of statement 6 in the slice leads to the inclusion of statements 3, 7, and 2 as well, even though two of the data dependencies of statement 6—on statement 7 for variable Y and on itself for variable Z—are never activated for this test-case.

In general, a statement may have multiple reaching definitions of a variable because there could be multiple execution paths leading up to that statement, and each of these paths may have different statements assigning a value to the same variable. For any single

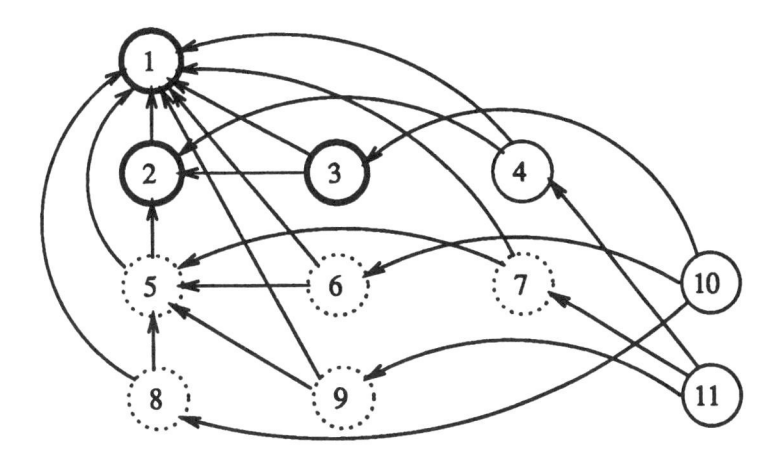

Figure 4: Dynamic Slice using Approach 1 for the program in Figure 1, test-case X = −1, with respect to variable Y at the end of the execution. All nodes are drawn as dotted in the beginning. A node is made solid if it is ever executed; and is made bold if it gets traversed while determining the slice.

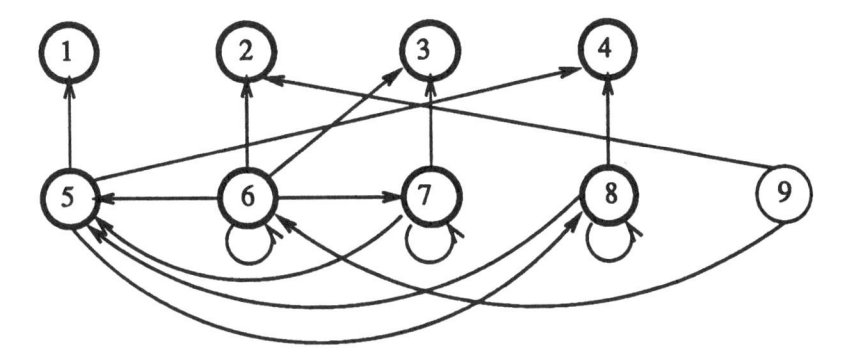

Figure 5: Dynamic slice using Approach 1 for the program in Figure 3, test-case N = 1, for variable Z, at the end of execution. Node 7 should not belong to the slice!

path, there can be at most one reaching definition of any variable at any statement; and since, in dynamic slicing, we are interested in examining dependencies for the single execution path under the given inputs, inclusion of a statement in the dynamic slice should lead to inclusion of only those statements that actually defined values used by it under the current test-case. This suggests our Approach 2 to computing dynamic slices:

> Mark the edges of the Program Dependence Graph as the corresponding dependencies arise during the program execution; then traverse the graph only along the marked edges to find the slice.

Consider again the program in Figure 3 and the test-case N = 1. Using Approach 2 on its execution history <1, 2, 3, 4, 5^1, 6, 7, 8, 5^2, 9> for variable Z yields the dynamic slice {1, 2, 3, 4, 5, 6, 8}. This is depicted in Figure 6. Imagine all edges to be drawn as dotted lines in the beginning. As statements are executed, edges corresponding to the new dependencies that occur are changed to solid lines. Then the graph is traversed only along solid edges and the nodes reached are made bold. The set of all bold nodes at the end gives the desired slice. Note that statement 7 that was included by Approach 1 in the slice is not included under this approach.

If a program has no loops then the above approach would always find accurate dynamic slices of the program (see [AH89] for details). In the presence of loops, the slice may sometimes include more statements than necessary. Consider the program in Figure 7 and the test-case where N = 2 and the two values of X read are −4 and 3. Then, for the first time through the loop statement 6, the **then** part of the **if** statement, is executed and the second time through the loop statement 7, the **else** part, is executed. Now suppose the execution has reached just past statement 9 second time through the loop and the second value of Z printed is found to be wrong. The execution history thus far is <1, 2, 3^1, 4^1, 5^1, 6, 8^1, 9^1, 10^1, 3^2, 4^2, 5^2, 7, 8^2, 9^2>. If we used Approach 2 to find the slice for variable Z for this execution history, we

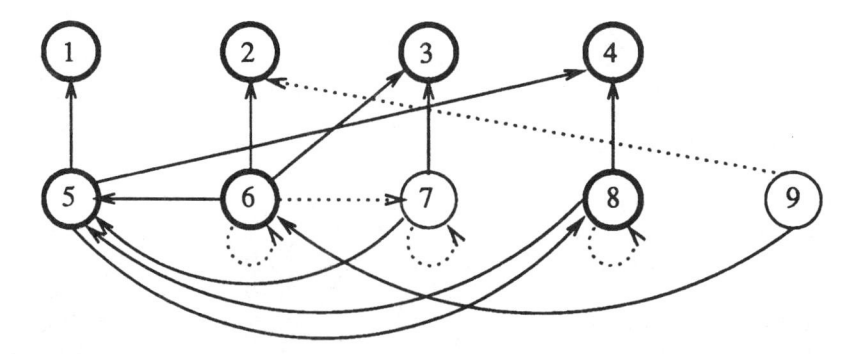

Figure 6: Dynamic Slice using Approach 2 for the program in Figure 3, test-case N = 1, for variable Z, at the end of execution. All edges are drawn as dotted at the beginning. An edge is made solid if the corresponding dependency is ever activated during execution. Only solid edges are traversed while slicing; nodes in the bold denote the slice obtained.

```
          begin
S1:           read(N);
S2:           I := 1;
S3:           while (I <= N)
              do
S4:              read(X);
S5:              if (X < 0)
                 then
S6:                  Y := f_1(X);
                 else
S7:                  Y := f_2(X);
                 end_if;
S8:              Z := f_3(Y);
S9:              WRITE(Z);
S10:             I := I + 1;
              end_while;
          end.
```

Figure 7: Example Program 3

would have both statements 6 and 7 included in the slice, even though the value of Z in this case is only dependent on statement 7. Figure 8 shows a segment of the Program Dependence Graph (only statements 4, 6, 7, 8, and 9) along with the effect of using Approach 2. The data dependence edge from 8 to 6 is marked during the first iteration, and that from 8 to 7 is marked during the second iteration. Since both these edges are marked, inclusion of statement 8 leads to inclusion of both statements 6 and 7, even though the value of Z observed at the end of second iteration is only affected by statement 7.

It may seem that the difficulty with the above approach will disappear if, before marking the data-dependence edges for a new occurrence of a statement in the execution history, we first *unmarked* any outgoing dependence edges that are already marked for this statement. This scheme will work for the above example, but unfortunately it may lead to wrong dynamic slices in other situations. Consider, for example, the program in Figure 9. Consider the case when the loop is iterated twice, first time through statements 7 and 11, and second time through statement 8 but skipping statement 11. If we obtain the dynamic slice for A at the end of execution, we will have statement 8 in the slice instead of statement 7. This is because when statement 9 is reached second time through the loop, the dependence edge from 9 to 7 (for variable Y) is unmarked and that from 9 to 8 is marked. Then, while finding the slice for A at statement 13, we will include statement 11, which last defined the value of A. Since statement 11 used the value of Z defined at statement 9, 9 is also included in the slice. But inclusion of 9 leads to inclusion of 8 instead of 7, because the dependence edge to the latter was unmarked during the second iteration. Value of Z at statement 11, however, depends on value of Y defined by statement 7 during the first iteration, so 7 should be in the slice, not 8. Thus the scheme of unmarking previously marked edges with every new occurrence of a statement in the execution history does not work.

3.3 Dynamic Slicing: Approach 3

Approach 2 discussed above sometimes leads to over-large dynamic slices because a statement may have multiple occurrences in an execution history, and different occurrences of the statement may have different reaching definitions of the same variable used by the statement. The Program Dependence Graph does not distinguish between these different occurrences, so inclusion of a statement in the dynamic slice by virtue of one occurrence may lead to the inclusion of statements on which a different occurrence of that

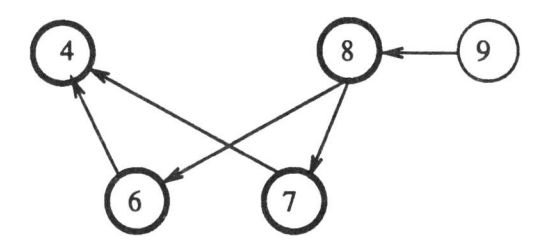

Figure 8: A subset of the dynamic slice obtained using Approach 2 for the program in Figure 7, test-case (N = 2, X = −4, 3), for Variable Z. Node 6 should not be in the slice!

```
         begin
S1:          read(N);
S2:          A := 0;
S3:          I := 1;
S4:          while (I <= N)
             do
S5:              read(X);
S6:              if (X < 0)
                 then
S7:                  Y := f₁(X);
                 else
S8:                  Y := f₂(X);
                 end_if;
S9:              Z := f₃(Y);
S10:             if (Z > 0)
                 then
S11:                 A := f₄(A, Z);
                 else
                 end_if;
S12:             I := I + 1;
             end_while;
S13:         write(A);
         end.
```

Figure 9: Example Program 4

statement is dependent. In other words, different occurrences of the same statement may have different dependencies, and it is possible that one occurrence contributes to the slice and another does not. Inclusion of one occurrence in the slice should lead to inclusion of only those statements on which this occurrence is dependent, not those on which some other occurrences are dependent. This suggests our third approach to dynamic slicing:

> Create a separate node for each occurrence of a statement in the execution history, with outgoing dependence edges to only those statements (their specific occurrences) on which this statement occurrence is dependent.

Every node in the new dependence graph will have at most one out-going edge for each variable used at the statement. We call this graph the *Dynamic Dependence Graph*. A program will have different dynamic dependence graphs for different execution histories. Miller and Choi also define a similar dynamic dependence graph in [MC88]; however, their approach differs from ours in the way the graph gets constructed (see Section 4).

Consider, for example, the program in Figure 7, and the test-case (N = 3, X = −4, 3, −2), which yields the execution history <1, 2, 3^1, 4^1, 5^1, 6^1, 8^1, 9^1, 10^1, 3^2, 4^2, 5^2, 7^1, 8^2, 9^2, 10^2, 3^3, 4^3, 5^3, 6^2, 8^3, 9^3, 10^3, 3^4>. Figure 10 shows the Dynamic Dependence Graph for this execution history. The middle three rows of nodes in the figure correspond to the three iterations of the loop. Notice the occurrences of node 8 in these rows. During the first and third iterations, node 8 depends on node 6 which corresponds to the dependence of statement 8 for the value of Y assigned by node 6, whereas during the second iteration, it depends on node 7 which corresponds to the dependence of statement 8 for the value of Y assigned by node 7.

Once we have constructed the Dynamic Dependence Graph for the given execution history, we can easily obtain the dynamic slice for a variable, *var*, by first finding the node corresponding to the last definition of *var* in the execution history, and then finding all nodes in the graph reachable from that node. Figure 10 shows the effect of using this approach on the Dynamic Dependence Graph of the program in Figure 7 for the test-case (N = 3, X = −4, 3, −2), for variable Z at the end of the execution. Nodes in bold belong to the slice. Note that statement 6 belongs to the slice whereas statement 7 does not. Approach 2, on the other hand, would have included statement 7 as well.

3.4 Dynamic Slicing: Approach 4

The size of a Dynamic Dependence Graph (total number of nodes and edges) is, in general, *unbounded*.

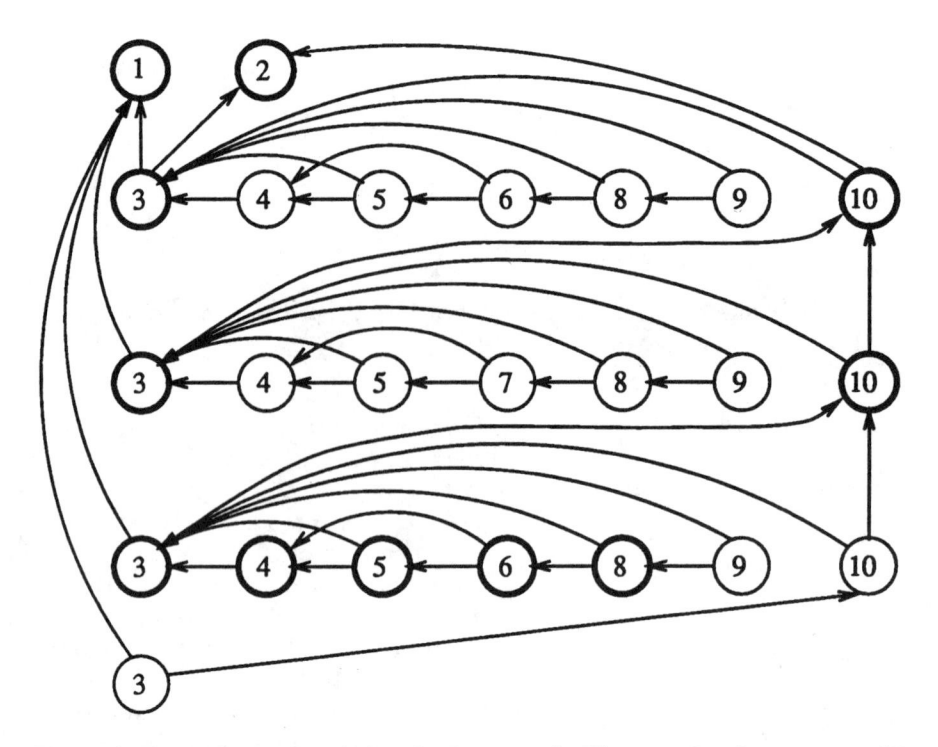

Figure 10: Dynamic Dependence Graph for the Program in Figure 7 for the test-case (N = 3, X = −4, 3, −2). Nodes in bold give the Dynamic Slice for this test-case with respect to variable Z at the end of execution.

This is because the number of nodes in the graph is equal to the number of statements in the execution history, which, in general, may depend on values of run-time inputs. For example, for the program in Figure 3 the number of statements in its execution history, and hence the size of its Dynamic Dependence Graph, depends on the value read by variable N at statement 1. On the other hand, we know that every program can have only a finite number of possible dynamic slices — each slice being a subset of the (finite) program. This suggests that we ought to be able to restrict the number of nodes in a Dynamic Dependence Graph so its size is not a function of the length of the corresponding execution history. Our fourth approach exploits the above observation:

> Instead of creating a new node for every occurrence of a statement in the execution history, create a new node only if another node with the same transitive dependencies does not already exist.

We call this new graph the *Reduced Dynamic Dependence Graph*. To build it without having to save the entire execution history we need to maintain two tables called *DefnNode* and *PredNode*. *DefnNode* maps a variable name to the node in the graph that last assigned a value to that variable. *PredNode* maps a control predicate statement to the node that corresponds to the last occurrence of this predicate in the execution history thus far. Also, we associate a set, *ReachableStmts*, with each node in the graph. This set consists of all statements one or more of whose occurrences can be reached from the given node. Every time a statement, S_i, gets executed, we determine the set of nodes, D, that last assigned values to the variables used by S_i, and the last occurrence, C, of the control predicate node of the statement. If a node, n, associated with S_i already exists whose immediate descendents are the same as $D \cup C$, we associate the new occurrence of S_i with n. Otherwise we create a new node with outgoing edges to all nodes in $D \cup C$. The *DefnNode* table entry for the variable assigned at S_i, if any, is also updated to point to this node. Similarly, if the current statement is a control predicate, the corresponding entry in *PredNode* is updated to point to this node.

If there were no circular dependencies in the dependence graph then the above scheme of looking for a node with the same set of immediate descendents would work fine. But in presence of circular dependencies (i.e., in presence of loops in the program dependence graph), the graph reduction described above won't occur: for every iteration of a loop involving circular dependencies we will have to create new node occurrences. We can avoid this problem, if whenever we need to create a new node, say for statement S_i, we first determine if any of its immediate descendents, say node v, already has a dependency on a previous occurrence of S_i and if the other immediate descendents of the new occurrence of S_i are also reachable from v. This is easily done by checking if the *ReachableStmts* set to be associated with the new occurrence is a subset of the *ReachableStmts* set associated with v. If so, we can merge the new occurrence of S_i with v. After this merge, during subsequent iterations of the loop the search for a node for S_i with same immediate descendents will always succeed.

Consider again the program in Figure 7, and test-case (N = 3, X = −4, 3, −2), which yields the execution history $<1, 2, 3^1, 4^1, 5^1, 6^1, 8^1, 9^1, 10^1, 3^2, 4^2, 5^2, 7^1, 8^2, 9^2, 10^2, 3^3, 4^3, 5^3, 6^2, 8^3, 9^3, 10^3, 3^4>$. Figure 11 shows the Reduced Dynamic Dependence Graph for this execution history. Every node in the graph is annotated with the set of all reachable statements from that node. Note that there is only one occurrence of node 10 in this graph, as opposed to three occurrences in the Dynamic Dependence Graph for the same program and the same test-case. Also note that the second occurrence of node 3 is merged with its immediate descendent node 10 because the *ReachableStmts* set, $\{1, 2, 3, 10\}$, of the former was a subset of that of the latter. The third occurrence of node 3 in the execution history has node 1 and node 10 as immediate descendents. Since these immediate dependencies are also contained in the merged node (10,3), the third occurrence of node 3 is also associated with this node.

Once we have the Reduced Dynamic Dependence Graph for the given execution history, to obtain the dynamic slice for any variable *var* we first find the entry for *var* in the *DefnNode* table. The *ReachableStmts* set associated with that entry gives the desired dynamic slice. So we don't even have to traverse the Reduced Dynamic Dependence Graph to find the slice. For example, the dynamic slice for variable Z in case of the Reduced Dynamic Dependence Graph in Figure 7 is given by the *ReachableStmts* set, $\{1, 2, 3, 4, 5, 6, 8, 10\}$, associated with node 8 in the last row, as that was the last node to define value of Z.

4 Related Work

The concept of program slicing was first proposed by Weiser [Wei84, Wei82]. His solution for computing static program slices was based on iteratively solving data-flow equations representing inter-statement influences. Ottenstein and Ottenstein later presented a much neater solution for static slicing in terms of graph reachability in the Program Dependence Graph [OO84], but they only considered the intra-procedural case. Horwitz, Reps, and Binkley have proposed extending the Program Dependence Graph representation to what they call System Dependence Graph to find inter-procedural static slices under the same graph-reachability framework [HRB88]. Dependence Graph representation of programs was first proposed by Kuck et al. [KKL+81]; several variations of this concept have since been used in optimizing and parallelizing compilers [FOW87] besides their use in program slicing.

Korel and Laski extended Weiser's static slicing algorithms based on data-flow equations for the dynamic case [KL88]. Their definition of a dynamic slice may yield unnecessarily large dynamic slices. They require that if any one occurrence of a statement in the execution history is included in the slice then all other occurrences of that statement be automatically included in the slice, even when the value of the variable in question at the given location is unaffected by other occurrences. The dynamic slice so obtained is executable and produces the same value(s) of the variable in question at the given location as the original program. For our purposes, the usefulness of a dynamic slice lies not in the fact that one can execute it, but in the fact that it isolates only those statements that affected a particular value observed at a particular location. For example, in the program of Figure 7 each loop iteration computes a value of Z, and each such computation is totally independent of computation performed during any other iteration. If the value of variable Z at the end of a particular iteration is found be incorrect and we desire the dynamic slice for Z at the end of that iteration, we would like only those statements to be included in the slice that affected the value of Z observed at the end of that iteration, not during all previous iterations, as the previous iterations have no effect on the current iteration. It is interesting to note that our Approach 2 (which may yield an overlarge dynamic slice) would obtain the same dynamic slice as obtained under their definition. So our algorithm for dynamic slicing based on the graph-reachability framework may be used to obtain dynamic slices under their definition, instead of using the more expensive algorithm based on iterative solutions of the data-flow equations.

Miller and Choi also use a dynamic dependence graph, similar to the one discussed in Section 3.3, to perform flow-back analysis [Bal69] in their Parallel Program Debugger PPD [MC88]. Our approach, however, differs from theirs in the way the graph is constructed. Under their approach, separate data-dependence graphs of individual basic blocks are constructed. The dynamic dependence graph is build by combining, in order, the data-dependence graphs of all basic blocks reached during execution and in-

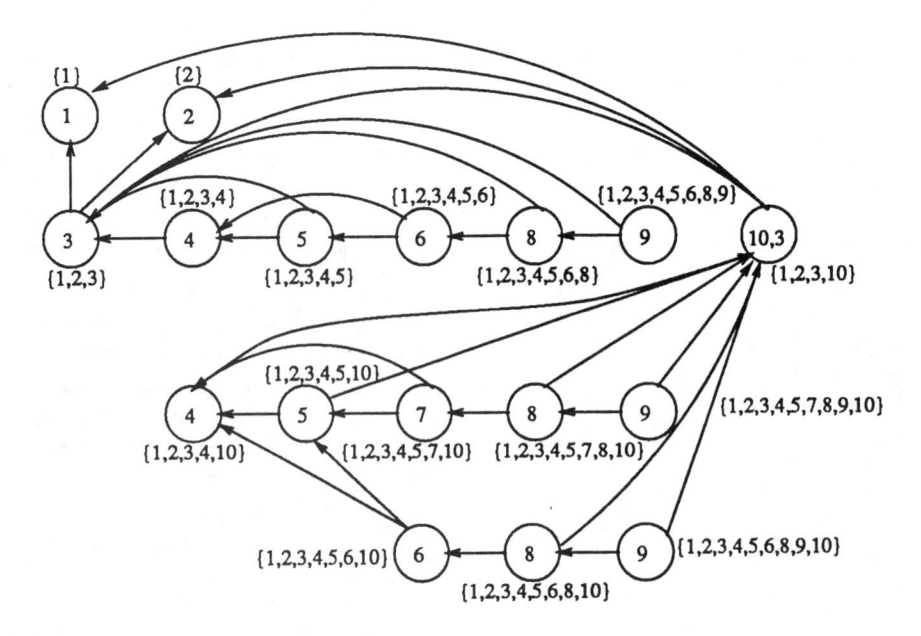

Figure 11: The Reduced Dynamic Dependence Graph for the Program in Figure 7 for the test-case (N = 3, X = −4, 3, −2), obtained using Approach 4. Each node is annotated with *ReachableStmts*, the set of all statements reachable from that node.

serting appropriate control dependence edges among them. They use a notion of incremental tracing where portions of the program state are checkpointed at the start and the end of segments of program-code called emulation-blocks. Later these emulation blocks may be reexecuted to build the corresponding segments of the dynamic dependence graph. The size of their dynamic dependence graph may not be bounded for the same reason as that discussed in Section 3.4.

5 Summary

In this paper we have examined four approaches for computing dynamic program slices. The first two are extensions of static program slicing using Program Dependence Graph. They are simple and efficient; however, they may yield bigger slices than necessary. The third approach uses Dynamic Dependence Graph to compute accurate dynamic slices but the size of these graphs may be unbounded, as it depends on the length of execution history. Knowing that every program execution can have only a finite number of dynamic slices it seems unnecessary having to create a separate node in the Dynamic Dependence Graph for each occurrence of a statement in the execution history. We then proposed the notion of a Reduced Dynamic Dependence Graph where a new node is created only if it can cause a new dynamic slice to be introduced. The size of the resulting graph is proportional to the actual number of dynamic slices that arose during the execution and not to the length of the execution.

Acknowledgements

We would like to thank Rich DeMillo, Stu Feldman, Gene Spafford, Ryan Stansifer, and Venky Venkatesh for their many helpful comments on an earlier draft of this paper.

References

[AH89]   Hiralal Agrawal and Joseph R. Horgan. Dynamic program slicing. Technical Report SERC-TR-56-P, Software Engineering Research Center, Purdue University, West Lafayette, Indiana, November 1989.

[ASU86] Alfred V. Aho, Ravi Sethi, and Jeffrey D. Ullman. *Compilers: Principles, Techniques, and Tools*. Addison-Wesley, 1986.

[Bal69] R. M. Balzer. Exdams—extendable debugging and monitoring system. In *AFIPS Proceedings, Spring Joint Computer Conference*, 1969, volume 34, pages 567–580.

[FOW87] Jeanne Ferrante, Karl J. Ottenstein, and Joe D. Warren. The program dependence graph and its uses in optimization. *ACM Transactions on Programming Languages and Systems*, 9(3):319–349, July 1987.

[HPR89] Susan Horwitz, Jan Prins, and Thomas Reps. Integrating noninterfering versions of programs. *ACM Transactions on Programming Languages and Systems*, 11(3):345–387, July 1989.

[HRB88] Susan Horwitz, Thomas Reps, and David Binkeley. Interprocedural slicing using dependence graphs. In *Proceedings of the ACM SIGPLAN'88 Conference on Programming Language Design and Implementation*, Atlanta, Georgia, June 1988. SIGPLAN Notices, 23(7):35–46, July 1988.

[KKL+81] D. J. Kuck, R. H. Kuhn, B. Leasure, D. A. Padua, and M. Wolfe. Dependence graphs and compiler optimizations. In *Conference Record of the Eighth ACM Symposium on Principles of Programming Languages*, Williamsburg, Virginia, January 1981. pages 207–218.

[KL88] Bogdan Korel and Janusz Laski. Dynamic program slicing. *Information Processing Letters*, 29:155–163, October 1988.

[MC88] Barton P. Miller and Jong-Deok Choi. A mechanism for efficient debugging of parallel programs. In *Proceedings of the ACM SIGPLAN'88 Conference on Programming Language Design and Implementation*, Atlanta, Georgia, June 1988. SIGPLAN Notices, 23(7):135–144, July 1988.

[OO84] Karl J. Ottenstein and Linda M. Ottenstein. The program dependence graph in a software development environment. In *Proceedings of the ACM SIGSOFT/SIGPLAN Symposium on Practical Software Development Environments*, Pittsburgh, Pennsylvania, April 1984. SIGPLAN Notices, 19(5):177–184, May 1984.

[Wei82] Mark Weiser. Programmers use slices when debugging. *Communications of the ACM*, 25(7):446–452, July 1982.

[Wei84] Mark Weiser. Program slicing. *IEEE Transactions on Software Engineering*, SE-10(4):352–357, July 1984.

II. Foundations of Software Merging

Semantic merging and decision support

The goal of semantic merging is to guarantee correctness sufficient to ensure that the results of automatic merging can be trusted in the absence of error messages. This is beyond the capabilities of current commercial merging tools, such as Merge Ahead (Prescient Software) or ClearCase (Atria Software), which rely on the engineers using the tools to guarantee the semantic integrity of the merge.

The current generation of commercial tools uses graphics and multiple simultaneous views to provide convenient interactive interfaces for the engineers to inspect the results of a text-based merge and to correct the errors they find. These tools are language-independent, and therefore insensitive to a language's semantics. They support presentation and manipulation of information related to merging. They can construct plausible merges and report problems in cases where several updates affect the same piece of text, but they do not provide real decision support to the engineers and are not capable of checking a merge's consistency. In particular, semantic merging conflicts can occur even if all updates affect only disjoint areas of the program text.

The papers in this section describe mathematical models of the correctness of software merging that can serve as the basis for guarantees of semantic correctness and future decision support tools for merging. We believe that such a formal basis is needed if merging tools are to approach the maturity level of modern compilers, which can automatically check properties such as type consistency and the absence of accesses to uninitialized data.

Overview of the papers

In the first paper in this section, Berzins presents the earliest formulation of semantic correctness for merging, in terms of a semantic lattice. This model applies to the special case of compatible extensions to functions, and talks about merging versions, rather than merging changes to versions. Artificial conflict elements are used to formally locate inconsistencies between versions that conflict. The paper also presents some merging methods for functional programs, including recursion but not state changes or loops.

In the second paper, Ramalingam and Reps develop a model of change merging that can represent incompatible modifications as well as extensions. They introduce functional modification algebras that model changes to software as second order functions, and shows the relationship to Browerian Algebras. This formalism is linked to the method for merging changes to while-programs described in the Horwitz, Prins, and Reps paper in Section III. The paper also contains an analysis of the problem of reversing a change while preserving a later change.

In the third paper, Berzins proposes a model of change merging that is a uniform extension of standard denotational semantics. This model handles merging of arbitrary changes to programs and contains a suitably extended set of conflict elements to support formal location of inconsistencies. The model is used to determine some general properties of merging, and in particular to explore the degree to which changes to the components of a functional composition (modules related by data flow relations) can be merged independently. Examples show that this is not possible in the general case, and proofs establish some special cases where it is possible.

Remaining challenges

Formal models of the requirements for semantic merging of sequential programs and some kinds of parallel programs are available. The third paper shows why none of the current modeling approaches (Boolean and Browerian algebras) can apply to languages whose semantics require an Egli-Milner power domain. We need this construction for languages that feature nondeterministic parallel execution together with possible nonterminating computations, if we want the meaning of a program (that is, the mathematical function that it computes) that sometimes works correctly and sometimes diverges to be different from the meaning of a program that always diverges and also different from the meaning of a program that always works correctly. In this context, a program's meaning is the mathematical function the program computes.

On Merging Software Extensions

Valdis Berzins

Computer Science Department, University of Minnesota, Minneapolis, MN 55455, USA

Summary. The problem of combining independent updates to a program is examined in the context of applicative programs. A partial semantic merge rule is given together with the conditions under which it is guaranteed to be correct, and the conditions under which a string merge corresponds to a semantic merge are examined. The theoretical work reported here contains initial steps towards a solution of the software merging problem and is not sufficient for producing a practical system.

1. Introduction

A typical software system evolves in a long series of extensions and modifications, in response to new requirements and discovered faults. Most useful systems are too large to be maintained by just one person, so that concurrent extensions and modifications to a system must be coordinated. This paper is concerned with automatic methods for merging two versions of a program that guarantee correctness of the result or at least pinpoint potential inconsistencies. We characterize the desired semantics of the merged program in terms of the semantics of the original programs and give several rules for constructing a merged program that is correct whenever it terminates cleanly. These results allow us to explore the conditions under which a string merge of the kind produced by sccs and rcs is semantically correct. We limit our discussion to applicative programs, and treat program *extensions* but not program *modifications*. A program extension extends the domain of a partial function without altering any of the initially defined values, while a modification redefines values that were defined initially. An applicative program consists of a set of recursive function definitions and an expression to be evaluated. Function definitions have a conventional form "name (parameters) = expression", and an expression is a constant, variable, function application, or conditional expression, as usual. We assume the desired semantics of a function can be characterized by a continuous predicate on pairs of values from the domain and range of the function.

The software merge problem was recognized in [1], which claimed a layered design database was needed but did not say how to do the merge. The source code control system (sccs) [2] of the Unix Programmer's Workbench [3] and the revision control system (rcs) [4] both have facilities for automatically merging a number of updates to source text, treated as an uninterpreted text string. Conflicts are reported where there is physical overlap of the substrings that are modified. We are not aware of other solutions ensuring the correctness of the merged document with respect to semantic criteria. The pioneering work of Scott [5] recognized the relevance of lattices and approximation orderings for modeling design extensions, but as far as we know this work has not been previously applied to the software merge problem. A different approach to computer-aided software maintenance is reported in [6]. This approach requires proving the correctness of the code, keeping the proofs on line, and using them to trace the effects of code modifications. The system directs the designer to the places in a design that are invalidated by a modification, but it does no synthesis or program modification. Our goal has been to explore the degree of automation that can be attained without requiring the explicit construction and processing of formalized specifications.

2. Correctness of Merges

The result of merging two programs should be a new program that has all the capabilities of each of the original programs. The notion of program merging can be formalized by using the approximation ordering introduced by Scott [5]. If $p \sqsubseteq q$ we say that p *approximates* q and that q is a *extension* of p. This means that q agrees with p everywhere p is defined and that q may be defined in some cases where p is not.

We take the problem of merging of two specifications (functions, programs) p and q to be the same as finding the *least common extension* of p and q[1], written $p \sqcup q$ where $\sqcup$ denotes the least upper bound with respect to the $\sqsubseteq$ ordering. We refer to p and q as the *base specifications* (functions, programs) and to $p \sqcup q$ as the *merged specification* (function, program). The least common extension of two versions is an extension of each, so it must exhibit the behavior of both. Since the least common extension must approximate all other common extensions, it can exhibit only behavior dictated by the requirement to conform with both p and q.

In the rest of this section we develop the required formalism and prove that a merging scheme is correct if it results in a program computing some common extension of the functions computed by the base programs.

2.1. Domains

We are concerned with four kinds of domains: specifications, functions, programs, and data types. Specifications characterize the intended behavior of programs, while (mathematical) functions represent the actual behavior of (applicative) programs. Programs are algorithms defining partial functions. Data types,

---

[1] The least common extension is not computable in the general case, so an approximation is needed in practice

the sets on which programs operate, concern us only indirectly. We treat all these domains as lattices with respect to the approximation ordering $\sqsubseteq$ (a lattice is a partially ordered set containing a least upper bound and a greatest lower bound for any pair of elements).

Each data type D_0 is made into a lattice $D = D_0 \cup \{\bot, \top\}$ by adding a pair of artificial elements $\bot$ (pronounced "undefined" or "bottom") and $\top$ (pronounced "inconsistent" or "top"). The extension relation for data types is the flat ordering defined by

$$x \sqsubseteq y \text{ iff } (\bot \equiv x) \text{ or } (x \equiv y) \text{ or } (y \equiv \top).$$

The undefined element $\bot$ approximates everything, so that replacing $\bot$ with any proper element of the domain is a valid extension. The inconsistent element $\top$ is an extension of every proper element, so that $\top$ cannot be replaced by a proper data element in any valid extension. The approximation ordering for the domain of truth values *Bool* is illustrated below.

$$\begin{array}{c} \top \\ / \ \backslash \\ \mathbf{T} \quad \mathbf{F} \\ \backslash \ / \\ \bot \end{array}$$

In Scott's work on the lattice of flow diagrams [5] the bottom element of the domain represents an undefined part of the program (flowchart), while in other work using approximation lattices [7, 8, 9] it represents the result of a nonterminating computation. We use the first interpretation for programs. For functions and specifications we generalize the second interpretation slightly, taking $\bot$ to represent the result of an unsuccessful computation. This includes infinite computations and computations that terminate abnormally or terminate with an error message in lieu of an answer. We take $\top$ to represent the result of merging two incompatible specifications (functions, programs), indicating a situation where no proper value can satisfy both specifications simultaneously. Such situations are bound to occur in practice. The best an automated merging facility can achieve is to detect and report the inconsistency. The value $\top$ is detectable both at merging time and at run-time and should produce an error message if produced at either time.

We view each data type as a heterogeneous algebra [10]. Each primitive operation f of the algebra is extended to the full lattice by requiring it to be doubly strict:

$x_i \equiv \bot \Rightarrow f(x_1, \ldots, x_i, \ldots, x_n) \equiv \bot,$ and
$x_i \equiv \top \& x_j \not\equiv \bot \quad \text{for } 1 \leq j \leq n \Rightarrow f(x_1, \ldots, x_i, \ldots, x_n) \equiv \top, \quad \text{for } 1 \leq i \leq n.$

The strong equality relation $x \equiv y$ gives **T** if x and y are the same element and **F** otherwise, even if x or y are improper elements. Conditional expressions are extended to the full lattice by the following rules:

$$(\text{if } \bot \text{ then } x \text{ else } y) \equiv \bot, \quad (\text{if } \top \text{ then } x \text{ else } y) \equiv \top$$

where the first rule is conventional [11]. The function and specification domains are defined as

$$Func = D \to R, \quad Spec = [D \times R] \to Bool$$

where D and R are data type domains of the form described above and where $X \to Y$ denotes the set of continuous functions with respect to the approximation ordering $\sqsubseteq$. A function f is continuous iff $f(\sqcup S) = \sqcup f(S)$ for all directed sets S. A set S is directed iff every finite subset of S has an upper bound in S. The orderings on these domains are defined as usual:

$$f \sqsubseteq g \text{ iff } \forall x \in D[f(x) \sqsubseteq g(x)], \quad s \sqsubseteq t \text{ iff } \forall x \in D, y \in R[s(x, y) \sqsubseteq t(x, y)]$$

where f and g are functions and s and t are specifications. The limitation to continuous functions is not a serious restriction with respect to *Func* and *Spec* because all computable functions are continuous with respect to $\sqsubseteq$ [8]. While undecidable specifications may have some theoretical interest, testing considerations indicate that practical specifications should be decidable.

Two specifications can be consistently merged only if they agree at all points where both are defined. We are interested in specifications that leave part of the input space unconstrained, to allow room for merging them with other specifications. This consideration motivates the following definitions, which say what it means for an input value to be in the domain of a specification and for a function to satisfy a specification.

$$Dom: Spec \to Powerset[D], \quad Dom(s) = \{x \in D \mid \exists y \in R[\mathbf{T} \sqsubseteq s(x, y)]\}$$
$$Sat: [Func \times Spec] \to Bool_0, \quad Sat(f, s) \text{ iff } \forall x \in Dom(s)[\mathbf{T} \sqsubseteq s(x, f(x))]$$

The domain of a specification $Dom(s)$ is the set of input data values for which an acceptable response has been specified and possibly overconstrained. If a specification for a function f is applied to a pair (x, y) then the result is $\mathbf{T}$ if y is an acceptable value for $f(x)$, $\mathbf{F}$ if y is not an acceptable value for $f(x)$, $\bot$ if the specification does not give any information about whether y is an acceptable value for $f(x)$, and $\top$ if the specification is inconsistent with respect to whether y is an acceptable value for $f(x)$. The last case can arise if two conflicting specifications are merged. A function satisfies a specification ($Sat(f, s)$) if the output of the function is either acceptable or overconstrained for every input in the domain of the specification, where the second case can arise only for inconsistent specifications. An inconsistent specification may overconstrain the outputs for only a subset of the input space and may be perfectly meaningful for other input values. We take a function to be acceptable with respect to a specification if it satisfies all the satisfiable constraints, which we believe is a practical approach.

An example of a specification for a square root function on real numbers with precision ε is

$$\lambda(x, y). \text{ if } 0 \leq x \text{ then } abs(y - x^2) \leq \varepsilon \text{ else } \bot.$$

The specification yields $\bot$ if $x < 0$, in which case a correct function may produce any result. This is a partial specification, with no constraints on responses to illegal inputs.

2.2. Correctness Theorem

We have identified the least common extension as the desired semantics for merging specifications and noted that the least common extension is not computable in general. The following theorem justifies the use of approximate methods of computing program merges based on common extensions that are not necessarily the least ones.

Theorem (Correctness of Extensions). *If s, t are monotonic, $f \sqsubseteq h$, $g \sqsubseteq h$, $Sat(f, s)$, and $Sat(g, t)$ then $Sat(h, (s \sqcup t))$*

Proof.

Suppose $x \in Dom(s \sqcup t)$.
Then $\exists y \in R [\mathbf{T} \sqsubseteq (s \sqcup t)(x, y)]$ Definition of $Dom(s \sqcup t)$
$\Rightarrow \exists y \in R [\mathbf{T} \sqsubseteq s(x, y) \sqcup t(x, y)]$ Property of $\sqcup$
$\Rightarrow \exists y \in R [\mathbf{T} \sqsubseteq s(x, y) \text{ or } \mathbf{T} \sqsubseteq t(x, y)]$ Case analysis on $s(x, y), t(x, y) \in Bool$

Therefore $x \in Dom(s)$ or $x \in Dom(t)$.

Suppose $x \in Dom(s)$. Then
$\mathbf{T} \sqsubseteq s(x, f(x))$ Definition of $Sat(f, s)$
$\sqsubseteq s(x, h(x))$ Monotonicity of s
$\sqsubseteq s(x, h(x)) \sqcup t(x, h(x))$ Property of $\sqcup$
$\equiv (s \sqcup t)(x, h(x))$ Property of $\sqcup$
So $Sat(h, (s \sqcup t))$.

The case $x \in Dom(t)$ is similar. □

Our correctness theorem depends on the assumption that specifications are monotonic. A function f is monotonic iff $x \sqsubseteq y$ implies $f(x) \sqsubseteq f(y)$. We are using an order-theoretic notion of continuity such that every continuous function is also monotonic (see [8]). The correctness theorem follows from essentially the same proof if we expand the definition of specifications as follows:

$$Spec = [D \times R \times Func] \to Bool$$

An example of a monotonic specification in the extended form is

$$\lambda(x, y, f). \text{ if } pre(x) \text{ then } post(x, y) \mathscr{S} y = f(y) \text{ else } \bot.$$

This specification says that under the precondition *pre* function f satisfies postcondition *post* and is idempotent ($f(f(x)) = f(x)$). The weak equality relation $=$ is the doubly strict extension of the equality relation on proper data elements, so that $(\bot = \bot) \equiv \bot$ and $(\mathbf{T} = \mathbf{T}) \equiv \mathbf{T}$. The monotonicity of this specification depends on the fact that the $=$ operator is doubly strict. Non-monotonic specifications can arise if quantifiers or non-strict operators such as $\sqsubseteq$ are used.

3. Calculating Program Merges

The least common extension of two functions is not computable in the general case, because the least upper bound can be used to check if a recursive function f terminates for a given input x by taking the least upper bounds with respect to two different constant functions c_1, and c_2, and evaluating both at x. Both $(c_1 \sqcup f)(x)$ and $(c_2 \sqcup f)(x)$ terminate, because they are extensions of functions known to be total (constants). If $f(x)$ terminates, at least one of the least upper bounds yields a $\top$, while both give proper constant values if $f(x)$ fails to terminate, since $\bot \sqcup c \equiv c$. This reduces a known undecidable problem to the construction of a least common extension, demonstrating that least common extension are not computable in general.

Useful programs must not give incorrect results without warning, because then there would be not way to distinguish a correct output from a meaningless one. An acceptable merge rule may therefore deliver a proper value only if that proper value is also delivered by the least common extension. The correctness theorem of the previous section says any common extension will do, which amounts to reporting an inconsistency ($\top$) in some cases where the least common extension would give a proper value. If a proper value cannot be determined, a $\top$ is preferable to a $\bot$ because it produces an error message at merge time, while a $\bot$ may produce an infinite computation. However, giving a $\top$ in all cases where successful termination cannot be determined *a priori* gives unnecessarily merge weak rules, leading us to look for partially correct approximations that are not extensions in the strict sense.

3.1. Merging Applicative Programs

An applicative program consists of a set of named recursive definitions of functions and an expression. The result of merging two programs is a set containing a definition for each function appearing in either of them where functions are matched up by name. If a function appears in one program but not the other, it appears in the merged program unchanged. If a function appears in both programs, with a different number of arguments in each, then a syntax error has occurred and the formal argument list should appear as $\top$ in the merged program to indicate the location of the error. Otherwise the formal parameters of one function are renamed if necessary to make the formal parameters of both definitions coincide, and the expressions in the bodies of the two definitions are merged to produce the body of the function in the merged program. Several different merge rules for expressions are described in the rest of this Section.

3.2. Operator Tree Merge Rule for Expressions

The simplest way to calculate expression merges, by taking the least common extension in the domain of operator trees, is correct but impractically weak.

The tree domain is defined by

$$Tree = Leaf + Sequence[Tree]$$
$$Sequence[X] = Nil + [X \times Sequence[X]]$$
$$Nil = \{\bot, nil, \top\}$$

where $+$ denotes disjoint.[2] The orderings for the cross product domain $D_1 \times D_2$ and the disjoint union domain $D_1 + D_2$ are given by the usual rules:

$$x \sqsubseteq y \text{ iff } x_1 \sqsubseteq_1 y_1 \,\&\, x_2 \sqsubseteq_2 y_2$$
$$x \sqsubseteq y \text{ iff } (x \in D_1 \,\&\, y \in D_1 \,\&\, x \sqsubseteq_1 y) \quad or$$
$$(x \in D_2 \,\&\, y \in D_2 \,\&\, x \sqsubseteq_2 y) \quad or \quad x \equiv \bot \quad or \quad y \equiv \top$$

where x_1 and x_2 represent the first and second elements of the pair x and where $\sqsubseteq_1$ and $\sqsubseteq_2$ are the approximation orderings of the domains D_1 and D_2. These rules imply that a tree t_1 approximates a tree t_2 if both have the same number of subtrees and each subtree of t_1 approximates the corresponding subtree of t_2. The leaf nodes of an operator tree have a flat ordering.

Least upper bounds for operator trees are computed pointwise, yielding a tree with the least upper bounds of corresponding subtrees as descendents if the original trees have the same number of descendents and yielding $\top$ otherwise. Least upper bounds for the leaf nodes are determined by the usual rules for a flat ordering:

$$(\bot \sqcup x) \equiv (x \sqcup \bot) \equiv x, (x \sqcup x) \equiv x, (\top \sqcup x) \equiv (x \sqcup \top) \equiv \top, x \not\equiv y \Rightarrow (x \sqcup y) \equiv \top.$$

For example, these rules allow us to determine that $f(g(x), \bot) \sqcup f(\bot, h(y)) \equiv f(g(x), h(y))$.

The operator tree $\sqcup$ operation is a correct merge rule because the value computed by $p_1 \sqcup p_2$ is a common extension of the values computed by the programs p_1 and p_2. (The property is obvious for constants and variables and holds for more complex programs because the composition, conditional, and least fixed point operators are monotonic, see [8].) Such a merge rule is not strong enough to be useful because it usually produces inconsistencies when two syntactically different extensions of a program are merged. For example, consider the two conditional expressions shown below.

$$\text{if } p(x) \text{ then } x \text{ else if } q(x) \text{ then } g(x) \text{ else } \bot$$
$$\text{if } p(x) \text{ then } x \text{ else if } r(x) \text{ then } h(x) \text{ else } \bot.$$

These programs are different extensions of their greatest common approximation,

$$\text{if } p(x) \text{ then } x \text{ else } \bot.$$

The least common extension of these programs with respect to the operator tree ordering is

$$\text{if } p(x) \text{ then } x \text{ else if } \top \text{ then } \top \text{ else } \bot = \text{if } p(x) \text{ then } x \text{ else } \top.$$

---

[2] For technical reasons (cf. [8]) we use separated sums rather than coalesced sums

The ⊤ indicates an inconsistency in the case where $p(x)$ is false, because neither q and r nor g and h are syntactic extensions of each other. The semantic least common extension of the two programs need not yield ⊤ in this case however, depending on the behavior of the functions q, r, g, and h. The rules given below do better.

3.3. Reducing Conditional Expressions

Improved merge rules are based on the semantic domain *Func* rather than the syntactic domain of programs. In this subsection we discuss how to merge conditionals more accurately. Conditionals have special importance with respect to program merging because if-then-else is the only construct in our language that is not doubly strict. Expressions containing only function applications must be completely defined to be useful since strictness guarantees that the value of the entire expression must be ⊥ if any of the subexpressions are ⊥. In contrast a conditional can have a proper value even if one of its arms is ⊥. This makes it possible to merge two useful but partially defined programs to produce a more complete program without necessarily producing an inconsistency.

The following relation can be derived from the basic properties of conditional expressions.

$$(\text{if } p(x) \text{ then } h_1(x) \text{ else } h_2(x)) \sqcup E$$
$$\text{if } p(x) \sqsubseteq \bot \text{ then } E \text{ else if } p(x) \text{ then } h_1(x) \sqcup E \text{ else } h_2(x) \sqcup E.$$

This rule is exact but not useful. The test $p(x) \sqsubseteq \bot$ cannot be computed in general, since it is equivalent to determining whether or not the computation of $p(x)$ terminates. An approximate but computable rule for reducing conditional can be derived using the following law (see [12]).

$$(\text{if } p(x) \text{ then } g(h_1(x)) \text{ else } g(h_2(x))) \sqsubseteq g(\text{if } p(x) \text{ then } h_1(x) \text{ else } h_2(x))$$

where p, g, h_1, and h_2 are monotonic and where equality holds in case $g(\bot) \equiv \bot$ or $p(x) \not\equiv \bot$. We use this law to define an approximate merge operator **m**. Taking $g(e) \equiv e\,\mathbf{m}\,E$ in the law above gives us the recurrence shown below for calculating the merge of a conditional and another expression E in terms of merges involving subexpressions of the conditional.

$$(\text{if } p(x) \text{ then } h_1(x)\,\mathbf{m}\,E \text{ else } h_2(x)\,\mathbf{m}\,E) \sqsubseteq (\text{if } p(x) \text{ then } h_1(x) \text{ else } h_2(x))\,\mathbf{m}\,E.$$

This relation can be used as a rewrite rule, where instances of the right hand side are to be replaced by the corresponding instance of the left hand side. Since the rule is based on an inequality rather than an identity, it results in an approximation rather than an exact least common extension. When used in concert with the operator tree merge rules for constants, variables, and function calls the above rule always produces a merged function that is *compatible* with the least common extension, where

$$compatible(f, g) \text{ iff } \forall x [f(x) \sqsubseteq g(x) \text{ or } g(x) \sqsubseteq f(x)].$$

Informally, two comparable functions must agree whenever both produce a proper data value.

We use part of the example of the previous section to illustrate the application of this rule.

(if $q(x)$ then $g(x)$ else $\bot$) $\mathbf{m}$ (if $r(x)$ then $h(x)$ else $\bot$)
  $\equiv$ if $q(x)$ then $(g(x) \mathbf{m}$ (if $r(x)$ then $h(x)$ else $\bot$))
     else $(\bot \mathbf{m}$ (if $r(x)$ then $h(x)$ else $\bot$))
  $\equiv$ if $q(x)$ then (if $r(x)$ then $(g(x) \mathbf{m} h(x))$ else $(g(x) \mathbf{m} \bot)$)
     else (if $r(x)$ then $(\bot \mathbf{m} h(x))$ else $(\bot \mathbf{m} \bot)$)
  if $q(x)$ then (if $r(x)$ then $\top$ else $g(x)$) else (if $r(x)$ then $h(x)$ else $\bot$).

The result in the example is approximate in two senses. First, the operator tree merge gives $\top$ for $g(x) \mathbf{m} h(x)$, because they are syntactically incompatible, but it might be the case that the programs g and h compute the same function. This is an instance of a common extension that is not necessarily the least one. Second, in the merged program, the result depends on *both* $q(x)$ and $r(x)$, and therefore diverges if either of those predicates does. This may lead to a partial implementation, because it might be that $q(x)$ and the first base program terminates properly for some value of x, but that $r(x)$ and therefore also the merged program diverges for the same value of x. In this case the merged program is less defined than the least common extension of the base functions.

3.4. Normal Forms

The tree merging rule says that a variable merged with another variable results in $\top$ unless the two variables are syntactically the same. This is sometimes overly restrictive, because two expressions can be consistently merged as long as they have the same value, irrespective of how that value is calculated.

The problem of general program equivalence is undecidable, but we can get a stronger rule than tree merging by making use of the conditional replacement law introduced in [11], which states that an occurrence of the expression e may be replaced by another expression e' in a conditional expression if the premise of that occurrence in the conditional expression implies that $e \equiv e'$. The premise is the condition under which the occurrence of the expression is evaluated, which is a conjunction of the positive or negated forms of the tests that lead to the arm of the conditional containing the occurrence.

The conditonal replacement law can be used to define a normal form for expressions. The improved merge rule first reduces both expressions to their normal forms and then does an ordinary operator tree merge. This rule gives stronger results because two equivalent expressions may have the same normal form even if they are syntactically distinct. A convenient way to arrive at a normal form is to treat all of the equalities in the premise as rewrite rules. To ensure that the term rewriting process terminates, each equation is applied in only one direction, where longer expressions are replaced by shorter ones. In case the expressions on both sides of an equation have the same length, the rule is oriented in the direction producing the expression earliest in the lexicographic ordering on terms induced by an arbitrary ordering on variable and operator names (alphabetic order will do).

For example, the premise $x = y + w \,\&\, w = z$ leads to the rewrite rules $y + w \to x$ and $z \to w$. These rewrite rules reduce the expression $x \times (y + z)$ to the normal form $x \times x$ in two steps. Under this reduction, the following conflict-free merge can be obtained.

(if $x = y + w \,\&\, w = z$ then $x \times (y + z)$ else $\bot$) **m**
   (if $x = y + w \,\&\, w = z$ then $x \times (y + w)$ else 0)
$\equiv$ if $x = y + w \,\&\, w = z$ then $x \times x$ else 0.

The tree merge rule gives if $x = y + w \,\&\, w = z$ then $\top$ else 0, which contains an inconsistency.

The normal form may depend on the order in which the rewrite rules are applied. A simple implementation can apply the rules in some arbitrary fixed order, and a more sophisticated one can use the Knuth-Bendix completion procedure [13, 14] to first transform the rules into a form where the result does not depend on the order in which the rules are applied. The Knuth-Bendix procedure has the advantage of producing rules that determine a canonical form if it succeeds and the disadvantage of running forever on some sets of rules. In practical cases some time limit must be imposed to ensure termination, resulting in a non-canonical rule set in case time runs out before the procedure is done.

Normal form merging can also be made stronger by adding rewrite rules based on theorems about the data type on which the program operates, such as $x + 0 = x$, if such information is available, and if the extra computation time is felt to be justified. Such an approach recognizes equivalences that depend on properties of the type rather than just the properties of equality and the control structures of the programming language.

3.5. Merging Function Calls

The operator tree merge rule says that two function calls can be merged consistently only if both calls are syntactically the same. If we apply a normal form reduction we can have different expressions in corresponding places as long as the expressions are probably equivalent. Calls to two functions which do not have equivalent semantics can sometimes be merged consistently by constructing a new function. This is possible in case the two functions have consistent interfaces (the same number of arguments in our context). If the interfaces of the two functions are not the same the result of the merge is $\top$.

The principle is best illustrated by an example. The function merge of $f(a)$ and $g(b)$ would be $h(a \sqcup b)$, where h is a fresh function name. If the definitions of f and g are $f(x) = E_f$ and $g(y) = E_g$ then the definition $h(z) = E_f[f \leftarrow h][x \leftarrow z] \,\mathbf{m}\, E_g[g \leftarrow h][y \leftarrow z]$ is generated for h, where z is a fresh variable name and $e[x \leftarrow y]$ denotes the result of substituting y for every occurrence of x in the expression e. The rule for functions with multiple arguments is similar.

If the merge of the two definition bodies gives ⊤ then the merged call is reduced to ⊤. To keep the process from diverging for mutually recursive functions, it is important to avoid constructing the merged definitions for a given pair of functions more than once, which can be done using a lookup table.

4. Comparison to Text Merging

Systems like rcs [4] perform feature merging on text strings without regard for the semantics of the text. We refer to such a string based merge as a *text merge*. In this section we explore the circumstances under which text merging leads to correct results, and those where it does not.

A text merge operation involves three versions of a document, two of which define a delta, which is applied to the third. A delta is a transformation that maps the first version into the second. The rcs system defined text deltas in terms of the operations of adding, deleting, or replacing lines of text at a given place in the document. Analogous operator tree deltas can be defined in terms of replacing subtrees, where a text addition corresponds to replacing a ⊥ with a proper subtree and a text deletion corresponds to replacing a subtree with ⊥. Since operator trees usually correspond to context free grammars, a replacement that is syntactically correct in one context is syntactically correct in another. Context sensitive semantic constraints can lead to problems. For example a delta that changes variable a to variable b leads to a semantic error if applied to a program where b is not declared.

Let us return to the example of Sect. 3.2, where we use the greatest common approximation and the first extension to define the operator tree delta illustrated below.

$$\text{if } p(x) \text{ then } x \text{ else } \bot \rightarrow \text{if } p(x) \text{ then } x \text{ else if } r(x) \text{ then } h(x) \text{ else } \bot.$$

The delta replaces the ⊥ in the first program with a conditonal expression occupying the corresponding place in the second. If we apply this delta to the other extension

$$\text{if } p(x) \text{ then } x \text{ else if } q(x) \text{ then } g(x) \text{ else } \bot$$

we get the following plausible-looking merge:

$$\text{if } p(x) \text{ then } x \text{ else if } q(x) \text{ then } g(x) \text{ else if } r(x) \text{ then } h(x) \text{ else } \bot.$$

Applying the method of Sect 3.3 to the same problem yields

$$\text{if } p(x) \text{ then } x \text{ else if } q(x) \text{ then } (\text{if } r(x) \text{ then } \top \text{ else } g(x))$$
$$\text{else } (\text{if } r(x) \text{ then } h(x) \text{ else } \bot)$$

which reduces to the result of the text merge under the condition $q(x) \Rightarrow \text{not } r(x)$. In general text merging fails to account for overlapping conditions, arbitrarily picking one of the possible values rather than reporting a conflict.

We can see that text merging works for applicative programs in cases where the two new features to be merged deal with disjoint regions of the input space, and where the code affected by the changes uses disjoint sets of variables and calls disjoint sets of functions. All of these conditions can be violated even if the regions of the program text affected by each extension do not overlap.

5. Conclusions

Systems with the capabilities of doing syntactic merging of updates to text documents have been found to be useful even without a guarantee that the syntactic merge is meaningful. Such systems are more useful if they can be used without relying on skilled programmers to review the output for errors.

We have presented some results that shed some light on the circumstances under which text merges are valid, and we have given some rules are guaranteed to preserve the semantics of applicative programs in an automatic merging scheme. We believe more work in the areas described below will lead to more flexible software systems.

5.1. Areas for Future Work

This study addressed only pure extensions to the behavior of programs, which is just one aspect of the problem. It is important to address modifications as well as pure extensions. A modification can be described as a combination of a deletion and an extension. We believe that the approach reported here can be extended to handle deletions. The current work applies to applicative programs with uninterpretated data types. Merging of abstract data types and programs with state changes should also be investigated.

It may be productive to consider restrictions on design that allow lossless automatic merges for a family of system features. This capability is most important for software products that must exist in many configurations, and with different sets of options. Maintaining such a family of systems is so difficult that automated aid may justify substantial restrictions on how such a system is designed. Language features supporting explicit undefined segments of a program would make it easier to automatically combine and select system features, because pure extensions could be recognized with a relatively shallow syntactic analysis. Explicitly undefined code segments have a place in production software, because they indicate the places where planned expansion is to occur. Language support for modular and flexible definition of the error message associated with undefined or overconstrained code would be useful.

References

1. Goldstein, I.P., Bobrow, D.G.: Descriptions for a Programming Environment. Proc. Conf. of the National Association for Artificial Intelligence, 187–189 (1980)
2. Rochkind, M.J.: The Source Code Control System. IEEE Trans. Software Eng. **SE-1**, 364–370 (1975)
3. Ivie, E.L.: The Programmer's Workbench – A Machine for Software Development. CACM **20**, 746–753 (1977)
4. Tichy, W.F.: Design, Implementation, and Evaluation of a Revision Control System. Proc. of the 6th Int. Conf. on Software Engineering, IEEE, 58–67 (1982)
5. Scott, D.: The Lattice of Flow Diagrams. Technical Monograph PRG-3, Oxford University 1970
6. Moriconi, M.S.: A Designer/Verifier's Assistant. IEEE Trans. Software Eng. **SE-5**, 387–401 (1979)
7. Scott, D.: Data Types as Lattices. SIAM J. Comput. **5**, 522–587 (1976)

8. Stoy, J.: Denotational Semantics: The Scott-Strachey Approach to Programming Language Theory. Cambridge: MIT Press 1977
9. Milne, R., Strachey, C.: A Theory of Programming Language Semantics. Sommerset, NJ: Halstead Press 1976
10. Birkhoff, G., Lipson, J.D.: Heterogeneous Algebras. J. Comb. Theory **8**, 115–133 (1970)
11. McCarthy, J.: A Basis for a Mathematical Theory of Computation. Computer Programming and Formal Systems. Amsterdam, London: North Holland 1963
12. Manna, Z., Ness, S., Vuillemin, J.: Inductive Methods for Proving Properties of Programs. CACM **16**, 491–502 (1973)
13. Knuth, D.E., Bendix, P.B.: Simple Word Problems in Universal Algebras. Computational Problems in Abstract Algebra, pp. 263–297. New York: Pergamon Press 1970
14. Huet, G.: A Complete Proof of Correctness of the Knuth-Bendix Completion Algorithm. J. Comput. Syst. Sci. **23**, 11–21 (1981)

Received May 15, 1985 / July 14, 1986

A Theory of Program Modifications

G. Ramalingam *Thomas Reps*
Computer Sciences Department
University of Wisconsin—Madison
1210 W. Dayton Street
Madison, WI 53706 USA

Abstract

The need to integrate several versions of a program into a common one arises frequently, but it is a tedious and time consuming task to merge programs by hand. The program-integration algorithm proposed by Horwitz, Prins, and Reps provides a way to create a *semantics-based* tool for integrating a base program with two or more variants. The integration algorithm is based on the assumption that any change in the *behaviour*, rather than the *text*, of a program variant is significant and must be preserved in the merged program. An integration system based on this algorithm will determine whether the variants incorporate interfering changes, and, if they do not, create an *integrated* program that includes all changes as well as all features of the base program that are preserved in all variants.

This paper studies the algebraic properties of the program-integration operation, such as whether there is a law of associativity. (For example, in this context associativity means: "If three variants of a given base are to be integrated by a pair of two-variant integrations, the same result is produced no matter which two variants are integrated first.") Whereas an earlier work that studied the algebraic properties of program integration formalized the Horwitz-Prins-Reps integration algorithm as an operation in a *Brouwerian algebra*, this paper introduces a new algebraic structure in which integration can be formalized, called *fm-algebra*. In *fm*-algebra, the notion of integration derives from the concepts of a *program modification* and an operation for *combining modifications*. (Thus, while earlier work concerned an algebra of *programs*, this paper concerns an algebra of *program modifications*.)

The potential benefits of an algebraic theory of integration, such as the one developed in this paper, are actually three-fold:

(1) It allows one to understand the fundamental algebraic properties of integration—laws that express the "essence of integration." Such laws allow one to reason formally about the integration operation.

(2) It provides knowledge that is useful for designing alternative integration algorithms whose power and scope are beyond the capabilities of current algorithms.

(3) Because such a theory formalizes certain operations that are more primitive than the integration operation, an implementation of these primitive operations can form the basis for a more powerful program-manipulation system than one based on just the integration operation.

This work was supported in part by a David and Lucile Packard Fellowship for Science and Engineering, by the National Science Foundation under grant DCR-8552602, by the Defense Advanced Research Projects Agency, monitored by the Office of Naval Research under contract N00014-88-K-0590, as well as by grants from IBM, DEC, and Xerox. G. Ramalingam was supported by an IBM graduate fellowship.

"A Theory of Program Modifications" by G. Ramalingam and T. Reps, from *Proc. Colloquium on Combining Paradigms for Software Development*, LNCS 494, Springer-Verlag, New York, N.Y., 1991, pp. 137–152. Copyright © 1991 Springer-Verlag, reprinted with permision.

1. Introduction

The need to integrate several versions of a program into a common one arises frequently: when a system is "customized" by a user and simultaneously upgraded by a maintainer, and the user desires a customized, upgraded version; when a system is being developed by multiple programmers who may simultaneously work with separate copies of the source files; when several versions of a program exist and the same enhancement or bug-fix is to be made to all of them. A tool that provides automatic assistance in tackling such problems would obviously be useful.

The program-integration algorithm proposed by Horwitz, Prins, and Reps [Horwitz89]—referred to hereafter as the HPR algorithm—provides a way to create a *semantics-based* tool for integrating two or more variants of a base program. The HPR algorithm is based on the assumption that any change in the *behaviour*, rather than the *text*, of program components in a variant is significant and must be preserved in the merged program. By the "behaviour" of a program component on some initial state σ, we mean the sequence of values produced at the component when the program is executed on σ. By the "sequence of values produced at a component," we mean: for a predicate, the sequence of boolean values to which the predicate evaluates; for an assignment statement, the sequence of values assigned to the target variable.

Given variants *a* and *b* of program *base*, the HPR algorithm first determines whether the changes made to *base* to produce *a* and *b* interfere; for example, one condition that causes interference is when there is a component of *base*, *a*, and *b* that has different behaviours in the three different programs. If there is no interference the algorithm produces a merged program that incorporates the changed behaviour of *a* with respect to *base*, the changed behaviour of *b* with respect to *base*, and the unchanged behaviour common to *base*, *a*, and *b*. To achieve this, the HPR algorithm employs a program representation that is similar to the *program dependence graphs* that have been used previously in vectorizing and parallelizing compilers [Kuck81, Ferrante87]. The algorithm also makes use of Weiser's notion of a *program slice* [Weiser84, Ottenstein84] to find the statements of a program that determine the behaviour of potentially affected program components.

One of the main features of the HPR algorithm that distinguishes it from text-based integration tools, such as the UNIX[1] utility *diff3*, is its semantic property described above. One has no guarantees about the way the program that results from a purely *textual* merge behaves in relation to the behaviour of the programs that are the arguments to the merge. The HPR algorithm, on the other hand, provides exactly such a semantic guarantee. This obviates the need to check the integrated program for conflicts that might have been introduced by the integration algorithm.

Though not as apparent, the algebraic properties of an integration algorithm play an equally important role in justifying various of its uses, particularly those that involve compositions of integrations. A two-variant program-integration algorithm defines a ternary (partial) function, denoted by $\_[\_]\_$, on the set of programs. (The expression $a[base]b$ denotes the result of integrating variants *a* and *b* with respect to program *base*.) An obvious use of $\_[\_]\_$ is in

---
[1] UNIX is a trademark of AT&T Bell Laboratories.

integrating three variants, say a, b, and c, of a program *base*, by a pair of two-variant integrations. This may be done in various ways; for instance, $(a\,[base\,]b)[base\,]c$ and $a\,[base\,](b\,[base\,]c)$ are two of the possible solutions. This raises the obvious question: is _[_]_ "associative"? That is, if three variants of a given base program are to be integrated by a pair of two-variant integrations, does it matter which two variants are integrated first? Other questions about the algebraic properties of integration arise similarly from various other applications of integration.

Reps [Reps90] addressed a variety of such questions about the HPR algorithm by reformulating the HPR algorithm as an operation in a Brouwerian algebra constructed from sets of dependence graphs. (A Brouwerian algebra is a distributive lattice with an additional binary operation, denoted by $\dot{-}$, which is a kind of difference operation [McKinsey46]). In this algebra, the program-integration operation can be defined solely in terms of $\sqcup$, $\sqcap$, and $\dot{-}$. By making use of the rich set of algebraic laws that hold in Brouwerian algebras, a number of algebraic properties of the integration operation were established. For instance, it was possible to show that the integration operation is associative.

One of the advantages of such an abstract approach is its potential applicability to other integration algorithms. Thus, for instance, showing that a given algorithm can be formulated as an integration operation in some Brouwerian algebra is sufficient to show that the properties proved in [Reps90] hold for the given algorithm too. Such abstract approaches are necessitated by the development of extensions and modifications to the basic HPR algorithm (intended to extend the set of language constructs to which the integration algorithms apply [Horwitz90, Horwitz89a] and to incorporate some alternative techniques [Yang90]). Unfortunately, the integration algorithm proposed in [Yang90] is not associative (and is thus not covered by the Brouwerian-algebraic framework).

This brings out another potential benefit of an algebraic theory of integration. Some properties of integration, such as associativity, are so important that they could be considered as an algebraic criterion the integration algorithms are required to satisfy. An algebraic theory of integration should not be considered as merely a tool to analyse proposed integration algorithms to discover their algebraic properties. Rather, it should provide knowledge that is of use in the design of new integration algorithms, knowledge that can ensure that these algorithms have certain algebraic properties.

Yet another of the benefits of a theory like the one developed in this paper is that it formalizes certain operators that are more primitive than the integration operation. These operators can form the basis for a more powerful program-manipulation system than one based on just the integration operation.

In this paper, we present a new approach to studying program-integration algorithms. In particular, we introduce a new algebraic structure, *fm-algebra*. Here, the concept of program integration derives from the concept of *program modifications* and the idea of *combining* program modifications. If each variant is thought of as having been obtained by performing a certain modification to the base program, an integration algorithm creates a merged program by first combining all the modifications and then applying the resultant modification to the base program. Thus, while the work reported in [Reps90] is based on an algebra of *programs*, the work reported here is based on an algebra of *program modifications*.

These ideas are formalized in Section 2, by treating "program modifications" as functional elements, by introducing an operator that combines two modifications, and by defining the integration operator in terms of these more primitive concepts. This provides us with a framework for studying the algebraic properties of integration. In Section 3, certain simple classes of *fm*-algebras are defined axiomatically. In Section 4, some properties of the integration operator (of these classes) are derived from the axioms satisfied by the basic operators. Section 5 shows that this approach to integration is very general. More specifically, it is shown there that any integration operator satisfying some simple properties can be constructed in the suggested fashion from appropriately defined "program-modification" elements and a "modification-combination" operator that satisfies the proposed axioms. The construction of models of the axioms also demonstrates their consistency. We illustrate our approach with an example in Section 6. Section 7 discusses a problem related to program integration, that of separating consecutive edits on some base program into individual edits on the base program. Section 8 compares our approach with related work.

2. Functional-modification algebras

Consider what it means to integrate a set of variants with respect to a base program. If each variant is thought of as having been obtained by performing a certain modification to the base program, an integration algorithm creates a merged program by combining all the modifications and incorporating the resultant modification in the base program. Given this interpretation, the design of an integration algorithm begins by answering the following questions: What is a program? (What program representation is to be used?) What is a program-modification? (What kinds of program modifications are to be handled by the integration algorithm?) If program a is a variant developed from program *base*, what program modification represents this development? (that is, performing which modification to *base* yields a?) What does it mean to combine (the effects of) two modifications? What does it mean to perform a modification m on some program *base*? We formalise these questions through the following definition.

Definition. A *modification algebra* is an algebra with two sets P and M, and three operations Δ, $+$, and $<>$, with the following functionalities:

$\Delta: P \times P \rightarrow M$
$+: M \times M \rightarrow M$
$<>: M \times P \rightarrow P.$

For our purposes, we may interpret the components of a modification algebra as follows. P denotes the set of programs; M denotes a set of allowable program-modification operations; $\Delta(a, base)$ yields the program modification done to *base* to obtain a; operation $m_1 + m_2$ combines two modifications m_1 and m_2 to give a new modification; $m <base>$ denotes the program obtained by performing modification m on program *base*. Thus, answering the questions listed previously amounts to defining a particular modification algebra.

We now consider a particular kind of modification algebra in which the modifications (elements of M) happen to be certain functions from P to P, and <> is just ordinary function application. (In what follows P $\rightarrow$ P is the set of all functions from P to P.)

Definition. A *functional-modification algebra* (abbreviated *fm*-algebra) is an algebra with two sets P and M, where M is a subset of P $\rightarrow$ P. There are three operations: Δ, +, and function application, where Δ and + have the following functionalities:

$$\Delta : P \times P \rightarrow M$$
$$+ : M \times M \rightarrow M.$$

In the next section, we define two varieties of *fm*-algebra – S-algebra and W-algebra (for *strong* and *weak fm*-algebra, respectively) – which have somewhat different axioms for Δ and +.

The intuitive description of integration given at the beginning of this section may be formalised through the following definition of a ternary integration operator $\_[\![\_]\!]\_ : P \times P \times P \rightarrow P$ of an *fm*-algebra.

Definition. $a[\![base]\!]b \triangleq (\Delta(a, base) + \Delta(b, base))(base)$.

Remark: More generally, we can let the elements of M be partial functions from P to P. This may be more convenient in modeling interference among modifications, and does not affect the following results. We restrict our attention to *fm*-algebras in the following sections, but the definitions and results may be directly generalised for modification algebras.

3. Axiomatisation of functional-modification algebras

The above definition formalises our intuitive explanation of program integration. In this section we look at properties that we might reasonably expect of Δ and +, given our interpretation of these operations. We utilise collections of such properties in axiomatically defining varieties of *fm*-algebras, and then study these classes. In what follows, I denotes the identity function from P to P. (Thus, it may be interpreted as the empty or null modification.)

Definition. An *S-algebra* is a functional-modification algebra that satisfies the following axioms:

S1. $\Delta(a, a) = I$
S2. $\Delta(a, base)(base) = a$
S3-S6. $<M, +>$ is a join-semi-lattice with I as the least element. This expands into the following four axioms:
    S3. + is commutative.
    S4. + is idempotent.
    S5. I is the identity element with respect to +.
    S6. + is associative.
S7. $\Delta(a[\![base]\!]b, base) = \Delta(a, base) + \Delta(b, base)$.

Axioms S1-S6 can be justified intuitively. Axiom S7 is a formalisation of our intuitive expectation of the integrated program (*e.g.*, the axiom can be read as: $a[\![base]\!]b$ is the element x such that $\Delta(x, base)$ is the combination of $\Delta(a, base)$ and $\Delta(b, base)$). Axiom S7 is discussed again later.

In Section 4 we derive some simple properties of the integration operator of an S-algebra. We first consider a weaker form of axioms S3-S7 that is sufficient to derive these various properties. This weaker set of axioms is motivated by the following observation: as the definition of _[[_]]_ indicates, we are not interested in "combining" *arbitrary* elements of M, but only modifications to the *same base* program. More formally, define

$$M_{base} \triangleq \{ \Delta(a, base) : a \in P \}.$$

We are interested in combining two modifications only if both are elements of some M_{base}. Hence, the axioms S3-S7 above may be weakened as follows.

Definition. A *W-algebra* is a functional-modification algebra that satisfies the following axioms:

W1. $\Delta(a,a) = I$
W2. $\Delta(a, base)(base) = a$
W3-W7. For every $base \in P$, $<M_{base}, +>$ is a join-semi-lattice with I as the least element. This expands into the following five axioms:
    W3. $\Delta(a, base) + \Delta(b, base) = \Delta(b, base) + \Delta(a, base)$.
    W4. $\Delta(a, base) + \Delta(a, base) = \Delta(a, base)$.
    W5. $I + \Delta(a, base) = \Delta(a, base) = \Delta(a, base) + I$.
    W6. $(\Delta(a, base) + \Delta(b, base)) + \Delta(c, base) = \Delta(a, base) + (\Delta(b, base) + \Delta(c, base))$.
    W7. $\Delta(a, base) + \Delta(b, base) \in M_{base}$.

We now show that axiom S2 (= W2) implies that the axioms S7 and W7 are equivalent.

Proposition. If an *fm*-algebra satisfies axiom S2, then it satisfies axiom S7 iff it satisfies axiom W7.

PROOF.
    Let S2 be true. We need to show that
    $\Delta(a[[base]]b, base) = \Delta(a, base) + \Delta(b, base) \Leftrightarrow \Delta(a, base) + \Delta(b, base) \in M_{base}$.
    => This is trivial since $\Delta(a[[base]]b, base) \in M_{base}$ by definition.
    <= We have $\Delta(a, base) + \Delta(b, base) = \Delta(c, base)$, for some c.
    $(\Delta(a, base) + \Delta(b, base))(base) = \Delta(c, base)(base)$
    $a[[base]]b = c$
    □

In particular, every W-algebra satisfies axiom S7, and every S-algebra satisfies axiom W7; thus, every S-algebra is also a W-algebra.

4. Properties of _[[_]]_

The _[[_]]_ operator of a W-algebra satisfies the following properties.

Proposition. $a[[base]]b = b[[base]]a$.
PROOF.

$$a[\![base]\!]b = (\Delta(a, base) + \Delta(b, base))(base)$$
$$= (\Delta(b, base) + \Delta(a, base))(base) \qquad \text{(axiom W3)}$$
$$= b[\![base]\!]a$$

□

Proposition. $a[\![base]\!]a = a$.

PROOF.
$$a[\![base]\!]a = (\Delta(a, base) + \Delta(a, base))(base)$$
$$= (\Delta(a, base))(base) \qquad \text{(axiom W4)}$$
$$= a \qquad \text{(axiom W2)}$$

□

Proposition. $a[\![base]\!]base = a$.

PROOF.
$$a[\![base]\!]base = (\Delta(a, base) + \Delta(base, base))(base)$$
$$= (\Delta(a, base) + I)(base) \qquad \text{(axiom W1)}$$
$$= (\Delta(a, base))(base) \qquad \text{(axiom W5)}$$
$$= a \qquad \text{(axiom W2)}$$

□

Definition. The *simultaneous integration* of elements $x_1, x_2, ..., x_n$ with respect to element *base* is the element $(x_1[\![base]\!]x_2, ..., x_n)$ defined by
$$(x_1[\![base]\!]x_2, ..., x_n) \triangleq (\Delta(x_1, base) + \Delta(x_2, base) + \cdots + \Delta(x_n, base))(base).$$

Note: The above definition makes sense as long as + is associative, at least when restricted to M_{base}.

Proposition. $(a_1[\![base]\!]a_2, ..., a_n)$ is symmetric in $a_1, ..., a_n$.
PROOF. Follows directly from axioms W3 and W6.

□

Proposition. $(x[\![base]\!]y)[\![base]\!]z = (x[\![base]\!]y, z)$.

PROOF.
$$(x[\![base]\!]y)[\![base]\!]z = (\Delta(x[\![base]\!]y, base) + \Delta(z, base))(base)$$
$$= (\Delta(x, base) + \Delta(y, base) + \Delta(z, base))(base) \qquad \text{(axiom S7)}$$
$$= (x[\![base]\!]y, z).$$

□

As an immediate consequence, we get the following associativity theorem.

THEOREM. $(x[\![base]\!]y)[\![base]\!]z = x[\![base]\!](y[\![base]\!]z) = (x[\![base]\!]z)[\![base]\!]y = x[\![base]\!]y, z$.

Note that $\_[\![\_]\!]\_$ is a ternary operator. By saying that $\_[\![\_]\!]\_$ is associative we mean that for any *base* the curried binary operator $\_[\![base]\!]\_$ is associative. We intuitively expect program integration to be associative: associativity justifies integrating multiple variants of a base program by performing a succession of two-variant integrations (in any order).

5. From integration to *fm*-algebras

The previous sections outline one possible way of constructing integration operators satisfying some simple properties from binary operators Δ and $+$ that form an S-algebra or W-algebra. A natural question that arises is: how general is this approach? Is it reasonable to assume that integration operators may always be constructed in such a fashion? In this section we show the generality of this approach by showing that any integration operator satisfying certain simple properties can be constructed in such a fashion. Assume that $\_[\_]\_:(P \times P \times P) \rightarrow P$ is a ternary operator on P satisfying the following properties (we expect most integration operators to satisfy these properties):

L1. $a[base]b = b[base]a$.
L2. $a[base]base = a$.
L3. $a[base]a = a$.
L4. $(a[base]b)[base]c = a[base](b[base]c)$.

Define $\Delta:(P \times P) \rightarrow (P \rightarrow P)$ by currying $\_[\_]\_$ as below:
$$\Delta(a,base) \triangleq \lambda b.(a[base]b).$$

In the following subsections we consider two different definitions of $+$, the operator for combining modifications. In each case the corresponding $\_[\![\_]\!]\_$ operator is shown to be the same as $\_[\_]\_$. We show that Δ and the first version of $+$ yield a W-algebra. We then show that Δ and the second version of $+$ yield an S-algebra, assuming that $\_[\_]\_$ satisfies one additional property (stated below as L5).

5.1. Definition 1

Define $+$ to be function composition. Let M be the range of Δ closed under function composition. Consider the resulting *fm*-algebra $<P,M,\Delta,+>$.

THEOREM. $a[\![base]\!]b = a[base]b$

PROOF.
$a[\![base]\!]b = (\Delta(a,base) + \Delta(b,base))(base)$
$= \Delta(a,base)(\Delta(b,base)(base))$
$= a[base](b[base]base)$
$= a[base]b$

□

THEOREM. $<P,M,\Delta,+>$ is a W-algebra.

PROOF.
W1. $\Delta(a,a) = \lambda b.(a[a]b)$
$= \lambda b.b$
$= I$

W2. $\Delta(a,base)(base) = a[base]base$
$= a$

W3. $\Delta(a,base) + \Delta(b,base) = (\lambda c.\ a[base]c) + (\lambda c.\ b[base]c)$
$= \lambda c.\ a[base](b[base]c)$
$= \lambda c.\ (a[base]b)[base]c$

$$= \lambda c. \ (b\,[base\,]a)[base\,]c$$
$$= \Delta(b, base) + \Delta(a, base)$$

W4. $\Delta(a, base) + \Delta(a, base) = (\lambda b.\ a\,[base\,]b) + (\lambda b.\ a\,[base\,]b)$
$$= \lambda b.\ a\,[base\,](a\,[base\,]b)$$
$$= \lambda b.\ (a\,[base\,]a)[base\,]b$$
$$= \lambda b.\ a\,[base\,]b$$
$$= \Delta(a, base)$$

W5. I is the identity with respect to function composition.

W6. Function composition is associative.

S7. $\Delta(a\,[\![base]\!]b, base) = \Delta(a\,[base\,]b, base)$
$$= \lambda c.\ (a\,[base\,]b)[base\,]c$$
$$= \lambda c.\ a\,[base\,](b\,[base\,]c)$$
$$= (\lambda c.\ a\,[base\,]c) + (\lambda c.\ b\,[base\,]c)$$
$$= \Delta(a, base) + \Delta(b, base)$$

W7. This follows directly from S7 above.

□

5.2. Definition 2

We assume in this subsection that _[_]_ satisfies the following property, in addition to the properties L1-L4 listed at the beginning of this section:

L5. $(a\,[base\,]c)\,[c\,]\,(c\,[base\,]b) = (a\,[base\,]b)[base\,]c$.

Property L5 says that $(a\,[base\,]c)\,[c\,]\,(c\,[base\,]b)$ is another correct way of integrating three variants a, b, and c with respect to $base$. Define $+$ as follows:
$$m_1 + m_2 \stackrel{\Delta}{=} \lambda p.\ m_1(p)\,[p\,]\,m_2(p).$$
Let M be the range of Δ closed under $+$.

THEOREM. $a\,[\![base]\!]b = a\,[base\,]b$

PROOF.
$a\,[\![base]\!]b = (\Delta(a, base) + \Delta(b, base))\,(base)$
$$= (\Delta(a, base)(base))\,[base\,]\,(\Delta(b, base)(base))$$
$$= (a\,[base\,]base)\,[base\,]\,(b\,[base\,]base)$$
$$= a\,[base\,]b$$

□

THEOREM. $<P, M, \Delta, +>$ is an S-algebra.

PROOF.
S1. $\Delta(a, a) = I$ (as in the previous subsection)
S2. $\Delta(a, base)(base) = a$ (as in the previous subsection)
S3. $m_1 + m_2 = \lambda p.\ m_1(p)\,[p\,]\,m_2(p)$
$$= \lambda p.\ m_2(p)\,[p\,]\,m_1(p)$$
$$= m_2 + m_1$$
S4. $m + m = \lambda p.\ m(p)\,[p\,]\,m(p)$
$$= \lambda p.\ m(p)$$
$$= m$$
S5. $m + I = \lambda p.\ m(p)\,[p\,]\,I(p)$

$$\begin{aligned}
&= \lambda p.\ m(p)\ [p\,]\ p \\
&= \lambda p.\ m(p) \\
&= m
\end{aligned}$$

S6. $(m_1 + m_2) + m_3 = \lambda p.\ (m_1(p)\ [p\,]\ m_2(p))\ [p\,]\ m_3(p)$
$ = \lambda p.\ m_1(p)\ [p\,]\ (m_2(p)\ [p\,]\ m_3(p))$
$ = m_1 + (m_2 + m_3)$

S7. $\Delta(a[\![base]\!]b, base) = \Delta(a\,[base\,]b, base)$
$ = \lambda c.\ (a\,[base\,]b)[base\,]c$
$ = \lambda c.\ (a\,[base\,]c)\,[c\,]\,(c\,[base\,]b)$ (using property L5)
$ = \lambda c.\ \Delta(a, base)(c)\,[c\,]\,\Delta(b, base)(c)$
$ = \Delta(a, base) + \Delta(b, base)$

□

Reps [Reps90] defines an integration operator _[_]_ and shows that it satisfies the properties L1-L5 listed in this section. (The definition of _[_]_ from [Reps90] is briefly summarised at the beginning of the next section.) Hence, the construction above shows the existence of non-trivial models of the axioms of S-algebra and W-algebra.

Remark: Observe that if _[_]_ were a partial ternary operator, then the elements of M of the *fm*-algebras constructed above could be partial functions.

6. *Fm*-algebras for the HPR algorithm

In this section, we look at an example of constructing an integration algorithm from an *fm*-algebra. We develop the integration algorithm first proposed by Horwitz, Prins and Reps [Horwitz89] (the HPR algorithm) and later expressed in an algebraic framework by Reps [Reps90]. The algorithm makes use of a program representation called a *program dependence graph* [Kuck81, Ferrante87]. Let s be a vertex of a program dependence graph G. The *slice* of G with respect to s, denoted by G/s, is a graph containing all vertices on which s has a transitive flow or control dependence. A dependence graph is a *single-point slice* iff it is the slice of some dependence graph with respect to some vertex (*i.e.*, equivalently, iff $G = G/v$ for some vertex v in G). The algebraic framework is based a partial order $\leq$ on single-point slices that denotes the relation "is-a-subslice-of". Thus, if a and b are single-point slices, $b \leq a$ iff b is a slice of a with respect to some vertex in a (*i.e.*, iff $b = a/v$ for some vertex v in a). Given a set A of single-point slices, the *downwards–closure* of A, $DC(A)$, is defined as
$$DC(A) \triangleq \{\,b : \exists a \in A.\,(b \leq a)\}.$$
It can be seen that $DC(A \cup B) = DC(A) \cup DC(B)$. A set A is said to be *downwards–closed* if $DC(A) = A$. The operation of *upwards–closure* is similarly defined as
$$UC(A) \triangleq \{\,b : \exists a \in A.\,(a \leq b)\}.$$
In this framework, a program is represented by the set of all single-point slices of the program. P, the domain of program representations, is taken to be the set of all downwards-closed sets of single-point slices. Let ⊤ denote the set of all single-point slices, and ⊥ the empty set. Let ∪, ∩, and − denote the set-theoretic union, intersection and difference operators. P is closed with respect to ∪ and ∩. P is not closed under −, but is closed under the

pseudo-difference operator $\dot{-}$ defined as follows:
$$X \dot{-} Y = DC(X-Y)$$
P is also closed under a similar (dual) operator $\dot{\div}$ defined as follows, where $\bar{}$ denotes the set-theoretic complement with respect to $\top$.
$$X \dot{\div} Y = \overline{UC(Y-X)}$$
Reps [Reps90] shows that $(P, \cup, \cap, \dot{-}, \dot{\div}, \top)$ is a double Brouwerian algebra and that the HPR integration algorithm can be represented by the ternary operator $\_[\_]\_$ defined by:
$$a[base]b \triangleq (a \dot{-} base) \cup (a \cap base \cap b) \cup (b \dot{-} base)$$
Here we see how the approach outlined in Section 2 can be used to arrive at the same definition.

The HPR algorithm considers the following two types of modifications: addition of slices and deletion of slices. Consider the modification of *base* to a. The set difference $(a-base)$ represents the slices that have been added to the *base* program. This suggests the possibility of representing this "addition of $(a-base)$" by the function $\lambda p.p \cup (a-base)$. Unfortunately, this function does not necessarily map downwards-closed sets to downwards-closed sets and hence may not be an element of $(P \rightarrow P)$. Similarly, $(base-a)$ represents the set of slices that have been deleted and we would like to represent this deletion by the function $\lambda p.p-(base-a)$. This function too may not be an element of $(P \rightarrow P)$. In what follows, we look at two different ways of changing these functions so that they do map downwards-closed sets to downwards-closed sets.

6.1. Definition 1

(Note that in what follows a, *base* and p are downwards-closed sets.) The addition of $(a-base)$ can be represented by the function $\lambda p.DC(p \cup (a-base)) = \lambda p.p \cup DC(a-b) = \lambda p.p \cup (a \dot{-} base)$. Thus, the addition of $(a-base)$ is interpreted as the addition of $DC(a-base)$. The deletion of $(base-a)$ can be represented by the function $\lambda p.DC(p-(base-a)) = \lambda p.DC(p \cap \overline{(base \cap \bar{a})}) = \lambda p.DC(p \cap \overline{(base \cup a)}) = \lambda p.DC((p \cap \overline{base}) \cup (p \cap a)) = \lambda p.DC(p-base) \cup (p \cap a) = \lambda p.(p \dot{-} base) \cup (p \cap a)$. The combination of the addition and deletion can be represented by the composition of the above two functions. (By applying the laws that relate $\cup$, $\cap$, and $\dot{-}$ in Brouwerian algebra, it can be shown that these two functions commute with each other with respect to function composition. We denote the composed function $\lambda x.f(g(x))$ by $f \circ g$.) Thus, we arrive at the following definition of Δ:
$$\Delta(a,base) \triangleq (\lambda p.p \cup (a \dot{-} base)) \circ (\lambda p.(p \dot{-} base) \cup (p \cap a)).$$
We define $+$ to be function composition. Let M be the closure of the range of Δ under $\circ$. Then, it can be shown that $<P, M, \Delta, +>$ is a W-algebra whose integration operator $\_[\![\_]\!]\_$ is the same as the integration operator in Brouwerian algebra. A short way of demonstrating this is to see that the above definition of Δ simplifies to

$$\begin{aligned}
\Delta(a,base) &= \lambda p.(a \dot{-} base) \cup (p \cap a) \cup (p \dot{-} base) \\
&= \lambda p.(a \dot{-} base) \cup (p \cap a \cap base) \cup ((p \cap a) \dot{-} base) \cup (p \dot{-} base) \\
&\quad (\text{since } x = (x \dot{-} y) \cup (x \cap y)) \\
&= \lambda p.(a \dot{-} base) \cup (p \cap base \cap a) \cup (p \dot{-} base) \\
&\quad (\text{since } (p \cap a) \dot{-} base \subseteq (p \dot{-} base)) \\
&= \lambda p.a[base]p
\end{aligned}$$

Hence, the desired result follows from the results of Section 5.

6.2. Definition 2

In Section 6.1, the addition of $(a-base)$ was interpreted as the addition of $DC(a-base)$, giving us the function $\lambda p.p \cup (a \dotdiv base)$. Analogously, the deletion of $(base-a)$ can be interpreted as the deletion of $UC(base-a)$, since the absence of $(base-a)$ in any downwards-closed set automatically implies the absence of $UC(base-a)$. Hence, this deletion can be represented by the function $\lambda p.p - UC(base-a) = \lambda p.p \cap \overline{UC(base-a)} = \lambda p.p \cap (a \div base)$. Any modification can be considered to be a combination of additions and deletions. This suggests the following definitions. Let M, the set of allowable modifications, be $\{ <x,y> : x, y \in P \}$, where $<x,y>$ denotes the function $\lambda z.(z \cup x) \circ \lambda z.(z \cap y)$. Δ is defined as follows:

$$\Delta(a, base) \stackrel{\Delta}{=} <a \dotdiv base, a \div base>.$$

The operator $+$ is defined as follows:

$$<x_1, y_1> + <x_2, y_2> \stackrel{\Delta}{=} <x_1 \cup x_2, y_1 \cap y_2>.$$

(An ordered pair $<x,y>$ is a representation for a modification. The above definition defines $+$ for such representations. The representation used for a modification $m \in M$ is $<m(\bot), m(\top)>$.) The motivation for the above definition is as follows. Consider the modification $<x_1, y_1>$. The addition component of this modification is the function $<x_1, \top>$, while the deletion component is the function $<\bot, y_1>$. The two additions $<x_1, \top>$ and $<x_2, \top>$ composed (in either order) yield $<x_1 \cup x_2, \top>$. Similarly, the two deletions $<\bot, y_1>$ and $<\bot, y_2>$ composed yield $<\bot, y_1 \cap y_2>$. It can be verified that whenever $<x_1, y_1>$ and $<x_2, y_2>$ commute with respect to $\circ$, $<x_1, y_1> \circ <x_2, y_2>$ is $<x_1 \cup x_2, y_1 \cap y_2>$. If the two do not commute with respect to $\circ$, then the "addition" performed by one of them conflicts with the "deletion" performed by the other. (*i.e.*, some slices get added by one of them, while the same slices get deleted by the other.) The above definition of $+$ resolves the conflict in favour of the "addition." This follows from the interpretation of the pair $<x, y>$: the deletion is done first, followed by the addition.

The definition of $\_[\![\_]\!]\_$ gives us the following:

$$\begin{aligned}
a[\![base]\!]b &= (\Delta(a, base) + \Delta(b, base))(base) \\
&= (<a \dotdiv base, a \div base> + <b \dotdiv base, b \div base>)(base) \\
&= <(a \dotdiv base) \cup (b \dotdiv base), (a \div base) \cap (b \div base)>(base) \\
&= (a \dotdiv base) \cup ((a \div base) \cap base \cap (b \div base)) \cup (b \dotdiv base) \\
&= (a \dotdiv base) \cup (a \cap base \cap b) \cup (b \dotdiv base) \qquad \text{(since } (x \div y) \cap y = x \cap y) \\
&= a[base]b
\end{aligned}$$

Though this definition of Δ and $+$ yields the same integration operator as the definitions in Section 6.1, the Δ and $+$ themselves do not satisfy the same set of axioms: operators Δ and $+$ satisfy axioms S1-S6, but they do not satisfy axiom S7. (This suggests that studying sets of axioms weaker than S1-S7 might be potentially useful.)

Figure 1 illustrates various values in this *fm*-algebra. Each program in the figure contains an *end statement* that names a list of variables used in the program. The programs are used in the figure as a representation for a set of single-point slices, namely the slices of the respective programs with respect to the final value computed for each of the variables listed in the end statement.

7. Separating consecutive edits

Program integration deals with the problem of reconciling "competing" modifications to a base program. A different, but related, problem is that of separating *consecutive* edits to a base program into individual edits on the base program. Consider the case of two consecutive

base	a	b	a⟦base⟧b
$DC\lceil$program $\rceil$ $\mid x := 4 \mid$ $\mid y := 2 \mid$ $\mid s := x+y \mid$ $\lfloor$end$(s)\rfloor$	$DC\lceil$program $\rceil$ $\mid x := 4 \mid$ $\mid y := 2 \mid$ $\mid s := x+y \mid$ $\mid p := x*y \mid$ $\lfloor$end$(s,p)\rfloor$	$DC\lceil$program $\rceil$ $\mid x := 4 \mid$ $\mid y := 2 \mid$ $\mid r := x/y \mid$ $\lfloor$end$(r)\rfloor$	$DC\lceil$program $\rceil$ $\mid x := 4 \mid$ $\mid y := 2 \mid$ $\mid r := x/y \mid$ $\mid p := x*y \mid$ $\lfloor$end$(r,p)\rfloor$

$\Delta(a,base)$	$\Delta(b,base)$	$\Delta(a,base) + \Delta(b,base)$
$<DC\lceil$program$\rceil,\top>$ $\mid x := 4 \mid$ $\mid y := 2 \mid$ $\mid p := x*y\mid$ $\lfloor$end$(p)\rfloor$	$<DC\lceil$program$\rceil,\overline{UC\lceil$program$\rceil}>$ $\mid x := 4 \mid\mid x := 4 \mid$ $\mid y := 2 \mid\mid y := 2 \mid$ $\mid r := x/y\mid\mid s := x+y\mid$ $\lfloor$end$(r)\rfloor\lfloor$end$(s)\rfloor$	$<DC\lceil$program$\rceil,\overline{UC\lceil$program$\rceil}>$ $\mid x := 4 \mid\mid x := 4 \mid$ $\mid y := 2 \mid\mid y := 2 \mid$ $\mid r := x/y\mid\mid s := x+y\mid$ $\mid p := x*y\mid\lfloor$end$(s)\rfloor$ $\lfloor$end$(r,p)\rfloor$

c	$\Delta(b,base)(c)$
$DC\lceil$program $\rceil$ $\mid x := 4 \mid$ $\mid y := 2 \mid$ $\mid q := y/x \mid$ $\lfloor$end$(q)\rfloor$	$DC\lceil$program $\rceil$ $\mid x := 4 \mid$ $\mid y := 2 \mid$ $\mid q := y/x \mid$ $\mid r := x/y \mid$ $\lfloor$end$(q,r)\rfloor$

Figure 1. An illustration of various values in the *fm*-algebra defined in Section 6.2.

edits to a program *base*; let *a* be obtained by modifying *base*, and *c* be obtained by modifying *a*. By "separating consecutive edits," we mean creating a program *b* that includes the second modification but not the first.

One approach to separating consecutive edits, suggested in [Reps90], is based on the assumption that the desired program *b* should satisfy the equation $a[\![base]\!]b = c$. Thus, the problem is related to solving an equation of the form $a[\![base]\!]x = c$ for x. In what follows, we look at solutions of this equation in W-algebra.

LEMMA. x is a solution to $a[\![base]\!]x = c$ iff $x = m(base)$ where $m \in M_{base}$ is a solution to the equation $\Delta(a,base) + m = \Delta(c,base)$.

PROOF. Note that $x = m(base)$ for some $m \in M_{base}$ iff $\Delta(x,base) = m$.
=> Let $a[\![base]\!]x = c$.
   Then, $\Delta(a[\![base]\!]x,base) = \Delta(c,base)$.
   Hence $\Delta(a,base) + \Delta(x,base) = \Delta(c,base)$, using axiom S7.
<= $\Delta(a,base) + \Delta(x,base) = \Delta(c,base)$.
   $\Delta(a[\![base]\!]x,base) = \Delta(c,base)$, using axiom S7.
   $a[\![base]\!]x = c$, applying both sides to *base* and using axiom W2.
   □

The above lemma shows that solving the equation $a[\![base]\!]x = c$ can be reduced to solving an equation of the form $p + y = q$ in the join-semi-lattice M_{base} of modifications to *base*. The following result concerns equations of the latter form.

THEOREM. Let <M, +> be a join-semi-lattice. Let $\sqsubseteq$ denote the corresponding partial order on M. Let $p, q \in$ M. Then,
1. The equation $p + x = q$ has a solution iff q itself is a solution iff $p \sqsubseteq q$.
2. If x_1 and x_2 are solutions of $p + x = q$ and $x_1 \sqsubseteq y \sqsubseteq x_2$, then y is a solution too.
3. If x_1 and x_2 are solutions of $p + x = q$, then $x_1 + x_2$ is a solution too.
4. The solutions to $p + x = q$ form a sub-semi-lattice of M with q as the maximum element (assuming that a solution exists).

PROOF.
1. Let x satisfy $p + x = q$. Then,
$$p + q = p + (p + x) = (p + p) + x = p + x = q$$
Hence, q is a solution to $p + x = q$. By the definition of $\sqsubseteq$, this is equivalent to $p \sqsubseteq q$.
2. $x_1 \sqsubseteq y \sqsubseteq x_2$. Hence, $p + x_1 \sqsubseteq p + y \sqsubseteq p + x_2$. i.e., $q \sqsubseteq p + y \sqsubseteq q$. Hence, y is a solution.
3. Since $p + x_1 = q$, $x_1 \sqsubseteq q$. Similarly, $x_2 \sqsubseteq q$. Hence, $x_1 \sqsubseteq (x_1 + x_2) \sqsubseteq q$. It follows from 1 and 2 that $x_1 + x_2$ is a solution.
4. Follows from 3.

THEOREM.
1. $a[\![base]\!]x = c$ has a solution iff c itself is a solution.
2. If x_1 and x_2 are solutions to $a[\![base]\!]x = c$ then, $x_1[\![base]\!]x_2$ is also a solution.

PROOF

1. This follows directly from the previous results.

2. This follows from the previous results as below. Since x_1 and x_2 are solutions of $a[\![base]\!]x = c$, it follows from the first lemma that $\Delta(x_1, base)$ and $\Delta(x_2, base)$ are solutions of the equation $\Delta(a, base) + m = \Delta(c, base)$. From the second lemma, it follows that $\Delta(x_1, base) + \Delta(x_2, base)$ is also a solution to the latter equation. Hence, $(\Delta(x_1, base) + \Delta(x_2, base))(base)$, i.e., $x_1[\![base]\!]x_2$ is a solution to $a[\![base]\!]x = c$ (from the first lemma). □

From the construction in the Section 5, it can be seen that the above theorem holds for any _[_]_ satisfying the properties L1-L4 (listed at the beginning of Section 5).

8. Relation to previous work

This paper has presented new techniques for studying program-integration algorithms. We introduced a new formalism for expressing integration, based on the following ideas:
(1) Program modifications are formalized as functions from programs to programs.
(2) The process of performing a modification on some program *base* is formalized as the application of a modification function m to *base*.
(3) There is an operation $\Delta(a, base)$ that produces a modification function that maps *base* to a.
(4) There is an operation $m_1 + m_2$ that combines two modification functions m_1 and m_2 to give a new modification function.

The formalization of the concept of a modification leads to a different way of looking at the problem of program integration, by shifting the focus from the domain of programs to the domain of program-modifications. We feel that the framework of modification algebra and *fm*-algebra is general enough to model different integration algorithms. The study of different classes of *fm*-algebras, characterised by the properties that the operators Δ and $+$ satisfy, arises naturally, as a means of establishing the properties of different integration algorithms. The discussions in Section 4 concerning the associativity of integration and in Section 7 concerning the problem of separating consecutive edits show that *fm*-algebra is a useful abstraction for studying the algebraic properties of program integration. It is worth noting that this paper is really about a theory of modifications, since it is immaterial whether the objects being modified are programs or not.

The work most closely related to the work presented in this paper is [Reps90], which also uses algebra to study program integration. There, the set of downwards-closed sets of single-point slices is shown to form a Brouwerian algebra; an integration operation is defined for Brouwerian algebra; and the integration operation for the Brouwerian algebra of downwards-closed sets of single-point slices is shown to correspond to the HPR integration algorithm.

This paper makes use of the results of [Reps90] in the following way: the constructions in Sections 5 and 6 show that the integration operation in a Brouwerian algebra—and hence, by the correspondence established in [Reps90], the HPR integration algorithm as well—corresponds to the integration operation in appropriately defined *fm*-algebras.

However, the S- and W-algebras studied in this paper are substantially different from Brouwerian algebra. Brouwerian algebra deals with one kind of element (which in [Reps90] formalizes the space of program representations). In contrast, *fm*-algebra has two kinds of elements; in our context, the two kinds of elements formalize the space of program representations and the space of program modifications. In other words, *fm*-algebra explicitly formalizes the notion of a *modification*, for which there is no corresponding notion in Brouwerian algebra.

REFERENCES

Ferrante87.
> Ferrante, J., Ottenstein, K., and Warren, J., "The program dependence graph and its use in optimization," *ACM Transactions on Programming Languages and Systems* 9(3) pp. 319-349 (July 1987).

Horwitz89a.
> Horwitz, S., Pfeiffer, P., and Reps, T., "Dependence analysis for pointer variables," *Proceedings of the ACM SIGPLAN 89 Conference on Programming Language Design and Implementation*, (Portland, OR, June 21-23, 1989), *ACM SIGPLAN Notices*, (1989).

Horwitz89.
> Horwitz, S., Prins, J., and Reps, T., "Integrating non-interfering versions of programs," *ACM Trans. Program. Lang. Syst.* 11(3) pp. 345-387 (July 1989).

Horwitz90.
> Horwitz, S., Reps, T., and Binkley, D., "Interprocedural slicing using dependence graphs," *ACM Trans. Program. Lang. Syst.* 12(1) pp. 26-60 (January 1990).

Kuck81.
> Kuck, D.J., Kuhn, R.H., Leasure, B., Padua, D.A., and Wolfe, M., "Dependence graphs and compiler optimizations," pp. 207-218 in *Conference Record of the Eighth ACM Symposium on Principles of Programming Languages*, (Williamsburg, VA, January 26-28, 1981), ACM, New York, NY (1981).

McKinsey46.
> McKinsey, J.C.C. and Tarski, A., "On closed elements in closure algebras," *Annals of Mathematics* 47(1) pp. 122-162 (January 1946).

Ottenstein84.
> Ottenstein, K.J. and Ottenstein, L.M., "The program dependence graph in a software development environment," *Proceedings of the ACM SIGSOFT/SIGPLAN Software Engineering Symposium on Practical Software Development Environments*, (Pittsburgh, PA, Apr. 23-25, 1984), *ACM SIGPLAN Notices* 19(5) pp. 177-184 (May 1984).

Reps90.
> Reps, T., "Algebraic properties of program integration.," in *Proceedings of the Third European Symposium on Programming*, (Copenhagen, Denmark, May 15-18, 1990), *Lecture Notes in Computer Science*, Vol. 432, ed. N. Jones,Springer-Verlag, New York, NY (1990).

Weiser84.
> Weiser, M., "Program slicing," *IEEE Transactions on Software Engineering* SE-10(4) pp. 352-357 (July 1984).

Yang90.
> Yang, W., Horwitz, S., and Reps, T., "A program integration algorithm that accommodates semantics-preserving transformations," *Proceedings of the 4th ACM SIGSOFT Symposium on Software Development Environments*, (Irvine, CA, December 3-5, 1990), *ACM SIGSOFT Software Engineering Notes*, (1990).

Software Merge: Semantics of Combining Changes to Programs

VALDIS BERZINS
Naval Postgraduate School

We present a language-independent semantic model of the process of combining changes to programs. This model extends the domains used in denotational semantics (complete partial orders) to Boolean algebras, and represents incompatible modifications as well as compatible extensions. The model is used to define the intended semantics of change-merging operations on programs and to establish some general properties of software merging. We determine conditions under which changes to subprograms of a software system can be merged independently and illustrate cases where this is not possible.

Categories and Subject Descriptors: D.2.7 [**Software Engineering**]: Distribution and Maintenance—*enhancement*; *version control*; D.3.1 [**Programming Languages**]: Formal Definitions and Theory—*semantics*; F.3.2 [**Logics and Meaning of Programs**]: Semantics of Programming Languages—*denotational semantics*; I.2.2 [**Artificial Intelligence**]: Automatic Programming—*program modification*; *program synthesis*; *program transformation*

General Terms: Languages

Additional Key Words and Phrases: Domains, semantics, software change merging, software maintenance

---

1. INTRODUCTION

Practical software systems have many different versions, all of which are constantly changing in response to changes in user needs, the operating environment, and the discovery of faults. Such changes often have to be developed concurrently and then combined, or the "same" change has to be applied to several different versions of the system. We call the process of combining several changes *software change merging*. Tool support for this process is desirable, possibly in the form of automated assistant to a designer [Rich and Waters 1990]. However, a production-quality tool should always produce either a correct result or an indication of failure together with diagnostic information. A clear and precise model of change merging is needed to build such tools and to demonstrate that they achieve the required degree of "correctness."

This research was supported in part by the Army Research Office under grant ARO-145-91.
Author's address: Computer Science Department, Naval Postgraduate School, Monterey, CA 93943; email: berzins@cs.nps.navy.mil.
Permission to copy without fee all or part of this material is granted provided that the copies are not made or distributed for direct commercial advantage, the ACM copyright notice and the title of the publication and its date appear, and notice is given that copying is by permission of the Association for Computing Machinery. To copy otherwise, or to republish, requires a fee and/or specific permission.

"Software Merge: Semantics of Combining Changes to Programs" by V. Berzins from *ACM Trans. Programming Languages and Systems*, Vol. 16, No. 6, Nov. 1994, pp. 1875–1903. Copyright 1994, Association for Computing Machinery, Inc., reprinted with permission.

This article provides such a model and determines some of its characteristics. Since our goal is to formulate a language-independent definition of the requirements for change merging, we focus on merging changes to the *meaning* of a program (rather than changes to the concrete representation of a program). This is only part of the problem: a practical tool must operate on concrete representations of programs and produce a concrete program whose meaning agrees with our model, unless it explicitly reports failure. Methods for change merging that operate on concrete representations of programs are outside the scope of this article. A concrete method for change merging that is based directly on a special case of the models presented here can be found in Berzins [1991].

We achieve language independence via the constructions used in denotational semantics to define the meanings of programming languages. The domains used in traditional denotational semantics do not have enough structure to provide a general definition of change merging. The main contribution of this article is a set of extended domain constructions that can support such a definition and a formalization of the notion of a *semantic conflict* between changes. Since exact merging is not computable [Berzins 1986], the set of inputs of which a merging tool reports a failure and the semantic merging model produces a conflict-free result is one criterion for comparing different merging tools. We also explore some semantic limitations on merging that are related to functional decomposition.

Section 2 reviews some relevant previous work. Section 3 presents the construction of semantic domains appropriate for program merging, first reviewing the basic properties of approximation lattices, then extending these lattices to Boolean algebras and showing the relation to Browerian algebras. The purpose of these structures is to extend the ordinary semantic domains to include improper values representing combinations of incompatible design decisions. This lets us model software merging as a total operation on these extended domains, and enables the change merging in the domain of program meanings to identify semantic conflicts in cases where changes cannot be consistently combined. Section 4 uses the algebraic structures developed in Section 3 to support a formal definition of an ideal operation for combining the semantics of software modifications, and determines some of the properties of this formal model. Section 5 presents some conclusions and directions for future work.

2. Previous Work

The problem of combining two versions of a functional program was formalized as constructing the least common extension of two partial functions in Berzins [1986]. This is a simplified version of the problem considered in this article, which includes incompatible modifications as well as compatible extensions. The intended semantics of merging compatible extensions was expressed using lattices and the approximation ordering $\sqsubseteq$ used in traditional approaches toward denotational semantics of programming languages [Roscoe 1992; Stoy 1977].

These lattice structures were refined into larger Boolean algebras to model incompatible changes via a suitable difference operation in Berzins [1991]. The idea behind the domain construction was sketched briefly, and was limited to primitive domains, cross products, and a rough approximation to function spaces that was limited to additive functions [Stoy 1977, p. 105]. The current article repairs the deficiencies in the Boolean function space construction and introduces Boolean versions of an extended sum constructor, two of the three main power domain constructors, and recursively defined domains (solutions to reflexive domain equations). The current article also formalizes the idea of semantic conflicts and explores properties of the change-merging model related to functional composition as well as the conditions under which the result of a set of changes is independent of the order in which they are applied. We also show that change merging does not preserve monotonicity (or computability).

We view changes as transformations from versions to versions as was done in Berzins [1991] and prove a minimality property suggested there. Change transformations have been developed in a different way in Ramalingam and Reps [1991].

This article characterizes the intended semantics of change merging but does not address concrete methods for change merging. Specific methods for change merging are briefly surveyed here. See Berzins [1993] for more information. The first semantically based methods for combining two versions of a functional program were given in Berzins [1986]. A method for merging versions of Prolog programs is in Sterling and Lakhotia [1988]. An approach to combining both modifications and compatible extensions to while programs based on data flow analysis and operations on program dependency graphs is described by Horowitz et al. [1989], and this approach was subsequently improved [Yang et al. 1990]. Another method for solving this problem that produces fewer spurious conflict reports is described in Berzins [1991]. A method for merging changes to prototypes with concurrent actions and hard real-time constraints is described in Dampier et al. [1993].

3. SEMANTIC DOMAINS FOR SOFTWARE MERGING

This section explores semantic domains that can support change-merging operations. A difference operation is desirable for this purpose, and at least a pseudodifference operation seems to be needed. Since the domains used commonly in denotational semantics do not in general provide such operations, we explore refinements to those domains.

Section 3.1 reviews some relevant properties of the domains used in denotational semantics. Section 3.2 presents a construction that extends a class of complete partial orders used commonly in denotational semantics to *atomic Boolean algebras* (which provide a difference operation). Section 3.3 explores the relation of this effort to Browerian algebras (which provide a pseudodifference operation).

Every atomic Boolean algebra is a Boolean algebra as well as a lattice, and satisfies all of the usual laws of Boolean algebras. It is possible to understand

Lattice	Boolean Algebra	Interpretation
$\top$	**1**	Conflict
$\bot$	**0**	Undefined
$x \sqsubseteq y$	$x \sqsubseteq y$	Compatible extension predicate
$x \sqcup y$	$x + y$	Compatible combination
$x \sqcap y$	xy	Common part
	$\bar{x}$	Complement
	$x - y$	Difference

Fig. 1. Correspondence between lattice notation and Boolean notation.

most of the later parts of this article in terms of the interpretations for the Boolean operations summarized in Figure 1, without knowledge of the special properties of the atomic Boolean algebras constructed in Section 3.2, although some parts of the proofs depend on these properties.

3.1 Lattices and Approximation Orderings

The domains used in denotational semantics are all partially ordered sets with an approximation ordering $\sqsubseteq$. Typical domains are special kinds of function spaces whose elements represent meanings of programs. An approximation $f \sqsubseteq g$ means that g is a compatible extension of f: g agrees with f whenever f is defined, and g may be defined in cases where f is not. Our model of change merging uses lattices that are special cases of this kind of structure.

A lattice is a partially ordered set that contains least upper bounds and greatest lower bounds for all finite subsets. Lattices have a least upper bound operation $\sqcup$, a greatest lower bound operation $\sqcap$, a least element $\bot$, and a greatest element $\top$.

All of the features of a lattice are relevant to change merging. The least upper bound merges all of the information contained in two elements. The greatest lower bound extracts the information common to both elements. The least element $\bot$ denotes the absence of information, and is used together with $\sqcap$ to indicate that two elements do not contain any common information. The greatest element $\top$ represents an inconsistency: the result of merging (all possible) incompatible information.

Denotational semantics was originally formulated using special kinds of lattices. Later formulations were recast in terms of cpos (complete partial orders) that are subsets of the original lattices. This was done partially to avoid overconstrained elements such as $\top$, which do not have a natural interpretation for individual programs. In the context of change merging, overconstrained elements represent conflicts between semantically incompatible changes. Since independently developed changes can easily be semantically incompatible, overconstrained elements have natural interpretations in our context.

Since lattice operations are applied to functions independently at each point, overconstrained elements may be useful for localizing semantic incompatibilities and diagnosing their causes. A simple example illustrates the idea.

$$[\bot, 1, 2, 3] \sqcup [4, 1, \bot, 5] = [4, 1, 2, 3 \sqcup 5].$$

Here we use sequences of length four as idealized finite examples of semantic functions representing meanings of programs. The least upper bound merges the information in the two functions to produce a third, which has normal data values in the first three positions and an overconstrained value in the fourth. The presence of the overconstrained value indicates a semantic conflict; its location indicates the part of the input space that is affected (the fourth value in the index set for the sequence); and the overconstrained value itself indicates the nature of the conflict (the same output has been simultaneously constrained to have two different and incompatible values, 3 and 5). Thus we have a semantic model for an idealized error-reporting facility.

It is of course much easier to merge the semantics of programs than it is to materialize the concrete programs corresponding to the merged semantics, and the problem of diagnosing and locating conflicts between changes is far from being solved in practice. However, it does help to have a clear idea of an idealized goal for error reporting. A partial change-merging method that can in some cases derive a program representation with overconstrained program elements in the parts of the program that produce semantic conflicts is described in Berzins [1991]. Representations of such overconstrained program elements are detectable by syntactic operations and could be used as a basis for generating concrete error messages.

3.2 Atomic Boolean Algebras

To model incompatible changes to the semantics of a program, we need a difference operation to describe the information that was removed from a software object. If we treat the partial functions computed by our programs as sets of pairs, then the set difference operation captures this idea for first-order functions. Together with $\subseteq$, $\cup$, $\cap$, and set complementation this structure forms a Boolean algebra, which is a simple and typical example of the extended semantic domains we will be using. Boolean algebras provide natural generalizations that cover higher-order functions as well. The motivation for our choice of algebraic structures is discussed further in Section 3.3. This section reviews the basic properties of Boolean algebras and shows how to construct the Boolean algebras for higher-order function spaces.

There are many equivalent definitions of Boolean algebras [Halmos 1963]. Every Boolean algebra is a complemented distributive lattice with respect to the partial ordering defined by the relations $x \sqsubseteq y \Leftrightarrow xy = x \Leftrightarrow x + y = y$. In addition to the lattice operations a Boolean algebra has a complement operation, which can be used to define a binary difference operator $x - y = x\bar{y}$ that obeys the algebraic properties of set difference. These structures are important for our goals of finding minimal compatible extensions and finding minimal change transformations.

We use notations for operations on Boolean algebras common in circuit design. Unfortunately, these notations are not the same as those used for lattice operations in the context of denotational semantics. The correspondence is shown in Figure 1 [Berzins 1991].

We will be working with a special class of Boolean algebras, those that are atomic. An *atom* is an element that is distinct from the bottom element **0** and has no lower bounds other than itself and **0**. A Boolean algebra is *atomic* if every element is the least upper bound of the set of atoms it dominates [Halmos 1963, Lemma 1, p. 70].

Every atomic Boolean algebra is isomorphic to the power set of its atoms, which becomes a Boolean algebra when $\sqcup$, $\sqcap$, and complement are interpreted as the union, intersection, and complement operations on sets [Halmos 1963, Theorem 5]. This isomorphism demonstrates that the difference operator of an atomic Boolean algebra really is the same as set difference. It also implies that every atomic Boolean algebra is complete and that its structure is determined by its cardinality. A Boolean algebra (or any lattice) is *complete* if and only if it has least upper bounds and greatest lower bounds for arbitrary subsets, not just the finite ones.

The Boolean algebras used in digital circuit design are atomic and finite: elements can be represented as fixed-length vectors of bits; the atoms are all zero except at one bit position; and the cardinality of the value set is equal to a power of two. The Boolean algebras we use for semantic domains are mostly function spaces, and the cardinality of the value set is typically infinite.

An example of a Boolean algebra that is neither atomic nor complete is the set of all finite unions of half-open real intervals of the form $\{x \mid a \leq x < b\}$ where $0 \leq a \leq b \leq 1$ and a and b are rational numbers. The operations of the algebra are ordinary set-theoretic unions, intersections, and complements; the ordering is subset; the bottom element is the empty set (any interval with $a = b$); and the top element is the interval with $a = 0$ and $b = 1$. To see that this Boolean algebra does not have any atoms, note that there is an infinite descending chain below every element other than the empty set. To see that it is not complete, note that any infinite set of pairwise disjoint intervals does not have a least upper bound.

We will find that isomorphic Boolean algebras can be given quite different interpretations, and that some properties relevant to change merging, such as whether or not a given element represents a semantic conflict, can depend on the intended interpretation as well as on the structure of the algebra. Since the intended interpretation of a domain is determined by how the domain was constructed, we label implicitly each domain with the operation that was used to construct it and consider algebras constructed in different ways to be distinct. To keep our conventions simple we will follow this convention uniformly and explicitly mention all isomorphisms, although this introduces some distinctions that are not significant. For example, the domains $A \times (B \times C)$ and $(A \times B) \times C$ are considered to be different even though they are isomorphic and have essentially the same meaning.

Our domain construction will proceed as follows. We will take some domains to be given a priori, and we will label them as primitive. All other domains will be constructed from the primitive domains using a fixed set of domain constructors and possibly reflexive domain equations. The domain constructors are cross products, extended disjoint sums, and function spaces. Section 3.3 extends this by adding power domain constructors.

3.2.1 *Primitive Domains.* The domains representing ordinary data types will be treated as primitive. By an ordinary data type we mean a set whose values are either completely defined or completely undefined. Ordinary data types can include composite data structures as long as it is not possible for some subcomponents to be defined while others are not. An example of a data type that is not ordinary is a list type with lazy evaluation for the element extraction operation, since some components might be well defined while an attempt to extract other components might cause the program to go into an infinite loop.

In denotational semantics, ordinary data types are represented as flat lattices or flat cpos. The Boolean algebra representing an ordinary data type is the power set of the type with the usual set operations.

Each element of this Boolean algebra is a set of values of the data type that represents the least upper bound of those values. Proper values of the type are represented as singleton sets of the algebra, and these are the atoms of the Boolean algebra. The approximation relation $\sqsubseteq$ is interpreted as the subset relation, and the operations $x + y$, xy, and $x - y$ are interpreted as union, intersection, and set difference operations. The completely undefined element **0** is represented as the empty set, and the completely overconstrained element **1** is represented as the set of all values of the data type.

For the primitive domains, semantic conflicts are represented by sets containing more than one element. An element x of a primitive domain is *conflict free* if and only if $x \sqsubseteq a$ for some atom a. Note that the undefined element **0** is conflict free as well as the proper values of the type.

The relation between the lattice construction and the Boolean algebra construction is illustrated in Figure 2 [Berzins 1991] for a discrete type representing the states of a traffic light. Our construction preserves the structure of flat lattices everywhere except for the top element $\top$, which is refined into a set of distinct improper elements in the Boolean algebra. The Boolean algebra can support a total- and single-valued difference operator because the least upper bounds of distinct sets of proper data elements are all distinct. It is not possible to define such a difference operator for flat lattices with more than two elements because all of these upper bounds are identified with the single element $\top$ in the flat lattice.

3.2.2 *Domain Construction: Cross Products.* We use the same product space constructor used in denotational semantics, since the product of two atomic Boolean algebras is an atomic Boolean algebra. The atoms of the product space are the tuples that have an atom as one component and undefined elements for all of the other components.

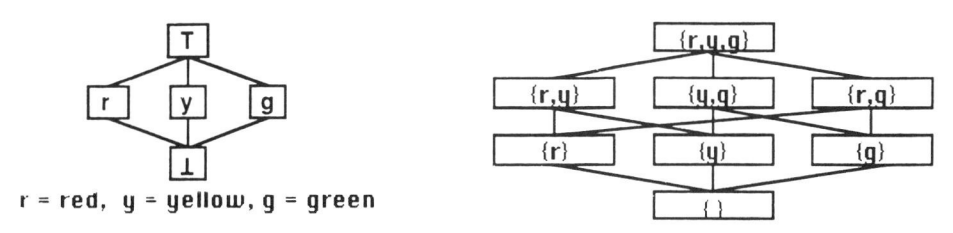

Fig. 2. A flat lattice and the corresponding Boolean algebra.

An element of a product space contains a semantic conflict if one of its components does: a tuple $t \in D_1 \times D_2$ is *conflict free* if and only if t_1 and t_2 are conflict free. Note that product spaces contain conflict-free elements that are not atoms and are not **0**. Since we can have a product space isomorphic to a primitive domain, we can see that the "conflict-free" property need not be preserved by isomorphism.

3.2.3 *Domain Construction: Extended Sums.* The domains produced by the classical disjoint sum construction are not in general Boolean algebras, nor can they be embedded in Boolean algebras. This is so because all Boolean algebras are distributive, but disjoint sums do not in general produce distributive lattices. To see this let A and B be atomic Boolean algebras and consider any elements $a, a' \in A$, and $b \in B$ that are ordered as shown in Figure 3. Such elements exist whenever A contains at least three distinct atoms and B at least two distinct atoms. These elements fail to satisfy the distributive law:

$$a + (a'b) = a + \mathbf{0} = a \neq a' = a'\mathbf{1} = (a + a')(a + b).$$

Since an embedding must preserve least upper bounds and greatest lower bounds, these elements will also violate the distributive law in any other lattice in which the sum domain can be embedded.

Therefore we reexamine disjoint sums in the context of change merging. To represent semantic conflicts accurately, we would like every pair of proper data values in our semantic domains to have a distinct least upper bound. This suggests that it is not really desirable to keep sum domains completely disjoint: certainly we want the parts of the domains containing the proper elements to be disjoint, but we would like to have distinct representations for all of the possible conflicts between the maximal proper elements from the different components of the sum. So we suggest using cross products under the usual ordering (Section 3.2.2) to encode extended disjoint sums.

This is not as unreasonable as it may at first appear: if we restrict our attention to the subset of the pairs that have an undefined element **0** in at least one component, the ordering on the cross product space is exactly the same as the ordering on a coalesced sum domain. The elements outside this subset all represent conflicts between elements from different components of the disjoint sum, and can be treated as not belonging to either component of the "sum." If we "encode" disjoint sums as product domains, the injection

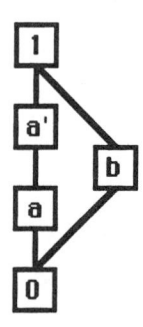

Fig. 3. Disjoint sums are not distributive.

functions in_i, the discrimination functions is_i, and the projection functions out_i that are usually used in the definitions of semantic functions involving sum domains can be defined as follows.

$in_1(x) = (x, \mathbf{0})$ \qquad $in_2(x) = (\mathbf{0}, x)$
$is_1(p) = (p_1 \neq \mathbf{0}) \,\&\, (p_2 = \mathbf{0})$ \qquad $is_2(p) = (p_1 = \mathbf{0}) \,\&\, (p_2 \neq \mathbf{0})$
$out_i(p)$ if $is_i(p)$ then p_i else if $p = (\mathbf{0}, \mathbf{0})$ then $\mathbf{0}$ else $\mathbf{1}$

Thus the encoding appears to be a workable (though not very elegant) solution that allows domain constructions involving sum constructors to be simulated by using cross products, which do yield Boolean algebras.

An element of an extended sum domain contains a conflict if either component has a conflict or if we do not have a $\mathbf{0}$ in at least one component: an element $x \in D_1 + D_2$ is *conflict free* if and only if x_1 and x_2 are conflict free and either $x_1 = \mathbf{0}$ or $x_2 = \mathbf{0}$.

3.2.4 *Domain Construction*: *Function Spaces*. The continuous-function-space constructor of denotational semantics does not preserve Boolean algebras, but the function space construction used in ordinary mathematics does. If A and B are atomic Boolean algebras, then the complete function space $A \to B$ is the atomic Boolean algebra whose elements are *all* of the functions from A to B with the natural pointwise ordering. The ordering, distinguished elements, and operations of the function space are described by the following relationships.

(a) $f \sqsubseteq g \Leftrightarrow \forall x \in A[f(x) \sqsubseteq g(x)]$
(b) $\mathbf{0}(x) = \mathbf{0}$
(c) $\mathbf{1}(x) = \mathbf{1}$
(d) $(f + g)(x) = f(x) + g(x)$
(e) $(fg)(x) = f(x)g(x)$
(f) $(\bar{f})(x) = \overline{f(x)}$
(g) $(f - g)(x) = f(x) - g(x)$

The relation (a) is the standard ordering for function spaces in denotational semantics, and implies relations (b)–(g). The relations (b) and (c) describe the connection between the top and bottom elements of the function space $A \to B$ and the top and bottom elements of its range algebra B. The relations (d)–(g) are homomorphic extension rules, which define the operations of the function space in terms of the operations of its range algebra. The operations are well defined because B is complete, so that least upper bounds exist for all subsets of its atoms. The Boolean algebra properties are satisfied for the function space because they are satisfied by the values of the functions at each point in A.

The resulting function space is an atomic Boolean algebra. The atoms of $A \to B$ are functions $g[x, y]$ that are undefined at all points of the input space A except for the point x, and have the value y at that point, where x can be any point in A and y can be any atom of B:

$$g[x, y](z) = \text{if } x = z \text{ then } y \text{ else } \mathbf{0}.$$

Every element of the function space is the least upper bound of the atoms it dominates because the corresponding property is true in B for the values of those functions at every point in A, since B is an atomic Boolean algebra.

The classical function space construction used in denotational semantics produces subsets of our function spaces. Note that we cannot limit the construction to just the monotonic functions (or just the continuous functions), because a Boolean algebra must be closed under complements, and the complement of a monotonic function is antimonotonic.

Since our function spaces are complete, they satisfy the weaker completeness properties needed to show the existence of least fixed points of continuous functions. They also contain all of the continuous functions, and hence support recursive definitions for elements of the function spaces.

A function contains a conflict if its value at some meaningful point contains a conflict: a function $f : D_1 \to D_2$ is *conflict free* if and only if $f(x)$ is conflict free for all conflict-free $x \in D_1$. We restrict our attention to the conflict-free points in D_1 because computable (monotonic) functions can be expected to produce conflicts at overdefined points.

3.2.5 *Domain Construction: Reflexive Domains.* Reflexive domains are the solutions to recursive domain equations, in which equality is interpreted as lattice isomorphism. Since our function spaces contain all functions, our function space constructor strictly increases the cardinality of the space, so we cannot hope to find spaces that are isomorphic to their own function spaces. This is one of the classical problems in denotational semantics, and it implies that the function space construction of Section 3.2.4 cannot be used in recursive domain equations. However, if we are willing to restrict ourselves to distributive lattices and embed solutions to domain equations in larger Boolean algebras, there is a way out via the space of continuous functions used in denotational semantics.

We start with a lemma that relates properties of domain constructors to the properties of reflexive domains defined using those constructors.

LEMMA 3.2.5.1. *If $\mathbf{F}$ is a continuous domain constructor [Roscoe 1992] that preserves distributiveness then the minimal solution to the domain equation $D = \mathbf{F}(D)$ exists and is distributive. Indeed, any property that is* *preserved by the domain constructors and can be expressed as an equation or inclusion between expressions denoting elements of a domain is satisfied in D.*

PROOF. D exists by Roscoe [1992, Theorem 4.2.8]. The minimal domain $\bot$ contains only one point, so all inclusions and equations on elements are trivially satisfied, and in particular we have $x \sqcup (y \sqcap z) = (x \sqcup y) \sqcap (x \sqcup z)$ and $x \sqcap (y \sqcup z) = (x \sqcap y) \sqcup (x \sqcap z)$ for all $x, y, z \in \bot$. So the domain $\bot$ is distributive. Since **F** preserves distributiveness, the approximating domains $\mathbf{F}^n(\bot)$ are distributive for all natural numbers n, by induction. By Roscoe [1992, Lemma 4.2.5], $x \sqsubseteq y \Leftrightarrow \forall n[\pi_n^*(x) \sqsubseteq \pi_n^*(y)]$, where π_n^* are the projection functions from D into $\mathbf{F}^n(\bot)$ defined in Roscoe 1992]. (Two elements of the limiting domain are ordered if and only if their projections into all of the approximation domains are ordered in the same way.) This implies $x \sqcup y = z$ in $D \Leftrightarrow \forall n[\pi_n^*(x) \sqcup \pi_n^*(y) = \pi_n^*(z)]$ and similarly for $\sqcap$. Since $x = y \Leftrightarrow x \sqsubseteq y\ \&\ y \sqsubseteq x$ we also have $x = y$ in $D \Leftrightarrow \forall n[\pi_n^*(x) = \pi_n^*(y)]$. By structural induction it follows that any equation among finite expressions built using variables, $\sqcup$, and $\sqcap$ is satisfied in the limit domain D if and only if the expression with each variable v replaced by the corresponding projection $\pi_n^*(v)$ it is satisfied in all the approximating domains $\mathbf{F}^n(\bot)$. So D must be distributive, since all of the approximating domains are distributive.

Now we can proceed to the main theorem. □

THEOREM 3.2.5.2. *The solution to any domain equation composed of given Boolean algebras and domain constructors that preserve distributiveness can be embedded in a Boolean algebra.*

PROOF. Boolean algebras are distributive lattices by definition. Lemma 3.2.5.1 says that the solution to a domain equation composed of domain constructors that preserve distributiveness is also a distributive lattice. Every distributive lattice can be extended to a Boolean algebra [MacNeille 1937, p. 450 ff.]. So the result follows. □

The primitive domains of Section 3.2.1 are all Boolean algebras. Cross products and function spaces of distributive lattices are distributive [Maclane and Birkhoff 1967, Theorem 13, Ch. 14]. The lattice of continuous functions is distributive because it is a sublattice of the full function space. Extended disjoint sums are encoded as cross products in Section 3.2.3. So the solution to any domain equation expressed using these constructs will be a distributive lattice, which can be embedded in a Boolean algebra. This Boolean algebra is a good candidate for hosting change-merging operations because it is a natural completion of the semantic domain that contains distinct representations for all possible conflict elements.

The solution to a reflexive domain equation is labeled with the outermost domain constructor on its right-hand side, and the appropriate definition of conflict-free elements is determined accordingly.

These constructions allow us to formulate change-merging operations for most of the programming languages covered by classical denotational semantics. This does not include the class of languages with parallel or nondeterministic operations, which are considered briefly in the next section.

3.3 Browerian Algebras

Boolean algebras are sufficient for modeling the semantics of change merging for the programming languages whose semantics can be expressed using the constructions of Section 3.2. Some work on concrete methods for change merging has been based on a more general class of Browerian algebras [Reps 1991]. This section discusses the role of Browerian algebras in modeling the semantics of change merging.

A Browerian algebra is a lattice with a pseudodifference operation $\dot{-}$ that satisfies the property $x \dot{-} y \sqsubseteq z \Leftrightarrow x \sqsubseteq y + z$. Every Boolean algebra becomes a Browerian algebra when it is equipped with a difference operator as defined in Section 3.2, but there exist Browerian algebras that are not Boolean algebras. In particular, Browerian algebras need not satisfy the law $\bar{\bar{x}} = x$. The difference operator of a Boolean algebra must satisfy both of the following properties.

(P1) $(x - y) + (xy) = x$

(P2) $(x - y)y = \mathbf{0}$

The pseudodifference operator of a Browerian algebra must satisfy P1, which says that all of the information in x is either contained in y or is contained in the part of x that is not in y: $(x \dot{-} y) + (xy) = ((x \dot{-} y) + x)(x \dot{-} y) = x(x + y) = x$ if we note that $x \dot{-} y \sqsubseteq x$ and use Proposition A.12 from Reps [1991]. However, the pseudodifference operator may fail to satisfy P2, which says that the result of removing y from x does not contain any of the information in y. It is easy to see that this disjointness property holds in a Boolean algebra: $(x - y)y = x\bar{y}y = x\mathbf{0} = \mathbf{0}$. The pseudodifference operator is thus not really a difference operator, because it may not remove all of the information contained in y, although it must remove as much as possible without violating property P1. This means that the underlying lattice of a Browerian algebra need not have sufficiently fine resolution to separate x and y, in the sense that it may not be possible to remove all of the information in y from x without also removing some information in x that is not contained in y.

We have worked with Boolean algebras because (1) they provide a natural representation for identifying precisely the sources of semantic conflicts, (2) proofs are simpler, and (3) the extra generality of Browerian algebras is not needed to express the semantics of change merging for most programming languages. Separating the elements of the semantic domains in the sense of the previous paragraph is usually not an issue because the data values of most programming languages are disjoint (can be modeled as a flat cpo) or can be assembled from disjoint parts (using cross products or functions).

Browerian algebras were used in Reps [1991] because the concrete dependence graph representations of programs do not have a Boolean algebra structure. However, we note that the semantic correctness of the HPR algorithm [Horowitz et al. 1989] as well as of the variant in Reps [1991] is not derived from the Browerian algebra structure of the dependence graph representations of the programs, but rather from the concrete properties of program slices.

A realistic example of a semantic domain that should be modeled properly as a Browerian algebra is the domain of maximum execution times (METs) for a language with hard real-time constraints such as PSDL [Dampier et al. 1994]. Since a larger number represents a weaker timing constraint, the approximation ordering $\sqsubseteq$ for this domain is the total ordering $\geq$ on numerical values. This is an extreme example of lack of separability because two constraints cannot be disjoint unless one of them is the vacuous constraint ∞ (the bottom element of the lattice). The lattice of MET values is a Browerian algebra with $x \dotdiv y = $ if $x \sqsubseteq y$ then ∞ else x. Since every Browerian algebra is a distributive lattice [McKinsey and Tarski 1946, Theorem 1.3], every Browerian algebra, including the MET domain, can be extended to a Boolean algebra by MacNeille [1937, p. 450 ff.]. A fragment of the MET domain and its embedding in a Boolean algebra are shown in Figure 4, where proper elements have bold lines and the artificial elements added by the embedding have thin lines. Unlike the extended data domains of Section 3.2, where the artificial elements represent conflicts between distinct proper elements, the extra elements in this extension to a Boolean algebra provide artificial differences between proper elements that do not have realistic interpretations. Change merging in this Boolean algebra can result in an improper element, while change merging in the Browerian algebra yields a proper element that dominates the result in the Boolean algebra. For example, merging the change from 2 to 1 with the change from 2 to 3 according to the model explained in Section 4 yields the improper element $(1 - 2) + (1)(3) + (3 - 2) = 3 + (1 - 2)$ in the extended Boolean algebra and the dominating proper element $(1 \dotdiv 2) + (1)(3) + (3 \dotdiv 2) = 1$ in the Browerian algebra, where $+$ and $-$ denote the operations from these algebras instead of the usual operations from arithmetic. This suggests Browerian algebras may provide appropriate change-merging models for data domains with overlapping proper elements that cannot be separated into disjoint proper components.

A standard construction for Browerian algebras involves topological closure operations [McKinsey and Tarski 1944]. A topological closure operation on a Boolean algebra of sets is a function from sets to sets that satisfies the following properties for all sets x and y in the domain of the Boolean algebra:

(C1) $x \subseteq C(x)$,
(C2) $C(C(x)) = C(x)$,
(C3) $C(x \cup y) = C(x) \cup C(y)$, and
(C4) $C(\{\ \}) = \{\ \}$.

Note that many "closure" operations used commonly in computer science are not topological closure operations. For example, the transitive closure of a graph does not satisfy condition C3. A set x is closed relative to C if $C(x) = x$. The closed elements of any Boolean algebra of sets with a topological closure operation C forms a Browerian algebra under the operation $x \dotdiv y = C(x - y)$ [McKinsey and Tarski 1946, Theorem 1.14], and every

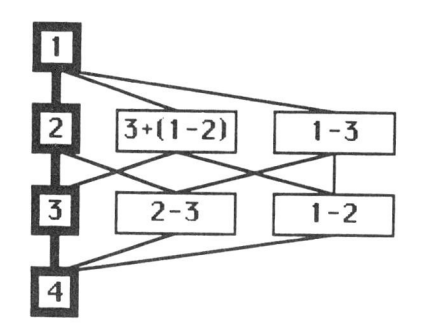

Fig. 4. Extending the MET Browerian algebra to a Boolean algebra.

Browerian algebra is isomorphic to an algebra constructed in this way [McKinsey and Tarski 1946, Theorem 1.15]. The connection to topology is that every topological space is a Browerian algebra, and every Browerian algebra is isomorphic to a subalgebra of the algebra of closed sets of a topological space [McKinsey and Tarski 1946, Theorem 1.19].

In particular, the set of all downward closed subsets of any lattice forms a Browerian algebra under the construction outlined above. The downward closure is defined by $DC(s) = \{y \mid \exists x \in s . y \sqsubseteq x\}$ and easily can be seen to satisfy the properties of a topological closure operation. Similar results hold for the upward closure $UC(s) = \{y \mid \exists x \in s . x \sqsubseteq y\}$. These properties turn out to be relevant to power domains.

3.3.1 *Domain Construction: Power Domains.* We saw in Section 3.2 how the semantic domains for many classical programming languages can be naturally embedded in Boolean algebras. The constructions of Section 3.2 do not cover languages with parallelism and nondeterministic constructs, whose semantic domains usually include power sets (power domains). Several varieties of power domain constructions have been proposed for defining the semantics of programming languages with parallelism. The approximation orderings on these domains are only quasiorderings, and the relation $x \equiv y \Leftrightarrow x \sqsubseteq y \,\&\, y \sqsubseteq x$ is an equivalence relation that is weaker than equality. The approximation relation becomes a partial ordering on equivalence classes in the quotient lattices with respect to this equivalence relation, but it is less cumbersome to represent each equivalence class by its largest member (the set with the most elements). There are three main variations on the power domain construction: the Hoare power domain, the Smyth power domain, and the Egli-Milner power domain. It turns out that the equivalence classes for the Hoare power domain are represented by the downward closed subsets of the underlying lattice; those for the Smyth power domain are represented by the upward closed subsets; and those for the Egli-Milner power domain are represented by the convex closed subsets [Roscoe 1992].

Since the downward and upward closure satisfy the topological closure properties C1–C4 above, the Hoare and Smyth power domains have a natural Browerian algebra structure, which implies that they are distributive lattices and can be extended to Boolean algebras. This implies that our model of the semantics of change merging can be applied to both the Hoare and Smyth

(a) Boolean Algebra (b) Derived Power Domain

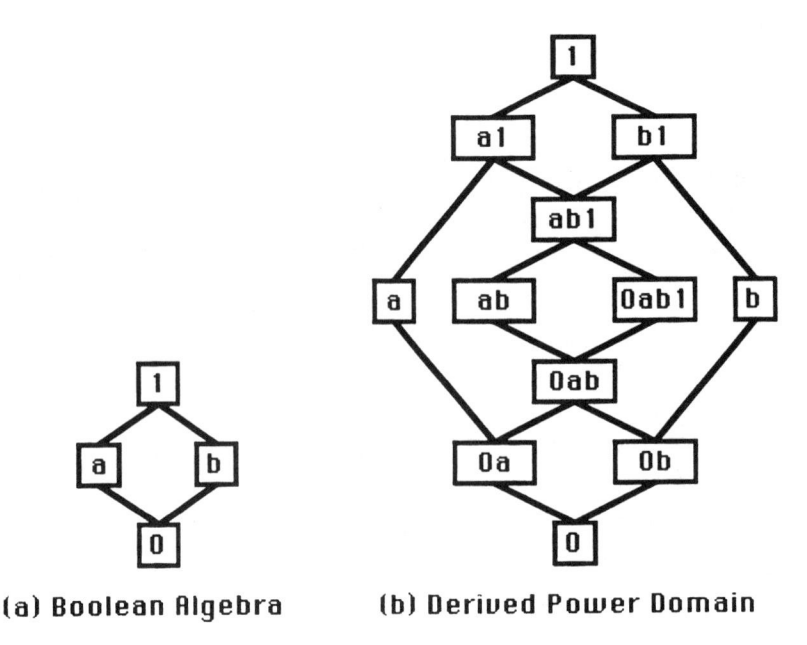

Fig. 5. The Egli-Milner power domain is not distributive.

power domains, and that Theorem 3.2.5.2 can be applied to reflexive domain equations containing these power domain constructors. We leave open the question of whether the Browerian or the Boolean model of change merging is more appropriate for these domains.

An element of a power domain represents a set of possible outcomes. Such an element has a semantic conflict if any of the possible outcomes have a conflict: a set $s \in P(D)$ is *conflict free* if and only if x is conflict free for all $x \in s$.

We note that the convex closure $CC(s) = \{y \mid \exists x, z \in s . x \sqsubseteq y \sqsubseteq z\}$ does not satisfy the topological closure property C3 above, so it is not a topological closure operation and does not support the Browerian algebra construction. In fact, the Egli-Milner power domain is not in general a distributive lattice, as demonstrated by the following counterexample. Figure 5 shows a four-element Boolean algebra (a) and the Egli-Milner power domain derived from it (b). This power domain is not a distributive lattice because $\{a, b\} \sqcup (\{a, b, 1\} \sqcap \{a\}) = \{a, b\} \sqcup \{0, a\} = \{a, b\} \neq \{a, b, 1\} = \{a, b, 1\} \sqcap \{a, 1\} = (\{a, b\} \sqcup \{a, b, 1\}) \sqcap (\{a, b\} \sqcup (\{a\}))$ where the least upper bounds and greatest lower bounds are taken with respect to the Egli-Milner ordering [Roscoe 1992] shown in Figure 5b. Since every Browerian algebra is a distributive lattice, Egi-Milner power domains cannot be extended to Browerian (or Boolean) algebras.

We conclude that none of the known models of change merging apply to languages whose semantics involve Egi-Milner power domains, since all of these models depend on (at least) a Browerian algebra structure. This issue is relevant to applications where programs that can fail to terminate must interact in a nondeterministic way (typically via parallel processing). The formulation of an appropriate model of change merging for this class of languages is left as an open problem.

4. LANGUAGE-INDEPENDENT MODEL OF SOFTWARE MERGING

This section discusses some properties of the change-merging operator in Berzins [1991], which is defined as follows.

$$f[g]h = (f - g) + fh + (h - g) \qquad \text{(M1)}$$

We know that $(f - g) + fh + (h - g) = (f - g) + fgh + (h - g)$ because $fh = fh(g + \bar{g}) = fgh + f\bar{g}h$ and $f\bar{g}h \sqsubseteq \bar{g}h = (h - g)$ (this equivalence holds also for Browerian algebras, but the proof is longer). Thus our definition of $f[g]h$ coincides with the negmajority operation $f[g]h$ defined in Hoare [1985] and the integration operation $f[g]h$ defined in Reps [1991]. The name "negmajority" was motivated by a propositional calculus interpretation of a Boolean operator that is true if and only if a majority of the three values is true after the middle value is negated. Our operator defines the same Boolean function, but it is interpreted in a much larger Boolean algebra representing the space of meaning functions for programs, rather than in the two-valued Boolean algebra of propositional calculus. Reps' version of $f[g]h$ is defined in terms of the pseudodifference operation of a Browerian algebra, instead of the difference operation of a Boolean algebra, because the graphs used to represent programs in his algorithm do not satisfy all the properties of a Boolean algebra. However, we have seen in Section 3 that the semantic domains for sequential programs can be extended to Boolean algebras.

4.1 The Relation to Minimal Change Transformations

Informally, an operation for combining changes to functions should be able to apply the change defined by the difference between two versions g and f of a function to some other version h. Berzins [1991] showed how to infer a mapping from versions to versions from the effect of a change on a particular base version g. This was done by characterizing the change from a function g to a function f in terms of the common part fg, the part that was added $f - g$, and the part that was removed $g - f$, as illustrated in Figure 6 [Berzins 1991]. These components were shown to be disjoint and to contain all of the information in the functions f and g, so that any change to a function can be characterized by the part that was added and the part that was removed.

We formalize the idea of a transformation $f[g]$ that changes a base version g into a modified version f as follows. We propose that change transformations should be functions of the form $\mathbf{T}[a, b]$ where $\mathbf{T}[a, b](x) = (x - a) + b$ for all x, and seek the smallest transformation such that $\mathbf{T}[a, b](g) = f$ (relative to the ordering defined by $\mathbf{T}[a_1, b_1] \sqsubseteq \mathbf{T}[a_2, b_2] \Leftrightarrow a_1 \sqsubseteq a_2 \,\&\, b_1 \sqsubseteq b_2$). This is based on the following assumptions:

(1) The information added as well as the information removed by a given change transformation should not depend on what version the change transformation is applied to.

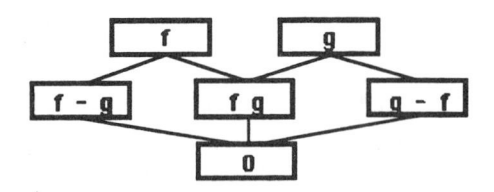

Fig. 6. Characterizing software changes.

(2) The only additions and removals included in the change transformation should be those necessary to transform g into f.

As was suggested in Berzins [1991], these assumptions uniquely determine $f[g]$: $f[g] = \mathbf{T}[g - f, f - g]$. To see that this change transformation maps g into f note that $\mathbf{T}[g - f, f - g](g) = (g - (g - f)) + (f - g) = g\overline{g\bar{f}} + f\bar{g} = g\bar{g} + g\bar{f} + \bar{g}f = \mathbf{0} + (g + \bar{g})f = f$. To see that it is the smallest such transformation, suppose that $(g - a) + b = f$. Then $f - g = f\bar{g} = (g\bar{a} + b)\bar{g} = g\bar{g}\bar{a} + b\bar{g} = b\bar{g} \sqsubseteq b$ and $g - f = g\bar{f} = g\overline{(g\bar{a} + b)} = g(\bar{g} + a)\bar{b} = a\bar{b} \sqsubseteq a$. So $\mathbf{T}[g - f, f - g] \sqsubseteq \mathbf{T}[a, b]$.

This minimality property suggests that change merging should be defined by $f[g]h = (h - (g - f)) + (f - g)$. This was shown to be equivalent to (M1) in Berzins [1991].

We now assess the adequacy of our formalization of the change-merging process. By identifying programs with the functions they compute, we have ignored nonfunctional attributes such as computational efficiency and program understandability. The result of a change-merging operation must certainly compute the correct function, and it may be subject to other constraints. These other constraints are beyond the scope of the current article. Change merging that involves efficiency-improving modifications is addressed in Berzins [1991], which suggests a method for program change merging that can accommodate efficiency-improving changes as well as changes in program behavior. This method prefers program realizations from the changed versions over those in the base program in cases where several different realizations of the same semantic (sub)function are present. The difficulty of recognizing efficiency-improving changes increases sharply with the size of the change and is undecidable in general. Automated capabilities in this area are necessarily limited, and can be augmented with declarations of programmer intent in the form of optional specifications for program fragments.

A related concern is the treatment of programs that do not terminate. Our formalization of change merging is intended to apply to any programming language that can be modeled by meaning functions over a fairly wide class of semantic domains, as described in Section 3.2. The effect of the change-merging function defined in this section depends on the semantic model of the programming language being discussed. These models can differ considerably. In a simple imperative language whose programs denote functions from states to states, a program that immediately enters an infinite loop is equivalent to one that causes some state changes and then enters an infinite loop, because in both cases there is no final state, and hence there are no observable results. Thus a change from the first program to the second would have no effect on program behavior, since we would have $g - f = \mathbf{0} = f - g$. For languages with I/O facilities, programs can denote functions from pairs (containing an input sequence and a state) to pairs (containing an output sequence and a state). In such a model, a program that enters an infinite loop computes immediately a different function than a program that first produces some output and then enters an infinite loop. A change from one to the other would have definite effect on program behavior in such a case. A different approach toward specifying the semantics of programs that are not intended to terminate can be found in Berzins and Luqi [1991].

4.2 Change Merging Does Not Preserve Monotonicity

In Section 3 we motivated the need for function spaces containing functions that are not monotonic via a rather indirect argument. Now we are in a position to show that change merging can produce nonmonotonic functions from monotonic ones. The following example shows three simple monotonic functions that produce a nonmonotonic function via change merging.

x	$f(x)$	$g(x)$	$h(x)$	$(f[g]h)(x)$
2	2	2	$\bot$	$\bot$
$\bot$	2	2		

Since every computable function is monotonic, this shows that the result of merging changes from computable functions to computable functions need not be computable. Thus the presence of conflicts is not the only factor that can lead to a situation where there does not exist any program that realizes the merge defined by a base program and two modified programs. This also shows that the domains of traditional denotational semantics must be extended to treat change merging as a total operation.

4.3 Commmutativity and Order Dependence

Some of the known properties [Hoare 1985; Reps 1991] of the change-merging operation are shown below.

(1) $b[a]c = c[a]b$
(2) $(b[a]c)[a]d = b[a](c[a]d)$

If we treat [a] as a binary operation, the first property says [a] is commutative, and the second says that [a] is associative. These properties imply that the order in which a set of changes to *the same base version* is combined does not matter.

We can see also that in general two change transformations commute whenever neither one removes information that the other adds. We can view the change-merging operation as the application of a function $\mathbf{T}[a, b]$ to a program. Since $(f - g)(g - f) = \mathbf{0}$ we know that every change-merging operation corresponds to a change transformation $\mathbf{T}[a, b]$ for which $ab = \mathbf{0}$. This says that in a minimal change transformation, none of the information that is removed is added back. We have

$$\mathbf{T}[a_2, b_2](\mathbf{T}[a_1, b_1](x)) = (((x - a_1) + b_1) - a_2) + b_2 = x\overline{a_1 a_2} + b_1\overline{a_2} + b_2,$$
$$\mathbf{T}[a_1, b_1](\mathbf{T}[a_2, b_2](x)) = (((x - a_2) + b_2) - a_1) + b_1 = x\overline{a_2 a_1} + b_2\overline{a_1} + b_1.$$

Clearly these are the same if $b_1\overline{a_2} = b_1$ and $b_2\overline{a_1} = b_2$. These conditions are equivalent to $b_1 \sqsubseteq \overline{a_2}$ and $b_2 \sqsubseteq \overline{a_1}$, which are equivalent to $b_1 a_2 = \mathbf{0}$ and $b_2 a_1 = \mathbf{0}$. So these conditions are sufficient for the transformations to commute. To see they are necessary, assume the transformations commute, and substitute a_1 for x:

$$a_1\overline{a_1 a_2} + b_1\overline{a_2} + b_2 = a_1\overline{a_2 a_1} + b_2\overline{a_1} + b_1,$$
$$\mathbf{0} + b_1\overline{a_2} + b_2 = \mathbf{0} + b_2\overline{a_1} + b_1,$$
$$b_1\overline{a_2} + b_2 = b_2\overline{a_1} + b_1.$$

If we multiply both sides by a_1 we get

$$a_1 b_1 \overline{a_2} + a_1 b_2 = b_2 a_1 \overline{a_1} + a_1 b_1,$$
$$\mathbf{0} + a_1 b_2 = \mathbf{0} + \mathbf{0},$$
$$a_1 b_2 = \mathbf{0}.$$

Similarly, $a_2 b_1 = \mathbf{0}$. Thus we have shown that $f[g](t[u]x) = t[u](f[g]x)$ if and only if $(f - g)(u - t) = \mathbf{0}$ and $(t - u)(g - f) = \mathbf{0}$.

This result tells us what we must check to see whether a set of changes will give us the same result independently of the order in which the changes are merged. In case some changes override each other, in the sense that one removes information that another adds, then applying the same changes in a different order can intuitively be expected to give different results: the last transformation to be applied gets the final say about what should be done about the disputed information (to add or to remove). In such cases, human guidance is needed to resolve the relative priority between the two changes, possibly by going back to the requirements and the underlying justifications, and determining which change is more important.

4.4 Properties Related to Functional Composition

Independent modules are a basic requirement for programming on a large scale. We would like to have localized methods for analyzing the processing programs, so that the analysis can be decomposed into smaller independent subproblems. Such decoupling makes human understanding of large systems possible, as well as concurrent team efforts. It leads also to computational efficiency and opportunities for parallel computation in automated processing of programs. Thus, to shed some light on the feasibility of change merging for large systems, we consider the interaction between program merging and functional composition, which we denote by $f \circ g$ where $(f \circ g)(x) = f(g(x))$. The urge to divide and conquer leads us to investigate the following distributive property.

$$(?) \ (f_2 \circ f_1)[(g_2 \circ g_1)](h_2 \circ h_1) = (f_2[g_2]h_2) \circ (f_1[g_1]h_1)$$

This expression describes two changes to an implementation that consists of two modules, where the output of the front end module g_1 is connected with the input of the back end module g_2. The left-hand side represents the result of merging two changes to the system in one big operation, while the right-hand side merges the changes to the front end and the changes to the back end in two independent operations and then connects the merged versions together. Although this distributive property appears to be plausible, it turns out to be false, as illustrated by the following example over the data values {1, 2, 3, 4}.

Example 4.4.1.

x	f_2	g_2	h_2	$f_2[g_2]h_2$	f_1	g_1	h_1	$f_1[g_1]h_1$	$f_2[g_2]h_2 \circ f_1[g_1]h_1$
1	1	1	1	1	1	1	1	1	1
2	3	2	2	3	3	3	2	2	3
3	4	4	4	4	4	4	4	4	2
4	2	3	3	2	2	2	3	3	4

x	$f_2 \circ f_1$	$g_2 \circ g_1$	$h_2 \circ h_1$	$(f_2 \circ f_1)[g_2 \circ g_1](h_2 \circ h_1)$
1	1	1	1	1
2	4	4	2	2
3	2	3	3	3
4	3	2	4	3 ⊔ 4

This example shows that the desired distributive property can be false even for well-behaved functions and changes that do not conflict (compare the results for $x = 2$ or $x = 3$). This negative result is somewhat surprising, because it implies that changes to subfunctions can interfere even for purely functional programs. The interference effect demonstrated above is, thus, completely unrelated to classical concerns about coupling between modules due to side effects or state changes.

Although the interference effect comes from different coincidences of equal values in different versions of the functions, it is not caused by several different values being mapped to the same value by the individual functions: note that all of the individual functions in Example 1, as well as their compositions and the results of the merges, are one-to-one. Thus the problem lies in the relationships between the versions, and is unlikely to be preventable via localized restrictions that can be applied to each of the versions independently.

The circumstances in which this interference effect shows up are complex and not very intuitive. For example, one case where the interference effect shows up without producing any local or global conflicts is when there is some input value x for the front end for which the first change does not affect either the output of the front end ($f_1(x) = g_1(x)$) or the output of the entire system ($f_2(f_1(x)) = g_2(g_1(x))$), and the second change transforms the output of the front end into a value affected by the first change to the back end but not affected by the second change to the back end ($f_2(h_1(x)) \neq g_2(h_1(x)) = h_2(h_1(x))$).

A concrete example of this is a simple text formatter composed of two parts. The front end determines which words go on each line, and the base version puts as many words as will fit. The back end adds extra space between the words, and the base version adds enough space to make the right margin even on every line except the last line of a paragraph. The first change affects only the back end, which is changed to adjust the right margin of the last line of a paragraph in those cases where the space left at the end of the line is strictly less than a given tolerance T, where $T > 1$. The second change affects only the front end, which is changed so that if the space left on a line when no more words from the following text will fit is greater than the space left on the previous line plus the length of the last word on the previous line, then the last word of the previous line is moved up to the current line. The interference effect will show up for an input where the space left on the last line of the paragraph is exactly equal to the tolerance T; the previous line is completely full; and the last word on the previous line is one character long. If we merge the two changes in a single global operation, then the merged version will move up the last word of the previous line and will not adjust the right margin of the last line. If we merge the two changes in isolation and combine the results, then the resulting program will adjust the right margin of the last line in addition to moving up the last word of the previous line. The two results are clearly different.

Also note that it is possible for the true merge of the compositions to contain a conflict even if the independent merges of the changes to corresponding subfunctions are conflict free (compare the results of Example 4.4.1 for $x = 4$). Approximate change-merging methods must be safe to be practically useful: they must never silently turn a real conflict into a proper (but incorrect) result, although they may occasionally report potential conflicts that are not really there. This implies that unrestricted changes to different subprograms cannot in practice be merged independently, and that interprocedural analysis is necessary for reliable change merging. Thus correct divide-and-conquer methods for unrestricted change merging cannot exist, at least relative to modularizations based on functional decomposition.

This is quite unwelcome news for those concerned with the evolution of large software systems, because functional decomposition is the modularization principle underlying many widely used approaches to systems analysis and software design, such as structured analysis. We discuss the implications of this for the practitioner at the end of this section, after examining in more detail the conditions under which change merging can and cannot be performed independently for the components of functional decompositions.

Some weaker distributive properties related to change merging do hold.

The following calculation (property P3) shows that functional composition distributes over the program merge operation from the right.

(P3) $(f[g]h) \circ c = (f\bar{g} + fh + \bar{g}h) \circ c$
$= (f \circ c)(\bar{g} \circ c) + (f \circ c)(h \circ c) + (\bar{g} \circ c)(h \circ c)$
$= (f \circ c)[g \circ c](h \circ c)$

The derivation uses the fact that $\bar{g} \circ c = \overline{g \circ c}$. This property says that the result of merging two changes is the same, independently of whether the inputs to the module that has been changed are supplied directly or come from another module. This is what most programmers would expect. We note that composition on the right may mask some conflicts in $f[g]h$, because the range of c may be a strict subset of the domains of f, g, and h that may not include some potential conflicts between those functions.

Functional composition does not always distribute over program merging from the left, but half of a distributive law is possible for conflict-free monotonic functions on primitive domains restricted to conflict-free portions of the input space. The restriction to monotonic functions is reasonable because every computable function is monotonic. The restriction to conflict-free functions is also reasonable because conflicts can be introduced only by a process of combining changes that operates in an extended syntactic domain: for every programming language we have seen, every program that follows the syntax rules of the programming language is conflict free. The restriction to conflict-free inputs is reasonable because there is no way to create self-contradictory input values on real computer systems. The restriction to primitive domains is less desirable, but it is necessary, as we demonstrate below. We start with a definition, which summarizes characterizations of semantic conflicts from Section 3, and a lemma.

Definition 4.4.2. An element x of a primitive domain (Section 3.2.1) is *conflict free* if and only if $x \sqsubseteq a$ for some atom a. A tuple $x \in D_1 \times D_2$ is *conflict free* if and only if x_1 and x_2 are conflict free. An element $x \in D_1 + D_2$ of an extended sum domain (encoded as a cross product) is *conflict free* if and only if x_1 and x_2 are conflict free and either $x_1 = \mathbf{0}$ or $x_2 = \mathbf{0}$. A function $f: D_1 \to D_2$ is *conflict free* if and only if $f(x)$ is conflict free for all conflict-free $x \in D_1$. A set $s \in P(D)$ is *conflict free* if and only if x is conflict free for all $x \in s$, where $P(D)$ can denote either the Hoare power domain construction or the Smyth power domain construction (Section 3.3.1).

LEMMA 4.4.3. *If f, $g : D_1 \to D_2$ are restricted to the conflict-free portion of D_1, $c : D_2 \to D_3$ is monotonic, f is conflict free, and D_2 is a primitive domain then $(c \circ f)(\bar{c} \circ g) \sqsubseteq (c \circ f)(c \circ \bar{g})$.*

PROOF.

> Since f is conflict free, $f(x)$ is conflict free for all conflict-free $x \in D_1$.
> Let $x \in D_1$. Then $f(x) \sqsubseteq a$ for some atom a, since D_2 is a primitive domain.
>> Case 1: $a \sqsubseteq g(x)$. Then $f(x) \sqsubseteq g(x)$.
>>> So $c(f(x)) \sqsubseteq c(g(x))$ and $c(f(x))\bar{c}(g(x)) = \mathbf{0} \sqsubseteq c(f(x))c(\bar{g}(x))$.

Case 2: $ag(x) = \mathbf{0}$. Then $f(x)g(x) = \mathbf{0}$ since $f(x)g(x) \sqsubseteq ag(x)$.
  Then $f(x) \sqsubseteq \bar{g}(x)$, $c(f(x)) \sqsubseteq c(\bar{g}(x))$, and $c(f(x)) = c(f(x))c(\bar{g}(x))$,
  so $c(f(x))\bar{c}(g(x)) \sqsubseteq c(f(x)) = c(f(x))c(\bar{g}(x))$.
Since a is an atom, cases 1 and 2 cover all possibilities.
So $(c \circ f)(\bar{c} \circ g) \sqsubseteq (c \circ f)(c \circ \bar{g})$ since $c(f(x))\bar{c}(g(x)) \sqsubseteq c(f(x))c(\bar{g}(x))$ for all x. □

THEOREM 4.4.4. *If f, g, $h: D_1 \to D_2$ are restricted to the conflict-free portion of D_1, $c: D_2 \to D_3$ is monotonic, f and h are conflict free, and D_2 is a primitive domain then $(c \circ f)[c \circ g](c \circ h) \sqsubseteq c \circ (f[g]h)$*

PROOF.

$(c \circ f)[c \circ g](c \circ h)$

$= (c \circ f)\overline{(c \circ g)} + (c \circ f)(c \circ h) + \overline{(c \circ g)}(c \circ h)$ Definition of .[.].

$\sqsubseteq (c \circ f)(c \circ \bar{g}) + (c \circ f)(c \circ h) + (c \circ \bar{g})(c \circ h)$ Lemma 4.4.3.

$\sqsubseteq c \circ (f\bar{g}) + c \circ (fh) + c \circ (\bar{g}h)$ Monotonicity of c

$\sqsubseteq c \circ (f\bar{g} + fh + \bar{g}h)$ Monotonicity of c

$= c \circ (f[g]h)$ Definition of .[.].

□

The following example shows that the inequality in Theorem 4.4.4 is sometimes strict.

Example 4.4.5.

f	g	h	$c(1)$	$c(2)$	$c(3)$
1	2	3	4	4	5

$c(f)[c(g)]c(h) = 4[4]5 = 5$
$c(f[g]h) = c(1[2]3) = c(1 \sqcup 3) = c(1) \sqcup c(3) = 4 \sqcup 5 \neq 5$

Together with property P3, Theorem 4.4.4 says that if two changes affect *only one module* of a system, and we merge the two changes to the module in isolation, then the result of replacing the original module with the doubly changed one in the system is consistent with the (ideal) result of merging the corresponding versions of the entire system. The fact that Theorem 4.4.4 is an inclusion rather than an equality means that some conflicts that appear when merging the changes to the module in isolation might not really be conflicts if the change-merging operation were expanded to act on the context c (the system in which the module is embedded) in addition to the base version g and the two modified versions f and h of the impacted module. This seems natural enough, since the context c is free to map two incompatible intermediate values $f(x)$ and $h(x)$ into the same value.

Theorem 4.4.4 behaves like a partial correctness result even though the inclusion appears to go in the wrong direction, because it is not possible in practice (under the hypotheses of the theorem) for the left-hand side to be undefined and the right-hand side to be a proper value unless the isolated merge $f[g]h$ produces a conflict. We can see this as follows. A strict inequality in Theorem 4.4.4 is possible at a given point in D_1 only if the values of f,

g, and h are all distinct, because $c(f[g]g) = c(f) = c(f)[c(g)]c(g)$ and $c(f[g]f) = c(f) = c(f)[c(g)]c(f)$. If c is computable we must have $c(\bot) = \bot$ except when c is a constant function, and in that case Theorem 4.4.4 becomes an equality. This gives us $c(\bot[g]h) = c(h) = \bot[c(g)]c(h) = c(\bot)[c(g)]c(h)$. Thus, strict inequality is possible only when the values of f, g, and h are all distinct and $f \neq \bot \neq h$, and in that case the value of $f[g]h$ at the given point represents a semantic conflict, since D_2 is a primitive domain.

Most programmers would expect these properties to be true in general. However, this is not the case: we have proved Theorem 4.4.4 only when the intermediate domain D_2 is primitive, and it turns out that the theorem does not hold if we remove that restriction. To see that Theorem 4.4.4 need not hold if we relax the requirement that D_2 is a primitive data domain, consider the following example, in which D_1 and D_3 are primitive domains containing numbers and D_2 contains 6-tuples of numbers.

Example 4.4.6.

$\mathbf{T}_1 = f(2) = [2, 2, \bot, \bot, \bot, 2]$ $\qquad c(\mathbf{T}_1) = 2$
$\mathbf{T}_2 = g(2) = [2, \bot, 2, \bot, 2, \bot]$ $\qquad c(\mathbf{T}_2) = 2$
$\mathbf{T}_3 = h(2) = [\bot, 2, 2, 2, \bot, \bot]$ $\qquad c(\mathbf{T}_3) = 2$
$\mathbf{T}_4 = f(2)[g(2)]h(2) = [2, 2, 2, \bot, \bot, \bot]$ $\qquad c(\mathbf{T}_4) = 3 \neq 2 = c(\mathbf{T}_1)[c(\mathbf{T}_2)]c(\mathbf{T}_3)$

In this example the tuples $\mathbf{T}_1$–$\mathbf{T}_4$ are all incomparable, so that monotonicity does not impose any relationships between their images under the function c. The fact that Theorem 4.4.4 need not hold for all conflict-free monotonic functions may be even more surprising than Example 1, because it shows that there can be interference between functional composition and a *single* program change that produces a conflict-free result when carried out in isolation. This can happen if the intermediate domain D_2 contains partial functions or partial data structures (which are realized via lazy evaluation in some functional programming languages). Although the computations in Example 4.4.6 are somewhat unusual, the function c can be realized (via several applications of a nondeterministic operation that evaluates two expressions in parallel and returns the value of the first one that terminates).

Some positive results are also possible for the simpler subproblem of combining compatible extensions to a program [Berzins 1986]. The simplification that occurs when merging compatible extensions is described by Lemma 4.4.7.

LEMMA 4.4.7. *If $g \sqsubseteq f$ and $g \sqsubseteq h$ then $f[g]h = f + h$.*

PROOF.

$$\begin{aligned}
f[g]h &= f\bar{g} + fgh + \bar{g}h \\
&= f\bar{g} + fgh + fgh + \bar{g}h \\
&= f\bar{g} + fg + gh + \bar{g}h \qquad \text{since } g = fg = gh = fgh \\
&= f(\bar{g} + g) + (g + \bar{g})h \\
&= f + h
\end{aligned}$$

□

The following distributivity properties (P4 and P5) hold for the special case of compatible extensions.

(P4) $(f \circ c) + (g \circ c) = (f + h) \circ c$

(P5) $(c \circ f) + (c \circ h) \sqsubseteq c \circ (f + h)$

Property P4 follows from the definition of $+$ on function spaces. Property P5 follows from the monotonicity of c (all computable functions are monotonic), and becomes an equality for additive [Stoy 1977, p. 105] functions c. The special case of additive functions has some practical interest: functions computed by conflict-free subprograms on primitive data domains are additive. The restriction to primitive domains (which also appears in Theorem 4.4.4) holds for subsets of programming languages that do not allow subprograms to be passed as parameters, do not support partially defined data structures, and pass all parameters by value or by reference (i.e., no higher-order functions, lazy evaluation, or call by name).

We can get half of a distributivity law for compatible extensions from properties P4 and P5.

THEOREM 4.4.8. *If* $g_2 \sqsubseteq f_2, h_2$ *and* $g_1 \sqsubseteq f_1, h_1$ *then*

$$(f_2 \circ f_1)[g_2 \circ g_1](h_2 \circ h_1) \sqsubseteq (f_2[g_2]h_2) \circ (f_1[g_1]h_1).$$

PROOF.

Suppose $g_2 \sqsubseteq f_2, h_2$ and $g_1 \sqsubseteq f_1, h_1$.
Then $g_2(g_1(x)) \sqsubseteq g_2(f_1(x)) \sqsubseteq f_2(f_1(x))$ for all x, so $g_2 \circ g_1 \sqsubseteq f_2 \circ f_1$.
Similarly $g_2 \circ g_1 \sqsubseteq h_2 \circ h_1$.

$f_2 \circ f_1[g_2 \circ g_1]h_2 \circ h_1 = (f_2 \circ f_1) + (h_2 \circ h_1)$ Lemma 4.4.7
$\sqsubseteq (f_2 \circ f_1) + (f_2 \circ h_1) + (h_2 \circ f_1) + (h_2 \circ h_1)$
$\sqsubseteq f_2 \circ (f_1 + h_1) + h_2 \circ (f_1 + h_1)$ Property P5
$= (f_2 + h_2) \circ (f_1 + h_1)$ Property P4
$= (f_2[g_2]h_2) \circ (f_1[g_1]h_1)$ Lemma 4.4.7   □

Theorem 4.4.8 can serve as the basis for an approximate method for merging compatible extensions that impact different modules of a system that are connected by data flows. This covers a situation in which methods based on program slicing, as in Horowitz et al. [1989], would always report a conflict. Since Theorem 4.4.8 is an inclusion rather than an equation, such a method may report some extraneous conflicts (see Example 4.4.5 and the following discussion).

Our results impact current software development practices in some environments. Common sense suggests that a change to a module can affect all of the other modules that can receive data from the modified module. However, in informal conversations, several practicing software engineers have described real projects in which different people were routinely assigned to make concurrent changes to modules with apparently unrelated functions, and the results of such updates were combined simply by linking the new versions of both modules into the system after both updates appeared to have been implemented correctly. This practice appears to be based on belief in the (incorrect) distributivity property marked with a (?) at the beginning of this section, or on the unquestioned assumption that if both engineers did their job correctly, then all should be well. The results of this section show that this assumption is not always sound, and that the situation is far from simple in the general case.

Example 4.4.1 shows that the results of combining changes to several different modules that are correct for each module in isolation can produce incorrect results when the modules are assembled into a system in such a way that the output of one changed module can reach the input of another changed module. More surprisingly, two changes to the same module that are consistent and produce correct results when the module is considered in isolation can produce an incorrect system-level result when the module is embedded in a larger system where nothing else has been changed (Example 4.4.6), although the conditions under which this can occur are rather exotic.

Some special cases where independent changes can be combined in isolation and then can be safely embedded in a larger system are identified in Theorems 4.4.4 and 4.4.8. In other cases, when changes are combined, all modules whose inputs can be affected by the outputs of the changed modules must be checked together to establish the mutual correctness of the combined changes. The correctness of the combined changes must be checked explicitly, in addition to checking the correctness of each change in isolation, since in the general case the combination can be incorrect even if each individual change produces correct results when considered in isolation from the other changes. The required check necessitates interprocedural analysis that can span large subsets of the system, even if only a few modules of the system have actually been changed. Such checking can be quite expensive if it is to be done manually. This consideration provides some support for test strategies that use program slicing to determine the impact of a change and to guide the selection of test data.

It is natural to ask why this problem has not been noticed before, if it really is potentially serious. One relevant point is that the desired distributivity property is almost true, in the sense that it was fairly difficult to find counterexamples. We succeeded in doing so only by explicitly analyzing the merging formula and several failed attempts to prove that the property was true. Thus, failures due to this mechanism might not be easy to detect using small sets of test cases. Another point is that large systems, in practice, are subject to failures that do not have clearly understood causes: "integration problems" during system-level testing are common, as is "software rot" that gradually appears as systems go through a long series of changes. Although these problems are undoubtably due in part to human error, the counterexamples to the distributivity law suggest that there may be other factors involved as well. At the current state of the art it would take a tedious experimental effort to gauge accurately how important these effects are in actual practice. This should become easier after reliable tools for semantically based change merging are developed that can adequately treat at least one programming language used in large software development and maintenance activities.

It is also natural to ask what practitioners can do to avoid merging problems before reliable change-merging tools become available. Our results indicate that in the general case changes cannot be combined reliably without including the context of the change. If accurate behavioral specifications for submodules are available, then these can be used to break some of the dependency chains, thus reducing the size of the part of the context that must be considered when implementing and checking a change [Luqi 1990]. This enables a higher degree of concurrency between the work of designers engaged in different changes without giving up serializability of the updates. In such an approach, each change must be checked with respect to only one context (the one defined by the serialization order, and identified as the primary input of the top-level step in Luqi [1990]) because each change becomes part of the context for the next change in the serialization order.

5. CONCLUSIONS AND FUTURE WORK

We have provided a characterization of the semantic properties of an operation for combining changes to software objects, and have shown that the formal model has some of the properties that we would intuitively expect. This characterization is independent of the programming language in which the software objects are described and can be applied in many contexts. We note that the HPR algorithm [Horowitz et al. 1989] is correct with respect to our characterization for the cases in which it does not report any conflicts. One advantage of our formal model is that it provides a natural representation for conflicts in the cases where the given changes cannot be consistently combined. The model can be applied to requirements and specifications in addition to programs, if we accept the view that a specification is a predicate that characterizes the set of all acceptable system behaviors, although the details of this are not explored in the current article.

In related work [Dampier 1990], we have applied our model of the change combination process to propose a new method for integrating changes to PSDL programs. PSDL is a language for prototyping large, real-time systems, which is based on an enhanced data flow model of computation [Luqi et al. 1988]. This language includes features for expressing concurrency and real-time constraints. A formal semantics of PSDL can be found in Kraemer et al. [1993]. An initial version of a method for combining changes to PSDL programs has been developed [Dampier 1990; Dampier et al. 1994]. We are also investigating the application of this framework to the development of program transformations that change the semantics of a program in a disciplined way [Berzins et al. 1993]. Such transformations are important in software evolution and form a complement to the meaning-preserving transformations that are used in implementing executable specification languages and in program optimization.

The results presented in this article establish a clear correctness criterion for software change merging. Much more work remains to be done before automated change merging can be realized in practice. In particular, the fact that the program merging operation does not distribute over functional composition (see Section 4.4) implies that changes to "independent" modules cannot, in general, be processed independently. This may provide some objective support for the common belief that software maintenance is difficult to do, and suggests that significant computational capacity may be required to combine changes reliably to large software systems. Section 4.4 determines some of the conditions under which changes to subfunctions can be merged independently.

Since the exact solution to the program-merging problem is undecidable, future work should explore the tradeoff between computational efficiency and the size of the subspace for which an algorithm can produce exact results. We would like to have reliable approximation algorithms that produce few spurious warnings and succeed in finding conflict-free merges in most of the cases where they exist. An initial step in this direction has been based on program dependency graphs [Horowitz et al. 1989]. A calculus for deriving change merges with fewer spurious conflicts and the capability to merge speedup transformations successfully with other changes is described in Berzins [1991]. More work is needed to develop representations of programs that can support accurate program merge algorithms with wide coverage. The crux of the problem is to recognize equivalent program fragments that are not identical. Normal forms and transformation technology [Guttag et al. 1982] are likely to be important for this aspect of the problem.

ACKNOWLEDGMENT

The author would like to thank Mike Mislove, for kindly communicating that nondistributivity of the Egli-Milner power domain is part of the folklore of domain theory, and the referees for their perceptive comments, which led to substantial improvements to the article.

REFERENCES

BERZINS, V, ED. 1993. *Proceedings of the ARO/AFOSR/ONR Workshop on Increasing the Practical Impact of Formal Methods for Computer-Aided Software Development: Software Slicing, Merging, and Integration.* U.S. Naval Postgraduate School, Monterey, Caif.

BERZINS, V. 1991. Software merge: Models and methods. *Int. J. Syst. Integr. 1*, 2 (Aug.), 121-141.

BERZINS, V. 1986. On merging software extensions. *Acta Informatica 23*, 6 (Nov.), 607-619.

BERZINS, V., AND LUQI. 1991. *Software Engineering with Abstractions.* Addson-Wesley, Reading, Mass.

BERZINS, V., LUQI, AND YEHUDAI, A. 1993. Using transformations in specification-based prototyping. *IEEE Trans. Softw. Eng. 19*, 5 (May), 436-451.

DAMPIER, D. 1990. A model for merging different versions of a PSDL program. M. S. thesis, Dept. of Computer Science, Naval Postgraduate School, Monterey, Caif.

DAMPIER, D., LUQI, AND BERZINS, V. 1994. Automated merging of software prototypes. *J. Syst. Integr. 4*, 1 (Feb.), 33-49.

DAMPIER, D., LUQI, AND BERZINS, V. 1993. Automated merging of software prototypes. In *Proceedings of the 5th International Conference on Software Engineering and Knowledge Engineering* (San Francisco, June 16-18). Knowledge Systems Institute, Skokie, Ill., 604-611.

GUTTAG, J. V., KAPUR, D., AND MUSSER, D. R. 1982. Derived pairs, overlap closures, and rewrite dominoes: New tools for analyzing term rewriting systems. In *Lecture Notes in Computer Science.* Springer-Verlag, New York, 300-312.

HALMOS, P. 1963. *Lectures on Boolean Algebras*. Van Nostrand, Princeton, N.J.

HOARE, C. A. R. 1985. A couple of novelties in the propositional calculus. *Zeitschrift für Mathematische Logik und Grundlagen der Mathematik 31*, 2, 173-178.

HOROWITZ, S., PRINS, J., AND REPS, T. 1989. Integrating noninterfering versions of programs. *ACM Trans. Program Lang. Syst. 11*, 3 (July), 345-387.

KRAEMER, B., LUQI, AND BERZINS, V. 1993. Compositional semantics of a real-time prototyping language. *IEEE Trans. Softw. Eng. 19*, 5 (May), 453-477.

LUQI. 1990. A graph model for software evolution. *IEEE Trans. Softw. Eng. 16*, 8 (Aug.), 917-927.

LUQI, BERZINS, V., AND YEH, R. 1988. A prototyping language for real-time software. *IEEE Trans. Softw. Eng. 14*, 10 (Oct.), 1409-1423.

MACNEILLE, H. 1937. Partially ordered sets. *Trans. Am. Math. Soc. 42*, 416-460.

MACLANE, S., AND BIRKHOFF, G. 1967. *Algebra*. Macmillan, New York.

MCKINSEY, J., AND TARSKI, A. 1946. On closed elements in closure algebras. *Ann. Math. 47*, 1 (Jan.), 122-162.

MCKINSEY, J., AND TARSKI, A. 1944. The algebra of topology. *Ann. Math. 45*, 1 (Jan.), 141-191.

RAMALINGAM, G., AND REPS, T. 1991. A theory of program modifications. In *Proceedings of the Colloquium on Combining Paradigms for Software Development*. Lecture Notes in Computer Science, vol. 494. Springer-Verlag, New York, 137-152.

REPS, T. 1991. Algebraic properties of program integration. *Sci. Comput. Program. 17*, 1-3 (Dec.), 139-215.

RICH, C., AND WATERS, R. 1990. *The Programmer's Apprentice*. Addison Wesley, Reading, Mass.

ROSCOE, W. 1992. *Lecture Notes on Domain Theory*. Programming Research Group, Oxford University.

STERLING, L., AND LAKHOTIA, A. 1988. Composing prolog meta-interpreters. In *Logic Programming: Proceedings of the 5th International Conference and Symposium*. MIT Press, Cambridge, Mass., 386-403.

STOY, J. 1977. *Denotational Semantics: The Scott-Strachey Approach to Programming Language Theory*. MIT Press, Cambridge, Mass.

YANG, W., HOROWITZ, S., AND REPS, T. 1990. A program integration algorithm that accommodates semantics-preserving transformations. In *Proceedings of the 4th ACM Software Engineering Notes Symposium on Software Development Environments*. ACM, New York, 133-143.

Received November 1990; revised January 1994; accepted March 1994

III. Merging Imperative Programs

Overview of the papers

The two papers in this section represent the two major known approaches to merging imperative programs. In the first paper, Horwitz, Prins, and Reps explain the approach to merging *while-programs* using program dependence graphs and slices. This method is efficient and semantically sound. Although part of the process (reconstructing the program from the program dependence graph) is NP complete, the program structure whose occurrences lead to this effect is pathological and should almost never occur in practice. Observed execution times are quite reasonable. The main weakness of the method is that it can report unnecessary conflicts. This stems from two effects.

- Disjoint execution path conditions are not recognized.
- Behavioral equivalences between distinct computation sequences are not recognized.

In the second paper, Berzins presents a merging method based on program meaning functions. This method improves merging accuracy at the expense of computing time. It can surmount both obstacles noted above, and should in principle be capable of deriving any semantically valid merge. However, the method can run forever if it is not restricted. This method needs heuristics to constrain the search for practical use.

Evaluation of the methods

As stated, both methods operate on a simplified programming language. Both can be extended to handle programming languages used in practice. Neither has yet been developed into a commercial merging tool. A prototype implementation of the method described in Horwitz, Prins, and Reps has been developed at the University of Wisconsin for the simple language described in the paper.

It should be possible to develop a version of the first merging method (based on program-dependence graphs) that covers practical programming languages and is efficient enough for commercial applications. Such a tool will report some unnecessary conflicts in addition to all the real ones. The interactive merging tools currently available can be useful for manually examining and resolving conflicts. The second method (based on meaning functions) is more accurate than the first, and derivatives of that method may be useful for diagnosing and resolving some of the unnecessary conflicts reported by the first method. More investigation is needed to determine whether it is more attractive to use the slower and more accurate method only for conflicts detected by the first method, or whether heuristics exist that can make the second method perform as well as the first.

If the accuracy and performance of automated merging methods can reach acceptable levels in practice, then we can expect their use in combining concurrent updates in practical development efforts. A representative from Atria Software reported that they use text-based merging to combine results of concurrent development efforts, and that they have successfully applied this method to programs with more than a million lines of code by using people and compilers to check the integrity of the results. Semantic merging tools should increase the accuracy of this process. It is difficult to quantify the practical benefits of semantic merging on a realistic scale at this time because production quality merging tools for commercial programming languages are not yet available.

Remaining challenges

To bring the methods into practice, we need to create production-quality implementations and experiments that determine the frequency of unnecessary conflict reports for the first method, to decide if the complexity of the second method is necessary. The fundamental open issues for merging include those for slicing: generic programs, procedural parameters, data structures, persistent storage, abstract data types, inheritance, and parallel programs.

At a higher level, decision support for resolving merging conflicts would be useful. This will require analyzing and maintaining the connections between the code and the corresponding specifications and requirements, and will involve both engineering tradeoffs and requirements changes to achieve feasible and desirable merges. Efficient methods for mechanical reasoning will be required to support this process. These problems are difficult and we cannot expect completely automated solutions in the near future.

Integrating Noninterfering Versions of Programs

SUSAN HORWITZ, JAN PRINS, and THOMAS REPS
University of Wisconsin, Madison

The need to integrate several versions of a program into a common one arises frequently, but it is a tedious and time consuming task to integrate programs by hand. To date, the only available tools for assisting with program integration are variants of *text-based* differential file comparators; these are of limited utility because one has no guarantees about how the program that is the product of an integration behaves compared to the programs that were integrated.

This paper concerns the design of a *semantics-based* tool for automatically integrating program versions. The main contribution of the paper is an algorithm that takes as input three programs A, B, and $Base$, where A and B are two variants of $Base$. Whenever the changes made to $Base$ to create A and B do not "interfere" (in a sense defined in the paper), the algorithm produces a program M that integrates A and B. The algorithm is predicated on the assumption that differences in the *behavior* of the variant programs from that of $Base$, rather than differences in the *text*, are significant and must be preserved in M. Although it is undecidable whether a program modification actually leads to such a difference, it is possible to determine a safe approximation by comparing each of the variants with $Base$. To determine this information, the integration algorithm employs a program representation that is similar (although not identical) to the *dependence graphs* that have been used previously in vectorizing and parallelizing compilers. The algorithm also makes use of the notion of a *program slice* to find just those statements of a program that determine the values of potentially affected variables.

The program-integration problem has not been formalized previously. It should be noted, however, that the integration problem examined here is a greatly simplified one; in particular, we assume that expressions contain only scalar variables and constants, and that the only statements used in programs are assignment statements, conditional statements, and while-loops.

Categories and Subject Descriptors: D.2.2 [**Software Engineering**]: Tools and Techniques—*programmer workbench*; D.2.3 [**Software Engineering**]: Coding—*program editors*; D.2.6 [**Software Engineering**]: Programming Environments; D.2.7 [**Software Engineering**]: Distribution and Maintenance—*enhancement, restructuring, version control*; D.2.9 [**Software Engineering**]:

A preliminary version of this paper appeared in the *Conference Record of the Fifteenth ACM Symposium on Principles of Programming Languages* (San Diego, Calif., Jan. 13-15, 1988), ACM, New York, 1988 [16].

This work was supported in part by a David and Lucile Packard Fellowship for Science and Engineering, by the National Science Foundation under grants DCR-8552602 and DCR-8603356, by the Defense Advanced Research Projects Agency, monitored by the Office of Naval Research under contract N00014-88-K-0590, as well as by grants from IBM, DEC, Siemens, and Xerox.

Authors' current addresses: S. Horwitz and T. Reps, Computer Sciences Department, University of Wisconsin, 1210 W. Dayton St., Madison, WI 53706; Jan Prins, Department of Computer Science, Sitterson Hall 083a, University of North Carolina, Chapel Hill, NC 27514.

Permission to copy without fee all or part of this material is granted provided that the copies are not made or distributed for direct commercial advantage, the ACM copyright notice and the title of the publication and its date appear, and notice is given that copying is by permission of the Association for Computing Machinery. To copy otherwise, or to republish, requires a fee and/or specific permission.

"Integrating Noninterfering Versions of Programs" by S. Horwitz, J. Prins, and T. Reps from *ACM Trans. Programming Languages and Systems*, Vol. 11, No. 3, July 1989, pp. 345–387. Copyright 1989, Association for Computing Machinery, Inc., reprinted with permission.

Management—*programming teams, software configuration management*; D.3.4 [**Programming Languages**]: Processors—*compilers, interpreters, optimization*; E.1. [**Data**]: Data Structures—*graphs*

General Terms: Algorithms, Design, Languages, Management, Theory

Additional Key Words and Phrases: Control dependence, data dependence, data-flow analysis, dependence graph, program integration, program slice

---

1. INTRODUCTION

Programmers are often faced with the task of integrating several related, but slightly different, variants of a system. One of the ways in which this situation arises is when a base version of a system is enhanced along different lines, either by users or maintainers, thereby creating several related versions with slightly different features. To create a new version that incorporates several of the enhancements simultaneously, one has to check for conflicts in the implementations of the different versions and then merge them in a manner that combines their separate features.

The task of integrating different versions of programs also arises as systems are being created. Program development is usually a cooperative activity that involves multiple programmers. If a task can be decomposed into independent pieces, the different aspects of the task can be developed and tested independently by different programmers. However, if such a decomposition is not possible, the members of the programming team must work with multiple, separate copies of the source files, and the different versions of the files must be merged into a common version.

The program-integration problem also arises in a slightly different guise when a family of related versions of a program has been created (for example, to support different machines or different operating systems), and the goal is to make the same enhancement or bug-fix to all of them. Such a change cannot be developed for one version and blindly applied to all other versions, since the differences among the versions might alter the effects of the change.

Anyone who has had to reconcile divergent lines of development will recognize these situations and appreciate the need for automatic assistance. Unfortunately, at present, the only available tools for integration are variants of differential file comparators, such as the UNIX® utility *diff*. The problem with such tools is that they implement an operation for merging files as strings of text.

A text-based approach has the advantage of being applicable to merging documents, data files, and other text objects as well as to merging programs. Unfortunately, this approach is necessarily of limited utility for integrating programs because the manner in which two programs are merged is not *safe*. One has no guarantees about the way the program that results from a purely *textual* merge behaves in relation to the behavior of the programs that are the arguments to the merge. The merged program must, therefore, be checked carefully for conflicts that might have been introduced by the merge.

® UNIX is a trademark of AT&T Bell Laboratories.

This paper describes a radically different approach based on the assumption that any change in the *behavior*, rather than the *text*, of a variant with respect to the base program is significant and must be preserved in the merged program. We present an algorithm, called *Integrate*, that could serve as the basis for building an automatic program-integration tool. Algorithm Integrate takes as input three programs A, B, and *Base*, where A and B are two variants of *Base*.[1] Algorithm Integrate either determines that the changes made to *Base* to produce A and B may interfere (in a sense defined in Sections 2 and 4.4), or it produces a new program M that integrates A and B with respect to *Base*. To find those components of a program that represent potentially changed behavior, algorithm Integrate makes use of *dependence graphs*, similar to those that have been used previously for representing programs in vectorizing and parallelizing compilers [2, 4, 11, 22], and an operation on these graphs called *program slicing* [24, 30].

A preliminary implementation of a program-integration tool based on the algorithm presented here has been embedded in a program editor created using the Synthesizer Generator [25, 26]. Data-flow analysis on programs is carried out according to the editor's defining attribute grammar and used to construct the programs' dependence graphs. An integration command invokes the integration algorithm, reports whether the variant programs interfere, and, if there is no interference, creates the integrated program.

To the best of our knowledge, the program-integration problem has not been formalized previously. It should be noted, however, that the integration problem examined here is a greatly simplified one; in particular, algorithm Integrate operates under the simplifying assumptions that expressions contain only scalar variables and constants and that the only statements used in programs are assignment statements, conditional statements, and while-loops.

The paper is organized into seven sections. Section 2 discusses criteria for integratability and interference. Section 3 illustrates some of the problems that can arise when programs are integrated using textual comparison and merging operations.

Sections 4.1 through 4.5 correspond to the five steps of algorithm Integrate. The first step is to build the dependence graphs that represent the programs *Base*, A, and B (the dependence graph that represents program P is denoted by G_P). Section 4.1 defines program dependence graphs and the operation of program slicing. The second step, discussed in Section 4.2, uses program slicing to determine sets of *affected points* of G_A and G_B as computed with respect to G_{Base}. These sets capture the essential differences between *Base* and the variant programs. The third step, described in Section 4.3, combines G_A and G_B to create a merged dependence graph G_M, making use of the sets of affected program points that were computed by the second step. The fourth step uses G_A, G_B, the affected points of G_A and G_B, and G_M to determine whether A and B interfere with respect to *Base*; interference is defined and discussed in Section 4.4. The fifth step, which is carried out only if A and B do not interfere, determines whether G_M corresponds to some program and, if it does, creates an appropriate program from G_M.

---

[1] In fact, the approach we describe can accommodate any number of variants, but for the sake of exposition we consider the common case of two variants A and B.

Although, as we have shown in [18], the problem of determining whether G_M corresponds to some program is NP-complete, we conjecture that the backtracking algorithm given for this step in Section 4.5 will behave satisfactorily on actual programs. Section 4.6 summarizes algorithm Integrate, states a theorem that characterizes how the semantics of the integrated program relates to the semantics of programs *Base*, A, and B, and discusses the algorithm's complexity.

Section 5 discusses applications of program integration in program-development environments. Section 6 describes related work, concentrating on the technical differences between the kind of dependence graphs we employ and the dependence representations that have been defined by others. Section 7 discusses some of the issues we have addressed in extending our work and outlines some problems for future research.

2. CRITERIA FOR INTEGRATABILITY AND INTERFERENCE

Two versions A and B of a common *Base* may, in general, be arbitrarily different. To describe the integrated version M, we could say that the developers of A and B each have in mind their own *specification* and that M should be constructed so as to satisfy *both* specifications. For example, following the view of specifications as pairs of pre- and post-condition predicates [8, 13], given programs A and B that satisfy $\{P_A\} A \{Q_A\}$ and $\{P_B\} B \{Q_B\}$, respectively, A and B are integratable if there exists a program M that halts such that $\{P_A\} M \{Q_A\}$ and $\{P_B\} M \{Q_B\}$.

Under certain circumstances, it is not possible to integrate two programs; we say that such programs *interfere*. One source of interference for the integration criterion given above can be illustrated by restating the criterion as follows: M integrates A and B if M halts and satisfies the three triples $\{P_A \wedge P_B\} M \{Q_A \wedge Q_B\}$, $\{P_A \wedge \neg P_B\} M \{Q_A\}$, and $\{P_B \wedge \neg P_A\} M \{Q_B\}$. A and B interfere if the formula $P_A \wedge P_B$ is satisfiable, but $Q_A \wedge Q_B$ is unsatisfiable; under this circumstance, it is impossible to find an M that halts, such that the specification $\{P_A \wedge P_B\} M \{Q_A \wedge Q_B\}$ is satisfied.

An integration criterion based on program specifications leaves a great deal of freedom for constructing a suitable M, but would be plagued by the familiar undecidable problems of automated program synthesis. Moreover, the requirement that programs be annotated with specifications would make such an approach unusable with the methods of system development currently in use. Consequently, this integration criterion is not suitable at the present time as the basis for building a usable program-integration system.

Given the problems inherent in specification-based integration, we chose to investigate a different definition of the program-integration problem (with a different interference criterion). While specification-based integration ignores program *Base*, *Base* plays an important role in our approach. Our basic assumption is that any change in the *behavior* of the variants with respect to *Base* is significant and must be preserved in M. A further assumption is that the integrated version M must be composed of exactly the statements and control structures that appear as components of *Base*, A, and B.

Our notion of changed behavior in program A (respectively, B) with respect to *Base* is roughly the following: if there exists an initial state and variable x for which the final value of x computed by *Base* is different from the final value computed by A (B), then the computation of x is considered to be a change in behavior of A (B) with respect to Base. The goal of program integration is to produce a program M that preserves the changed behaviors of both A and B with respect to Base (i.e., if Base and A (B) disagree on the final value of x, then M agrees with A (B)) and also preserves the behaviors that are *unchanged* in both A and B with respect to Base (i.e., if Base, A, and B all compute the same final value of x, then M also computes that final value). Variants A and B *interfere* with respect to Base if there exists an initial state and variable x such that Base, A, and B each compute different final values for x.

Although it is undecidable whether a program modification actually leads to a change in behavior, it is still possible to base an algorithm on this definition of program integration. In particular, it is possible to determine a safe approximation of (i.e., a superset of) the set of changed computations. To compute this information, we use a *dependence-graph* representation of programs similar to those used previously for representing programs in vectorizing and parallelizing compilers [2, 4, 11, 22]. We also use *program slices* [24, 30] to find just those components of a program that determine the values of potentially affected variables. (In both cases, these ideas have been adapted to the particular needs of the program-integration problem.)

To simplify the program-integration problem to a manageable level, we allow ourselves two further assumptions. First, we confine our attention to a simplified programming language with the following characteristics:[2] expressions contain only scalar variables and constants; statements are either assignment statements, conditional statements, while loops, or a restricted kind of "output statement" called an *end statement*, which can only appear at the end of a program. An end statement names one or more of the variables used in the program. The variables named in the end statement are those whose final values are of interest to the programmer; when execution terminates, the final state is defined on only those variables in the end statement. Thus a program is of the form:

program
   stmt_list
end(*id**)

Second, we make two assumptions about the editor used to create variants A and B from copies of Base.

(1) The editor provides a tagging capability so that common components (i.e., statements and predicates) can be identified in all three versions. Each component's tag is guaranteed to persist across different editing sessions and machines; tags are allocated by a single server, so that two different editors cannot allocate the same new tag.

(2) The operations on program components supported by the editor are insert, delete, and move. When editing a copy of Base to create a variant, a newly inserted component is given a previously unused tag; the tag of a component that is deleted is never reused; a component that is moved from its original position in Base to a new position in the variant retains its tag from Base.

---

[2] We believe that our approach to program integration can be extended to more realistic programming languages. For example, we have made some progress in extending the algorithm to handle languages with procedure calls [19] and with pointer variables [15].

A tagging facility meeting these requirements can be supported by language-based editors, such as those that can be created by such systems as MENTOR [9], GANDALF [12, 23], and the Synthesizer Generator [25, 26].

An additional goal for an integration tool, although one of secondary importance, is ensuring that the program M that results from integrating A and B resembles A and B as much as possible. There is one aspect of this goal that is not addressed by the algorithm described in this paper. In particular, when the final step of the integration algorithm determines the order of statements in M, it does not make direct use of the order in which statements occur in A or B. Consequently, it may not preserve original statement order, even in portions of the programs that are unaffected by the changes made to the base program to create A and B. Our integration method *does* preserve the original variable names used in A, B, and *Base*; however, as discussed briefly in Section 4.5, it may be desirable to abandon this property and permit the final step of the integration algorithm to perform a limited amount of variable renaming.

3. THE PERILS OF TEXT-BASED INTEGRATION

Integrating programs via textual comparison and merging operations is accompanied by numerous hazards. This section describes some of the problems that can arise, and underscores them with an example that baffles the UNIX program *diff3*. (*Diff3* is a relative of *diff* that can be used to create a merged file when supplied a base file and two variants.)

One problem is that character- or line-oriented textual operations do not preserve syntactic structure; consequently, a processor like *diff3* can easily produce something that is syntactically incorrect. Even if the problem of syntactically erroneous output were overcome, there would still be severe drawbacks to integration by textual merging, because text operations do not take into account program semantics. This has two undesirable consequences:

(1) If the variants of the base program do interfere (under a semantic criterion), *diff3* still goes ahead and produces an "integrated" program.
(2) Even when the variants do not interfere (under a semantic criterion), the integrated program created using *diff3* is not necessarily an acceptable integration.

The latter problem is illustrated by the example given below. In this example, *diff3* creates an unacceptable integrated program despite the fact that it is only necessary to reorder (whole) lines to produce an acceptable one. The example concerns the following base program and two variants:

Base program
program
  if P **then** $x := 0$ **fi**
  if Q **then** $x := 1$ **fi**
  $y := x$
  if R **then** $w := 3$ **fi**
  if S **then** $w := 4$ **fi**
  $z := w$
end(y, z)

<pre>
        Variant A   Variant B
        program   program
          if Q then x := 1 fi   if S then w := 4 fi
          if P then x := 0 fi   if R then w := 3 fi
          y := x   z := w
          if R then w := 3 fi   if P then x := 0 fi
          if S then w := 4 fi   if Q then x := 1 fi
          z := w   y := x
        end(y, z)   end(y, z)
</pre>

In variant A, the conditional statements that have P and Q as their conditions are reversed from the order in which they appear in *Base*. In variant B, the order of the P–Q pair remains the same as in *Base*, but the order of the R–S pair is reversed; in addition, the order of the first and second groups of three statements have been interchanged.

Under UNIX, a program that (purportedly) integrates *Base*, A, and B can be created by the following operations:

diff3 −e *A Base B* > script
(cat script; echo '1,$p') | ed − *A*

The first command invokes the three-way file comparator *diff3*; the −e flag of *diff3* causes it to create an editor script as its output. This script can be used to incorporate in one of the variants (in this case, A) changes between the base program (*Base*) and the second variant (B). The second command invokes the editor to apply the script to variant A.

The program that results from these operations is

<pre>
        program
          if S then w := 4 fi
          if R then w := 3 fi
          z := w
          if P then x := 0 fi
          if Q then x := 1 fi
          y := x
        end(y, z)
</pre>

This program is exactly the same as the one given as variant B. Because it does not account for the differences in behavior between *Base* and variant A, this can hardly be considered an acceptable integration of *Base*, A, and B.

We now try a different tactic and exchange the positions of A and B in the argument list passed to *diff3*, thereby treating B as the "primary" variant and A as the "secondary" variant (*diff3* is not symmetric in its first and third arguments). The program that results is

<pre>
        program
          if Q then x := 1 fi
          if P then x := 0 fi
          y := x
        end(y, z)
</pre>

Clearly, this program is unacceptable as the integration of *Base*, A, and B.

This example illustrates the use of *diff3* to create an editing script that merges three documents whether or not there are "conflicts." Under some versions of

UNIX, it is also possible to have *diff3* produce an editing script that annotates the merged document at places where conflicts occur. At such places, the script inserts both versions of the text, and brackets the region of the conflict by "<<<<<<<" and ">>>>>>>." For instance, the outcome for the second case discussed above is

program
<<<<<<< B
   if S **then** $w := 4$ **fi**
   if R **then** $w := 3$ **fi**
   $z := w$
   if P **then** $x := 0$ **fi**
=======
>>>>>>> A
   if Q **then** $x := 1$ **fi**
   if P **then** $x := 0$ **fi**
   $y := x$
end(y, z)

When we apply the program-integration method that is described in this paper to this same example, there are several programs it might create, including the following three:

program	**program**	**program**
if S **then** $w := 4$ **fi**	**if** Q **then** $x := 1$ **fi**	**if** Q **then** $x := 1$ **fi**
if R **then** $w := 3$ **fi**	**if** P **then** $x := 0$ **fi**	**if** P **then** $x := 0$ **fi**
$z := w$	$y := x$	**if** S **then** $w := 4$ **fi**
if Q **then** $x := 1$ **fi**	**if** S **then** $w := 4$ **fi**	**if** R **then** $w := 3$ **fi**
if P **then** $x := 0$ **fi**	**if** R **then** $w := 3$ **fi**	$y := x$
$y := x$	$z := w$	$z := w$
end(y, z)	**end**(y, z)	**end**(y, z)

In contrast to the programs that result from text-based integration, any of the algorithm's possible products is a satisfactory outcome for integrating *Base*, *A*, and *B*.

4. AN ALGORITHM FOR INTEGRATING NONINTERFERING VERSIONS OF PROGRAMS

4.1 The Program Dependence Graph

Different definitions of program dependence representations have been given, depending on the intended application; they are all variations on a theme introduced in [21], and share the common feature of having an explicit representation of data dependences (see below). The "program dependence graphs" defined in [11] introduced the additional feature of an explicit representation for control dependences (see below). The definition of program dependence graph given below differs from [11] in two ways. First, our definition covers only the restricted language described earlier, and hence is less general than the one given in [11]. Second, because of the particular needs of the program-integration problem, we omit certain classes of data dependence edges and introduce one new class; reasons for these changes are provided in Section 6.1. Despite these differences, the structures we define and those defined in [11] share the feature of explicitly representing both control and data dependences; therefore, we refer to our graphs as "program dependence graphs," borrowing the term from [11].

The *program dependence graph* (or PDG) for a program P, denoted by G_P, is a directed graph whose vertices are connected by several kinds of edges.[3] Program dependence graph G_P includes four kinds of vertices:

(1) For each assignment statement and control predicate that occurs in program P, there is a vertex labeled with the assignment or predicate.
(2) There is a distinguished vertex called the *entry vertex*.
(3) For each variable x for which there is a path in the standard control-flow graph for P on which x is used before being defined (see [1]), there is a vertex called the *initial definition of x*. This vertex represents an assignment to x from the initial state. The vertex is labeled "$x := InitialState(x)$."
(4) For each variable x named in P's end statement, there is a vertex called the *final use of x*. This vertex represents an access to the final value of x computed by P, and is labeled "$FinalUse(x)$."

We assume that vertices of PDGs are also labeled with an additional piece of information (which is not shown in our examples). Recall that we have assumed that the editor used to modify programs provides a tagging capability. Vertices of a PDG are labeled with the tags of the corresponding program components.

The edges of G_P represent *dependences* between program components. An edge represents either a *control dependence* or a *data dependence*. Control dependence edges are labeled either **true** or **false**, and the source of a control dependence edge is always the entry vertex or a predicate vertex. A control dependence edge from vertex v_1 to vertex v_2, denoted by $v_1 \rightarrow_c v_2$, means that, during execution, whenever the predicate represented by v_1 is evaluated and its value matches the label on the edge to v_2, then the program component represented by v_2 will be executed (although perhaps not immediately). A method for determining control dependence edges for arbitrary programs is given in [11]; however, because we are assuming that programs include only assignment, conditional, and while statements, the control dependence edges of G_P can be determined in a much simpler fashion. For the language under consideration here, the control dependence edges reflect a program's nesting structure; program dependence graph G_P contains a *control dependence edge* from vertex v_1 to vertex v_2 iff one of the following holds:

(1) v_1 is the entry vertex, and v_2 represents a component of P that is not subordinate to any control predicate; these edges are labeled **true**.
(2) v_1 represents a control predicate, and v_2 represents a component of P immediately subordinate to the control construct whose predicate is represented by v_1. If v_1 is the predicate of a while-loop, the edge $v_1 \rightarrow_c v_2$ is labeled **true**; if v_1 is the predicate of a conditional statement, the edge $v_1 \rightarrow_c v_2$ is

---

[3] A *directed graph* G consists of a set of *vertices* $V(G)$ and a set of *edges* $E(G)$, where $E(G) \subseteq V(G) \times V(G)$. Each edge $(b, c) \in E(G)$ is directed from b to c; we say that b is the *source* and c the *target* of the edge.

labeled **true** or **false** according to whether v_2 occurs in the **then** branch or the **else** branch, respectively.[4]

Note that initial-definition and final-use vertices have no incoming control dependence edges.

A data dependence edge from vertex v_1 to vertex v_2 means that the program's computation might be changed if the relative order of the components represented by v_1 and v_2 were reversed. In this paper, program dependence graphs contain two kinds of data dependence edges, representing *flow dependences* and *def-order dependences*.

The data dependence edges of a program dependence graph are computed using data-flow analysis. For the restricted language considered in this paper, the necessary computations can be defined in a syntax-directed manner (see [14]).

A program dependence graph contains a *flow dependence* edge from vertex v_1 to vertex v_2 iff all of the following hold:

(1) v_1 is a vertex that defines variable x.

(2) v_2 is a vertex that uses x.

(3) Control can reach v_2 after v_1 via an execution path along which there is no intervening definition of x. That is, there is a path in the standard control-flow graph for the program [1] by which the definition of x at v_1 reaches the use of x at v_2. (Initial definitions of variables are considered to occur at the beginning of the control-flow graph, and final uses of variables are considered to occur at its end.)

A flow dependence that exists from vertex v_1 to vertex v_2 will be denoted by $v_1 \rightarrow_f v_2$. (When it is necessary to indicate that a dependence is due to a particular variable x, it will be denoted by $v_1 \rightarrow_f^x v_2$).

Flow dependences are further classified as *loop independent* or *loop carried* [3]. A flow dependence $v_1 \rightarrow_f v_2$ is carried by loop L, denoted by $v_1 \rightarrow_{lc(L)} v_2$, if in addition to (1), (2), and (3) above, the following also hold:

(4) There is an execution path that both satisfies the conditions of (3) above and includes a backedge to the predicate of loop L; and

(5) Both v_1 and v_2 are enclosed in loop L.

A flow dependence $v_1 \rightarrow_f v_2$ is loop independent, denoted by $v_1 \rightarrow_{li} v_2$, if in addition to (1), (2), and (3) above, there is an execution path that satisfies (3) above and includes *no* backedge to the predicate of a loop that encloses both v_1 and v_2. It is possible to have both $v_1 \rightarrow_{lc(L)} v_2$ and $v_1 \rightarrow_{li} v_2$.

A program dependence graph contains a *def-order dependence* edge from vertex v_1 to vertex v_2 iff all of the following hold:

(1) v_1 and v_2 are both assignment statements that define the same variable.

(2) v_1 and v_2 are in the same branch of any conditional statement that encloses both of them.

---

[4] In other definitions that have been given for control dependence edges, there is an additional edge for each predicate of a **while** statement—each predicate has an edge to itself labeled **true**. By including the additional edge, the predicate's outgoing **true** edges consist of every program element that is guaranteed to be executed (eventually) when the predicate evaluates to **true**. This kind of edge is unnecessary for our purposes, and hence is left out of our definition.

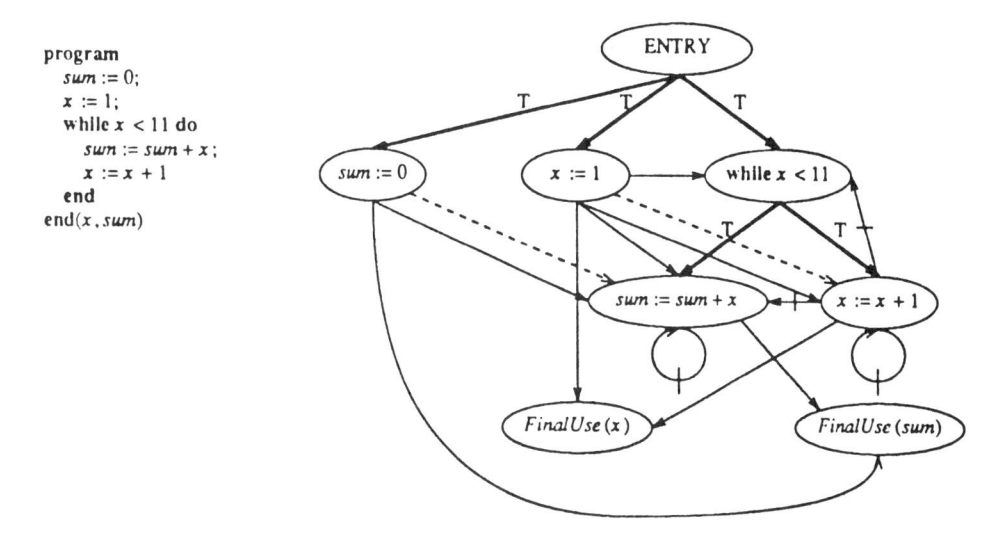

```
program
  sum := 0;
  x := 1;
  while x < 11 do
    sum := sum + x;
    x := x + 1
  end
end(x, sum)
```

Fig. 1. An example program, which sums the integers from 1 to 10 and leaves the result in the variable *sum*, and its program dependence graph. The boldface arrows represent control dependence edges, dashed arrows represent def-order dependence edges, solid arrows represent loop-independent flow dependence edges, and solid arrows with a hash mark represent loop-carried flow dependence edges.

(3) There exists a program component v_3 such that $v_1 \rightarrow_f v_3$ and $v_2 \rightarrow_f v_3$.

(4) v_1 occurs to the left of v_2 in the program's abstract syntax tree.

A def-order dependence from v_1 to v_2 is denoted by $v_1 \rightarrow_{do(v_3)} v_2$.

Note that a program dependence graph is a multigraph (i.e., it may have more than one edge of a given kind between two vertices). When there is more than one loop-carried flow dependence edge between two vertices, each is labeled by a different loop that carries the dependence. When there is more than one def-order edge between two vertices, each is labeled by a vertex that is flow-dependent on both the definition that occurs at the edge's source and the definition that occurs at the edge's target.

Example. Figure 1 shows an example program and its program dependence graph. The boldface arrows represent control dependence edges; dashed arrows represent def-order dependence edges; solid arrows represent loop-independent flow dependence edges; solid arrows with a hash mark represent loop-carried flow dependence edges.

4.1.1 *Def-order Dependences versus Anti- and Output Dependences.* Previous program dependence representations have included flow dependence edges as well as edges for two other kinds of data dependences, called *antidependences* and *output dependences*. (All three kinds may be further characterized as loop independent or loop carried.) Def-order dependences have not been previously defined. The definition of program dependence graphs given in Section 4.1 omits anti- and output dependences in favor of def-order dependences. Our reasons for using this definition are discussed in Section 6.1; this section merely clarifies the *differences* among these three kinds of dependences.

For flow dependences, antidependences, and output dependences, a program component v_2 has a dependence on component v_1 due to variable x only if execution can reach v_2 after v_1 and there is no intervening definition of x along the execution path by which v_2 is reached from v_1. There is a flow dependence if v_1 defines x and v_2 uses x (a "write-read" dependence); there is an antidependence if v_1 uses x and v_2 defines x (a "read-write" dependence); there is an output dependence if v_1 and v_2 both define x (a "write-write" dependence).

Although def-order dependences resemble output dependences in that they are both "write-write" dependences, they are two different concepts. An output dependence $v_1 \rightarrow_o v_2$ between two definitions of x can hold only if there is no intervening definition of x along some execution path from v_1 to v_2; however, there can be a def-order dependence $v_1 \rightarrow_{do} v_2$ between two definitions even if there is an intervening definition of x along *all* execution paths from v_1 to v_2. This situation is illustrated by the following example program fragment, which demonstrates that it is possible to have a program in which there is a dependence $v_1 \rightarrow_{do} v_2$ but not $v_1 \rightarrow_o v_2$, and *vice versa*:

```
[1]     x := 10
[2]     if P then
[3]             x := 11
[4]             x := 12
[5]     fi
[6]     y := x
```

The one def-order dependence, $[1] \rightarrow_{do([6])} [4]$, exists because the assignments to x in lines [1] and [4] both reach the use of x in line [6]. In contrast, the output dependences are $[1] \rightarrow_o [3]$ and $[3] \rightarrow_o [4]$, but there is no output dependence $[1] \rightarrow_o [4]$.

4.1.2 *Program Slices.* For a vertex s of a program dependence graph G, the *slice* of G with respect to s, written as G/s, is a graph containing all vertices on which s has a transitive flow or control dependence (i.e., all vertices that can reach s via flow or control edges): $V(G/s) = \{w \in V(G) \mid w \rightarrow^*_{c,f} s\}$. We extend the definition to a set of vertices $S = \bigcup_i s_i$ as follows: $V(G/S) = V(G/(\bigcup_i s_i)) = \bigcup_i V(G/s_i)$. It is useful to define $V(G/v) = \emptyset$ for any $v \notin G$.

The edges in the graph G/S are essentially those in the subgraph of G induced by $V(G/S)$, with the exception that a def-order edge $v \rightarrow_{do(u)} w$ is only included if, in addition to v and w, $V(G/S)$ also contains the vertex u that is directly flow dependent on the definitions at v and w. In terms of the three types of edges in a PDG, we have

$$\begin{aligned}
E(G/S) = &\{(v \rightarrow_f w) \in E(G) \mid v, w \in V(G/S)\} \\
\cup &\{(v \rightarrow_c w) \in E(G) \mid v, w \in V(G/S)\} \\
\cup &\{(v \rightarrow_{do(u)} w) \in E(G) \mid u, v, w \in V(G/S)\}
\end{aligned}$$

Example. Figure 2 shows the graph that results from slicing the program dependence graph from Figure 1 with respect to the final-use vertex for x.

4.1.3 *Program Dependence Graphs and Program Semantics.* In choosing which dependence edges to include in our program dependence graphs, our goal has been to characterize partially programs that have the same behavior—two inequivalent programs should not have the same program dependence graph, although two equivalent programs may have different program dependence graphs.

```
program
  x := 1;
  while x < 11 do
    x := x + 1
  end
end(x)
```

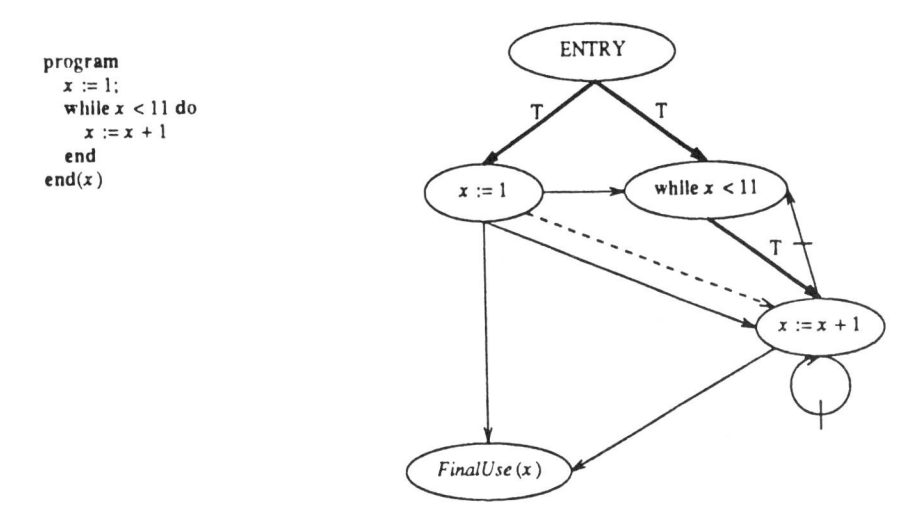

Fig. 2. The graph that results from slicing the example from Figure 1 with respect to the final-use vertex for x, together with the one program to which it corresponds.

This property is crucial to the correctness of our program-integration algorithm. In particular, the final step of the algorithm reconstitutes the integrated program from a program dependence graph. Because this graph may correspond to more than one program, we need to know that all such programs are equivalent.

The relationship between a program's PDG and the program's execution behavior has been addressed in [17, 18]. It is shown in [17, 18] that if the program dependence graphs of two programs are isomorphic, then the programs have the same behavior. It is also shown that if any of the different kinds of edges included in our definition of program dependence graphs were omitted, programs with different behavior could have the same program dependence graph. The concept of "programs with the same behavior" is formalized as the concept of *strong equivalence*, defined as follows:

Definition. Two programs P and Q are *strongly equivalent* iff for any state σ, either P and Q both diverge when initiated on σ or they both halt with the same final values for all variables. If P and Q are not strongly equivalent, we say they are *inequivalent*.

The term "divergence" refers to both nontermination (for example, because of infinite loops) and abnormal termination (for example, because of division by zero).

The main result of [17, 18] is the following theorem (we use the symbol ≈ to denote isomorphism between program dependence graphs):

THEOREM (Equivalence Theorem [17, 18]). *If P and Q are programs for which $G_P \approx G_Q$, then P and Q are strongly equivalent.*

Restated in the contrapositive, the theorem reads: Inequivalent programs have nonisomorphic program dependence graphs.

The relationship between a program's PDG and a slice of the PDG has been addressed in [27]. We say that G is a *feasible* program dependence graph iff G is the program dependence graph of some program P. For any $S \subseteq V(G)$, if G is a feasible PDG, the slice G/S is also a feasible PDG; it corresponds to the program P' obtained by restricting the syntax tree of P to just the statements and predicates in $V(G/S)$ [27].

THEOREM (Feasibility of Program Slices [27]). *For any program P, if G_S is a slice of G_P (with respect to some set of vertices), then G_S is a feasible PDG.*

Example. Figure 2 shows the one program that corresponds to the graph that results from slicing the graph in Figure 1 with respect to the final-use vertex for x.

The significance of a slice is that it captures a portion of a program's behavior in the sense that, for any initial state on which the program halts, the program and the slice compute the same sequence of values for each element of the slice [27]. In our case, a program point may be (1) an assignment statement, (2) a control predicate, or (3) a final use of a variable in an end statement. Because a statement or control predicate may be reached repeatedly in a program, by "computing the same sequence of values for each element of the slice," we mean: (1) for any assignment statement the same *sequence* of values is assigned to the target variable; (2) for a predicate the same *sequence* of Boolean values is produced; and (3) for each final use the same value for the variable is produced.

THEOREM (Slicing Theorem [27]). *Let Q be a slice of program P with respect to a set of vertices. If σ is a state on which P halts, then for any state σ' that agrees with σ on all variables for which there are initial-definition vertices in G_Q: (1) Q halts on σ', (2) P and Q compute the same sequence of values at each program point of Q, and (3) the final states agree on all variables for which there are final-use vertices in G_Q.*

4.2 Determining the Differences in Behavior of a Variant

In this section, we characterize (an approximation to) the difference between the behavior of *Base* and its variants. Since we do not know the specification of *Base* or its variants, we assume that *any* and *only* changes in the behavior of a variant with respect to *Base* are significant. The program dependence graphs are a convenient representation from which to determine these changes.

Recall the assumption made in Section 4.1 that the vertices of a PDG are labeled with the tags maintained by the editor on program components. These tags provide a means for identifying PDG vertices that correspond in all three versions. It is these tags that are used to determine "identical" vertices when we perform operations on vertices from different PDGs (e.g., $V(G') - V(G)$). Similarly, when we speak below of "identical slices," where the slices are actually taken in different graphs, we mean that the slices are isomorphic under the mapping provided by the editor-supplied tags.

If the slice of variant G_A at vertex v differs from the slice of G_{Base} at vertex v (i.e., they are different graphs), then values at v are computed in a different manner by the respective programs. This means that the values at v may differ, and we take this as our definition of changed behavior. We define the *affected points* $AP_{A,Base}$ of G_A as the subset of vertices of G_A whose slices in G_{Base} and G_A differ:

$$AP_{A,Base} = \{v \in V(G_A) \mid (G_{Base}/v) \neq (G_A/v)\}.$$

The slice $G_A/AP_{A,Base}$ captures the behavior of A that differs from *Base*. Note that when there is a vertex v that is present in G_{Base} but not in G_A, any vertex still present in G_A that in G_{Base} depends on v is an affected point of G_A; thus, although such "deleted" vertices are not themselves affected points, they may have indirect effects on $AP_{A,Base}$ (and hence on $G_A/AP_{A,Base}$).

Example. Figure 1 shows a program that sums the integers from 1 to 10 and its corresponding program dependence graph. We now consider two variants of this program, shown in Figure 3 with their program dependence graphs:

(1) In variant A, two statements have been added to the original program to compute the product of the integer sequence from 1 to 10.
(2) In variant B, one statement has been added to compute the mean of the sequence.

These two programs represent noninterfering extensions of the original summation program. The set $AP_{A,Base}$ contains three vertices: the assignment vertices labeled "*prod* := 1" and "*prod* := *prod* * *x*" as well as the final-use vertex for *prod*. Similarly, $AP_{B,Base}$ contains two vertices: the assignment vertex labeled "*mean* := *sum*/10" and the final-use vertex for *mean*. Figure 4 shows the slices $G_A/AP_{A,Base}$ and $G_B/AP_{B,Base}$, which represent the changed behaviors of A and B, respectively.

There is a simple technique to determine $AP_{A,Base}$ that avoids computing all of the slices stated in the definition. The technique requires at most two complete examinations of G_A, and is based on the following three observations:

(1) All vertices that are in G_A but not in G_{Base} are affected points.
(2) Each vertex w of G_A that has a different set of incoming control or flow edges in G_A than in G_{Base} gives rise to a set of affected points—those vertices that can be reached via zero or more control or flow edges from w.
(3) Each vertex w of G_A that has an incoming def-order edge $w' \to_{do(u)} w$ that does not occur in G_{Base} gives rise to a set of affected points—those vertices that can be reached via zero or more control or flow edges from u.

The justification for observation (1) is straightforward: for $w \in V(G_A) - V(G_{Base})$, G_{Base}/w is the empty graph, whereas $w \in V(G_A/w)$, so G_A/w is not empty. The justification for observation (2) is also straightforward. By the definition of slicing, when w differs in incoming flow or control edges, G_A/w and G_{Base}/w cannot be the same, hence w itself is affected. For any vertex v that is (directly or indirectly) flow or control dependent on w in G_A, the slice G_A/v contains the subgraph G_A/w. Therefore, if w is affected, all *successors* of w in G_A via control and flow dependences are also affected.

The justification for observation (3) is more subtle. When a def-order edge $w' \to_{do(u)} w$ occurs in G_A but not in G_{Base}, then the slice G_A/u will include both w' and w and the def-order edge between them, while G_{Base}/u will not include this edge. Hence u is affected. The reverse situation, where $w' \to_{do(u)} w$

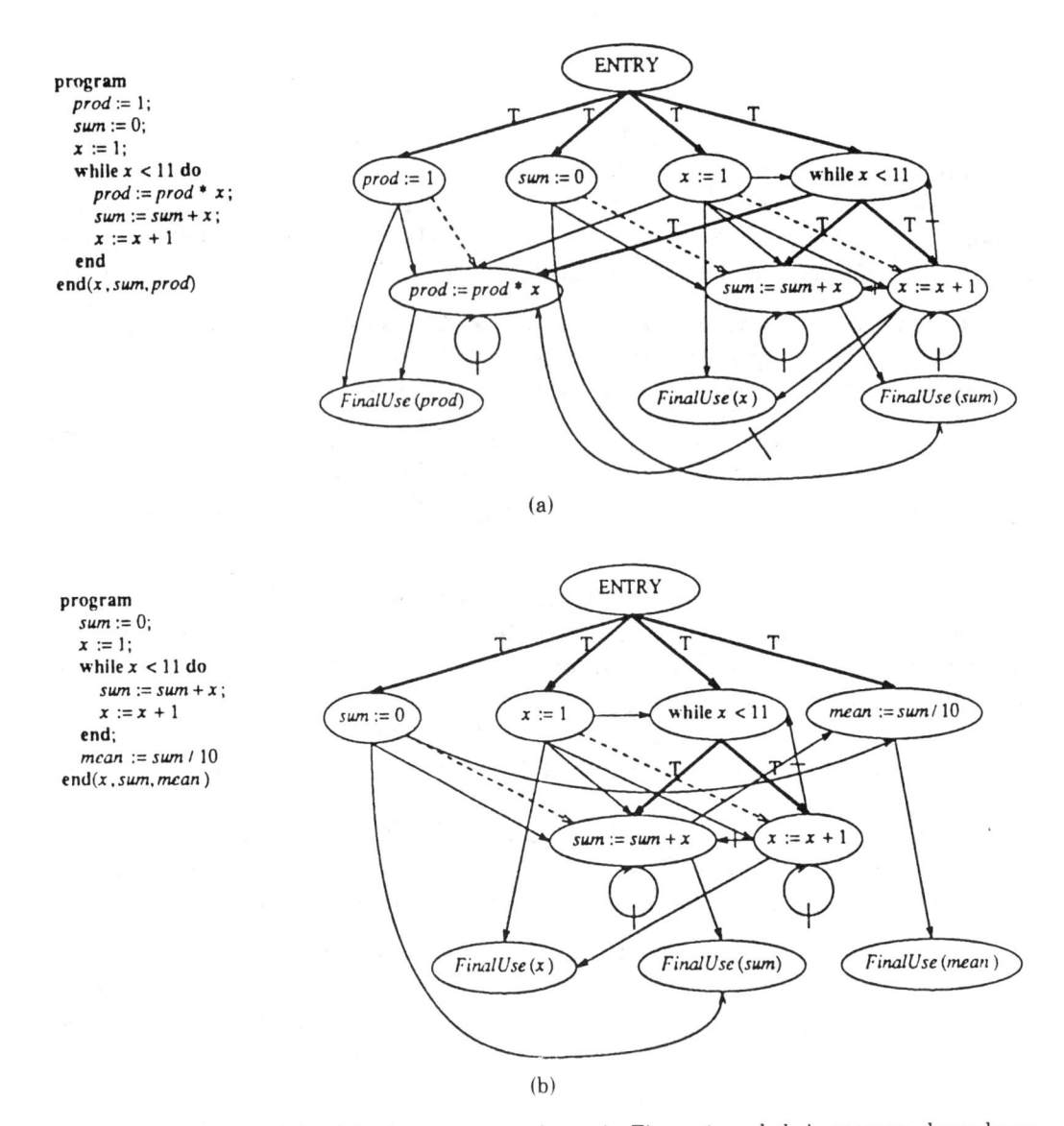

Fig. 3. Variants A and B of the base program shown in Figure 1, and their program dependence graphs.

occurs in G_{Base}, but not in G_A, means u is affected if $u \in V(G_A)$. But it is not necessary to examine this possibility since either $w' \rightarrow_{do(u)} w$ in G_{Base} is replaced by $w \rightarrow_{do(u)} w'$ in G_A, in which case $w' \in V(G_A)$ will contribute u as affected, or else one or both of the flow edges $w \rightarrow_f u$ and $w' \rightarrow_f u$ in G_{Base} will be missing in G_A, in which case u is affected by the change in incoming flow edges. As before, for any vertex v that is (directly or indirectly) flow or control dependent on u, the slice G_A/v contains the subgraph G_A/u; therefore, if u is affected, all *successors* of u via control and flow dependences are affected. Note that neither w' itself nor w itself is necessarily an affected point.

Observations (1), (2), and (3) serve to characterize the set of affected points. If $v \in V(G_A)$ is affected, there must be some w in G_A/v with different incoming edges in G_A and G_{Base}. By the arguments above, either w itself is an affected point

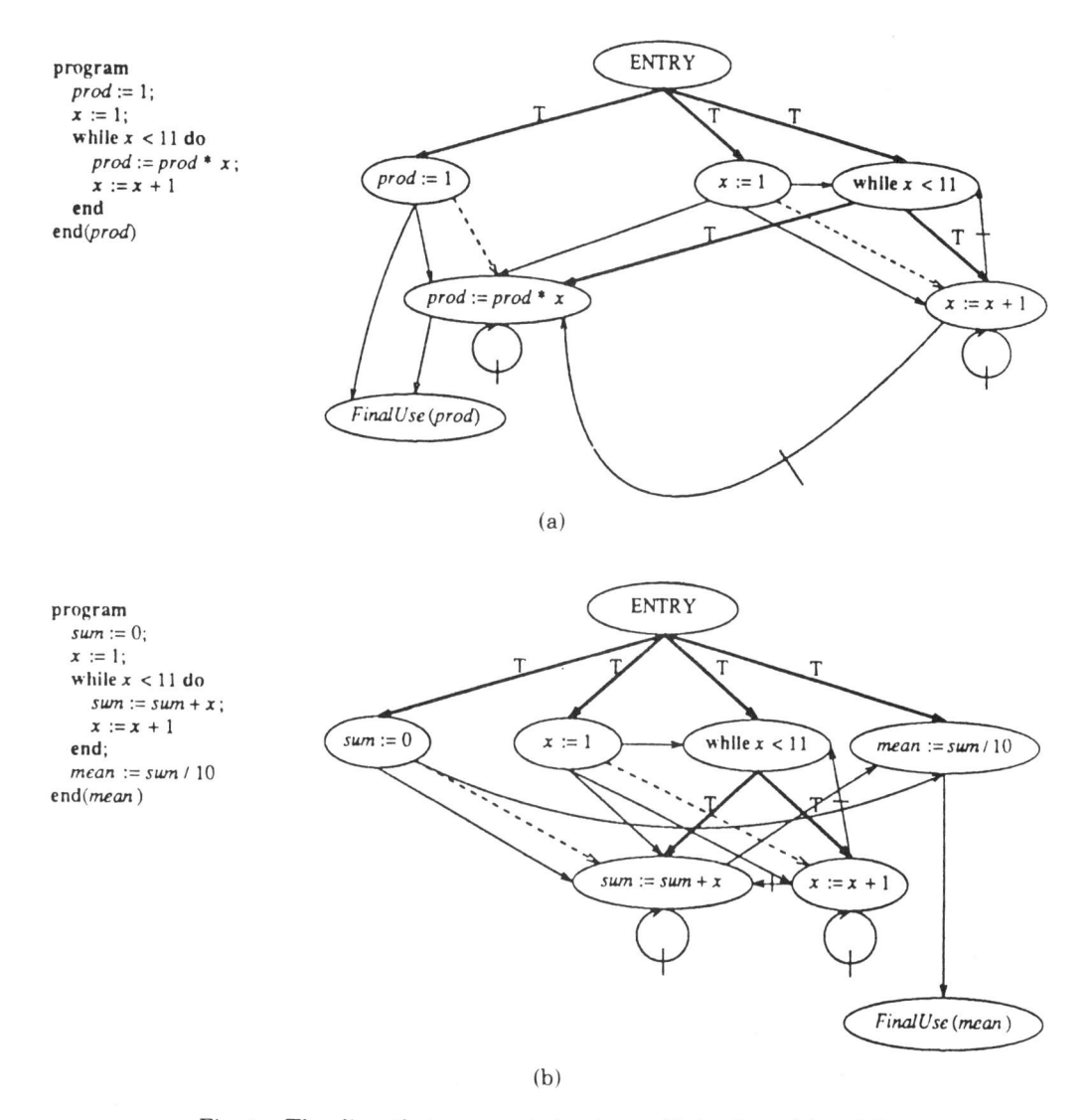

Fig. 4. The slices that represent the changed behaviors of A and B.

(cases (1) and (2)), or it contributes a vertex $u \in V(G_A/v)$ that is an affected point (case (3)); therefore, it is possible to identify v as an affected point by following control and flow edges. This latter observation forms the basis for the function AffectedPoints(G', G), given in Figure 5.

It computes the set of affected points of G' with respect to G by examining all vertices w in G' that have a different set of incoming edges in G' than in G, and collecting the affected points that each vertex contributes. Then a worklist algorithm is used to find all vertices reachable from this set by flow or control edges.

4.3 Merging Program Dependence Graphs

We now show how to create the merged program dependence graph G_M. Graph G_M is formed by taking the union of three slices; these slices represent the

```
function AffectedPoints(G', G) returns a set of vertices
declare
    G', G: program dependence graphs
    S, Answer: sets of vertices
    w, u, b, c: individual vertices
begin
    S := ∅
    for each vertex w in G' do
        if w is not in G then
            Insert w into S
        fi
        if the sets of incoming flow or control edges to w in G' are different from the incoming sets to w in G then
            Insert w into S
        fi
        for each def-order edge w' →_{do(u)} w that occurs in G' but not in G do
            Insert u into S
        end
    end
    Answer := ∅
    while S ≠ ∅ do
        Select and remove an element b from S
        Insert b into Answer
        for each vertex c such that b →_f c or b →_c c is an edge in G' and c ∉ (Answer ∪ S) do
            Insert c into S
        end
    end
    return(Answer)
end
```

Fig. 5. The function AffectedPoints determines the points in the program dependence graph G' that may yield different values in G' than in G.

changed behaviors of A and B with respect to *Base* and the behavior of *Base* that is preserved in both A and B.

The previous section discussed how to compute the slices $G_A/AP_{A,Base}$ and $G_B/AP_{B,Base}$, which represent the changed behaviors of A and B with respect to *Base*. The slice that represents preserved behavior is computed similarly. If the slice of G_{Base} with respect to vertex v is identical to the slices of G_A and G_B with respect to vertex v, then all three programs produce the same sequence of values at v. We define the *preserved points* $PP_{Base,A,B}$ of G_{Base} as the subset of vertices of G_{Base} with identical slices in G_{Base}, G_A, and G_B:

$$PP_{Base,A,B} = \{v \in V(G_{Base}) \mid (G_{Base}/v) = (G_A/v) = (G_B/v)\}.$$

The slice $G_{Base}/PP_{Base,A,B}$ captures the behavior of *Base* that is preserved in both A and B.

Example. When integrating the base program from Figure 1, variant A from Figure 3(a) and variant B from Figure 3(b), the slice $G_{Base}/PP_{Base,A,B}$ consists of G_{Base} in its entirety. That is, the graph that represents the behavior of the original program that is preserved in both variant A and variant B is identical to the graph shown in Figure 1.

The merged graph G_M is formed by taking the graph union of the slices that characterize the changed behavior of A, the changed behavior of B, and behavior of *Base* preserved in both A and B.

$$G_M = (G_A/AP_{A,Base}) \cup (G_B/AP_{B,Base}) \cup (G_{Base}/PP_{Base,A,B}).$$

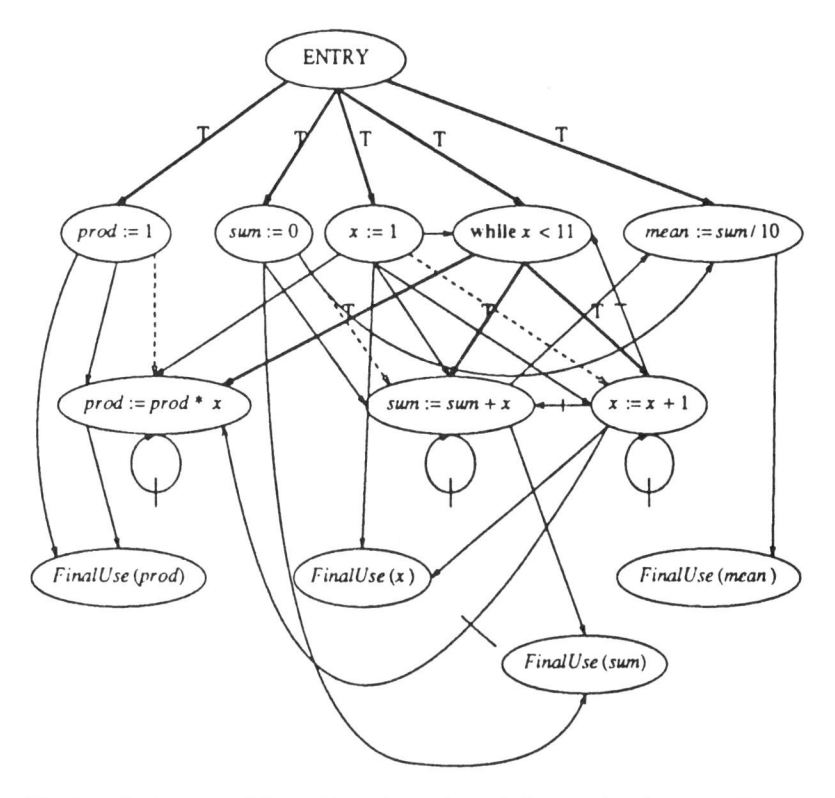

Fig. 6. G_M is created by taking the union of the graphs shown in Figures 4(a), 4(b), and 1.

Example. The merged graph G_M, shown in Figure 6, is formed by taking the union of the graphs shown in Figure 4(a), Figure 4(b), and Figure 1.

4.4 Determining Whether Two Versions Interfere

A merged program dependence graph, G_M, that is created by the method described in the previous section can fail to reflect the changed behavior of the two variants A and B in two ways. First, because the union of two feasible PDGs is not necessarily a feasible PDG, G_M may not be a feasible PDG. Second, it is possible that G_M will not preserve the differences in behavior of A or B with respect to *Base*. If either condition occurs, we say that A and B interfere. Testing for interference due to the former condition is addressed in Section 4.5; this section describes a criterion for determining whether a merged program dependence graph preserves the changed behavior of A and B.

To insure that the changed behavior of variants A and B is preserved in G_M, we introduce a noninterference criterion based on comparisons of slices of G_A, G_B, and G_M; the condition that must hold for the changed behavior of A and B to be preserved in G_M is

$$G_M/AP_{A,Base} = G_A/AP_{A,Base} \quad \text{and} \quad G_M/AP_{B,Base} = G_B/AP_{B,Base}.$$

On vertices in $PP_{Base,A,B}$ the graphs G_A and G_B agree, and hence G_M is correct for these vertices.

The verification of the invariance of the slices in G_M and the variant graphs is closely related to the problem of finding affected points: G_M must agree with

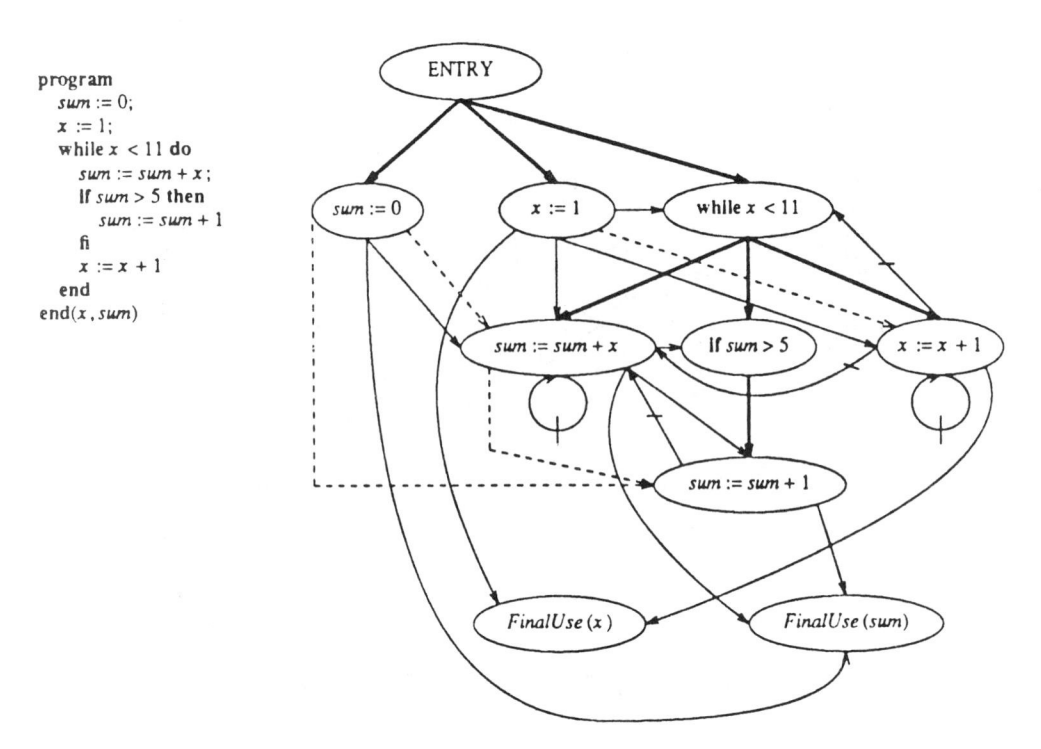

```
program
   sum := 0;
   x := 1;
   while x < 11 do
      sum := sum + x;
      if sum > 5 then
         sum := sum + 1
      fi
      x := x + 1
   end
end(x, sum)
```

Fig. 7. Variant C and its program dependence graph.

variant A on $AP_{A,Base}$ and with B on $AP_{B,Base}$. Therefore, an easy way to test for noninterference (using function AffectedPoints) is to verify that

$$AP_{M,A} \cap AP_{A,Base} = \emptyset \quad \text{and} \quad AP_{M,B} \cap AP_{B,Base} = \emptyset.$$

Example. An inspection of the merged graph shown in Figure 6 reveals that there is no interference; the slices $G_M/AP_{A,Base}$ and $G_M/AP_{B,Base}$ are identical to the graphs that appear in Figures 4(a) and 4(b), respectively.

To illustrate interference, consider integrating the base program of Figure 1, variant B from Figure 3(b), and variant C from Figure 7. As in the previous integration example, the slice $G_B/AP_{B,Base}$ is shown in Figure 4(b); the slice $G_C/AP_{C,Base}$ includes all of the vertices of variant C except for $FinalUse(x)$. The merged graph is shown in Figure 8.

Variants B and C interfere (with respect to *Base*) because B's changed behavior (with respect to *Base*) is not preserved in the merged graph G_M. In particular, the vertex "mean := sum/10" is an affected point of B with respect to *Base*, but the slice $G_M/$"mean := sum/10" includes vertices "sum := sum + 1" and "if sum > 5", which are not included in the slice $G_B/$"mean := sum/10."

4.5 Reconstituting a Program From the Merged Program Dependence Graph

The final step of the integration algorithm involves reconstituting a program from the merged program dependence graph. Given a program dependence graph G_M that was created by merging variants A and B, function ReconstituteProgram

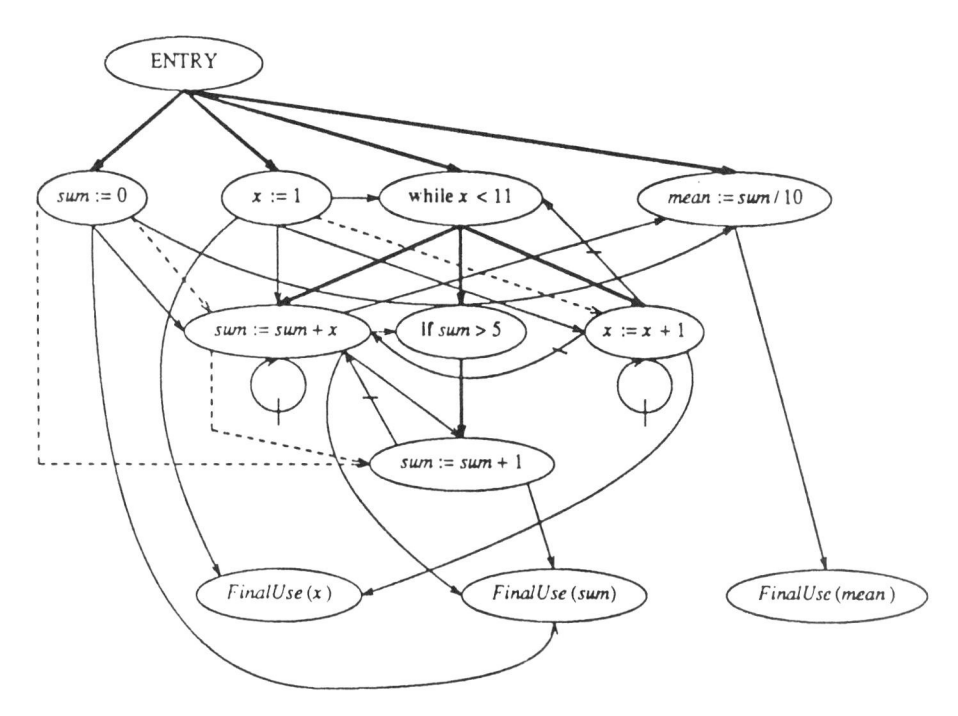

Fig. 8. The merged program dependence graph G_M resulting from the integration of Base, B, and C.

must determine whether G_M is feasible (i.e., corresponds to some program), and, if it is, create an appropriate program from G_M.

Example. The program dependence graph shown in Figure 6 is feasible and corresponds to the program:

```
program
  prod := 1;
  sum := 0;
  x := 1;
  while x < 11 do
    prod := prod * x;
    sum := sum + x;
    x := x + 1
  end;
  mean := sum/10
end(x, sum, prod, mean)
```

Because we are assuming a restricted set of control constructs, each vertex of G_M has at most one incoming control dependence edge (from a predicate vertex or the entry vertex), that is, the control dependences of G_M define a tree rooted at the entry vertex. The crux of the program-reconstitution problem is to determine, for each predicate vertex v (and for the entry vertex as well), an ordering on the targets of v's outgoing control dependence edges that is consistent with the data dependences of G_M. Once all vertices are ordered, the control dependence subgraph of G_M can be easily converted to an abstract-syntax tree.

Unfortunately, as we have shown in [18], the problem of determining whether it is possible to order a vertex's children is NP-complete. We have explored two

```
function ReconstituteProgram(G_M) returns a program or FAILURE
declare
    G_M, G, G_P: program dependence graphs
    v, w: vertices of G
begin
[1]     G := a copy of G_M
[2]     for each vertex v of G in a post-order traversal of the control-dependence subgraph of G do
[3]         if OrderRegion(G, { w | (v →_c^T w) ∈ E(G) }) fails then return( FAILURE ) fi
[4]         if v represents an if-predicate then
[5]             if OrderRegion(G, { w | (v →_c^F w) ∈ E(G) }) fails then return( FAILURE ) fi
[6]         fi
[7]     end
[8]     P := TransformToSyntaxTree(G);
[9]     if G_M = G_P then return( P )
[10]    else return( FAILURE )
[11]    fi
end
```

Fig. 9. The operation ReconstituteProgram(G_M) creates a program corresponding to the program dependence graph G_M by ordering all vertices, or discovers that G_M is infeasible.

approaches to dealing with this difficulty:

(1) For graphs created by merging PDGs of actual programs, it is likely that problematic cases rarely arise. We have explored ways of reducing the search space, in the belief that a backtracking method for solving the remaining step can be made to behave satisfactorily. These techniques are described in the remainder of this section.

(2) It is possible to sidestep completely the need to solve an NP-complete problem by performing a limited amount of variable renaming. This technique is described in Section 4.5.3, where it can be used to avoid any difficult ordering step that remains after applying the techniques outlined in approach (1).

The rest of this section describes the function ReconstituteProgram, which is invoked as step five of the program-integration algorithm. ReconstituteProgram is presented in outline form in Figure 9.

ReconstituteProgram alters graph G, which is a copy of G_M; G_M itself is saved, unaltered, for use in the test on line [9]. In the **for**-loop (lines [2]–[7]), the tree induced on G by its control dependences is traversed in postorder. For each vertex v visited during the traversal, an attempt is made to determine an acceptable order for v's children; this attempt is performed by the procedure OrderRegion, which is explained in detail below. We assume that a function, named TransformToSyntaxTree, has been provided to convert G with ordered vertices into the corresponding abstract-syntax tree.

ReconstituteProgram can fail in two different ways. Failure can occur because procedure OrderRegion determines that there is no acceptable ordering for the children of some vertex. Failure can also occur at a later point, after OrderRegion succeeds in ordering all vertices of G. In this case, TransformToSyntaxTree is used to produce program P from G, P's program dependence graph G_P is built, and G_P is compared to G_M; failure occurs if G_M and G_P are not identical. Examples of these kinds of failure are given in Section 4.5.4.

The correctness of ReconstituteProgram is captured by the following theorem.

THEOREM. *ReconstituteProgram(G_M) succeeds iff graph G_M is feasible.*

It is easy to show that ReconstituteProgram fails when G_M is infeasible: If G_M is infeasible, there is *no* program whose dependence graph is isomorphic to G_M; hence the test in step [9] of ReconstituteProgram (see Figure 9) must fail.

The proof that ReconstituteProgram fails *only* when G_M is infeasible is rather lengthy and is omitted here; the proof can be found in [5].

4.5.1 *Procedure OrderRegion: Ordering Vertices Within a Region.*

Definition. The subgraph induced on a collection of vertices, all of which are targets of control dependence edges from some vertex v, is called a *region*; v is the *region head*. If v represents the predicate of a conditional, v is the head of *two* regions; one region includes all statements in the "true" branch of the conditional, the other region includes all statements in the "false" branch of the conditional. For all vertices w, EnclosingRegion(w) is the region that includes w (*not* the region of which w is the head). Because the entry vertex and the vertices representing initial definitions and final uses of variables are not subordinate to any predicate vertex, they are not included in any region (however, the entry vertex is a region head).

Given region R, the main job of procedure OrderRegion (shown in Figure 10) is to find a total ordering of the vertices of R that preserves the flow and def-order dependences of G, or to discover that no such ordering is possible.

Note that simply using a topological ordering of the region is not satisfactory. For example, consider the dependence graph fragment shown in Figure 11.

A topological ordering of the vertices of the region subordinate to vertex C is F, D, G, E; however, the dependence graph of the program generated according to this ordering would incorrectly have flow edges from D to G and from D to H, rather than the ones from F to G and from F to H.

A secondary responsibility of OrderRegion is to project onto the head of R information from the vertices of R regarding variable uses, variable definitions, and incoming and outgoing edges. This projection ensures that, when the head of R is considered as a vertex in its enclosing region, it represents all uses and definitions that occur in R.

To order the vertices of R, OrderRegion calls procedures PreserveExposed-UsesAndDefs and PreserveSpans (discussed below). These procedures add edges to R to force an ordering of the vertices consistent with the region's data dependences. (This process is roughly that of introducing anti- and output dependences consistent with the flow and def-order dependences of region R. As explained in Section 6.1, there are fundamental problems in trying to perform integration with a dependence representation that includes anti- and output dependences; thus, OrderRegion must discover these dependences from the merged graph.) If this process introduces a cycle in R, OrderRegion fails; otherwise, a topological sort of region R produces an ordering consistent with the region's data dependences.

Information is projected onto the head of region R both by procedure PreserveExposedUsesAndDefs, which projects the loop-carried flow edges of R and the edges of G with only a single endpoint in R onto the region head, and by procedure ProjectUsesAndDefs, which projects onto the head of R information from the vertices in region R about variable uses and definitions. For example,

Fig. 10. Procedure OrderRegion adds new edges to the given region to ensure that dependences are respected, projects information onto the region head, and topologically sorts the vertices of the region.

```
procedure OrderRegion(G,R)
declare
    G: a graph
    R: a region of G
begin
    PreserveExposedUsesAndDefs(G,R)
    If PreserveSpans(R) fails then fail.else TopSort(R) fi
    ProjectUsesAndDefs(G,R)
end
```

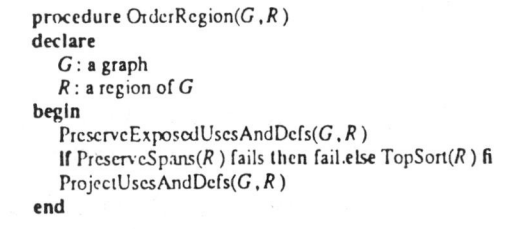

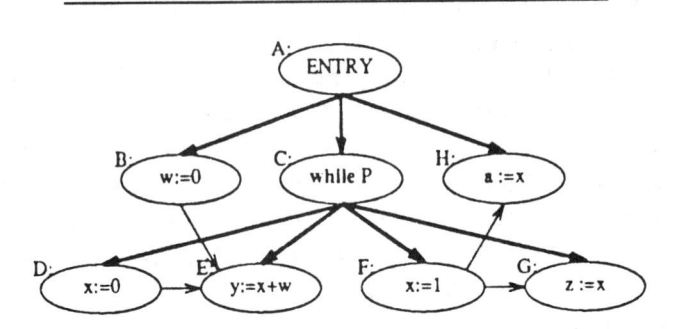

Fig. 11. Dependence graph fragment: Topological ordering F, D, E, G, of the vertices subordinate to vertex C is not acceptable.

procedure ProjectUsesAndDefs would designate vertex C of Figure 11 as representing uses of w and x and definitions of x, y, and z.

4.5.2 Procedure PreserveExposedUsesAndDefs: Preserving Upwards-Exposed Uses and Downwards-Exposed Definitions. For all variables x, a use of x that is upwards-exposed [1] within a region must precede all definitions of x within the region other than its loop-independent flow-predecessors (a use of x can be upwards-exposed and still have a loop-independent flow-predecessor that defines x within the region if the flow-predecessor represents a conditional definition). Vertex E in Figure 11 represents an upwards-exposed use of variable w.

Similarly, a definition of x that is downwards-exposed within a region must follow all other definitions of x within the region other than those to which it has a def-order edge (again, a definition of x can be downwards-exposed and still precede a conditional definition of x). Vertex F in the example of Figure 11 represents a downwards-exposed definition of variable x.

Procedure PreserveExposedUsesAndDefs uses flow edges of G having only one endpoint inside the given region R, and loop-carried flow edges having both endpoints inside R to identify exposed uses and definitions. It then adds edges to R to ensure that exposed uses and definitions are ordered correctly with respect to other definitions within the region. Finally, the edges used to identify exposed uses and definitions are removed from R and are projected onto the region head. Def-order edges with a single end-point inside R are also projected onto head(R). This ensures that the region that includes the head of R will be ordered correctly during a future call to OrderRegion. PreserveExposedUsesAndDefs performs the following four steps:

Step (1): Identify upwards-exposed uses. A vertex with an incoming loop-independent flow edge whose source is outside region R, or with an incoming

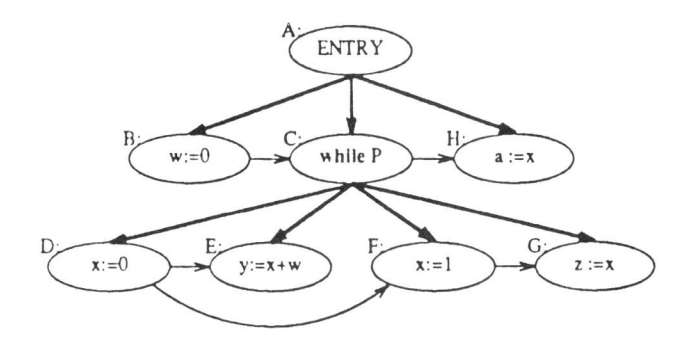

Fig. 12. Dependence graph fragment with new edge D → F added to preserve the downwards-exposed definition of x at vertex F.

loop-carried flow edge with arbitrary source, represents an *upwards-exposed use* of the variable x defined at the source of the flow edge. Mark each such vertex UPWARDS-EXPOSED-USE(x).

Step (2): Identify downwards-exposed definitions. A vertex that represents a definition of variable x and has an outgoing loop-independent flow edge whose target is outside region R, or has an outgoing loop-carried flow edge with arbitrary target, represents a downwards-exposed definition of x.[5] Mark each such vertex DOWNWARDS-EXPOSED-DEF(x).

Step (3): Preserve exposed uses and definitions. For each vertex n marked UPWARDS-EXPOSED-USE(x), add a new edge from n to all vertices m in the region such that m represents a definition of variable x, and m is not a loop-independent flow predecessor of n. For each vertex n marked DOWNWARDS-EXPOSED-DEF(x), add a new edge to n from all vertices m in the region, such that m represents a definition of x and there is no def-order edge from n to m.

Step (4): Project edges onto the region head. Let S stand for $R \cup \{head(R)\}$. Replace all flow and def-order edges with source outside of S and target inside S with an edge (of the same kind) from the source to $head(R)$. Replace all flow and def-order edges with source inside S and target outside of S with an edge (of the same kind) from $head(R)$ to the target. Consider each loop-carried flow edge $v_1 \to_{lc(L)} v_2$ such that both v_1 and v_2 are in S. If $head(R) = L$, then remove the edge; otherwise, replace the edge with a loop-carried flow edge $head(R) \to_{lc(L)} head(R)$.

Figure 12 shows the example dependence graph fragment of Figure 11 after the four steps described above have been performed on the region headed by vertex C.

The edge from D to F was added in Step (3), due to F being downwards-exposed, and this prevents F from preceding D in a topological ordering. The edges from B to C and from C to H were added in Step (4), replacing those from B to E and F to H, respectively.

---

[5] Our use of the term "downwards-exposed" is slightly nonstandard; we consider a definition to be downwards-exposed in code segment C only if it reaches the end of C and the variable it defines is live at the end of C.

4.5.3 *Dependences Induced by Spans.* To simplify this section's presentation, we begin by considering regions that only include assignment statements; under this restriction, each use of variable x within a region is reached by at most one definition of x that occurs within the region.

In the example dependence graph fragment of Figure 12, the ordering D, F, E, G of the vertices subordinate to vertex C is a topological ordering, but an unacceptable one for our purposes. The problem with this ordering is that it allows the definition of variable x at vertex F to "capture" the use of x at vertex E. The dependence graph of the program generated according to this ordering would incorrectly have a flow edge from F to E, rather than the one from D to E. In general, a definition d of variable x must precede all uses it reaches via loop-independent flow edges; other definitions of x must either precede d or follow all the uses reached by d. This observation leads to the following definition:

Definition. The *span* of a definition d, where d defines variable x, is the set $\{d\}$, together with all uses of x that are loop-independent flow targets of d and in the same region as d.

$$\text{Span}(d, x) = \{d\} \cup \{u \mid (d \rightarrow_{li}^{x} u) \in E(\text{EnclosingRegion}(d))\}.$$

Span(d, x) is called an x-span, and vertex d is its *head*.

Restating the observation above in terms of spans, a definition d_1 of variable x must precede all vertices in Span(d_1, x); other definitions of x must either precede d_1 or follow all vertices in Span(d_1, x). Furthermore, for any other x-span with head d_2, if *any* vertex in Span(d_1, x) must precede a vertex in Span(d_2, x), then *all* vertices in Span(d_1, x) must precede d_2.

Unacceptable topological orderings are excluded by considering, for each variable x, all pairs $\langle d_1, d_2 \rangle$ of definitions of x. If there is some vertex v in Span(d_1, x) that must precede some vertex w in Span(d_2, x), because of a path from v to w, then edges are added from all vertices in Span(d_1, x) − Span(d_2, x) to vertex d_2. Similarly, if there is a path from a vertex in Span(d_2, x) to a vertex in Span(d_1, x), edges are added from all vertices in Span(d_2, x) − Span(d_1, x) to vertex d_1. For example, in the graph fragment of Figure 12, the edge E → F would be added because the edge D → F (introduced by PreserveExposedUsesAndDefs) forms a path from Span(D, x) to Span(F, x), and vertex E is in Span(D, x) − Span(F, x).

The reason for taking the set difference Span(d_1, x) − Span(d_2, x) is that, even in regions containing only assignment statements, spans can overlap, as illustrated in Figure 13.

Because C is itself in Span(B, x), adding edges from *all* vertices in Span(B, x) to C would create a self-loop at C, making a topological ordering impossible.

Allowing vertices that represent loops and conditionals introduces the possibility that spans may overlap in two new ways, as illustrated in Figure 14.

In the first case in Figure 14 there must be a def-order dependence edge from d_1 to d_2, or *vice versa*, or the graph would fail the interference test of Section 4.4. In the second case there is a flow edge from d_1 to d_2. These edges force an ordering of the two spans. Thus, allowing conditionals and loops does not complicate PreserveSpans.

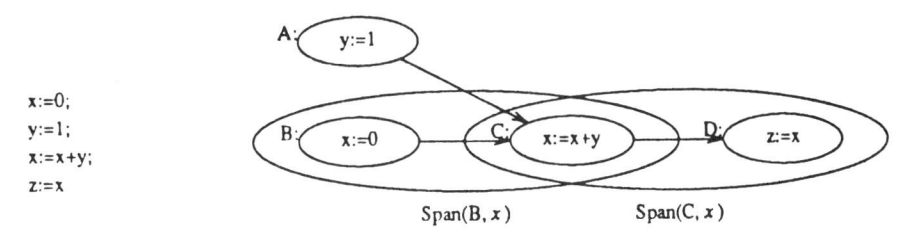

Fig. 13. Straight-line code fragment and corresponding dependence graph fragment (control edges omitted) with overlapping x-spans.

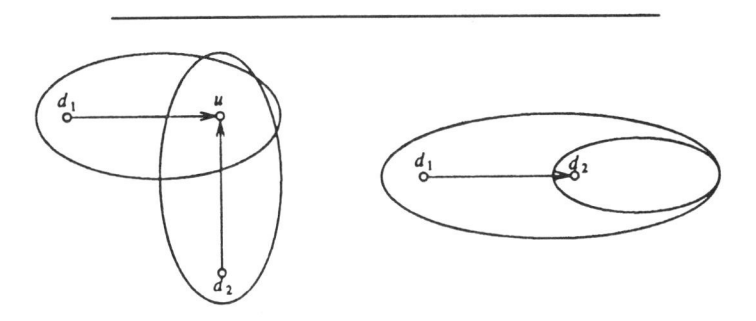

Fig. 14. Conditionals and loops can lead to the two additional kinds of overlapping spans shown above.

There may be pairs of spans, Span(d_1, x) and Span(d_2, x), such that there is no path in either direction between Span(d_1, x) and Span(d_2, x); such pairs are called *independent x-span pairs*. It is still necessary to add edges to force one span to precede the other so as to exclude unacceptable topological orderings. Although it might seem that an arbitrary choice can be made, Figure 15 gives an example in which making the wrong choice leads to the introduction of a cycle in a fragment of a feasible graph.

The fragment of Figure 15 includes two x-spans: Span(A, x) and Span(D, x), and two y-spans: Span(B, y) and Span(C, y). There are paths neither between the two x-spans nor between the two y-spans; thus, it appears that one is free to choose to add edges from the vertices of Span(A, x) to vertex D, or from the vertices of Span(D, x) to vertex A, or from the vertices of Span(B, y) to vertex C, or from the vertices of Span(C, y) to vertex B. However, while three out of these four choices lead to a successful ordering of the vertices, choosing to add edges from the vertices of Span(D, x) to vertex A leads to the introduction of a cycle. This is because the introduction of these new edges creates paths both from a vertex in Span(B, y) to a vertex in Span(C, y), and *vice versa*. Figure 16 shows the fragment of Figure 15 with the new edges added; the path from Span(C, y) to Span(B, y) is shown using dashed lines. The path from Span(B, y) to Span(C, y) is shown using dotted lines.

Unfortunately, as we have shown in [18], the problem of determining the right choice in a situation like the one illustrated in Figure 15 is NP-complete. However, we expect that in practice there will be very few such choices to be made, and a simple backtracking algorithm will suffice: if a cycle is introduced when ordering spans, procedure PreserveSpans backtracks to the most recent choice point and

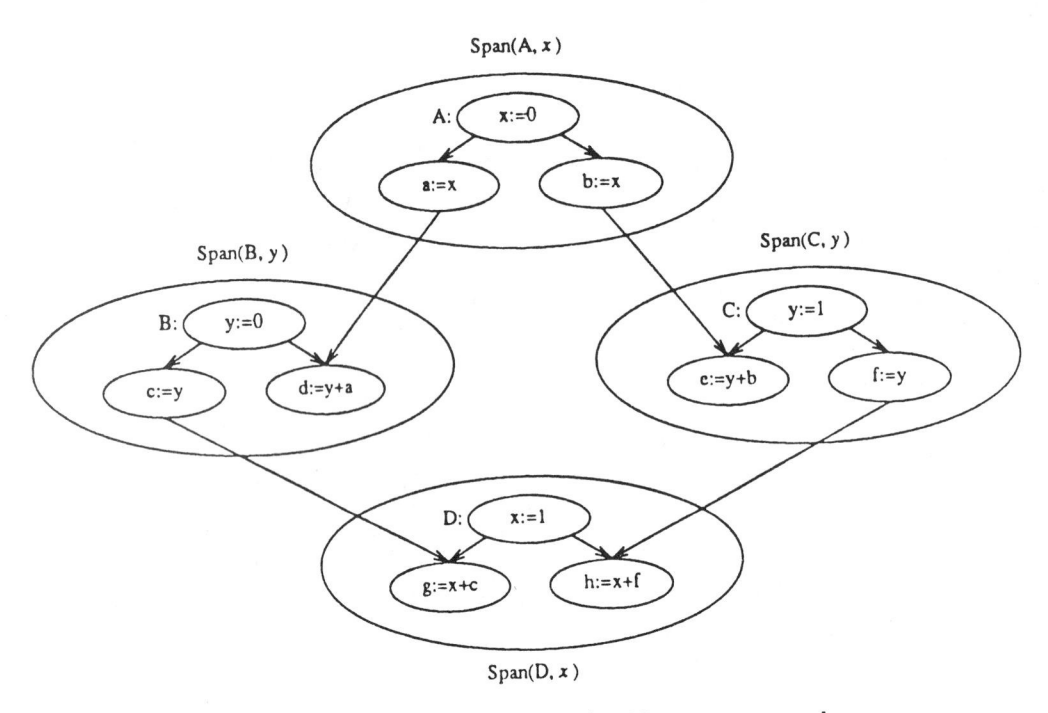

Fig. 15. Graph fragment (control edges omitted) with two x-spans and two y-spans.

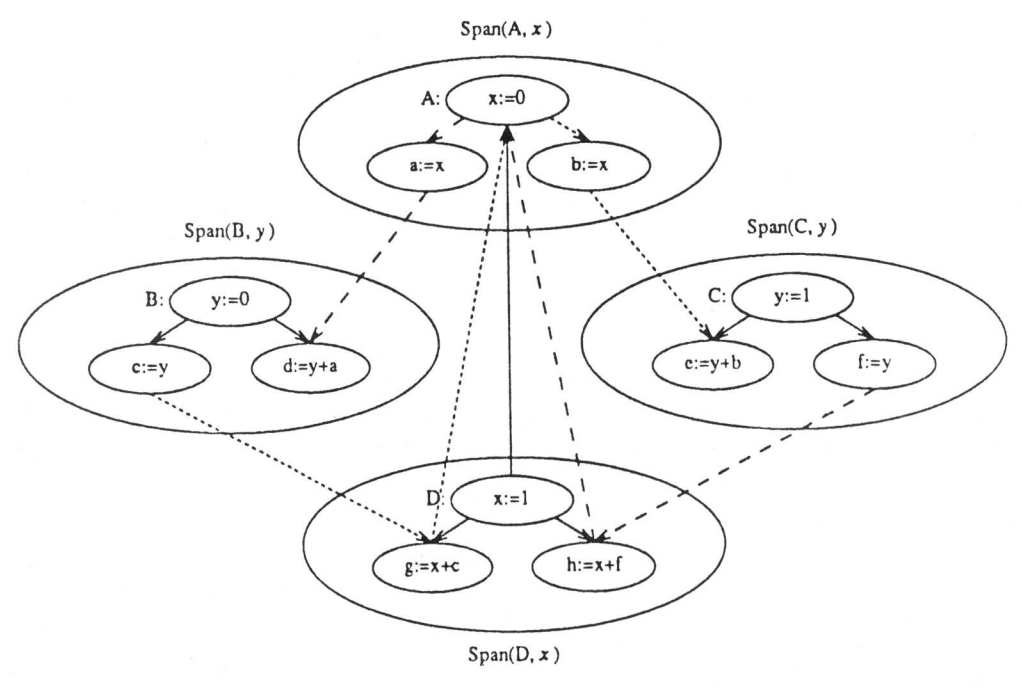

Fig. 16. Span(D, x) has been chosen to precede Span(A, x). Paths have been created from Span(B, y) to Span(C, y) and *vice versa*. The path from Span(C, y) to Span(B, y) is indicated using dashed edges; the path from Span(B, y) to Span(C, y) is indicated using dotted edges.

tries a different choice. If all choices lead to the introduction of a cycle, the graph is infeasible. Procedure PreserveSpans is presented in Figure 17.

PreserveSpans makes use of an auxiliary procedure, OrderDependentSpans, to order any span pairs of region R whose relative order is forced by a connecting

```
procedure PreserveSpans(R)
declare
    R: a region
    h₁, h₂: vertices of R
    Stack: a stack
begin
    TransitivelyClose(R)
    If R is cyclic then fail fi
    Unmark all edges of R
    OrderDependentSpans(R)
    Stack := EmptyStack()
    do
        R is acyclic and there exist independent x-span pairs (for some variable x) with heads h₁ and h₂ →
            Push(Stack, R, h₁, h₂)
            AddEdgeAndClose(R, (h₁, h₂))
            OrderDependentSpans(R)
    [] R is cyclic and Empty(Stack) → fail
    [] R is cyclic and ¬Empty(Stack) →
            R, h₁, h₂ := Pop(Stack)
            AddEdgeAndClose(R, (h₂, h₁))
            OrderDependentSpans(R)
    od
end

procedure OrderDependentSpans(R)
declare
    R: a region
    a, b, c, u, v, w: vertices of R
    A, B: sets of vertices
    x: a variable
begin
    while there exists an unmarked edge (v, w) in R do
[1]     Mark edge (v, w)
[2]     for each variable x ∈ (Defs(v) ∪ Uses(v)) ∩ (Defs(w) ∪ Uses(w)) do
            /* v is in an x-span and w is in an x-span */
            A := { u | v ∈ Span(u, x) }  /* heads of x-spans of which v is a member */
            B := { u | w ∈ Span(u, x) }  /* heads of x-spans of which w is a member */
[3]         for each vertex a ∈ A do
[4]             for each vertex b ∈ B do
[5]                 for each c ∈ (Span(a, x) − Span(b, x)) do
                        if (c, b) ∉ E(R) then AddEdgeAndClose(R, (c, b)) fi
                    end
                end
            end
        end
    end
end
```

Fig. 17. Procedure PreserveSpans introduces edges into region R to preserve the spans of R.

path. An invariant of the two procedures, established in the first line of PreserveSpans, is that graph R is transitively closed. The basic operation used in PreserveSpans and OrderDependentSpans is "AddEdgeAndClose(R, (a, b))", whose first argument is a graph and whose second argument is an edge to be added to the graph. AddEdgeAndClose(R, (a, b)) carries out two actions:

(1) edge (a, b) is inserted into R;
(2) any additional edges needed to transitively close R are inserted into R.

Because R is transitively closed, paths that force span orderings correspond to edges of R; furthermore, the cost of AddEdgeAndClose is quadratic (rather than cubic) in the number of vertices of R.

Each edge of R can be *marked* or *unmarked*; the edges added to R by AddEdgeAndClose (by either 1 or 2) are unmarked. Edges are marked at line [1] in OrderDependentSpans. An invariant of the **while**-loop in Order-DependentSpans is that, for each marked edge e, all spans for which e forces an ordering are appropriately ordered. Thus, after an unmarked edge (v, w) is selected (and marked), the invariant is reestablished as follows: line [2] generates all variables x for which both v and w are elements of an x-span (but not necessarily the same x-span); lines [3] and [4] iterate over all pairs of x-spans (represented by their heads), such that v is a member of the first span and w is a member of the second; line [5] orders the two spans as forced by the presence of edge (v, w).

The initial call on OrderDependentSpans in PreserveSpans serves to introduce edges for all forced span orderings. The **do-od**-loop then implements a backtracking algorithm that examines all choices for independent span pairs. Each pair of independent spans (represented by their span heads, say h_1 and h_2) represents two possibilities—the elements of Span(h_1, x) could precede the elements of Span(h_2, x), or *vice versa*. The first possibility is represented by the call AddEdgeAndClose(R, (h_1, h_2)), which introduces an edge directed from h_1 to h_2; the second possibility (which is tried only in the backtracking step, guarded by the condition "R is cyclic and ¬Empty(*Stack*)") is represented by the call AddEdgeAndClose(R, (h_2, h_1)). In both cases, OrderDependentSpans is called to introduce edges for all span orderings forced as a consequence of the new edge. (A single edge, such as (h_1, h_2), may force an ordering between spans other than those headed by h_1 and h_2.)

The information needed for backtracking is kept as a stack of triples: the graph R as it existed before a given "choice," span head h_1, and span head h_2. Backtracking terminates with failure if R is cyclic and the stack is empty, because no alternative remains to be tried. When R is cyclic but the stack is not empty, one entry is popped from the stack and the "choice" is tried in the opposite direction. (Since there are only two choices to be tried for each pair of span heads, there is no Push before continuing the search with the second alternative.) PreserveSpans terminates with success if R is acyclic and there remain no independent x-span pairs.

The cost of OrderDependentSpans can be expressed in terms of the following parameters:

- N the maximum number of vertices in a region,
- V the number of variables in the program,
- G the maximum number of spans of which any vertex is a member,
- S the maximum size of a span.

Our statement of the complexity of OrderDependentSpans is based on the assumption that the set operations Insert, Delete, and MemberOf have unit cost, and that Union, Intersection, and Difference can be performed with linear cost. At most N^2 edges can be inserted in R; for each edge, the processing cost is N^2: the cost of reclosing R, plus the product of the costs of lines [2], [3], [4], and [5], which are $O(V)$, $O(G)$, $O(G)$, and $O(S)$, respectively. Thus, the cost of OrderDependentSpans is bounded by $O(N^2 \cdot (N^2 + V \cdot G^2 \cdot S))$.

PreserveSpans performs at least one call on OrderDependentSpans; if backtracking is needed, there can be an additional factor of 2^P, where P is the number

```
    x := 0                   x := 0                  x := 0
    If P then x := 1 fi      If P then fi            If P then x := 2 fi
    y := x                                           z := x

      A                       Base                     B
```
(a)

(b)

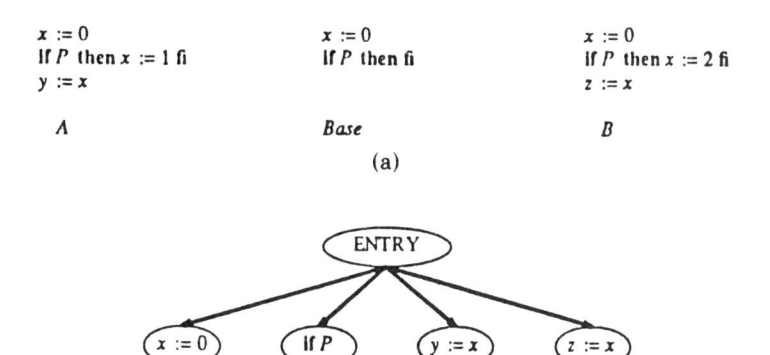

Fig. 18. Illustration of interference due to failure in OrderRegion. Fragments of a base program and two variants, and the infeasible merged program dependence graph. The vertices of G_M cannot be ordered so as to preserve both the flow edge from "$x := 1$" to "$y := x$", and the flow edge from "$x := 2$" to "$z := x$"

of pairs of independent spans that remain after the initial call on OrderDependentSpans.

It is possible to sidestep entirely the need for backtracking in PreserveSpans by allowing a limited amount of variable renaming to be performed. In particular, when two x-spans, s_1 and s_2, are independent, all occurrences of the name x in s_1 (as well as in any x-spans that overlap s_1 in the region) can be replaced by a new name not appearing elsewhere in the program. This renaming removes all problematic choices, and thus PreserveSpans need never backtrack. The disadvantage of this measure is that the integrated program will include variable names that did not appear in either variant, and thus conflicts with our goal that the integrated program be composed of exactly the statements and control structures that appear as components of the base program and its variants. Further work is needed to determine whether this technique will be necessary in practice.

4.5.4 *Examples of Interference Due to Infeasibility.* In this section, we illustrate the two ways in which ReconstituteProgram can fail. Failure can occur in procedure OrderRegion because there is no acceptable ordering for the children of some vertex of the merged program dependence graph G_M. This kind of infeasibility is illustrated in Figure 18.

An attempt to integrate any programs *Base*, *A*, and *B* that include the program fragments shown in Figure 18(a) would produce a merged PDG that includes the subgraph shown in Figure 18(b). OrderRegion would fail because the children of the vertex "**if** P" cannot be ordered so as to preserve both the flow edge from "$x := 1$" to "$y := x$" and the flow edge from "$x := 2$" to "$z := x$."

Failure can also occur in ReconstituteProgram after acceptable orderings are found for the children of every vertex in G_M. After all calls to OrderRegion

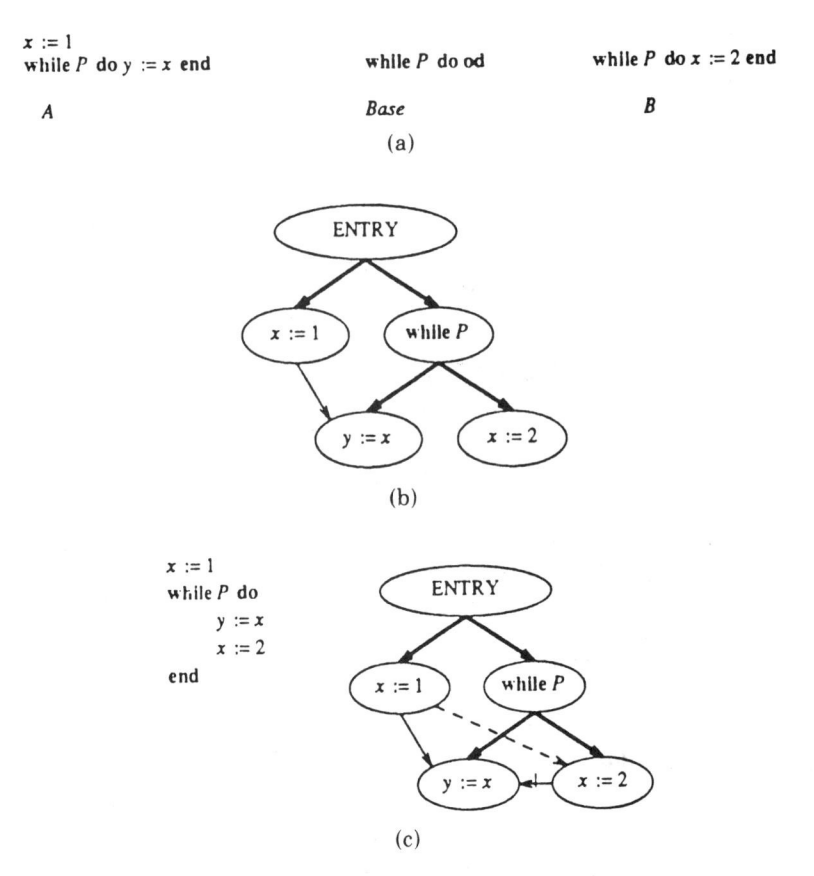

```
      x := 1
      while P do y := x end          while P do od          while P do x := 2 end

              A                         Base                          B
```
                                        (a)

```
                    ENTRY
                   /      \
              x := 1      while P
                   \     /       \
                    y := x       x := 2
```
                                        (b)

```
      x := 1
      while P do              ENTRY
          y := x             /      \
          x := 2        x := 1      while P
      end                  \       /       \
                            y := x  ←  x := 2
```
                                        (c)

Fig. 19. Illustration of interference discovered in the final step of ReconstituteProgram. The merged dependence graph G_M, shown in (b), is not identical to the dependence graph of program Q, shown in (c), which is the program generated from G_M by ReconstituteProgram.

succeed, TransformToSyntaxTree is used to produce a program P, P's program dependence graph G_P is built, and G_P is compared to G_M; failure occurs if G_M and G_P are not identical. This kind of infeasibility is illustrated in Figure 19.

Again, an attempt to integrate any programs Base, A, and B that include the program fragments shown in Figure 19(a) would produce a merged PDG that includes the subgraph shown in Figure 19(b). OrderRegion would succeed, and a program P that includes the program fragment shown in Figure 19(c) would be produced. P's program dependence graph would include the subgraph shown in Figure 19(c), which is not identical to the subgraph shown in Figure 19(b); thus ReconstituteProgram would fail.

4.6 Recap of the Program Integration Algorithm

The function Integrate, given in Figure 20, takes as input three programs, A, B, and Base, where A and B are variants of Base. Whenever the changes made to Base to create A and B do not interfere, function Integrate produces a program P that integrates A and B.

```
function Integrate(A,B,Base) returns a program or FAILURE
declare
    Base,A,B,M: programs
    G_Base, G_A, G_B, G_M: program dependence graphs
begin
    G_M := (G_A /AP_{A,Base}) ∪ (G_B /AP_{B,Base}) ∪ (G_Base /PP_{Base,A,B})
    If (G_M /AP_{A,Base} ≠ G_A /AP_{A,Base}) ∨ (G_M /AP_{B,Base} ≠ G_B /AP_{B,Base}) then return( FAILURE ) fi
    M := ReconstituteProgram(G_M)
    If M = FAILURE then return( FAILURE ) fi
    return(M)
end
```

Fig. 20. The function Integrate takes as input three programs A, B, and $Base$, where A and B are variants of $Base$. Whenever the changes made to $Base$ to create A and B do not interfere, function Integrate produces a program P that integrates A and B.

The following theorem characterizes the execution behavior of the integrated program produced by function Integrate in terms of the behaviors of the base program and the two variants [27, 28].

THEOREM (Integration Theorem [27, 28]). *If A and B are two variants of Base for which integration succeeds (and produces program M), then for any initial state σ on which A, B, and Base all halt, (1) M halts on σ; (2) if x is a variable defined in the final state of A for which the final states of A and Base disagree, then the final state of M agrees with the final state of A on x; (3) if y is a variable defined in the final state of B for which the final states of B and Base disagree, then the final state of M agrees with the final state of B on y; and (4) if z is a variable on which the final states of A, B, and Base agree, then the final state of M agrees with the final state of Base on z.*

Restated less formally, M preserves the changed behaviors of both A and B (with respect to $Base$) as well as the unchanged behavior of all three.

The cost of algorithm Integrate breaks down into three components: (1) building the program dependence graphs for $Base$, A, and B; (2) building the merged program dependence graph G_M and determining whether the changed behaviors of A and B are preserved in G_M; and (3) reconstituting a program from G_M.

(1) Building a program dependence graph is dominated by the cost of computing reaching definitions; for the limited language considered here, this has cost $O((\# \text{ program components}) \cdot (\# \text{ of assignment statements}))$.

(2) Function AffectedPoints (Figure 5) is linear in the size of its arguments; slicing a graph is linear in the size of the slice. Consequently, the cost of creating the merged graph G_M is linear in the sum of the sizes of G_{Base}, G_A, and G_B. Similarly, the cost of testing for interference by the test described in Section 4.4 is linear in the sum of the sizes of G_A, G_B, and G_M.

(3) The cost of ReconstituteProgram is dominated by the cost of the calls on PreserveSpans made by OrderRegion. If no backtracking is needed, the cost of ReconstituteProgram is $O(R \cdot N^2 \cdot (N^2 + V \cdot G^2 \cdot S))$, where R is the number of regions in the program, and other quantities are as described in

Section 4.5.3; backtracking can contribute an additional exponential factor for each region.

5. APPLICATIONS TO PROGRAMMING IN THE LARGE

An environment for programming in the large addresses problems of organizing and relating designs, documentation, individual software modules, software releases, and the activities of programmers. The manipulation of related versions of programs is at the heart of these issues. In many respects, program integration is the key operation in an environment to support programming in the large. Three specific applications for program integration are discussed below.

5.1 Propagating Changes Through Related Versions

The program-integration problem arises when a family of related versions of a program has been created (for example, to support different machines or different operating systems), and the goal is to make the same change (e.g., an enhancement or a bug-fix) to all of them. Our program-integration algorithm provides a way for changes made to the base version to be automatically installed in the other versions.

For example, consider the diagram shown in Figure 21, where Figure 21(a) represents the original development tree for some module (branches are numbered as in RCS [29]).

In Figure 21(b), the variant numbered "1.1.2.1" represents the enhanced version of the base program "1.1" (created by editing a copy of base program "1.1"). Variant "1.1.2.2," which is obtained by integrating "1.1.2.1" and "1.2" with respect to "1.1," represents the result of propagating the enhancement to "1.2." Figure 21(c) represents the new development history after all integrations have been performed and the enhancement has been propagated to all versions.

5.2 Separating Consecutive Program Modifications

Another application of program integration permits separating consecutive edits on the same program into individual edits on the original base program. For example, consider the case of two consecutive edits to a base program O; let $O + A$ be the result of the first modification to O and let $O + A + B$ be the result of the modification to $O + A$. Now suppose we want to create a program $O + B$ that includes the second modification but not the first. This is represented by situation (a) in the following diagram:

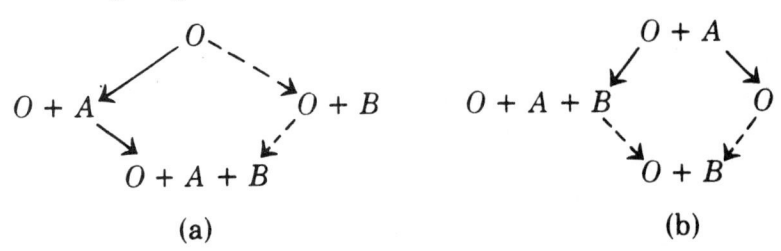

Under certain circumstances, the development-history tree can be rerooted so that $O + A$ is the root; the diagram is turned on its side and becomes a program-integration problem (situation (b)). The base program is now $O + A$, and the two

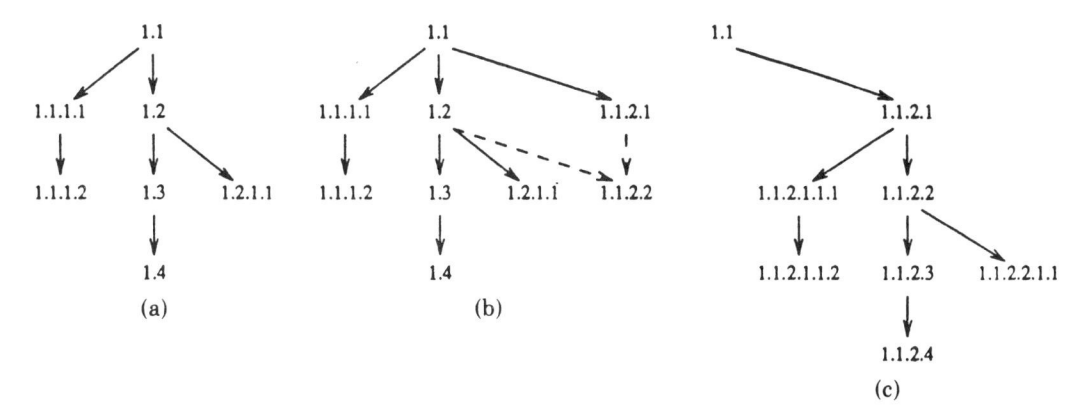

Fig. 21. Propagating changes through a development-history tree.

variants of $O + A$ are O and $O + A + B$. Instead of treating the differences between O and $O + A$ as changes that were made to O to create $O + A$, they are now treated as changes made to $O + A$ to create O. For example, when O is the base program, a statement s that occurs in $O + A$ but not in O is a "new" statement arising from an insertion; when $O + A$ is the base program, we treat the missing s in O as if a user had deleted s from $O + A$ to create O. Version $O + A + B$ is still treated as being a program version derived from $O + A$. $O + B$ is created by integrating O and $O + A + B$ with respect to base program $O + A$.

5.3 Optimistic Concurrency Control

An environment for programming in the large must provide concurrency control; that is, it must resolve simultaneous requests for access to a program. Traditional database approaches to concurrency control assume that transactions are very short-lived, and so avoid conflict using locking mechanisms. This solution is not acceptable in programming environments where transactions may require hours, days, or weeks.

An alternative to locking is the use of an *optimistic concurrency control* strategy: grant all access requests and resolve conflicts when the transactions complete. The success of an optimistic concurrency control strategy clearly depends on the existence of an automatic program-integration algorithm to provide acceptable conflict resolution.

6. RELATION TO PREVIOUS WORK

We are not aware of any other work that permits the integration of program variants so as to preserve changes to a base program's behavior. One piece of work that addresses a related, but different, problem is [7]; however, it treats the integration of program *extensions*, not program *modifications*:

> A program extension extends the domain of a partial function without altering any of the initially defined values, while a modification redefines values that were defined initially [7].

In [7], functions A and B are merged without regard to *Base*. The function that results from the merge preserves the (entire) behavior of *both*; thus, A and

```
        x := 10                              x := 11
        a := x                               b := x
        x := 12          x := 12             x := 12

          A              Base                  B
```

(a)

(b)

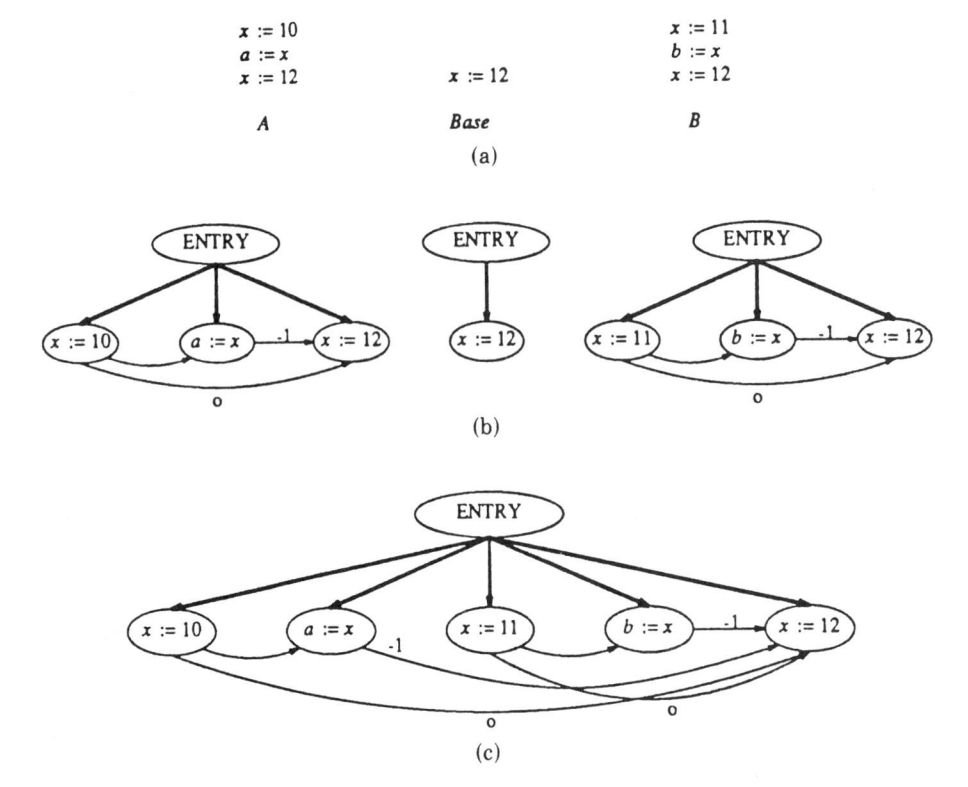

(c)

Fig. 22. A base program and two variants, the program dependence graphs that would be built for the three programs if program dependence graphs were to include anti- and output dependence edges, and the merged graph. Control dependence edges are shown in boldface; flow dependence edges are shown using (unlabeled) arrows; output dependence edges are shown using arrows labeled "o"; antidependence edges are shown using arrows labeled "−1".

B cannot be merged if they conflict at any point where both are defined. In contrast, this paper addresses the integration of *modifications* (in the sense defined in [7], quoted above). With our technique, a program that results from merging A and B preserves the *changed behavior* of A with respect to *Base*, the *changed behavior* of B with respect to *Base*, and the unchanged behavior common to all three.

In the rest of this section, we discuss some technical differences between the program dependence graphs and operations on them that are used in this paper and those used by others.

6.1 Program Dependence Graphs

There are several reasons for our use of program dependence graphs that include def-order dependence edges but omit anti- and output dependence edges. The basic problem is that, for the purposes of program integration, anti- and output dependences impose unnecessary ordering constraints. Two consequences of this problem are illustrated in Figures 22 and 23.

Figure 22 shows a base program and two variants, the program dependence graphs that would be built for the three programs if program dependence graphs

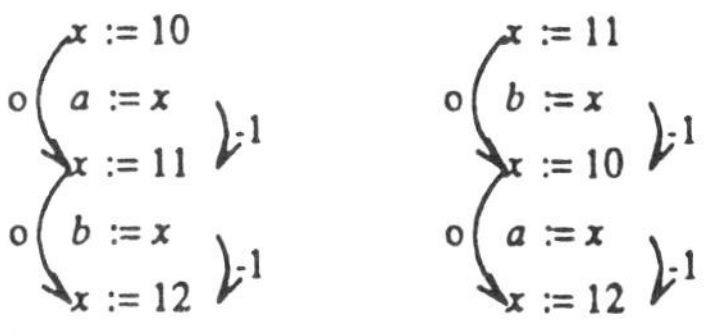

Fig. 23. Two strongly equivalent programs with different sets of anti- and output dependences (antidependences are shown to the right of the program using arrows labeled "−1"; output dependences are shown to the left of the program using arrows labeled "o"). The programs have the same (empty) sets of def-order dependences, and the same sets of flow dependences.

were to include anti- and output dependence edges, and the merged graph that combines the changed computations of the variants with the computation common to all three programs. The merged graph is infeasible; it is not possible to order the assignments to x so as to preserve the merged graph's anti- and output dependences. In contrast, if anti- and output dependences are omitted from the program dependence graphs of this example, the merged graph *is* feasible and corresponds to both of the programs shown in Figure 23 (ignore the anti- and output dependence annotations).

Figure 23 illustrates a second advantage of using def-order dependences rather than anti- and output dependences; using def-order dependences allows a larger class of equivalent programs to have the same program dependence graph. Figure 23 shows two strongly equivalent programs that have different sets of anti- and output dependences (and thus would have different program dependence graphs if such graphs included anti- and/or output dependences). The programs have the same (empty) sets of def-order dependences and the same sets of flow dependences; thus, they have the same program dependence graphs, using the definition from this paper.

6.2 Operations on Program Dependence Graphs

The problem of generating program text from a program dependence graph has previously been addressed only in a context that admits a considerably simpler solution. In previous work, the program dependence graph is known to correspond to some program. For example, in the work on program slicing, because the slice is derived from a program dependence graph whose text is known, when creating the textual image of a slice, it suffices to take the text of the original program and delete all tokens that do not correspond to components of the slice [24].

Our work requires a solution to a more general problem because the final program dependence graph is created by merging three other program dependence graphs. The merged program dependence graph may not correspond to any program at all, but even if it does, this program is not known *a priori*, when ReconstituteProgram is invoked. As shown in [18], the problem of deciding whether a PDG is feasible is NP-complete.

Ferrante and Mace describe an algorithm for generating sequential code for programs written in a language with a multiple GOTO operator and impose the condition that the algorithm not duplicate any code in this process [10]. Programs written in the language they consider have a close correspondence to the subgraph of control dependences of a program dependence graph. They discuss the application of their algorithm to compiling a program dependence graph for execution on a sequential machine; however, they assume that only a certain class of optimizing transformations has been applied to the original (feasible) PDG. They assert that the transformations of this class preserve the property that the resulting graph is feasible. Thus, while their results are relevant to generalizing ReconstituteProgram to work on PDGs generated from programs with arbitrary control flow [11], they will have to be extended to account for the possibility of infeasibility.

7. EXTENSIONS AND FUTURE WORK

In this paper, the problem of program integration is studied in an extremely simplified setting. For this reason, the algorithm described in the paper is not yet applicable to real programming languages; however, we feel that the approach that we have developed provides a strong foundation for creating a system that supports program integration. In this section, we describe some of the issues we have addressed in extending our work and outline some problems for future research.

7.1 Applicability to Realistic Languages

Among the obvious deficiencies of the present study are the absence of numerous programming constructs and data types found in languages used for writing "real" programs. Certainly, one area for further work is to extend the integration method to handle additional programming language constructs, such as declarations, **break** statements, and I/O statements, as well as other data types, such as records and arrays.

The major challenge when extending the integration method to handle other programming language constructs is devising a suitable extension of the program dependence representation. For example, the simplest way of handling arrays is to treat an update to any cell as a conditional update to the entire array. However, this strategy would preclude the integration of some noninterfering variants. Analyses of array index expressions developed for vectorizing compilers provide sharper information about the actual dependences among array references [2, 3, 6, 31]. Because the definition of program dependence graphs that we use for program integration differs from that used in previous work, previous results in this area will require adaptation.

We have recently made progress towards handling languages with procedure calls and pointer-valued variables. Our results in these areas are summarized below.

7.1.1 Interprocedural Slicing Using Dependence Graphs. As a first step toward extending our integration algorithm to handle languages with procedures, we have devised a multiprocedure dependence representation and developed a new algorithm for interprocedural slicing that uses this representation [19]. The algorithm generates a slice of an entire system, where the slice may cross the boundaries of procedure calls. It is both simpler and more precise than the one previous algorithm given for interprocedural slicing [30].

The method described in [30] does not generate a precise slice because it fails to account for the calling context of a called procedure. The imprecision of the method can be illustrated using the following example:

program *Main*
  sum := 0;
  x := 1;
  while *x* < 11 **do**
    call *Add*(*sum*, *x*);
    call *Add*(*x*, 1)
  end
end(*x*, *sum*)

procedure *Add*(*a*, *b*)
  a := *a* + *b*
return

Using the algorithm from [30] to slice this system with respect to variable *x* at the end of program *Main*, we obtain everything except the final use of *sum* at the end of program *Main*:

program *Main*
  sum := 0;
  x := 1;
  while *x* < 11 **do**
    call *Add*(*sum*, *x*);
    call *Add*(*x*, 1)
  end
end(*x*)

procedure *Add*(*a*, *b*)
  a := *a* + *b*
return

However, further inspection shows that the value of *x* at the end of program *Main* is not affected by the first call on *Add* in *Main*, nor by the initialization of *sum* in *Main*. The reason these components are included in the slice is (roughly) the following: the statement "**call** *Add*(*x*, 1)" in program *Main* causes the slice to "descend" into procedure *Add*. When the slice reaches the beginning of *Add*, it "ascends" to *all* sites that call *Add*, both the site in *Main* at which it "descended" as well as the (irrelevant) site "**call** *Add*(*sum*, *x*)."

In contrast, our algorithm for interprocedural slicing correctly accounts for the calling context of a called procedure; in the example give above, the first call on *Add* in *Main* and the initialization of *sum* in *Main* are both correctly left out of the slice:

program *Main*
  x := 1;
  while *x* < 11 **do**
    call *Add*(*x*, 1)
  end
end(*x*)

procedure *Add*(*a*, *b*)
  a := *a* + *b*
return

A key element of this algorithm is an auxiliary structure that represents calling and parameter-linkage relationships. This structure, called the *linkage grammar*, takes the form of an attribute grammar. Transitive dependences due to procedure calls are determined using a standard attribute-grammar construction: the computation of the nonterminals' *subordinate characteristic graphs*. These dependences are the key to the slicing algorithm; they permit the algorithm to "come back up" from a procedure call (e.g., from procedure *Add* in the above example) without first descending to slice the procedure (it is placed on a queue of procedures to be sliced later). This strategy prevents the algorithm from ever ascending to an irrelevant call site [19].

7.1.2 Dependence Analysis for Pointer Variables. To incorporate pointer-valued variables, an analysis of pointer usage is necessary; without the information that such an analysis provides, an update via a dereferenced pointer has to be considered a potential update to every location in memory.

We have devised a method for determining data dependences between program statements for programming languages that have pointer-valued variables (e.g., Lisp and Pascal). The method determines data dependences that reflect the usage of heap-allocated storage in such languages, which permits us to build (and slice) program dependence graphs for programs written in such languages. The method accounts for destructive updates to fields of a structure, and thus is *not* limited to simple cases where all structures are trees or acyclic graphs; the method is applicable to programs that build up structures that contain cycles.

Unlike the situation that exists for programs with (only) scalar variables—where there is a fixed "layout" of memory—for programs that manipulate heap-allocated storage, not all accessible memory locations are named by program variables. In the latter situation, new memory locations are allocated dynamically in the form of cells taken from the heap. To compute data dependences between constructs that manipulate and access heap-allocated storage, our starting point is the method described by Jones and Muchnick in [20], which, for each program point q, determines a set of structures that approximates the different "layouts" of memory that can possibly arise at q during execution. We extend the domain employed in the Jones–Muchnick abstract interpretation so that the (abstract) memory locations are labeled by the program points that set their contents. Flow dependences are then determined from these memory layouts according to the component labels found along the access paths that must be traversed to evaluate the program's statements and predicates during execution.

7.2 An Interactive Integration Tool

It remains to be seen how often integrations of real changes to programs of substantial size can be automatically accommodated by our integration technique. Due to fundamental limitations on determining information about programs via data-flow analysis and on testing equivalence of programs, both the procedure for identifying changed computations and the test for interference must be *safe* rather than *exact*. Consequently, the integration algorithm will report interference in some cases where no real conflict exists. Whether or not fully automatic integration is a realistic proposition can be determined only through experience; an integration tool must be built and used on real programs.

A successful integration tool will certainly have to provide facilities for programmers to cope with reported interference—facilities that would enable diagnosing spurious interference of the kind described above, as well as aids for resolving true conflicts. For these situations, it is not enough merely to detect and report interference; one needs a tool for *semiautomatic, interactive integration* so that the user can guide the integration process to a successful completion. Some rudimentary diagnostic facilities have been incorporated in a prototype program-integration tool embedded in an editor created using the Synthesizer Generator [25, 26]. The tool's integration command invokes the integration algorithm on a base program and two variants, and reports whether the variant programs interfere. If interference is reported, it is possible for the user to examine sites of potential conflicts—sites which may or may not represent actual conflicts. (Roughly speaking, the sites reported are those at which slices of the two variants become "intertwined" in the merged graph.) The tool's slice command makes it possible for the user to display the elements of program slices; slicing can be invoked to provide further information about potential integration conflicts.

Further work on this tool is needed to provide capabilities for the user to resolve conflicts and create a satisfactory merged program. Renaming program variables and suppressing dependences between program components would be two ways a user might interact with an interactive integration tool. Conflict-resolution facilities could operate directly on the merged program dependence graph, which is built by the integration algorithm whether or not the variants interfere.

7.3 Alternative Program-Integration Criteria

We anticipate that it will be useful to define variations on the technique presented in this paper. It will undoubtedly be desirable for users to be able to supply pragmas to furnish additional information to the program-integration system. For example, a user-supplied assertion that a change to a certain module in one variant does not affect its functionality (only its efficiency, for example) could be used to limit the scope of slicing and interference testing.

A somewhat different possibility exists when one can anticipate that a successfully integrated program will never have to be examined by a human programmer. Under these conditions, there are perhaps more liberal notions of program integration; for example, the integration procedure should be permitted to rename freely any variable that occurs in the program.

Finally, there may be cases where it is desirable for programs produced through integration to have somewhat different semantic properties than those guaranteed by the algorithm given above. For example, consider the integration of programs that contain I/O statements. I/O statements could be treated as accesses to two special objects *input* and *output*, which may be thought of as streams that are updated whenever operations are performed on them. For example, an output statement "**write** x" could be treated as an assignment "*output* := *output* | StringValueOf(x)," where the symbol " | " represents string concatenation. Consequently, output statements would be treated just like assignment statements in terms of detecting changes to a base program's behavior, and the relative order of output statements appearing in a program P would be captured in G_P by flow dependence edges [24]. Unfortunately, the integration of a base program with two variants that both affect the output stream would fail due to interference. Thus, it may be useful to develop an alternative representation for output statements in dependence graphs that would allow the creation of an integrated program that would not necessarily preserve the output stream of either variant, but instead produce an interleaving of their output streams. In cases where interleaved output is an appropriate property, this might make it possible to perform integrations that would otherwise fail.

ACKNOWLEDGMENTS

We would like to thank Dexter Kozen for his comments on an earlier version of the paper, the referees for their many helpful suggestions, and Thomas Bricker for his role in developing the prototype program-integration system.

REFERENCES

1. AHO, A. V., SETHI, R., AND ULLMAN, J. D. *Compilers: Principles, Techniques, and Tools.* Addison-Wesley, Reading, Mass., 1986.
2. ALLEN, J. R., AND KENNEDY, K. PFC: A program to convert Fortran to parallel form. Tech. Rep. MASC TR82-6, Dept. of Math. Sciences, Rice Univ., Houston, Tex., March 1982.
3. ALLEN, J. R. Dependence analysis for subscripted variables and its application to program transformations. Ph.D. dissertation, Dept. of Math. Sciences, Rice Univ., Houston, Tex., April 1983.
4. ALLEN, J. R., AND KENNEDY, K. Automatic loop interchange. In *Proceedings of the SIGPLAN 84 Symposium on Compiler Construction* (Montreal, June 20-22, 1984). ACM SIGPLAN Not. 19, 6 (June 1984), 233-246.
5. BALL, T., HORWITZ, S., AND REPS, T. Correctness of an algorithm for reconstituting a program from a dependence graph. Computer Sciences Dept., Univ. of Wisconsin, Madison. Tech. Rep. in preparation, Spring 1989.
6. BANNERJEE, U. Speedup of ordinary programs. Ph.D. dissertation and Tech. Rep. R-79-989, Dept. of Computer Science, Univ. of Illinois, Urbana, Oct. 1979.
7. BERZINS, V. On merging software extensions. *Acta Inf. 23* (1986), 607-619.
8. DIJKSTRA, E. W. *A Discipline of Programming.* Prentice-Hall, Englewood, Cliffs, N.J., 1976.
9. DONZEAU-GOUGE, V., HUET, G., KAHN, G., AND LANG, B. Programming environments based on structured editors: The MENTOR experience. In *Interactive Programming Environments*, D. Barstow, E. Sandewall, and H. Shrobe, Eds., McGraw-Hill, New York, 1984, 128-140.
10. FERRANTE, J., AND MACE, M. On linearizing parallel code. In *Conference Record of the Twelfth ACM Symposium on Principles of Programming Languages* (New Orleans, La., Jan. 14-16, 1985). ACM, New York, 1985, 179-189.
11. FERRANTE, J., OTTENSTEIN, K., AND WARREN, J. The program dependence graph and its use in optimization. *ACM Trans. Program. Lang. Syst. 9*, 3 (July 1987), 319-349.
12. HABERMANN, A. N., AND NOTKIN, D. Gandalf: Software development environments. *IEEE Trans. Softw. Eng. SE-12*, 12 (Dec. 1986), 1117-1127.
13. HOARE, C. A. R. An axiomatic basis for computer programming. *Commun. ACM 12*, 10 (Oct. 1969), 576-580, 583.
14. HORWITZ, S., PRINS, J., AND REPS, T. Integrating non-interfering versions of programs. TR-690, Computer Sciences Dept., Univ. of Wisconsin, Madison, March 1987.
15. HORWITZ, S., PFEIFFER, P., AND REPS, T. Dependence analysis for pointer variables. In *Proceedings of the ACM SIGPLAN 89 Conference on Programming Language Design and Implementation* (Portland, Ore., June 21-23, 1989). ACM, New York, 1989.
16. HORWITZ, S., PRINS, J., AND REPS, T. Integrating non-interfering versions of programs. In *Conference Record of the Fifteenth ACM Symposium on Principles of Programming Languages* (San Diego, Calif., Jan. 13-15, 1988), ACM, New York, 1988, 133-145.
17. HORWITZ, S., PRINS, J., AND REPS, T. On the adequacy of program dependence graphs for representing programs. In *Conference Record of the Fifteenth ACM Symposium on Principles of Programming Languages* (San Diego, Calif., Jan. 13-15, 1988). ACM, New York, 1988, 146-157.
18. HORWITZ, S., PRINS, J., AND REPS, T. On the suitability of dependence graphs for representing programs. Computer Sciences Dept., Univ. of Wisconsin, Madison, Aug. 1988. Submitted for publication.

19. HORWITZ, S., REPS, T., AND BINKLEY, D. Interprocedural slicing using dependence graphs. In *Proceedings of the ACM SIGPLAN 88 Conference on Programming Language Design and Implementation* (Atlanta, Ga., June 22-24, 1988). *ACM SIGPLAN Not. 23*, 7 (July 1988), 35-46.
20. JONES, N. D., AND MUCHNICK, S. S. Flow analysis and optimization of Lisp-like structures. In *Program Flow Analysis: Theory and Applications*, S. S. Muchnick and N. D. Jones, Eds., Prentice-Hall, Englewood Cliffs, N.J., 1981.
21. KUCK, D. J., MURAOKA, Y., AND CHEN, S. C. On the number of operations simultaneously executable in FORTRAN-like programs and their resulting speed-up. *IEEE Trans. Comput. C-21*, 12 (Dec. 1972), 1293-1310.
22. KUCK, D. J., KUHN, R. H., LEASURE, B., PADUA, D. A., AND WOLFE, M. Dependence graphs and compiler optimizations. In *Conference Record of the Eighth ACM Symposium on Principles of Programming Languages* (Williamsburg, Va., Jan. 26-28, 1981), ACM, New York, 1981, 207-218.
23. NOTKIN, D., ELLISON, R. J., STAUDT, B. J., KAISER, G. E., KANT, E., HABERMANN, A. N., AMBRIOLA, V., AND MONTANGERO, C. Special issue on the GANDALF project. *J. Syst. Softw. 5*, 2 (May 1985).
24. OTTENSTEIN, K. J., AND OTTENSTEIN, L. M. The program dependence graph in a software development environment. In *Proceedings of the ACM SIGSOFT/SIGPLAN Software Engineering Symposium on Practical Software Development Environments* (Pittsburgh, Pa., Apr. 23-25, 1984). *ACM SIGPLAN Not. 19*, 5 (May 1984), 177-184.
25. REPS, T., AND TEITELBAUM, T. The Synthesizer Generator. In *Proceedings of the ACM SIGSOFT/SIGPLAN Software Engineering Symposium on Practical Software Development Environments* (Pittsburgh, Pa., April 23-25, 1984). *ACM SIGPLAN Not. 19*, 5 (May 1984), 42-48.
26. REPS, T., AND TEITELBAUM, T. *The Synthesizer Generator: A System for Constructing Language-Based Editors.* Springer, New York, 1988.
27. REPS, T., AND YANG, W. The semantics of program slicing. TR-777, Computer Sciences Dept., Univ. of Wisconsin, Madison, June 1988.
28. REPS, T., AND YANG, W. The semantics of program slicing and program integration. In *Proceedings of the Colloquium on Current Issues in Programming Languages* (Barcelona, March 13-17, 1989). *Lecture Notes in Computer Science, 352.* Springer, New York, 1989, 360-374.
29. TICHY, W. F. RCS: A system for version control. *Softw. Pract. Exper. 15*, 7 (July 1985), 637-654.
30. WEISER, M. Program slicing. *IEEE Trans. Softw. Eng. SE-10*, 4 (July 1984), 352-357.
31. WOLFE, M. J. Optimizing supercompilers for supercomputers. Ph.D. dissertation and Tech. Rep. R-82-1105, Dept. of Computer Science, Univ. of Illinois, Urbana, Oct. 1982.

Received April 1987; revised January 1989; accepted February 1989

Software Merge: Models and Methods for Combining Changes to Programs

VALDIS BERZINS
Computer Science Department, Naval Postgraduate School, Monterey, CA 93943

(Received November 8, 1990, Revised February 25, 1991)

Abstract. We outline a model for programs and data and present a formal definition of an ideal change merging operation. This model is used to develop a new semantically based method for combining changes to programs. We also evaluate the appropriateness of the change merging operation and examine some circumstances where the specifications of a program as well as the implementations can be used to guide the change merging process in cases where the implementations conflict but the specifications do not.

Key Words: software merging, configuration management, maintenance.

1. Introduction

Combining changes to a system is a critical issue in software development and maintenance. Software systems are created and evolve in a series of extensions and changes as requirements are extended, reformulated, or dropped and as system faults are discovered and repaired. The versions of the system produced by this process can be arranged in a rooted acyclic graph representing the development history of the system [13]. A formalism is needed to develop accurate methods for automatically constructing new versions of the system by combining changes present in the development history. This article presents such a formalism and a derived method for combining changes to a program. An operation for combining changes can be useful in the contexts of parallel enhancements, alternative designs, and alternative implementations.

Different branches of the version history can represent *enhancements developed in parallel* by different engineers or teams. Semantically based tools for combining changes are useful for combining the results of such parallel efforts. Different people working concurrently on a large software system usually have incomplete knowledge of what the others are doing. Semantically based tools for combining changes are essential for preserving the integrity of such systems, since people can detect inconsistencies only if they have knowledge of conflicting decisions.

Different branches of the version history can represent *alternative designs* for the same enhancement. Automated tools for combining changes can be used to explore alternative choices for decisions in the context of software prototyping and exploratory design. The speed and accuracy provided by tool support can enable exploratory evaluations of design

This work was performed for the Office of Naval Research and funded by the Naval Postgraduate School.

"Software Merge: Models and Methods for Combining Changes to Programs" by V. Berzins from *J. Systems Integration*, Vol. 1, 1991, pp. 121–141. Copyright © 1991 Kluwer Academic Publishers, reprinted with permission.

alternatives based on experimental measurements. These processes may be impractically slow and expensive if done manually, especially when exploring combinations of several interacting design decisions.

Different branches of the version history can also represent *alternative implementations* of a system for different operating environments that are derived from a common base version of the system. An enhancement to such a software family can be developed once based on the common root version and propagated automatically to all of the environment-dependent variations by a tool for combining changes, as illustrated in Figure 1 for the case of just two alternative variations. The grey boxes represent the software components that could be automatically generated based on models and methods such as those proposed in this article. In general, there can be many branches of the development affected by a change, and there can be long chains of indirectly induced modifications, as discussed in [13]. Similar patterns of change propagation occur when a fault in a design decision is discovered only after several subsequent changes have been based on the faulty decision.

The problem of change propagation is also closely related to the treatment of inheritance in object-oriented programming languages. If a base version of an object-oriented program is represented by a set of class definitions and an enhancement by a set of subclasses that inherit from the subclasses comprising the base version, then updates to the base version should ideally be automatically propagated to the enhanced version. However, in the context of current object-oriented programming languages, the effect of such a process depends very much on the internal details of the design and implementation of both the original method and the enhanced method, and there is no guarantee that the results of the process will be predictable or correct. If the enhanced method completely overrides the base version of the method, then updates to the base version will be ignored, and if it uses the base version as a subroutine, then arbitrary changes to the base version are likely to invalidate the principles on which the design of the enhancement depends, unless all of the subclasses are reviewed and redesigned in response to each update of the superclass. The semantic model developed here may lead to automated assistance for such a review process. Methods for merging programs based on this model may also enable future object-oriented programming languages with multiple inheritance to successfully coalesce several inherited methods for the same message if they do not conflict, rather than always reporting an error or forcing the choice of just one of the inherited methods.

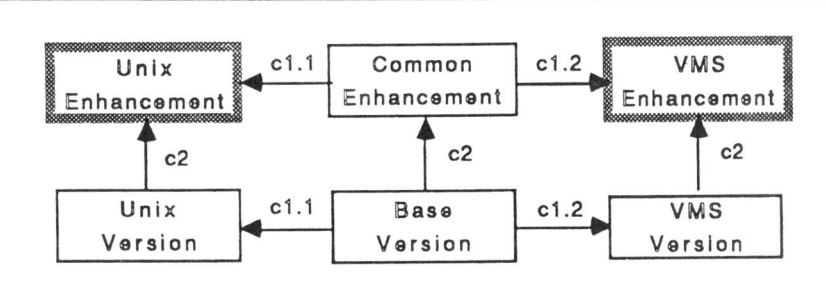

Figure 1. Automatically propagating changes to software families.

Many software errors can be attributed to the difficulty of understanding interactions between scattered pieces of code [10]. Global inconsistencies in large software systems can be particularly difficult to detect using manual approaches because no single person may be aware of all the decisions in a mutually inconsistent set. The goal of our work is to develop accurate and reliable methods for automatically combining *changes* to a system that either guarantee correctness of the combination or pinpoint conflicts if the changes to be combined conflict with each other. Such facilities should (1) make software development less error prone and (2) increase software productivity by reducing the need to repair inconsistencies introduced by system modification and reducing the amount of manual effort required for combining a set of changes into a consistent version of a system. We have focused on the semantic models defining the requirements for such a system and on formal systems for accurately deriving combinations of software changes. More work remains to develop efficient algorithms addressing complete programming languages in practical use.

Section 2 reviews some relevant previous work. Section 3 describes a semantic model for describing program behavior. This model extends approximation lattices to Boolean algebras. The purpose of these structures is to extend the ordinary data, program, and function domains to include improper values representing combinations of incompatible design decisions. This lets us formulate software merging as a total operation on this extended domain, which locates conflicts in cases where changes cannot be consistently combined. Section 4 uses the algebraic structures developed in Section 3 to provide a formal definition of an ideal operation for combining the semantics of software modifications, and determines some of the properties of this formal model. Section 5 uses the formal model developed in Section 4 to develop a new method for merging imperative programs and shows some examples of its application. Section 6 presents some conclusions and directions for future work.

2. Previous Work

There should be more work in this area because of its potential impact on software maintenance. However, this is a new and difficult area. A general theory of combining changes is hard to formulate because such a theory should be independent of the source language to have a wide area of application. A sound theoretical framework is needed to enable the construction of software tools for combining changes, since such tools must be trustworthy and accurate to be useful in practical applications.

Automatable methods for combining two versions of a functional program are given in [1], which addresses a simplified version of the problem considered in this article. The goal of the previous work was to construct the least common extension of two partial functions. This is a formalization of the problem of combining two upward-compatible extensions to a common base program. An upward-compatible extension preserves all of the behavior of the original version but adds new functionality in some cases where the original version is not defined (i.e., produces an error message or fails to terminate). The restriction to upwards-compatible extensions enabled a formulation [1] in terms of versions rather than in terms of changes between versions and allowed the common base program to remain implicit in the formulation. However, a solution to the restricted problem is not sufficient in many practical situations where software modifications are responses to changes in the requirements and produce incompatible changes. Such incompatible changes result in modified program behavior for some input values for which the previous version has a well-defined but inappropriate response. This article extends the earlier work to treat such incompatible changes, and addresses imperative programs in addition to functional programs.

The problem of merging compatible extensions is undecidable [1]. Since this problem is a special case of the problem addressed in the current work, the undecidability result and the conclusion that we must be content with reliable approximate solutions carry over to the current context. The intended semantics of merging compatible extensions was expressed using lattices and the approximation ordering $\sqsubseteq$ used in traditional approaches to denotational semantics of programming languages [15]. These lattice structures are also useful for formulating the intended semantics of combining incompatible changes, but they must be embedded in larger Boolean algebras to support a suitable difference operation, as explained in Section 3.

An approach to integrating both modifications and compatible extensions to while-programs is described in [7]. This approach defines the intended semantics of the combined program in terms of program slices [16] and proposes an algorithm for combining changes based on program-dependency graphs. The method is based on principles similar to those used in compilers for data flow analysis. This formulation gives a restricted view of correctness for the process of combining changes to programs, which is specific to the language of while-programs. The algorithm described in [7] has been shown to be partially correct with respect to this language-specific characterization of the desired semantics. The approximations used in the algorithm give partial but reliable results: in the cases for which the algorithm terminates without reporting conflicts, the results are correct with respect to reasonable criteria. Conflicts are reported when combining changes that can affect the same output variable.

This article characterizes the intended semantics of combining changes independently of the algorithms used and the programming languages on which they operate and proposes a method that can produce correct and conflict-free results in some cases where previous algorithms report conflicts [7].

3. Semantic Domains for Software Merging

This section describes the semantic domains used to construct a formal model of the software merging operation in the next section. We embed the normal data values on which our programs operate in larger mathematical structures containing additional improper data elements to let us define the software merging operation as a total function. This has the advantage of providing diagnostic information for conflicts, since our representation allows us to show exactly which parts of the programs to be combined contain conflicts, thus locating problems, and also to show exactly which constraints conflict for each problematic point. A merge operation succeeds without producing any conflicts when all of the components of the merged program are proper data elements.

We introduce improper data elements to represent overconstrained values and undefined values to let us represent programs that result from the combination of conflicting changes and programs that may diverge or terminate abnormally for some inputs. Specifically, our semantic domains are complete Boolean algebras that contain the complete lattices commonly used in the denotational semantics of programming languages as substructures.

A lattice is a partially ordered set that contains least upper bounds for all finite subsets. In denotational semantics, the partial ordering relation of a complete lattice is written $\sqsubseteq$, and $f \sqsubseteq g$ is interpreted to mean that g is a compatible extension of f. The semantic domains for traditional programming languages and the data domains corresponding to composite data structures are mostly special kinds of function spaces. If f and g are interpreted as elements of functions spaces or as composite data structures such as arrays or trees, $f \sqsubseteq g$ means that g agrees with f at all points where f is defined, and that g may be defined at some points where f is not.

A complete lattice has a least upper bound operation $\sqcup$, a greatest lower bound operation $\sqcap$, a least element $\bot$, and a greatest element $\top$. The complete lattices used in denotational semantics contain least upper bounds for some infinite sets as well as for all the finite ones. This completeness property guarantees the existence of minimal fixed points, which are used to provide well-defined interpretations for recursive definitions of elements of the lattice. The significance of the components of a complete lattice in the context of the change-merging problem can be outlined as follows.

1. The elements of the lattice represent the software objects to be combined. Different lattices are used to represent different kinds of objects, or different aspects of the same object. For example, the elements of a syntactic domain represent program texts, and the elements of the corresponding semantic domain represent the functions computed by the programs. The data value domains represent the data values on which the semantic functions act.
2. The bottom of the lattice $\bot$ represents a completely undefined (unconstrained) element, since every element of the lattice must be a compatible extension of $\bot$. The element $\bot$ can represent the result of a decision that has not yet been made, such as a fragment of a program text that is "to be determined," the result of a computation that diverges, or the result of a computation that terminates abnormally without delivering a result. The bottom element is an artificial value that represents the absence of useful information.
3. The top element $\top$ of the lattice represents a completely overconstrained element, since it must be a compatible extension of all the elements in the lattice. The element $\top$ can represent the result of merging incompatible elements and is useful in our context for representing and marking places where two or more software objects to be combined are in conflict with each other. The top element is an artificial value that represents an inconsistency.
4. The least upper bound $\sqcup$ of two elements in a lattice is the least common extension of the two elements, which represents the intended semantics of an ideal merging operation for compatible extensions. Any upper bound is simultaneously a compatible extension of both versions to be combined. The least upper bound must be compatible with every upper bound, and hence must have minimal information content. The least upper

bound of two software objects has all the features exhibited by at least one of the two objects, and no other features. For example, in a syntactic domain, the least upper bound of two versions of a program contains the parts of the text that appear in both versions, and the parts of the text in each version that correspond to an undefined element ⊥ in the other version. The result contains the overconstrained element ⊤ in all the places where both versions are well defined and incompatible with each other, and the undefined element ⊥ in all of the places where both versions are undefined. In a semantic domain the least upper bound produces a function whose graph agrees with the union of the pairs in the graphs of the two partial functions, except that input values that are associated with multiple output values by the union are associated with the overconstrained value ⊤ by the least upper bound.

5. The greatest lower bound ⊓ of two elements of the lattice represents their common part: both elements are compatible extensions of their greatest lower bound. The greatest lower bound operation is used in defining the meaning of incompatible changes. The greatest lower bound of two software objects has all of the features present in both objects, and no other features. For example, in a syntactic domain the greatest lower bound of two versions of a program represents the parts of the program text that appear in both versions and contains undefined elements ⊥ in the places where the texts of the two versions are incompatible. The greatest lower bound in the corresponding semantic domain is a partial function that is compatible with the functions computed by both programs. This function has a defined value only for those input values for which both versions of the program compute compatible values, and has the undefined value ⊥ in all other cases.

Lattice structures are sufficient for describing operations that combine versions or that combine compatible extensions of partially defined software objects [1]. Compatible extensions are monotonic in the sense that they add information without changing any previously defined features of the two versions. However, in practical situations, changes often remove or modify existing features of a software object in addition to adding new features. To model such nonmonotonic changes, we need a richer semantic structure.

Boolean algebras provide an appropriate structure for describing nonmonotonic modifications to software objects. Such modifications can change or remove previously defined functionality of a software object as well as adding new functionality. We use a class of countably based, complete Boolean algebras to model such modifications.

Every Boolean algebra is a lattice with respect to the partial ordering defined by the relations $x \sqsubseteq y \Leftrightarrow xy = x \Leftrightarrow x + y = y$. In addition to the lattice properties, a Boolean algebra also has a complement operation, which can be used to define a difference operator $x - y = x\bar{y}$. This difference operator is the additional primitive we need to model incompatible changes and to show how they can be combined.

We use notations for operations on Boolean algebras common in circuit design. Unfortunately, these notations are not the same as those used for lattice operations in the context of denotational semantics. The correspondence is shown in Figure 2. The notations for the Boolean constants and operators obey all the familiar algebraic properties of Boolean expressions. We have followed circuit designers in interpreting + as the inclusive-or operation, rather than as exclusive-or.[1] The properties of the difference operator are the same as those of the set difference operator in ordinary set theory.

Lattice	Boolean Algebra	Interpretation
⊤	1	Conflict
⊥	0	Undefined
$x \sqsubseteq y$	$x \sqsubseteq y$	Compatible extension predicate
$x \sqcup y$	$x + y$	Compatible combination
$x \sqcap y$	xy	Common part
	$\bar{x}$	Complement
	$x - y$	Difference

Figure 2. Correspondence between lattice notation and Boolean notation.

Although they obey the same algebraic laws, the Boolean algebras we are using have different interpretations than those used in digital circuit design, and typical models are larger. Circuit designers usually assume that the value sets of their Boolean algebras consist of the truth values T and F, or fixed-length vectors of truth values. For this class of models the cardinality of the value set is finite and equal to a power of two. In contrast, the Boolean algebras we use are mostly function spaces, and the cardinality of the value set is typically infinite. The spaces we use are closely related to those used by circuit designers in the sense that they are generated by countable sets of atoms. An *atom* is an element that is distinct from the bottom element 0 and has no lower bounds other than itself and 0.

The Boolean algebra representing a scalar data domain is constructed as follows. The value set of the Boolean algebra is the power set of the domain of proper data elements. The proper data values are represented as singleton sets, and these values are the atoms of the Boolean algebra. The approximation relation $\sqsubseteq$ is interpreted as the subset relation, and the operations $x + y$, xy, and $x - y$ are interpreted as union, intersection, and set difference operations in the model structures. The completely undefined element 0 is represented as the empty set, and the completely overconstrained element 1 is represented as the set of all the proper data values. Each set of proper data elements represents the least upper bound of those elements.

This construction is illustrated in Figure 3 for a traffic light data type whose proper values are given by the enumeration (red, yellow, green). The normal data values are represented by the atomic elements {red}, {yellow}, and {green} of the Boolean algebra. The undefined element 0 is represented by the empty set { } in this model. The improper element {red, yellow} represents the least upper bound {red} + {yellow}, which is an

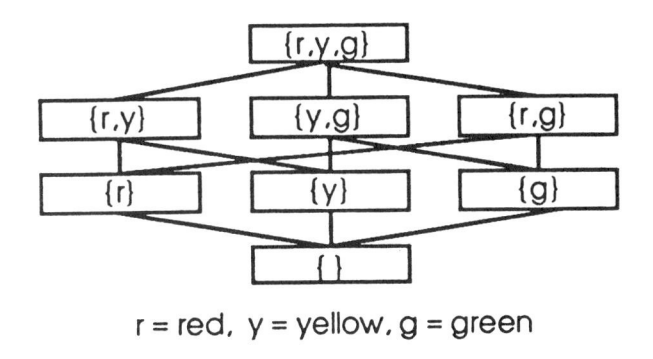

Figure 3. Boolean algebra induced by an atomic data type.

overconstrained element that is obliged to be simultaneously compatible with both of the normal data values {red} and {yellow}, and hence represents the result of combining two conflicting design decisions.

Function spaces are defined by pointwise extension based on the set of all functions from atoms (normal data values) to atoms, using the rule that the functions of the Boolean function space must preserve least upper bounds of arbitrary sets. Each atom of the function space is a function whose value is the undefined element 0 everywhere except for a set of points consisting of all upper bounds for a single atom of the Boolean algebra representing the domain of the function.

4. Language-independent Model of Software Merging

In this section we develop a formal definition of an operation for combining changes to software objects in terms of the operations of the Boolean algebras constructed in the previous section. We explore some of the properties of this definition to show that it correctly captures the informal intentions of software developers and to clarify some aspects of software evolution.

4.1. Definition of the Model of Software Merging

We identify the meaning of a program with the function it computes. These functions are treated as elements of the Boolean function spaces defined in the previous section. The Boolean function spaces contain all ordinary partial functions as a subset. The Boolean spaces have been completed to include additional improper functions whose results are overspecified by conflicting constraints. These improper functions represent results of combining conflicting versions of a program and contain information about the location and nature of the conflicting constraints. This provides a context in which the process of combining software objects can be treated as a total operation, and the results of that process can be analyzed to determine if they are free of conflicts, or to identify the parts of the input space of the combined object that produce results subject to conflicting constraints.

Informally, an operation for combining changes to software objects should be able to apply the change defined by the difference between two versions v_1 and v_2 of a software object to some other version v_3 of the software object. We can characterize the change between two software objects f and g by decomposing each version into a common part and a changed part, as illustrated in Figure 4. The diagram shows that the version g can be decomposed into two disjoint components, the greatest lower bound fg and the Boolean difference $g - f$. These two components contain all of the information in the g version because it can be recovered from them via the relation $g = (fg) + (g - f)$.

Derivation: $fg + (g - f) = fg + \bar{f}g = (f + \bar{f})g = 1g = g$

The two components are disjoint because they satisfy the relation $(fg)(g - f) = 0$.

Derivation: $fg(g - f) = fgg\bar{f} = ff\bar{g} = 0g = 0$

The software object fg represents the aspects of the object common to both versions f and g since $fg \sqsubseteq f$ and $fg \sqsubseteq g$. In terms of the functions computed by the software objects, fg is the partial function that gives the same result as both f and g for all inputs where the two versions agree and gives the undefined value 0 for all other inputs. The software object $g - f$ represents the part of version g that differs from version f. In terms of the functions computed by the software objects, $g - f$ is the partial function that agrees with g for all inputs where f and g differ and gives the undefined value 0 for all other inputs. The functions (fg) and $(g - f)$ are disjoint in the sense that there is no point in their domain for which both are defined (differ from the undefined element 0).

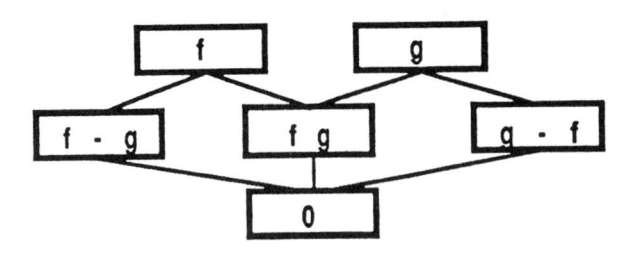

Figure 4. Characterizing software changes.

This decomposition views both versions f and g as compatible extensions of their greatest common subfunction fg. If we consider a change that transforms the initial version f into the new version g then the component $f - g$ represents a retraction: this is the behavior present in the original version f but not in the revised version g, which must be removed to transform f into g. This property is expressed by the relation $fg = f - (f - g)$.

Derivation: $f - (f - g) = \overline{f(f\bar{g})} = f(\bar{f} + \bar{\bar{g}}) = 0 + fg = fg$

Conversely, $g - f$ represents an extension: this is the new behavior added by a transformation from f to g. The roles of $f - g$ and $g - f$ are interchanged in the context of the reverse transformation from the new version g to the previous version f. The retraction and the extension characterizing a change are also disjoint from each other: $(f - g)(g - f) = 0$.

Derivation: $(f - g)(g - f) = f\bar{g}g\bar{f} = f0\bar{f} = 0$

In the special case where the change from f to g is a compatible exension ($f \sqsubseteq g$), the retraction is empty ($f - g = 0$) and the common part is the entire original version ($fg = f$).

The previous discussion characterized a change in terms of its effect on one particular version of a software object. If we wish to apply that change to a different software object, then we must have some criterion for determining the intended effects of the change on all possible objects. This is an extreme form of the inductive inference problem: we are trying to infer an entire function (the intended change transformation) from its effect at only one point (the give initial version f). Clearly, this problem does not have a unique solution. One plausible approach to our extrapolation problem is the principle of minimal change, according to which no behavior other than that contained in the retraction $f - g$ may be removed by the general change transformation, and no behavior other than that contained in the extension $g - f$ may be added. This principle suggests the change transformation $\Delta[f, g]$ induced by an initial version f and a revised version g should be defined as follows:

$$\Delta[f, g](h) = [h - (f - g)] + (g - f)$$

This transformation removes exactly the behavior contained in the retraction $(f - g)$ and adds exactly the behavior contained in the extension $(g - f)$. This operation is illustrated in terms of set-theoretic operations in Figure 5. The shaded portion shows the result of the change transformation. The diagram is simple because it shows an abstract view of the operation in terms of the power set representation of the Boolean algebra. The elements of the sets in the diagram are the atoms of a Boolean function space, and each set represents the least upper bound of the atomic functions in the set. More concrete examples follow after we explore some of the properties of change transformations.

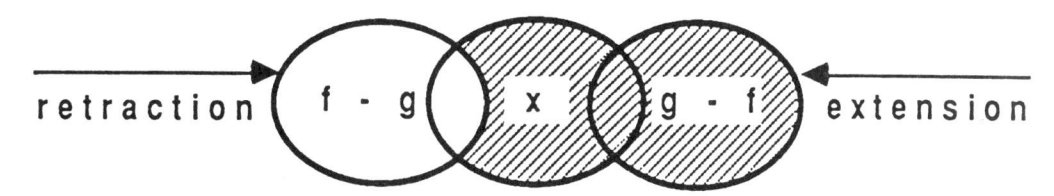

Figure 5. The change transformation $\Delta[f, g]$.

4.2. Properties of the Model

We can also express the change transformation as $(g - f) + gh + (h - f)$, since

$$\Delta[f, g](h) = [h - (f - g)] + (g - f)$$
$$= h\overline{(f\bar{g})} + g\bar{f}$$
$$= h(\bar{f} + \bar{\bar{g}}) + g\bar{f}$$
$$= h\bar{f} + hg + g\bar{f}$$
$$= (h - f) + hg + (g - f)$$
$$= (g - f) + gh + (h - f)$$

Since $gh = gh(f + \bar{f}) = gfh + g\bar{f}h$ and $g\bar{f}h \sqsubseteq \bar{f}h = (h - f)$, we note:

$$\Delta[f, g](h) = (g - f) + gh + (h - f) = (g - f) + gfh + (h - f) = g[f]h$$

where $g[f]h$ is the negmajority operation defined in [6] and corresponds to the integration operation defined in [14].[2] For economy and notational consistency, we will write $g[f]h$ for $\Delta[f, g](h)$ and $g[f]$ for $\Delta[f, g]$ in the rest of this article. We can check that the change transformation $g[f]$ has the expected effect on the initial version f as follows.

$$g[f]f = (g - f) + fg + (f - f) = g\bar{f} + gf + 0 = g$$

The intended use of a change transformation is to apply a change between two versions to a third version. However, there are two ways to do this, as illustrated in Figure 6(a). We can view the pair of versions a and b as defining the change transformation $b[a]$, which is applied to the version c, or we can view the pair of versions a and c as defining the change transformation $c[a]$, which is applied to the version b.

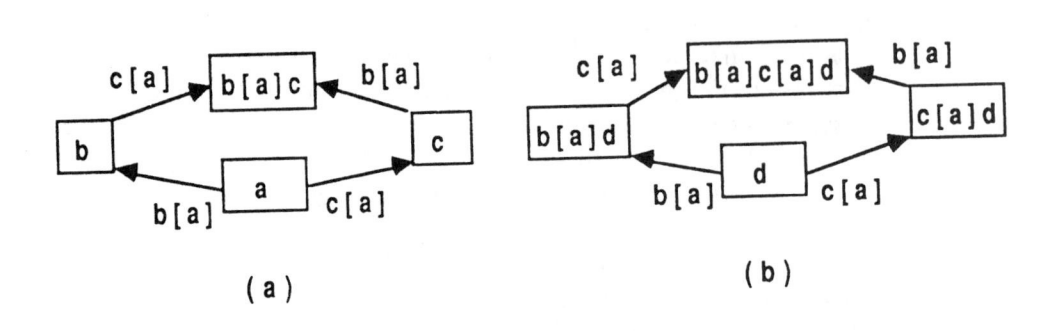

Figure 6. Commutativity of change transformations.

The following calculation shows these two processes are equivalent.

$$b[a]c = (b - a) + bc + (c - a) = (c - a) + cb + (b - a) = c[a]b$$

If we treat $[a]$ as a binary operation, this result says $[a]$ is commutative. A related question is whether the transformations $b[a]$ and $c[a]$ commute when applied to an arbitrary initial version, as illustrated in Figure 6(b). The following calculation shows this is indeed the case.

$$\begin{aligned}
b[a](c[a]d) &= (b - a) + b(c[a]d) + ((c[a]d) - a) \\
&= (b\bar{a}) + (c[a]d)(b + \bar{a}) \\
&= (b\bar{a}) + (c\bar{a} + cd + d\bar{a})(b + \bar{a}) \\
&= (b\bar{a})(1 + c + d) + (c\bar{a})(1 + d) + d\bar{a} + cbd \\
&= (b + c + d)\bar{a} + bcd \\
&= (b + c + d) - a] + bcd
\end{aligned}$$

Interchanging b and c in this result we get

$$c[a](b[a]d) = (c + b + d) - a + cbd = (b + c + d) - a + bcd = b[a](c[a]d)$$

We conclude that both diagrams in Figure 6 commute: the results do not depend on which of the two possible paths we follow. Using this result and the commutativity of $[a]$ we can show that the operation $[a]$ is also associative.

$$(c[a]d)[a]b = b[a](c[a]d) = [(b + c + d) - a] + bcd$$

Substituting $(b \rightarrow d, c \rightarrow b, d \rightarrow c)$ gives us

$$(b[a]c)[a]d = [(d + b + c) - a] + dbc = [(b + c + d) - a] + bcd = b[a](c[a]d)$$

The significance of these results is that a set of modifications to the same base version can be combined in any order without affecting the result. This lets us view change combination with respect to a common base version as a set operation. We extend our notation to represent the result of a set of changes $c_i (1 \leq i \leq N)$ to a base version b as follows:

$$[b] \sum_{i=1}^{N} c_i = \bigcup_{i=1}^{N} \bar{b} c_i + \bigcap_{i=1}^{N} c_i$$

5. A Method for Combining Programs

To develop a concrete method for combining changes to programs based on the theoretical framework developed in the previous section, we need a representation for the function represented by a program. For programs over a language whose states consist only of the values bound to the program variables, one candidate for such a representation is the program function notation proposed in [11]. This notation identifies the meaning of a program statement with a function from states to states, where a state consists of a value for each variable in the program. Meaning functions are represented as sets of pairs, and states are represented as n-tuples of values. By convention, we arrange the variables of the program in alphabetical order to determine a unique position in the state tuple for each variable.

We illustrate our approach by using the proposed representation to construct the semantic merge for the example shown in Figure 7 as follows. Our objective is to construct the merged version M = A[B]C, where B is the base version of the program, and A and C are two different modifications of B. The version M can be viewed as the result of applying the change A[B] to the version C, or equivalently of applying the change C[B] to the version A. We formally derive M via the meaning functions m(A), m(B), and m(C) corresponding to the versions A, B, and C. These meaning functions can be obtained from the program code as described in [11], with the following results.

$$m(B) = (x > 0 \rightarrow \{((x, y), (x, 1))\} | x \leq 0 \rightarrow \{((x, y), (x, -1))\})$$
$$m(A) = (x > 0 \rightarrow \{((x, y), (x, 1))\} | x \leq 0 \rightarrow \{((x, y), (x, 0))\})$$
$$m(C) = (x > 0 \rightarrow \{((x, y), (x, x))\} | x \leq 0 \rightarrow \{((x, y), (x, -1))\})$$

The state space of this program consists of pairs of values for the program variables (x, y). Thus the meaning of the base program B is a mapping that leaves the value of the state variable x invariant, and assigns either a 1 or a -1 to the state variable y, depending on the initial value of x. The notation is a shorthand for defining functions by cases, with a structure similar to guarded commands. For example, the expression $(p(a) \rightarrow \{(a, f(a))\} | q(a) \rightarrow \{(a, g(a))\})$ represents the set of pairs $\{(a, b) | (p(a) \text{ and } b = f(a)) \text{ or } (q(a) \text{ and } b = g(a))\}$, where a and b are program state tuples representing the initial state and the final state of the program, respectively.

We derive the meaning function for the merged program directly from our semantic definition of the change merging operation A[B]C using the interpretations of the Boolean algebraic operations as unions, intersections, and set differences with respect the the powerset construction for our extended semantic domains.

Base version B: if $x > 0$ then $y := 1$ else $y := -1$ fi

First changed version A: if $x > 0$ then $y := 1$ else $y := 0$ fi

Second changed version C: if $x > 0$ then $y := x$ else $Y := -1$ fi

Merged version M: if $x > 0$ then $y := x$ else $y := 0$ fi

Figure 7. Example of a conditional merge.

$$m(M) = m(A[B]C)$$
$$= m(A)[m(B)]m(C)$$
$$= (m(A) - m(B)) \cup (m(A) \cap m(C)) \cup (m(C) - m(B))$$

$$= (x > 0 \rightarrow \{((x, y), (x, 1))\} - \{((x, y), (x, 1))\}$$
$$| x \leq 0 \rightarrow \{((x, y), (x, 0))\} - \{((x, y), (x, -1))\}) \cup$$
$$(x > 0 \rightarrow \{((x, y), (x, 1))\} \cap \{((x, y), (x, x))\}$$
$$| x \leq 0 \rightarrow \{((x, y), (x, 0))\} \cap \{((x, y), (x, -1))\}) \cup$$
$$(x > 0 \rightarrow \{((x, y), (x, x))\} - \{((x, y), (x, 1))\}$$
$$| x \leq 0 \rightarrow \{((x, y), (x, -1))\} - \{((x, y), (x, -1))\})$$

$$= (x > 0 \rightarrow \{\} | x \leq 0 \rightarrow \{((x, y), (x, 0))\}) \cup$$
$$(x > 0 \rightarrow \{((x, y), (1, 1))\} | x \leq 0 \rightarrow \{\}) \cup$$
$$(x > 0 \rightarrow \{((x, y), (x, x)) | x \neq 1\} | x \leq 0 \rightarrow \{\})$$

$$= (x > 0 \rightarrow \{((x, y), (x, x))\} | x \leq 0 \rightarrow \{((x, y), (x, 0))\})$$

$$= m(\text{if } x > 0 \text{ then } y := x \text{ else } y := 0)$$

$$= m(M)$$

The first element of each pair of state tuples contains variables that are free to range over the entire state space, whereas the second element of the pair contains expressions in which all occurrences of the state variables are implicitly bound by their occurrences in the first element of the pair. For example, the function $\{((x, y), (x, 1))\}$ is equivalent to the set of pairs $\{((x, y), (z, w)) | z = x \text{ and } w = 1\}$. We obtained the intersection by unifying the range descriptions (x, x) and $(x, 1)$ to obtain the intersection $(1, 1)$ via the substitution $(x = 1)$. This kind of unification can be performed efficiently [8] and yields an exact result whenever the unification succeeds. In general, it is possible for two syntactically distinct symbolic expressions to denote the same value and in such cases the unification may fail even though the exact intersection may not be empty. Some stronger, but possibly costly, methods for recognizing the equivalence of two symbolic expressions are described in [1].

As noted in the introduction, we must be content with safe approximations or with exact methods that may in some cases fail to deliver a result because the exact change merging operation is not computable in general. It is safe but inexact to assume that intersections for which the unification fails are empty. Such inexact approximations can lead to merged programs that are partially correct but may be undefined in some cases where the exact change merging operation produces a proper result. An exact representation of an intersection of the form $\{(a, f1(a))\} \cap \{(a, f2(a))\}$ is $\{(a, b) | b = f1(a) \text{ and } b = f2(a)\}$, but this representation is not easy to transform back into a program.

After deriving the meaning function of the merged program, we must reconstruct the program text from the meaning function. In this case, the result is a program function representing a conditional statement, corresponding to the combined program shown in figure 7. Note that the result is a proper program even though both of the changes to be combined affect the same output variable y. There is no interference in this case because the two changes affect disjoint regions of the initial state space. Since the program function notation directly represents the functions computed by the programs, and the method for combining changes is directly based on the semantic definitions characterizing an ideal change combination process, correct results are assured whenever the symbolic expressions for the meaning function of the merged version can be transformed back into a program.

The transformation back into a program may be difficult or impossible to perform, and there may not be a unique solution. The conditions under which a meaning function can be realized by a program of a given form have been explored, and closed-form characterizations of these conditions can be found in [11]. Automating this part of the process is subject to a trade-off between the success rate and time spent on searching for possible solutions. The foregoing method is potentially capable of finding merged programs with algorithms and control structures that differ from both the base versions and the two modified versions, but such solutions may be computationally expensive. To find a practical resolution of this trade-off, we are exploring heuristics for guiding the search based on the structures of the three program versions to be combined and on estimates of the relative efficiency of different program structures.

The process we have described is more difficult to carry out for programs containing loops. An example is shown in figure 8. The meaning functions for this example follow.

$$m(B) = m(C) = (x \geq 0 \rightarrow \{((x, y, z), (0, y, x * y))\} \mid x < 0 \rightarrow \{((x, y, z), (x, y, 0))\})$$

$$m(A) = \{((x, y, z), (0, y, x * y))\}$$

The programs in the example are simple loops for implementing multiplication. Version C has the same meaning function as the base version B, but it has been transformed to prove efficiency. Both B and C implement multiplication for only positive values of the input variable x. Version A has been modified to implement multiplication for both positive and negative values. The meaning function for the desired merge is derived as follows:

$$\begin{aligned}
m(M) &= m(A[B]C) \\
&= m(A)[m(B)]m(C) \\
&= (m(A) - m(B)) \cup (m(A) \cap m(C)) \cup (m(C) - m(B)) \\
&= \{\ \} \cup (x \geq 0 \rightarrow \{((x, y, z), (0, y, x * y))\}) \cup \\
&\qquad (x < 0 \rightarrow \{((x, y, z), (0, y, x * y))\}) \\
&= \{((x, y, z), (0, y, x * y))\} \\
&= m(A)
\end{aligned}$$

We see that the meaning function for the merged version is the same as for the enhanced version A so that A is a possible candidate for the merged version. We have instead constructed the merged version M by replacing B by C in A. This is sound because we know B and C have the same meaning function. It is desirable because C is more efficient than

Base version B:
  $z := 0$; while $x > 0$ do $z := z + y$; $x := x - 1$ end

First changed version A:
  if $x < 0$ then $x := -x$; $y := -y$ end;
  $z := 0$; while $x > 0$ do $z := z + y$; $x := x - 1$ end

Second changed version C:
  $z := 0$;
  while $x > 0$ do
    if x mod $2 = 0$ then $x := x$ div 2; $y := y + y$
    else $z := z + y$; $x := x - 1$ end
  end

A merged version M:
  if $x < 0$ then $x := -x$; $y := -y$ end;
  $z := 0$;
  while $x > 0$ do
    if x mod $2 = 0$ then $x := x$ div 2; $y := y + y$
    else $z := z + y$; $x := x - 1$ end
  end

Figure 8. Example of merging loops.

B, and the replacement is suggested by a heuristic that prefers implemenation structures in the enhanced versions over the corresponding implementation structures in the base version.

We have made use of specification information in the above derivation, since we have identified the meaning of the loop with the multiplication function. The automatic procedures for deriving meaning functions give recursive equations for the meaning function of a program containing loops. We have taken the expected meaning function from the specification for the program and checked that it satisfies the recursive equation derived directly from the program according to the methods described in [11]. If specifications are not available, then it is sometimes possible to derive a closed form for the meaning function using techniques for solving difference equations. If the recursive equations cannot be solved in closed form, it is sometimes possible to check that two recursively defined functions are equal by showing that each satisfies the equations defining the other. This allows loops to be merged whenever one of the two changes preserves the meaning function of the loop, as in the foregoing example. This approach thus enables treatment of changes that improve the efficiency of a program.

Derivations involving loops can involve some difficult reasoning, and the method is not guaranteed to terminate in the general case. However, as we have illustrated, this method can be used to successfully merge changes to a program even if some of the changes involve choice of different algorithms. In previous approaches to this problem [7] the merged version is restricted to simulating the three original versions exactly (the same sequence of values must be read and written by corresponding program statements), where different statements in the merged version may come from different versions of the original program.

The transformation process we have described can also locate conflicts in changes that are not compatible with each other. In general, the result of the merging process is a set of pairs representing a relation on pairs of states (the initial and final states of the program). Although we would like this relation to be a function, this need not always be the case, because the union operations can associate more than one final state with an initial state. If the programs A, B, and C are free of conflicts themselves, then $m(A)$, $m(B)$, and $m(C)$ are functions, and $m(A)[m(B)]m(C)$ is a relation that associates at most two final states with each initial state. If the resulting relation is not a function, we say that it contains a conflict for each initial state that is associated with more than one final state. The programming language we consider is completely deterministic: the primitives are assignment statements, sequencing, if-then-else statements, and while-loops. Multiple-valued program relations resulting from the combination of several program modifications represent overconstrained rather than nondeterministic behavior: the program does not have a free choice of which final state to enter, but instead the unique final state of the program is required to be simultaneously compatible with all the final states associated with the initial state by the program relation. For this reason we adopt a rule that transforms multiple-valued program relations into improper functions as follows:

$$m(A[B]C)(\sigma) = \bigsqcup \{\tau | (\sigma, \tau) \in m(A)[m(B)]m(C)\}$$

where σ represents the initial program state and τ represents the final program state. A simple example illustrates a combined program relation containing conflicts, the improper program function it represents, and the corresponding improper program.

A: $x := 1$ $m(A) = \{((x), (1))\}$
B: $x := 2$ $m(A) = \{((x), (2))\}$
C: $x := 3$ $m(A) = \{((x), (3))\}$

$m(A)[m(B)]m(C)$
$= \{((x), (1))\} - \{((x), (2))\} \cup \{((x), (1))\} \cap \{((x), (3))\} \cup \{((x), (3))\} - \{((x), (2))\}$
$= \{((x), (1))\} \cup \{\} \cup \{((x), (3))\}$
$= \{((x), (y)) | y = 1 \text{ or } y = 3\}$
$= \{((x), (1 \sqcup 3))\}$
$= \{((x), (\{1\} \cup \{3\}))\}$
$= \{((x), (\{1,3\}))\}$
$= m(x := \{1,3\})$

We have converted the multiple-valued program relation into an improper function, assuming that the function space has been embedded in a Boolean algebra according to the construction explained in Section 3. The final form of the program function represents an assignment statement that binds an improper value to the variable x. This improper value pinpoints the two inconsistent design decisions in the modified versions A and C: the value must be simultaneously compatible with both 1 and 3 to carry out both modifications. Note that the value 2 does not appear because it has been superseded by both modifications.

A software designer has several alternative approaches to resolve a conflict situation such as the one just outlined, depending on whether or not the requirements changes motivating the modifications A and C are incompatible.

The requirements changes corresponding to A and C might be compatible even through the particular program functions A and C are not compatible because a requirement might only partially constrain program behavior and might thus be consistent with several different program functions. This situation is illustrated in figure 9. We represent a requirement by the set of program functions that satisfy it (thus a requirement is formalized as a predicate on program functions, which distinguishes conforming behaviors from nonconforming behaviors). In terms of this representation, two requirements are compatible if their intersection is nonempty. In such a situation, the designer may choose to merge the two modifications A[B] and C[B] to produce a program D, which computes a function D which is incompatible with both A and C, but which is compatible with both of the requirements that motivated the initial choices of the behaviors A and C. This kind of transformation requires knowledge of the requirements as well as the programs, and is likely to be difficult to automate, because it requires the derivation of an implementation of a completely new function D without much guidance from existing implementations of compatible subfunctions. We expect such situations to be handled in an interactive fashion, with the deeper reasoning performed by a skilled human designer and some of the more apparent details potentially derived by automated design support tools. Automation requires a formal approach at the conceptual modeling and functional specification stages [2, 4].

If the two requirements are incompatible, there are two ways to proceed: either evaluate the priorities of the goals supported by each and abandon the one with the lower priority, or examine the higher-level goals that motivated the requirements, and seek to loosen the requirements in such a way that the higher-level goals are still met but the loosened requirements have a nonempty intersection. This kind of process is likely to involve informal reasoning because the higher-level goals are usually not completely formalized. For this reason we expect this part of the process to be carried out mainly by skilled people rather than by software.

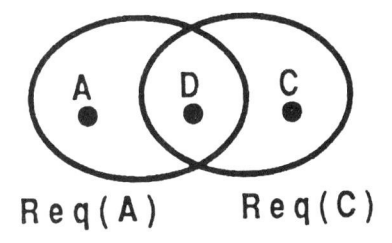

Figure 9. Partially overlapping requirements.

6. Conclusions and Future Work

Large programming projects are characterized by concurrent efforts of a group of software engineers. The new problems that arise on such a scale involve coordinating, propagating, and reconciling the consequences of design descisions made by different people. A reliable method for combining changes to programs is an essential aspect of the computer-aided design capabilities that should be provided by software development environments for large programs. Such a capability would enable different people to concurrently develop updates to the same software object without the need for locking or mutual exclusion and would allow the results to be combined after the independent updates have resulted in two alternative versions of the software object. Such situations may be common in large projects with aggressive schedules. A capability for combining changes is also useful in the situation where a design decision is found to be faulty after some subsequent decisions and software modifications have already been made. In such a case, the developer would back up to the version before the faulty decision, make an alternative enhancement corresponding to a different choice for the faulty decision, and then use the computer-aided change combination facilities to combine the alternative enhancement with the modifications that had been made based on the faulty decision. Such a tool would locate the places where these modifications conflict with the new design and would guarantee the integrity of the results if no conflicts were detected.

We have provided a characterization of the semantic properties of an operation for combining changes to software objects. This characterization is independent of the programming language in which the software objects are described, and can be applied in many contexts. For example, the algorithm in [7] is correct with respect to our characterization for the cases in which it does not report any conflicts. The theory can also be applied to requirements and specifications, if we accept the view that a specification is a predicate that characterizes the set of all acceptable system behaviors, although the details of this are not explored further here.

We have applied our ideal characterization of the change combination process to propose a new method for integrating changes to programs. The new method for combining changes is correct because it is based on direct representations of the functions computed by programs. Our approach has also been applied to other languages, notably the Prototype System Description Language PSDL. PSDL is a language for prototyping large, real-time systems, which is based on an enhanced data flow model of computation [12]. This language includes features for expressing concurrency and real-time constraints. A formal semantics of PSDL can be found in [9]. An initial version of a method for combining changes to PSDL programs has been developed [5]. We are also investigating the application of this framework to the development of program transformations that change the semantics of a program in a disciplined way [3]. Such transformations are important in software evolution and form a complement to the meaning-preserving transformations that are used in implementing executable specification languages and in program optimization.

This article outlines a method for merging changes to monolithic (small) imperative programs based on our semantic model. These results represent a single step towards reliable automated software merging and computer-aided configuration management. Much more work remains to be done before this technology can be routinely applied in large-scale software development projects.

Our vision of future facilities for software development and maintenance includes a configuration management system that provides more functions than most of the systems in current use. We expect such future systems to be sensitive to the semantics of the programming and specification languages used and to be capable of automatically merging changes and automatically analyzing the structure and content of a software design. In the long run such systems should have many capabilities related to the semantic compatibility relation $\sqsubseteq$ at the root of our model, such as factoring software objects into prime independent components and storing design histories in terms of prime decompositions of design decisions, with possible alternatives for each decision. A reliable change merging facility is needed to get the maximum benefit from such a vision because engineers cannot rely on mechanically merged versions of software objects unless they have predictable properties. Such a facility would enable automatic synthesis of system variants driven by different combinations of stored choices for sets of independent design decisions. Many of the combinations that could be realized by such a system will not have been explicitly created by human designers.

A representation for software systems that decomposes software objects into independent design decisions promises to be a more useful record of a design history that the chronological sequence of steps that lead to the current configuration because the logical dependencies are needed to understand and change a design. This logical structure may be only weakly related to the chronological order in which changes were made. It would be useful to formalize this logical structure to the point where computer-aided factoring and recombination of software objects becomes feasible. However, realizing this vision may require integrated change merging at the levels of software requirements and behavioral specifications as well as algorithms and data structures.

Notes

1. The exclusive-or interpretation for $+$ is used in the study of Boolean rings because this operation has all of the usual algebraic properties of addition.
2. The program integration operation is defined in terms of the pseudo-difference operation of a Browerian algebra, instead of the difference operation of a Boolean algebra because the graphs used in the algorithm do not satisfy all the properties of a Boolean algebra. Every Boolean algebra is a Browerian algebra, but Browerian algebras need not satisfy the law $1 - (1 - x) = x$.

References

1. V. Berzins, "On merging software extensions," *Acta Inform.*, 23, Fasc. 6, pp. 607–619, November 1986.
2. V. Berzins, M. Gray, and D. Naumann, "Abstraction-based software development," *Comm. of the ACM*, 29(5), pp. 402–415, May 1986.
3. V. Berzins, B. Kopas, Luqi, and A. Yehudai, "Transformations in specification-based software evolution," Technical Report NPS 52-90-034, Computer Science Department, Naval Postgraduate School, Monterey, CA, 1990.

4. A. Berztiss, "The set-function approach to conceptual modeling," in *Information System Design Methodologies*, T. Olle, H. Sol, and A. Verrigh-Stuart (Eds.), North-Holland, Amsterdam, 1986, pp. 107-144.
5. D. Dampier, "A model for merging different versions of a PSDL program," M.S. thesis, Dept. of Computer Science, Naval Postgraduate School, Monterey, CA, June 1990.
6. C.A.R. Hoare, "A couple of novelties in the propositional calculus," *Z. Mathematische Logik und Grundlagen der Mathematik*, 31, (2) (1985), 173-178.
7. S. Horowitz, J. Prins, and T. Reps, "Integrating non-interfering versions of programs," *Trans. Prog. Lang. Systems*, 11(3), pp. 345-387, July 1989.
8. D. Kapur, M. Krishnamoorthy, and P. Narendran, "A new linear algorithm for unification," Report 82CRD100, Corporate Research and Development, General Electric, Schenectady, New York, 1982.
9. B. Kraemer, Luqi, and V. Berzins, "Denotational semantics of a real-time prototyping language," Technical Report NPS 52-90-033, Computer Science Department, Naval Postgraduate School, Monterey, CA, 1990.
10. S. Letovsky and E. Soloway, "Delocalized plans and program comprehension," *IEEE Software*, 3(3), pp. 41-49, May 1986.
11. R.C. Linger, H.D. Mills, and B.I. Witt, *Structured Programming: Theory and Practice*, Addison-Wesley: Reading, MA, 1979.
12. Luqi, V. Berzins, and R. Yeh, "A prototyping language for real-time software," *IEEE Trans. Software Eng.*, 14 (10) pp. 1409-1423, October 1988.
13. Luqi, "A graph model for software evolution," *IEEE Trans. Software Eng.*, 16(8), pp. 917-927, August 1990.
14. T. Reps, "On the algebraic properties of program integration," Computer Sciences Technical Report 856, University of Wisconsin, Madison, 1989.
15. J. Stoy, *Denotational Semantics: The Scott-Strachey Approach to Programming Language Theory*, MIT Press: Cambridge, MA, 1977.
16. M. Weiser, "Program slicing," *IEEE Trans. Software Eng.*, SE-10(4), pp. 352-357, July 1984.

IV. Merging for Other Languages

Overview of the papers

The first paper in this section by Luqi explains the large-scale context of change merging and illustrates how a merging tool might fit into an integrated system for configuration management, project planning, project scheduling, and team coordination. A graph model represents the dependencies between different versions of a software system. Merging is used to recombine parallel lines of development, which appear as paths in the graph model. The model's novel feature is that it includes representations of development activities, as well as representations of the products produced by the activities.

In the second paper, Dampier, Luqi, and Berzins describe a merging method for the prototype description language PSDL. The novel features of this language are hard real-time constraints, parallel computation, and nondeterminism. The merging method is based on an extension of the slicing idea. Dampier describes an implementation of this method. Sterling and Lakhotia (1988) offer a merging method for Prolog, limited to compatible extensions. Berzins and Luqi (1991) describe a merging method for specifications that is part of the inheritance mechanism in the Spec language.

Remaining challenges

The main challenge for developing merging methods for languages with significantly different models of computation is to develop suitable semantic representations of programs that can efficiently support the operations of semantic union, semantic intersection, and semantic difference. For very large-scale systems problems arise in modeling and merging differences in interfaces (Berzins, Luqi, and Yehudai, 1993). Computational problems include transforming back and forth between concrete programs and the corresponding semantic representations; recognizing semantic equivalences between syntactically distinct programs; and determining semantic dependencies.

References

Sterling, L., and A. Lakhotia, "Composing Prolog Meta-Interpreters," *Logic Programming Proc. 4th Int'l Conf. and Symp.,* MIT Press, Cambridge, Mass., 1988, pp. 386–403.

Berzins, V., and Luqi, *Software Engineering with Abstractions,* Addison-Wesley, Reading, Mass., 1991, pp. 182–188.

Berzins, V., Luqi, and A. Yehudai, "Using Transformations in Specification-Based Prototyping," *IEEE Trans. Software Eng.,* Vol. 19, No. 5, May 1993, pp. 436–452.

A Graph Model for Software Evolution

LUQI

Abstract—This paper presents a graph model of software evolution. We seek to formalize the objects and activities involved in software evolution in sufficient detail to enable automatic assistance for maintaining the consistency and integrity of an evolving software system. This includes automated support for propagating the consequences of a change to a software system.

Index Terms—Configuration control, consistency, management, maintenance, software evolution.

I. Introduction

EVEN though the evolution of software systems accounts for the bulk of their cost, there is currently little automated support for evolution, especially when compared to other aspects of software development. This state of affairs is partially due to lack of tractable formal models for the process of software evolution. We propose a graph model of software evolution to help address this problem, and show how our model can help in maintaining the consistency of a changing system. We are particularly concerned with large and complex systems, which often have long lifetimes and undergo gradual but substantial modifications because they are too expensive to discard and replace. Computer assistance is essential for effective and reliable evolution of such systems because their representations and evolution histories are too complex for unaided human understanding. Computer-aided evolution is particularly important in rapid prototyping, where exploratory design and prototype demonstrations guide the development of the requirements via an iterative process that can involve drastic conceptual reformulations and extensive changes to system behavior [9].

Software evolution involves change requests, software systems, and evolution steps as well as customers, managers, and software engineers. Customers include the people and organizations who use software systems and have funded their development and evolution. Change requests come from customers, and the corresponding changes are controlled by the managers of the software system. Change requests that are approved by the management trigger evolution steps which produce versions of the system incorporating the requested changes. The evolution steps are scheduled by the management, and are carried out by the software engineers.

Both software systems and evolution steps typically have hierarchical structures. Software systems are viewed and manipulated as structured collections of software components of many different types, such as requirements, specifications, design descriptions, source code modules, test cases, manuals, etc. Similarly, evolution steps are viewed and scheduled as structured collections of related substeps, such as job assignments for organizations and individuals, and changes to subsystems and individual software objects. A software component or a step is *composite* if it can be viewed as a collection of related parts, and is *atomic* otherwise. The customers are usually directly concerned only with the top levels of these structures, which correspond to delivered systems and responses to change requests, respectively. Top-level components and steps can be either atomic or composite. For large systems, top-level components and steps are usually composite, with several levels of decomposition between the top level and the atomic parts.

As systems change, they go through many different versions. An *object* is a software component that is subject to change. Objects can be either composite or atomic, and can represent both systems and individual modules. A *version* is an immutable snapshot of an object. Versions have unique identifiers. New versions can be created, but versions cannot be modified after they are created. Objects can be changed only by creating new versions. Because previous versions are not destroyed when a new version is created, the state of an object consists of a partially ordered set of versions, rather than a single version.

This paper explores the general class of objects subject to version control. We view each type of software object—such as a specification or a program—as a subclass of the general class "versioned-object." Each subclass provides additional operations and properties relevant to each kind of software object. Our discussion is independent of the additional operations and properties provided by the more specific subclasses.

A distinguishing characteristic of versioned-objects is that they are persistent. Thus versioned-objects are more closely related to the objects in object-oriented databases than they are to the objects in object-oriented programming languages. In the rest of this paper we refer to versioned-objects simply as objects.

Large systems change gradually, in relatively small steps. The direct effect of each step in the evolution of a system is a change in one or more of the component objects comprising a system. These changes affect the functionality and the performance of the system as well as its

Manuscript received December 15, 1989; revised April 9, 1990. Recommended by M. Zelkowitz. This work was supported in part by the National Science Foundation under Grant CCR-8710737.

The author is with the Department of Computer Science, Naval Postgraduate School, Monterey, CA 93943.

IEEE Log Number 9036535.

representation, and must respect many dependencies between the components to avoid damaging the system. Considering the complexity of current software systems and the scope and frequency of the changes they typically undergo, complete and effective control over the set of configurations is imperative for successful system evolution. Two of the main objectives of version management are ensuring that consistency constraints are met and coordinating concurrent updates to subcomponents of a system.

Evolution steps can be represented as dependency relations between versions. There are often very many evolution steps in the lifetime of a system, and some of these steps may fork off new branches to create families of alternative versions of the system, which may differ in functionality of performance, and may interface to different operating environments, peripherals, or external systems. The complexity of this structure and the dependence of future changes on past design decisions makes it important to record the evolution history of a system.

We assume that each object has one or more alternative *variations*. A variation of an object is a totally ordered sequence of versions of the object which represents the evolution history of an independent line of development. Each version of an object belongs to exactly one variation. Each variation has a unique identifier. All variations of an object share some common properties which characterize the identity of the object. A new variation for an object is created when one of its lines of development branches. Different variations of an object have different properties of interest to the designers, such as those listed above. Variations can be organized using *generalization per category* [8], which provides a structure useful for supporting browsing tools and mapping values for sets of categorical properties meaningful to the users into internal unique identifiers, thus supporting retrieval and specification of variations based on information familiar to the users.

We seek to formalize the evolution history to provide computer aid for maintaining the consistency of the configurations in the product repository. After summarizing some relevant previous work in Section II and presenting the details of our formalized graph model in Section III, we describe the possibilities for computer aid in Section IV and present some conclusions in Section V.

II. Summary of Previous Work

We briefly review some recent work on configuration management, emphasizing the aspects most closely related to this paper. Our work adapts and extends some of the concepts and structures introduced in earlier models [3], [4]. This section concludes with a summary of the relevant aspects of these models. The rest of the paper refines and extends these concepts to reflect specifics of software evolution.

A. Related Work on Configuration Management

The goals of configuration management include recording the development history of evolving systems, maintaining the integrity of such systems, and aiding the management of the systems in guiding and controlling their evolution. Until relatively recently, configuration management was carried out via a combination of manual and administrative procedures. Early attempts at providing automated support for these functions were aimed at identifying and efficiently storing many versions of the same document, and at keeping versions of mechanically derived software objects up to date.

The problem of maintaining the integrity of an evolving configuration has been addressed more recently via module interconnection languages [12]. The purpose of a module interconnection language is to record the interdependencies between the components of a system. The approach reported in [12] includes specifications of functional properties of modules, in addition to the structural and syntactic properties captured by earlier approaches. This language provides a textual form for recording which versions are compatible with which other versions in a related family of software systems. A major contribution of this work is the recognition that specifications can be ordered by an upward compatibility relationship, and that one component can be substituted for another even in cases where the specifications of the components differ, provided that the specification of the new component is an upwards compatible extension of the specification for the original component. This idea is orthogonal to our contribution, and can be beneficially combined with the formulation presented in this paper. The Inscape environment [13] provides several refined versions of upward compatibility, as well as strict compatibility and implementation compatibility. Implementation compatibility is a weaker restriction than upward compatibility which allows one specification to be substituted for another in particular contexts. The concept of obligations in the Inscape environment also supports automatically determining whether an induced step needs to actually make any changes, and locating the aspects of a component that must be changed by an induced step.

Our work is concerned with clarifying the concepts associated with configurations to enable automated tool support for exploring design alternatives in the context of prototyping, for providing concurrency control in situations where many designers are simultaneously working on different aspects of the same system, and for aiding management in controlling and directing the evolution of complex systems at a conceptually manageable level of detail. Rather than introducing a special language for recording dependencies, we rely on existing specification languages to represent semantic constraints, and include specification objects in the configuration. This simplifies the dependencies between components, resulting in a graph structure that can be represented and maintained via established database technology, and can be treated uniformly for all types of software objects. Our work explicitly provides frozen versions, which are necessary to provide stability in a project setting, and applies to all kinds of software objects. The work reported in [12] is limited to just specifications and programs.

Other work has addressed the problem of maintaining mechanically-derivable software objects [6]. The main contribution of this work is to do opportunistic evaluation of derived components based on forward chaining and a set of rules and strategies that represent a model of the user's intentions and the systems capabilities. These rules can also be applied via backward chaining, which provides a mechanism for the system to deduce what tools must be applied to which components to achieve a state requested by the user. The problem of maintaining rederivable components is not addressed in this paper, and the solutions to these problems can be profitably integrated with our approach. The work reported in [6] does not directly address frozen versions and the details of managing configurations. Our view of dependencies between source objects can readily be encoded in rules of the style reported in [6], and our model can be implemented using the system described there. Transactions are considered in [7], which proposes some programming language constructs for realizing nested atomic transactions that can take long periods of time without blocking other concurrent activities. This work does not characterize the integrity properties of the software configuration that should be maintained, and does not link the commit protocols of the transactions to management controls. We provide a graph model that captures these integrity properties, and extend the transaction commit protocol to provide management controls on a high level that can be mechanically extended to the detailed evolution steps that realize a high level change.

The work described above [6], [7], [12], [13] appears to be based on the implicit assumption that only the current version of the object is useful. Our work focuses on maintaining the entire history of each object, not just the most current version. This is most important for groups of evolving systems that share evolving reusable components. Histories are considered in the Cosmos system [14], which provides a distributed database for supporting software development environments. This work is compatible with ours, and provides a means for realizing our graph model in a practical setting. Their consistent domains and domain relative addressing provide solutions for the problems of providing concurrency control that allows a high degree of concurrency in a distributed environment without risk of deadlock. Our work sheds some additional light on the properties of consistent domains, and indicates how the boundaries of a consistent domain might be established by automatic means: a consistent domain consists of the results of an evolution step and all of its induced steps. Nested steps give rise to nested consistent domains.

B. Concepts from the Model of Software Manufacture

The model of software manufacture [3] was developed to aid in managing versions of mechanically derived objects, with the goals of minimizing the number of objects that must be rederived in response to a change, and of automatically estimating the computing costs associated with installing a proposed change. Our main concern is with the source objects which are produced under the direct control of the software engineers. Several of the concepts of [3] can be readily adapted for formalizing evolution histories in addition to providing support for creating and managing mechanically derived objects.

The model of software manufacture formalizes the concept of a *configuration*. Configurations are intended to capture all of the information that can distinguish between two different versions of a system. The concept of a configuration is important in software evolution because each top-level evolution step produces a new configuration of the evolving system. A configuration is represented as a triple $[G, E, L]$, where $G = [C, S, I, O]$ is a bipartite directed acyclic graph, $E \subseteq C$ is a set of exported components, and L is a labeling function giving unique identifiers for both components and manufacturing steps. The nodes in the graph represent software components (C nodes) and manufacturing steps (S nodes), and the two kinds of nodes alternate on every path in the graph. The arcs in the graph represent input relations between components and manufacturing steps ($I \subseteq C \times S$), and output relations between manufacturing steps and components ($O \subseteq S \times C$).

Exported components correspond to the deliverable parts of a system. Each configuration contains all of the components that can affect the production of the deliverable parts of a specific version of a system, and no other components. The model of software manufacture has a broad view of components, which can include software tools such as compilers and flow analyzers, and tool inputs such as command line options as well as traditional software objects such as test data files and source code modules.

The unique identifiers assigned by the labeling function ensure that each component is the result of a unique manufacturing step. This can be expressed formally as follows.

$$\text{ALL}(m1\ m2:S,\ c:C::$$
$$[m1, c] \in O \ \& \ [m2, c] \in O \Rightarrow m1 = m2) \quad (1)$$

Different invocations of the computations representing a manufacturing step are considered to be distinct, have different unique id's, and produce two different sets of output components, which also have distinct id's. Thus two components are considered to be distinct if they have different derivation histories, if even if the values of the components happen to be the same. The model of software manufacture is constructed in this way to avoid the assumption that all manufacturing steps must be repeatable, so that derivations can involve computations which have persistent states or may be affected by transient hardware faults. The unique identifiers for components and manufacturing steps also allow the graphs corresponding to several different configurations to be combined via graph unions without loss of information. Since the labeling functions are required to give globally unique identifiers with respect to the set of all possible components and steps rather than with respect to just the components and steps in a single configuration, there is no possibility of losing the distinction between parts of different configurations.

The software components and manufacturing steps in the model of software manufacture correspond to our component versions and evolution steps. However, the model of software manufacture focuses on steps that can be completely automated, such as compilation, and on components that can be automatically generated, such as object code. A typical manufacturing step is illustrated in Fig. 1. Since we are concerned mainly with coordinating the activities of a team of people responsible for the evolution of a software system, rather than on the coordination of a set of programs, our model includes only source objects as component versions and activities involving human interaction as evolution steps. A typical evolution step is illustrated in Fig. 2.

The model of software manufacture provides formal definitions of some concepts useful for describing software evolution. The set of *primitive components* P consists of the components that are not produced by any step, and can be defined formally as follows.

$$P = \{c:C \mid ALL(s:S::[s, c] \notin O)\} \quad (2)$$

In the context of the model of software manufacture, primitive components are the source objects: those which cannot be mechanically generated. In the context of software evolution, the primitive components form the initial configuration of the system, as delivered by the developers. Modified versions of these original source objects are considered to be derived rather than primitive in our model of software evolution.

The dependency relation $D+$ is defined to be the transitive closure of the relation

$$D = (I \cup O) \quad (3)$$

induced by the arcs in the graph. Since the relation D is acyclic, $D+$ is a strict partial ordering. The dependency relation represents the dependencies among the components and the steps in terms of the derivation structure. For example, component $c1$ depends on component $c2$ if $[c2, c1] \in D+$ and step $m1$ depends on step $m2$ if $[m2, m1] \in D+$. This dependency relation plays a central role in both the model of software manufacture and in our model of software evolution. For example, it can be used to define the set of steps affected by a change in a component c as follows.

$$\text{affected-steps}(c:C) = \{s:S \mid [c, s] \in D+\} \quad (4)$$

This set is used to determine which derived components must be recomputed when the component c is changed [3]. In Section IV we develop a refinement of this concept suitable for identifying induced evolution steps.

The model of software manufacture must be extended to represent the issues relevant to software evolution because it does not include any representations for future plans, does not admit parts of derivations that do not lead

Fig. 1. A typical manufacturing step.

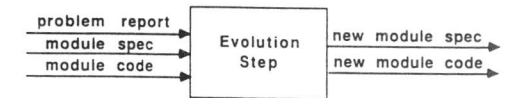

Fig. 2. A typical evolution step.

to delivered products, and does not include any representation of the hierarchical structures involved in software evolution. The relations between components in the model of software manufacture are limited to just the dependencies induced by the derivation history. In particular the model of software manufacture has no representation of whether or not two components are different versions of the same object, or whether one component is a part of another component.

C. Concepts from the Graph Transform Model

The motivation for the graph transform model [4] is similar to that for the model of software manufacture, and several of the concepts of that model are useful in our context. We classify software objects into two categories: *rederivable* and *nonrederivable*. Rederivable objects can be automatically reconstructed by applying a software tool to a set of software objects, without the need for human intervention. All other objects are nonrederivable. An example of a nonrederivable object is a representation of the user input guiding a computer-aided software design tool. The software objects in the graph transform model can have attributes, which can specify computational procedures that can be applied to the components to perform specific transformations.

There are two important relations between nonrederivable and rederivable objects: *uses* and *derives*. These relations have a direction and have natural representations as directed graphs, as illustrated in Fig. 3.

The relation "derives" is defined between general objects and rederivable objects. The relation represents possible transformations of one or more software objects into other objects (e.g., compilation of source code into object code). The "derives" transformations are associated with the use of software tools in the process of programming and are usually invisible to the management and the customers. In the applications of the graph transform model the set of transformations is usually fixed. Individual transformations from the set can be applied automatically using information about the type of the software object and the attributes associated with the objects. The "derives" relation is used for automatically managing derivable objects, which can be either stored or computed on demand depending on the relative importance of response time and use of storage space. This is an important function in a computer aided evolution environment, which

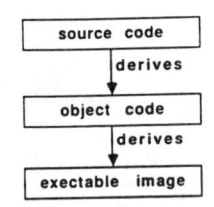

Fig. 3. The derives relation.

we propose to integrate with our approach via the "derives" relationship. The primary focus of our work, however, is the problem of managing the non-re-derivable components of an evolving system.

The "uses" relation is defined between non-re-derivable objects, and represents situations where the semantics or implementation of one software object depends on another software object. An example of this kind of relation is the dependency between Ada packages represented by Ada "with" statements. The "uses" relations between code modules are part of the module decomposition of a software system. These relations may be either defined directly in the components themselves via compiler directives or programming language constructs (e.g., "#include" in C, "with" in Ada, "COPY" in some Cobol dialects) or may be contained in externally specified attributes representing additional information used by the software tools (e.g., library specifications in linking commands). In both cases the relation is defined explicitly, and is not changed often in the evolution process compared to the properties of the individual components. The "uses" relation for implementation modules can be derived automatically from the source code and the external attributes for most programming languages.

In addition to recording dependencies between source code modules, the "uses" relation can include dependencies involving other types of software objects. For example, a clear box test case for a module "uses" the source code of the module, the source code of a module "uses" the behavioral specification for the module as well as the behavioral specifications and the concrete interfaces of the other modules it invokes, the behavioral specification of a module "uses" definitions of properties of the environment from the requirements model, a specification for a user function "uses" the requirements satisfied by the user function, and lower-level requirements "use" the higher-level goals they achieve. Similar relations expressing dependencies not directly related to the source code are that a user manual entry for a user function "uses" the specifications for the user function, and that a black box test case for a code module "uses" the behavioral specifications for the module. These relations are illustrated in Fig. 4. The relationship "a uses b" is denoted by an arrow directed from a to b. It is worth noting that in the event a composite module is decomposed into submodules, the implementation of the composite module uses the its own specification and the specifications of the submodules, *but not the implementations of the submodules*. This limits the impact of evolution steps

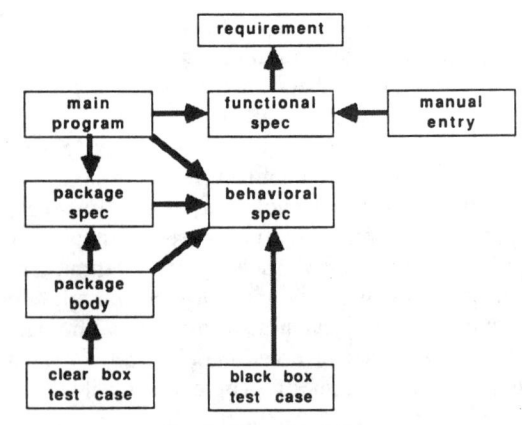

Fig. 4. The uses relation.

and provides in incentive for using formal specifications in software evolution. The uses relation can serve as the basis for automatically identifying inputs of proposed evolution steps and the identifying induced steps triggered by a proposed step, as indicated below.

III. Model of Software Evolution

The main objective of our model of software evolution is to provide a framework that integrates software evolution activities with configuration control. The model is not concerned with the mechanics and the details of the tasks carried out by the software engineers and evolution programmers. The model is a refinement of some recent work [11] based on a set of organizational paradigms consistent with the ANSI/IEEE standard on Software Configuration Management [1], which are summarized as follows:

1) The management of the software evolution organization exercises a formal type of change control, so that the system configuration changes only as a result of an evolution action authorized by the management.

2) A software configuration management system is used as a tool to coordinate evolution activities for a system.

3) All of the verified software objects are contained in a controlled software library (the configuration repository) and all changes to components of the configuration repository must be authorized by the management.

4) The actual programming work is done using the programmer's workspace, which is outside the configuration repository. When a programmer is assigned to perform an evolution activity, appropriate software objects are copied from configuration repository to the programmer's workspace, where the programmer has free access to them. Final results of the activity are transferred from the programmer's workspace to the configuration repository when the work has been tested, verified and accepted.

5) The deliverable products of the configuration (e.g., user manuals and executable software objects) are derived from the system's configuration repository and installed at the "production" site, which is outside the configuration repository. These software products are the "exports" of the configuration.

6) Since product derivation may be required at any point of time, the system's configuration must be consistent at all times, i.e., the derivation of deliverable objects may not be compromised at any time because of consistency problems in existing software objects.

Such organizational paradigms are common to most software development and evolution organizations that deal with medium and large sized software systems.

A. Definition of the Model

The model of software evolution is composed of two basic elements: system components and evolution steps. We refer to these as components and steps.

Components are versions of nonrederivable software objects: they are immutable, and correspond to the components in the model of software manufacture with the exception that the components must have concrete existence, since they cannot be automatically reconstructed on demand.

The evolution steps correspond to manufacturing steps of the model of software manufacture with the following differences.

1) A top-level evolution step is a representation of an organizational activity concerned with initiation, analysis and implementation of one request for a change in the system.

2) An evolution step may be either atomic or composite.

3) An atomic evolution step produces at most one new version of a system component.

4) The inputs and outputs of a composite step correspond to the inputs and outputs of its substeps.

5) The model of software evolution allows empty steps that do not produce any output components.

6) The model allows steps that do not lead to production of exported components. Such steps represent design alternatives that were explored but not incorporated into any configuration in the repository.

7) Automatic transformations are not considered to be evolution steps and are not represented in the model.

8) The model covers multiple systems which can share components, alternative variations for a single system, and a series of configurations representing the evolution history of each alternative variation of a system.

9) A scope is associated with each evolution step which identifies the set of systems and variations to be affected by the step.

The evolution history is an acyclic bipartite graph G with a global labeling function L, as defined in Section II-B. We interpret C nodes as system components and S nodes as evolution steps. The output edges O relate an evolution step to the components it produces. The input edges I relate a step to the set of system components which must be examined to produce output components that are consistent with the rest of the system. Cycles are not allowed in the graph G, so that sets of software objects with circular dependencies must be packaged as single atomic components in the repository. For example, a set of mutually recursive subprograms must be packaged as an atomic component, as must the data declaration and the operations comprising an abstract data type.

Every configuration in the repository consists of an initial subgraph of G, a set of exported components E, and the global labeling function L. The evolution history graph represents a snapshot of the evolution history at some point in time. New versions of this graph may be created only by consistent extension, i.e., all evolution history graphs representing past states must be initial subgraphs of the current evolution history graph, and must be subject to the same global labeling function.

We formalize some of the above principles and definitions. The set of input components and the set of output components of an evolution step are defined in terms of the arcs in the evolution history graph.

$$\text{input}(s:S) = \{c:C \,|\, [c, s] \in I\},$$
$$\text{output}(s:S) = \{c:C \,|\, [s, c] \in O\} \quad (5)$$

The "part-of" relation for steps represents the relationship between a substep of a composite step and the composite step. This relation defines a tree-structured decomposition for each top-level evolution step. Atomic steps are defined as follows.

$$\text{atomic}(s:S) = \neg \text{EXISTS}(s':S :: s' \text{ part-of } s) \quad (6)$$

We also need to introduce a relationship that captures indirect dependencies between components. One component *affects* another if both components are identical or if the first component is involved in the derivation of the second component, expressed formally as follows.

$$\text{ALL}(c1\ c2:C :: c1 \text{ affects } c2 \Leftrightarrow c2 \text{ uses* } c1) \quad (7)$$

The relation "uses*" is the reflexive transitive closure of the "uses" relation introduced in Section II-C. The "affects" relation can be derived from the structure of the non-primary inputs of the evolution steps for all components except for the primitive components in the initial configuration. The "uses" relations among the primitive components must be specified when the initial configuration is defined.

The restriction on inputs and outputs of steps can now be stated as follows.

$$\text{ALL}(s:S :: \text{atomic}(s) \Rightarrow |\text{output}(s)| \leq 1) \quad (8)$$

Atomic steps produce at most one output.

$$\text{ALL}(s1\ s2:S,\ c:C ::$$
$$s1 \text{ part-of } s2\ \&\ c \in \text{output}(s1) \Rightarrow c \in \text{output}(s2))$$
$$(9)$$

The output of a composite step includes all of the outputs of its substeps.

The inputs to both composite and atomic steps are restricted by their parent steps. The inputs to a composite step could be defined to consist of all the inputs of its substeps, but it is more useful to aggregate inputs using a kind of generalization based on the dependencies between components. This simplifies descriptions of composite steps, and supports planning via estimates of the expected sets of inputs to the top-level steps before implementation begins. We achieve this via the following restriction.

$$\text{ALL}\big(s1\ s2:S,\ c1:C ::$$
$$s1\ \text{part-of}\ s2\ \&\ c1 \in \text{inputs}(s1) \Rightarrow$$
$$\text{EXISTS}\big(c2:C :: (c2 \in \text{input}(s2)\ \&\ c2\ \text{affects}\ c1)\ \text{or}$$
$$(c2 \in \text{output}(s1)\ \&\ c2\ \text{uses}\ c1)\big)\big)$$

Every input to a substep must either be affected by some input to the parent step, or must affect some output of the substep. For example, if a high-level step changes the specification of a user function, then the substeps can take as input the specifications and code of the modules implementing the user function, since all of those components directly or indirectly "use" the specification of the user function. These indirect dependencies let the inputs to top-level steps be small sets of high-level components which are meaningful to managers, such as the set of requirements affected by the top-level step. If the substep corresponds to a major change that introduces subcomponents that were not used by the previous version, thus introducing some new dependencies, then the specifications of those additional subcomponents will also be inputs to the substep. This is an example of a situation where all of the inputs to the substeps cannot be anticipated in advance. This type of step need not introduce potentials for deadlocks, however, because there is no need to acquire new locks after a transition has started: either the additional subcomponents can be reused without any modifications, or they can be modified by branching off a new variation of the object in question, without affecting any of the other contexts where the object is used.

B. States of Evolution Steps

To model the dynamics of the evolution process, we associate states with evolution steps. We define the following five states of a evolution step.

1) Proposed: In this state a proposed evolution step is analyzed to determine costs, benefits, and potential impact on the system. This includes identifying the software objects in the step's input set. In this state implementation of the change has not yet been approved.

2) Approved: In this state the implementation of the change has been approved, but has not yet been scheduled, and references to generic input objects are not yet bound to particular versions.

3) Scheduled: In this state the implementation has been scheduled, the people responsible for doing the work have been assigned, all inputs of the step have been bound to particular versions, and the work may be in progress. When the step is in this state unique identifiers have been assigned for its output components, but the corresponding components are not yet part of the configuration repository.

4) Completed: In this state the outputs of the step have been verified, integrated, and approved for release. When a top-level step reaches this state, all output versions associated with the step and all of its direct and indirect substeps are incorporated in the configuration repository. This the final state for all successfully completed steps.

5) Abandoned: In this state the step has been canceled before it is completed. The outputs of the step do not appear as components in the evolution history graph or in the configuration repository. All partial results of the step and the reasons why the step was abandoned are stored as attributes of the step for future reference. The "abandoned" state is the final state for all evolution steps that were not approved by the Software Configuration Control Board or were canceled by the management in the "approved" or "scheduled" states.

Each state corresponds to several phases of the evolution process as they are defined in [10], and corresponding substates can be defined for each of the above states in a detailed implementation of the model.

Transitions of an evolution step from one state to another correspond to explicit decisions made by the management of the evolution organization. By controlling the states of the evolution steps, the management exercises direct control over both the software evolution process and the system configuration. The possible transitions are illustrated in Fig. 5. Evolution steps in the "scheduled" state can be "rolled back" into the "approved" state. Such an action corresponds to a long term delay in a step, and releases the bindings of generic input objects to specific versions. Since this may result in the loss of some or all of the work invested in the step, due to changes in the input objects that may occur before the step returns to the "scheduled" state, decisions to take such transitions should be made with insight and great care. This disadvantage can be reduced by tools for automatically applying a given change to another version of the object. However, automatically combining the results of several steps is the subject of current research [2], [5], and completely automated tools for performing this task reliably have not yet become available for practical use.

C. Constraints on State Transitions

Evolution steps have a tree structure described by the "part-of" relation. In order to ensure consistency in evolution histories containing both composite and atomic steps, we impose the following constraints on some state transitions of composite steps and their substeps:

1) When a step changes from the "proposed" to the "approved" state all of its substeps make the same transition automatically.

2) A step changes automatically from the "approved" state to the "scheduled" state if one of its substeps makes this transition.

3) When a step changes from the "scheduled" to the "approved" state all of its substeps make the same transition automatically.

4) A composite step changes automatically from the "scheduled" state to the "completed" state when all of its substeps have done so.

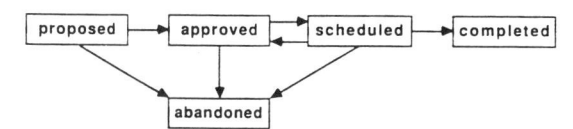

Fig. 5. State transitions for evolution steps.

(a) History of the affected object variation c(v) before the step:
[c(v, 1), ... , c(v, n)]

(b) History of the affected object variation c(v) after the step:
[c(v, 1), ... , c(v, n), c(v, n+1)]

Fig. 6. The effect of an atomic step.

5) A composite step changes automatically to the "abandoned" state when all of its substeps have done so.

6) When a step changes to the "abandoned" state all of its substeps make the same transition automatically.

7) When a new substep is created, it enters the same state as its parent superstep and inherits all version bindings associated with the parent step.

These rules help to ensure that inconsistent configurations are not entered into the repository and that the version bindings for a step are consistent with the version bindings of its substeps. They also reduce clerical effort by allowing management decisions to be explicitly recorded only for the largest applicable composite steps, with mechanical propagation down to the detailed substeps as appropriate.

D. Input Classification for Atomic Evolution Steps

The purpose of an atomic evolution step is to incorporate a single change in a single component of the system. The result of the change is the single output of the atomic step. In order to capture dependencies between different software objects, we distinguish between primary inputs and nonprimary inputs of an atomic step. An input to an atomic step is *primary* if and only if it is a version of the same variation of the same object as the output of the step. Recall that alternative variations of an object represent parallel lines of development for the object which correspond to alternative design choices. The most common case, in which there is exactly one primary input, is illustrated in Fig. 6. We use the notation $c(a, b)$ to denote version b of variation a of object c. The primary input of the step is $c(v, n)$, which is the most recent version of the affected object variation $c(v)$ before the step, and the next to most recent version after the step. The version $c(v, n + 1)$ represents the output from the step.

An atomic step without any primary inputs can arise in several situations. For example, an atomic step may create a new software object as part of a major change which affects the decomposition of the system. An atomic step can also create a new variation of an existing object in cases where the evolution of the object must split into two independent branches. Such a situation can arise in cases where a software object is shared between different systems, and an evolution step acting on one of these systems $S1$ has created a new version of an object which is not suitable for another system $S2$. This new version is therefore not incorporated in any configuration of $S2$. When a later step acting on $S2$ affects the same object, this change must be based on a version of the object that is not the most current one, thus creating a parallel branch in the development of the object, corresponding to a new alternative variation for the object. This is illustrated in Fig. 7. Primary inputs are shown as heavy arrows and nonprimary inputs are shown as thin arrows. Variations are represented as paths with heavy arrows. The versions $c(1, 1..n)$ are shared by systems $S1$ and $S2$, and all belong to variation 1 of the object c. Step $s1$ implements an enhancement to system $S1$ and produces a version $c(1, n + 1)$ which is compatible with system $S1$ but not with system $S2$. Steps $s2$ and $s3$ introduce later chnages in the object c for implementing enhancements to system $S2$. Step $s2$ creates the new variation with index 2, and cannot have a primary input because there are no versions belonging to variation 2 until after step $s2$ is completed. The later step $s3$ has a primary input $c(2, 1)$ which belongs to the same variation as the output version $c(2, 2)$.

We assume that an atomic step has at most one primary input, since it makes sense to include two different versions of an object as inputs to the same step only if those versions have different purposes, and in such a case the two versions should belong to two different alternative variations of the object. An atomic step which acts on several different variations of the affected object represents a change that combines the features of all the variations of a software object. Such a change can either be treated as an enhancement to one of the input variations, in which case there is one primary input corresponding to the existing variation associated with the output, or it can be treated as the creation of a completely new variation of the object, in which case there are no primary inputs.

We can formalize the concept of a primary input by introducing the attributes *object-id* and *variation-id*, both of which apply to versions, and yield unique identifiers for the object and variation associated with the version. Two versions belong to the same variation if they are versions of the same variation of the same object.

$$\text{ALL}(c1\ c2:C :: c1 \text{ same-variation } c2 \Leftrightarrow$$
$$\text{object-id}(c1) = \text{object-id}(c2) \ \&$$
$$\text{variation-id}(c1) = \text{variation-id}(c2)) \quad (11)$$

The property *primary-input* can then be defined as follows.

$$\text{ALL}(s:S, c1:C :: c1 \text{ primary-input } s \Leftrightarrow$$
$$c1 \in \text{input}(s) \ \&$$
$$\text{EXISTS}(c2:C :: c2 \in \text{output}(s) \ \&$$
$$c1 \text{ same-variation } c2)) \quad (12)$$

Some of the nonprimary inputs of an evolution step can be derived from the "uses" relation, since a step can depend on all of the components used by its primary input.

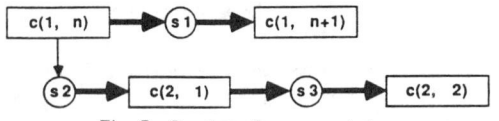

Fig. 7. Creation of a new variation.

This can be expressed formally as follows.

$$\text{ALL}(c1\ c2:C, s:S ::$$
$$c1 \text{ uses } c2 \ \&\ c1 \text{ primary-input } s \Rightarrow c2 \in \text{input}(s)) \tag{13}$$

The set of nonprimary inputs to a step should ideally contain all of the component versions used by the *output* of the step. The above rule approximates this set by the set of component versions used by the primary input of the step, and is intended to define a mechanically derived initial approximation to the set of nonprimary inputs. This initial approximation may need some manual adjustment, since design changes associated with the evolution step can introduce dependencies that did not exist in the previous version, and can remove some dependencies that did exist.

E. Specifying Inputs to Evolution Steps

Inputs to an evolution step can be specified by a reference to either a generic object or a specific version. Generic object references are usually the most common. Informally a generic object reference denotes the "current" version of the object.

Formally a generic object reference consists of an identifier for an object and an identifier for a variation of that object. Each variation of an object consists of a sequence of versions ordered by the dependency relation $D+$, or equivalently by the completion times of the versions. Generic object references for any step are bound to specific versions based on the scheduling of its top-level super-step, at the time the top-level step makes the transition from the "approved" state to the "scheduled" state. The top-level super-step top(s) is defined by the following properties:

$$s \text{ part-of* top}(s)\ \&\ \neg\ \text{EXISTS}(s':S::\text{top}(s) \text{ part-of } s') \tag{14}$$

where "part-of*" is the reflexive transitive closure of the irreflexive "part-of" relation. The top-level superstep is unique because a step cannot be "part-of" two different supersteps.

The inputs to a step can be specified by generic object references only while the step is in a "proposed" or "approved" state, and must be resolved to specific versions before the step can enter the "scheduled" or "completed" states. The version bindings of a composite step are inherited by its substeps to ensure consistency. Configurations in the repository are completely bound, in the sense that they do not contain any generic object references.

Specific object references are usually used to define inputs to steps in cases where the current version of an object has features that are not desirable for the proposed new configuration, and some earlier version of the object is acceptable. Specific object references often coincide with the creation of new variations, as discussed in Section III-D.

IV. Evolution Consistency

An important practical problem in the evolution of a large system is ensuring the consistency of each new configuration. While the certification of semantic consistency involves several computationally undecidable problems in the general case, some related consistency criteria based on structural considerations can be maintained automatically with practical amounts of computation. Such support should extend the abilities of an organization responsible for the evolution of a software system to maintain control over the system. We propose to base such support on the concept of an *induced evolution step*.

A. Induced Evolution Steps

A change in a component of a software system can require changes in other components to maintain the consistency of the system. We refer to those other changes as *induced evolution steps*. In this section we define some relationships that enable induced evolution steps to be identified mechanically. These relationships are based on structural considerations, and provide a conservative estimate of the impact of a change. A human designer must either examine the induced steps to determine if they need to produce new versions, or must define uniform policies similar to the "difference predicates" of [3] for filtering out some of the common cases where an induced step can be safely implemented by the identity transformation. Tools for automatically recognizing instances of upwards compatibility relationships [12] would also be useful for this purpose. The purpose of induced evolution steps is to alert the software engineers and the management to the impact of proposed changes and to prevent problems due to incomplete propagation of the consequences of a change. A change in one module can trigger a change in another, which can trigger further changes in a chain of indirect effects. The extent of such chains can be difficult to predict without computer assistance, especially for complex systems.

We call a step that originates such a chain an *inducing step*. The set of induced steps triggered by an inducing step updates the current versions of all components which are affected by the inducing step and are within the scope of the current top-level evolution step. There is need for concern about the scope because there may be multiple systems in the evolution history, which are distinct but may share components. We do not wish to create induced steps which implement unauthorized changes to systems that are not involved in the current top-level evolution step. The purpose of the induced steps is to produce versions of their primary inputs which are consistent with the output version of the inducing step.

A component is current if there is no later version of the same variation of the same object.

$$\text{ALL}(c1:C :: \text{current}(c1) \Leftrightarrow$$
$$\neg \text{ EXISTS}(c2:C :: c1 \ D + c2 \ \&$$
$$c1 \text{ same-variation } c2)) \quad (15)$$

The scope of a top-level step consists of the components affected by its inputs.

$$\text{scope}(s:S) = \{c1:C \mid \text{EXISTS}(c2:C ::$$
$$c2 \in \text{input}(\text{top}(s)) \ \& \ c2 \text{ affects } c1)\} \quad (16)$$

This formulation assumes that the inputs to the top-level steps are the highest-level objects that are affected by the step, such as the system requirements affected by the change.

The set of induced steps can now be characterized as follows.

$$\text{induced-steps}(s1) =$$
$$\{s2:S \mid \text{EXISTS}(c1 \ c2:C :: c1 \text{ primary-input } s1$$
$$\& \ c2 \text{ primary-input } s2 \ \& \ c1 \text{ affects } c2$$
$$\& \ \text{current}(c2) \ \& \ c2 \in \text{scope}(s1))\} \quad (17)$$

Since the inputs of a top-level step are bound to specific versions at the time the step is scheduled, the set of induced steps cannot be influenced by any changes due to parts of any other top-level steps that may be executed concurrently. The predicate "current" is evaluated in the state defined by the version bindings of the top-level step.

An example of induced steps in a small system implemented in Ada is shown in Fig. 8. The initial configuration of the system shown in the figure consists of the three components in the top row. The step $s1$ changes the main program without affecting the package specification, and does not trigger any induced steps. The step $s2$ changes the package body without affecting the package specification, and does not cause any induced steps because there are no other components that use the package body. The step $s3$ does change the package specification, and triggers induces steps $s3.1$ and $s3.2$, which must update the main program and the package body to conform to the new package specification. These induced steps can be derived from the "uses" relationships according to definitions (15)–(17). For all but the initial versions of the components, the "uses" relationships can be derived from the evolution history graph by reversing the directions of the nonprimary input relationships.

In realistic situations there can be longer chains of induced steps, corresponding to paths in the "uses" relation similar to those illustrated in Fig. 4. An example of indirectly induced steps is shown in Fig. 9. Step $s1$ triggers the induced step $s1.1$, which in turn triggers the indirectly induced step $s1.1.1$.

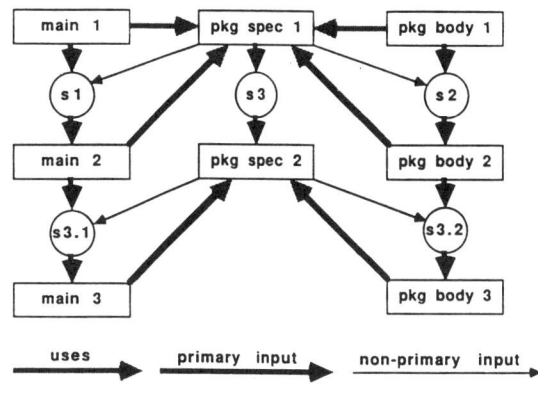

Fig. 8. Induced evolution steps.

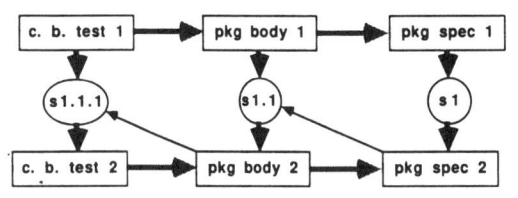

Fig. 9. Indirectly induced steps.

B. Induced State Transitions

To maintain the consistency of the configuration, an inducing step and all of the induced steps must be carried out as an atomic operation. This means that all of the steps in such a set must make their transitions from the "approved" to the "scheduled" states and from the "scheduled" to the "completed" states without other intervening transitions. This can be accomplished by the following rules.

1) An inducing step can enter the "completed" state only if all its induced steps are completed.

2) An induced step enters the "scheduled" state automatically when its inducing step does so.

3) Any "roll back" transition of an inducing step from the "scheduled" state to the "approved" state causes the same transition to be performed on all its induced steps.

4) An induced step can be "rolled back" only by "rolling back" all of its inducing steps.

5) Abandoning an inducing step causes all of its induced steps to be abandoned.

6) An induced step can be abandoned only by abandoning its inducing step.

The first rule ensures that the effects of an inducing step are entered into the repository together with the effects of all the directly and indirectly induced steps. The second rule ensures that the version bindings of the induced steps are consistent with those of the inducing steps. The remaining rules deal with propagating the effects of rollbacks and canceled steps.

V. Conclusion

A formal model of the process of software evolution is needed to serve as a basis for smarter software tools. This paper describes an initial version of such a model and indicates how the model can be used to help maintain the consistency of an evolving system and to help organize and coordinate the activities involved in the evolution of large systems. The model can support aspects of software evolution that are not described in detail in this paper. Some areas for future applications of the model include tools for estimating the cost of proposed changes, and scheduling approved evolution steps. We have found that ideas similar to those underlying techniques for automatically managing versions of automatically rederivable software objects can be applied to nonrederivable source objects, if dependencies between objects are recorded and maintained. We have refined previous approaches to opportunistic construction of derived objects by introducing a link to management approval via the scope of an evolutionary step, as defined in equation (16). This prevents unauthorized and unintended changes to systems caused by propagation of changes to components shared by several systems.

Our model can also serve as the basis for organizing the repository of configurations. Our work has suggested that the configuration repository should contain representations of the steps as well as of the resulting software products. The minimal set of attributes associated with a step are the sets of inputs and outputs. This information is useful for reconstructing the "uses" relation, which is needed in determining the set of induced steps triggered by a proposed evolution step. Other attributes that might be useful include records of time and effort spent on the step, and records of the justifications for the decisions made and the alternatives that were considered and rejected.

Work is needed to address the additional problem of providing computer-aided explanations of the evolution history to support the decisions of the software engineers. This problem is a natural extension of the questions addressed in this paper. Decision support of this type is needed because the groups of people responsible for building a system and those responsible for evolving it are often disjoint, and tend to serve in their positions for short periods of time relative to the lifetime of the system. Thus the evolution history should serve as a "corporate memory," and be capable of supporting current decisions by supplying relevant information about decisions made in the past about the design of the system and past evaluations of alternative designs that were not adopted. Effective representations and analysis procedures for providing adequate decision support for the engineers responsible for system evolution are important areas for future research. We believe such representations can be developed as compatible extensions of the model described in this paper.

REFERENCES

[1] *IEEE Guide to Software Configuration Management*, American National Standards Inst./IEEE, New York, Standard 1042-1987, 1988.
[2] V. Berzins, "On merging software extensions," *Acta Inform.*, vol. 23, no. 6, pp. 607-619, Nov. 1986.
[3] E. Borison, "A model of software manufacture," in *Advanced Programming Environments*, R. Conradi, T. Didriksen, and D. Wanvik, Eds. New York: Springer-Verlag, 1986, pp. 197-220.
[4] D. Heimbigner and S. Krane, "A graph transform model for configuration management environments," in *Proc. ACM Software Eng. Notes/SIGPLAN Notices Software Engineering Symp. Practical-Software Development Environments*, 1988, pp. 216-225.
[5] S. Horowitz, J. Prins, and T. Reps, "Integrating non-interfering versions of programs," *Trans. Program. Lang. Syst.*, vol. 11, no. 3, pp. 345-387, July 1989.
[6] G. Kaiser, P. Feiler, and S. Popovich, "Intelligent assistance for software development and maintenance," *IEEE Software*, pp. 40-49, May 1988.
[7] G. Kaiser, "Modeling configurations as transactions," in *Proc. 2nd Int. Workshop Software Configuration Management*, IEEE, Princeton, NJ, Oct. 1989, pp. 129-132.
[8] M. Ketabchi and V. Berzins, "Generalization per category: Theory and Application," in *Proc. Int. Conf. Information Systems*, 1986; also Tech. Rep. 85-29, Dep. Comput. Sci., Univ. Minnesota.
[9] Luqi, "Software evolution via rapid prototyping," *Computer*, vol. 22, no. 5, pp. 13-25, May 1989.
[10] R. Martin and W. Osborne, *Guidance on Software Maintenance*, Nat. Bureau Standards, U.S. Dep. Commerce, Dec. 1983.
[11] I. Mostov, Luqi, and K. Hefner, "A graph model of software maintenance," Dep. Comput. Sci., Naval Postgraduate School, Tech. Rep. NP552-90-014, Aug. 1989.
[12] K. Narayanaswamy and W. Scacchi, "Maintaining configurations of evolving software systems," *IEEE Trans. Software Eng.*, vol. SE-13, no. 3, pp. 324-334, Mar. 1987.
[13] D. Perry, "The Inscape Environment," in *Proc. 11th Int. Conf. Software Engineering*, IEEE, 1989, pp. 2-12.
[14] J. Walpole, G. Blair, J. Malik, and J. Nichol, "A unifying model for consistent distributed software development environments," *Software Eng. Notes (Proc. ACM Software Engineering Symp. Practical Software Development Environments)*, vol. 13, no. 5, pp. 183-190, Nov. 1988.

Automated Merging of Software Prototypes

DAVID A. DAMPIER DAMPIER@CS.NPS.NAVY.MIL
Computer Science Department, Naval Postgraduate School, Monterey, California 93943

LUQI
Computer Science Department, Naval Postgraduate School, Monterey, California 93943

VALDIS BERZINS
Computer Science Department, Naval Postgraduate School, Monterey, California 93943

(Received February 24, 1993; Revised May 25, 1993)

Abstract. As software becomes more complex, more sophisticated development and maintenance methods are needed to ensure software quality. Computer-aided prototyping achieves this via quickly built and iteratively updated prototypes of the intended system. This process requires automated support for keeping track of many independent changes and for exploring different combinations of alternative changes and refinements. This article formalizes the update and change merging process, extends the idea to multiple changes to the same base prototype, and introduces a new method of slicing prototypes. Applications of this technology include automatic updating of different versions of existing software with changes made to the baseline version of the system, integrating changes made by different design teams during development, and checking consistency after integration of seemingly disjoint changes to the same software system.

Key Words: Software, automation, computer-aided prototyping, maintenance, formal models, software engineering, software merging, change integration, case tools, slicing.

1. Introduction

Software development is an ever-increasing and complex industry. As software systems gain sophistication and maintaining them becomes more difficult, automated software development methods and the supporting formal models must be devised to increase reliability and decrease post-development maintenance effort.

Computer-aided prototyping is one such method to reduce maintenance costs by making the original requirements conform more closely to the real needs of the users. Systems correctly implementing an accurate set of requirements have lower maintenance costs because there are fewer surprises when the system is put into actual use. An appreciable part of the maintenance activity can be carried out by changing and updating the prototype rather than repeatedly updating the production version of the intended system. This is useful because the prototype description can be significantly simpler than the production code if the prototype is expressed in a notation tailored to support modifications, and the software tools in the computer-aided prototyping environment can help carry out the required modifications rapidly [12]. Prototyping a software system using tools decreases development time and increases maintainability because it reduces customer dissatisfaction with the delivered system [14].

The designers construct and change prototypes of the intended systems quickly to meet the customer's desires during the requirements analysis phase. The designers need automated tools that will allow several changes to a base version of a software prototype to be automatically combined as well as automatically propagated through multiple alternative versions of the prototype. Formal models are the keys and foundations for building such automated tools.

Change merging is the process of automatically combining the effects of several changes to a software system. Change merging has been studied in the context of software maintenance and conventional methods for software development. Early version control systems such as SCCS [18] and RCS [20] provide primitive change merging facilities based on string editing operations on the source text without considering the effects on program behavior. However automated tools must provide guarantees regarding program behavior to be trusted by designers. Semantically based change merging seeks to construct a program whose behavior agrees with the changed version in all situations where the behavior of a changed version differs from the behavior of the base version. The behavior of the constructed program should agree with the base version for all situations where the behaviors of all the changed versions agree with the behavior of the base. The problem for functional programs was considered in [2]. Semantically based change merging based on program slicing [21] and data-flow analysis has been studied for imperative while-programs [16, 10]. A general theory of change merging that can apply to any kind of programming language is described in [4], along with a high resolution approach to change merging for while-programs based on specifications and meaning functions [3]. An initial exploration of change merging models for the prototyping language PSDL can be found in [8].

Change merging is an important aspect of computer-aided prototyping because the prototyping process is characterized by rapid and extensive changes. The computer-aided prototyping system (CAPS) [12] is a computer-aided prototyping environment comprised of a software database system, an execution support system, and a user interface that helps designers to develop prototypes. The software database system manages changes to multiple versions of prototype designs and provides an expert system to select and retrieve reusable components from the software base. The design database provides concurrency control functions, which allow multiple designers to update the parts of the prototype without risk of unintentional interference. In the interests of minimizing delay, the design database will not lock out access to any part of the design, even while the design is being updated. Instead, the system will allow the previous version of the component to be examined and updated. Such a parallel update will split off a new branch or *variation* in the version history [13]. The system will provide a warning that a new version is currently in preparation and information about the reason the component is being modified (i.e., some particular new or modified requirement) on request. The methods proposed in this article provide automated support for combining both branches of a split resulting from parallel updates to produce a version that incorporates the effects of both of the updates.

Our goal is to develop a tool for the CAPS system that will support automatic merging of different versions of a prototype. We have developed a model that shows that it is possible to correctly perform a merge operation in most cases [8]. This article formalizes the change process for the Prototyping System Design Language (PSDL), a design-based language written specifically for CAPS, and uses this formalization to strengthen our merging model.

2. Prototyping in CAPS

Computer-aided prototyping allows the user to get a better handle on his or her requirements early in the conceptual phase of design development and use automated tools to rapidly create "a concrete executable model of selected aspects of a proposed system" [12], to allow the user to view the model and to make comments early. The prototype is then rapidly reworked and redemonstrated to the user over several iterations until the designer and the user have a precise view of what the system should do. This process produces a validated set of requirements that become the basis for implementing the final product [12]. The prototype can also become part of the final product. In some prototyping methodologies, the prototype is an executable shell of the final system, containing only a subset of the system's ultimate functionality. After the prototype is approved by the customer, the holes are filled in and the system is delivered. In this approach to computer-aided prototyping, software systems can be delivered incrementally as parts of the system become fully operational [12].

CAPS, a computer-aided software development environment, supports prototyping of embedded hard real-time systems [12]. CAPS reduces the effort of the prototype designer by providing an integrated set of tools that help design, translate, and execute the prototypes, along with a language in which to design and program the prototypes.

The Prototype System Description Language (PSDL) is the prototyping language associated with CAPS [11]. It was created to provide the designer with a simple way to abstractly specify software systems. A PSDL program is a set of PSDL operators and data types, containing zero or more of each. PSDL operators and types consist of a specification and an implementation. The specification defines the external interfaces of each operator through a series of interface declarations, provides timing constraints, and describes the functionality of the operator through the use of formal and informal descriptions. The implementation can either be in PSDL or Ada. PSDL implementations are data flow diagrams augmented with a set of data stream definitions and a set of control and timing constraints.

3. Changing Prototypes

A current focus of CAPS is formalization of the change process. To discuss the merging of changes made to a prototype, we must first provide a mathematical model of the change process.

PSDL prototypes can be considered iterative versions of a software system. If S is the intended final version of the software system, then each successive iteration of the prototype can be viewed as an element of a sequence S_i, where $\lim_{i \to \infty} S_i = S$. Each prototype S_i is modelled as a graph $G_i = (V_i, E_i, C_i)$, where

1. V_i is a set of vertices. Each vertex can be an atomic operator or a composite operator modelled as another graph.
2. E_i is a set of data streams. Each edge is labelled with the associated variable name. There can be more than one edge between two vertices. There can also be edges from an operator to itself, representing state variable data streams.

3. C_i is a set of timing and control constraints imposed on the operators in version **i** of the prototype.

The prototype designer repeatedly demonstrates versions of the prototype to users, and designs the next version based on user comments. The change from the graph representing the **i**th version of the prototype to the graph representing the **(i + 1)**st version can be described in terms of graph operations by the following equations:

$$S_{i+1} = (V_{i+1}, E_{i+1}, C_{i+1}) = S_i + \Delta S_i$$

$$\Delta S_i = (VA_i, VR_i, EA_i, ER_i, CA_i, CR_i) \text{ where}$$

$V_{i+1} - V_i = VA_i$: The set of vertices to be added to S_i.

$V_i - V_{i+1} = VR_i$: The set of vertices to be removed from S_i.

$E_{i+1} - E_i = EA_i$: The set of edges to be added to S_i.

$E_i - E_{i+1} = ER_i$: The set of edges to be removed from S_i.

$C_{i+1} - C_i = CA_i$: The set of timing and control constraints to be added to S_i.

$C_i - C_{i+1} = CR_i$: The set of timing and control constraints to be removed from S_i.

The + operation above is defined as follows:

$$V_{i+1} = V_i \cup VA_i - VR_i$$
$$E_{i+1} = E_i \cup EA_i - ER_i$$
$$C_{i+1} = C_i \cup CA_i - CR_i$$

The following figures show an example of a change made to a composite operator in PSDL. Figure 1 contains a graph representation for a prototype **Fishies** modelling a *fish-farm control system*. Figure 2 shows a change to be applied to Fishies to produce **Fishies$_A$**. Figure 3 shows a graph representation of **Fishies$_A$**, the result of applying the change to **Fishies**. The intent of this change is to provide a method for measuring bacterial levels in the fish tank.

4. Merging PSDL Prototypes

Merging different versions of a program is useful in performing automatic maintenance of software systems. In prototyping, it is common for different versions to evolve from the base system. If the system designer discovers a fault in the base version of the system, it would be desirable to have the capability to automatically apply that change to all of

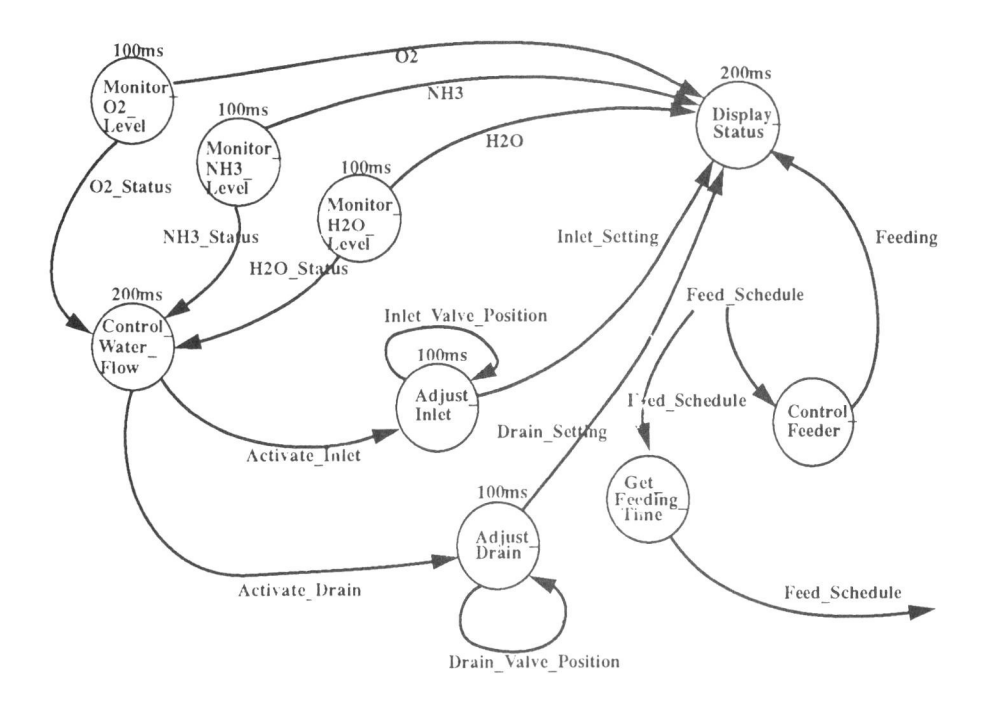

Fishies = ($V_{Fishies}$, $E_{Fishies}$, $C_{Fishies}$)

$V_{Fishies}$ = {Monitor_O2_Level, Monitor_NH3_Level, Monitor_H2O_Level, Control_Water_Flow, Display_Status, Adjust_Drain, Get_Feeding_Time, Control_Feeder, Adjust_Inlet}

$E_{Fishies}$ = {(O2_Status: Monitor_O2_Level -> Control_Water_Flow),
(NH3_Status: Monitor_NH3_Level -> Control_Water_Flow),
(H2O_Status: Monitor_H2O_Level -> Control_Water_Flow),
(O2: Monitor_O2_Level -> Display_Status),
(NH3: Monitor_NH3_Level -> Display_Status),
(H2O: Monitor_H2O_Level -> Display_Status),
(Activate_Inlet: Control_Water_Flow -> Adjust_Inlet),
(Activate_Drain: Control_Water_Flow -> Adjust_Drain),
(Inlet_Setting: Adjust_Inlet -> Display_Status),
(Drain_Setting: Adjust_Drain -> Display_Status),
(Inlet_Valve_Position: Adjust_Inlet -> Adjust_Inlet),
(Drain_Valve_Position: Adjust_Drain -> Adjust_Drain),
(Feed_Schedule: EXT -> Get_Feeding_Time),
(Feed_Schedule: EXT -> Control_Feeder),
(Feed_Schedule: Get_Feeding_Time -> EXT),
(Feeding: Control_Feeder -> Display_Status)}

$C_{Fishies}$ = {max_exec_time(Monitor_O2_Level, 100ms), max_exec_time(Monitor_NH3_Level, 100ms), max_exec_time(Monitor_H2O_Level, 100ms), max_exec_time(Adjust_Inlet, 100ms), max_exec_time(Adjust_Drain, 100ms), max_exec_time(Control_Water_Flow, 200ms), max_exec_time(Display_Status, 200ms), period((Control_Water_Flow, 2000ms)}

Figure 1. Example of a composite operator in PSDL.

the versions currently in use. To do this, the merging process must be able to apply the change to the common parts of each version without affecting the peculiar functionality in each one.

Δ_AFishies = {VA_A, VR_A, EA_A, ER_A, CA_A, CR_A}

VA_A = {Monitor_Bacteria_Level, Control_Water_Flow_2, Display_Status_2}

VR_A = {Control_Water_Flow, Display_Status}

EA_A = {(Bacteria_Status: Monitor_Bacteria_Level -> Control_Water_Flow_2),
    (Bacteria: Monitor_Bacteria_Level -> Display_Status_2)
    (O2_Status: Monitor_O2_Level -> Control_Water_Flow_2),
    (NH3_Status: Monitor_NH3_Level -> Control_Water_Flow_2),
    (H2O_Status: Monitor_H2O_Level -> Control_Water_Flow_2),
    (O2: Monitor_O2_Level -> Display_Status_2),
    (NH3: Monitor_NH3_Level -> Display_Status_2),
    (H2O: Monitor_H2O_Level -> Display_Status_2),
    (Activate_Inlet: Control_Water_Flow_2 -> Adjust_Inlet),
    (Activate_Drain: Control_Water_Flow_2 -> Adjust_Drain),
    (Inlet_Setting: Adjust_Inlet -> Display_Status_2),
    (Drain_Setting: Adjust_Drain -> Display_Status_2),
    (Feeding: Control_Feeder -> Display_Status_2)}

ER_A = {(O2_Status: Monitor_O2_Level -> Control_Water_Flow),
    (NH3_Status: Monitor_NH3_Level -> Control_Water_Flow),
    (H2O_Status: Monitor_H2O_Level -> Control_Water_Flow),
    (O2: Monitor_O2_Level -> Display_Status),
    (NH3: Monitor_NH3_Level -> Display_Status),
    (H2O: Monitor_H2O_Level -> Display_Status),
    (Activate_Inlet: Control_Water_Flow -> Adjust_Inlet),
    (Activate_Drain: Control_Water_Flow -> Adjust_Drain),
    (Inlet_Setting: Adjust_Inlet -> Display_Status),
    (Drain_Setting: Adjust_Drain -> Display_Status),
    (Feeding: Control_Feeder -> Display_Status)}

CA_A = {max_exec_time(Monitor_Bacteria_Level, 100ms),
    max_exec_time(Display_Status_2, 100ms),
    max_exec_time(Control_Water_Flow_2, 200ms),
    period(Control_Water_Flow_2, 2000ms)}

CR_A = {max_exec_time(Display_Status, 100ms),
    max_exec_time(Control_Water_Flow, 200ms),
    period(Control_Water_Flow, 2000ms)}

Figure 2. Example of a change made to **Fishies**.

Two compatible modifications of a semantic function can be merged as follows:

If the functions computed by the programs are represented as sets of pairs, then the result of merging two modifications A & C of a base version B is defined as:

$$M = A[B]C = (A - B) \cup (A \cap C) \cup (C - B)$$

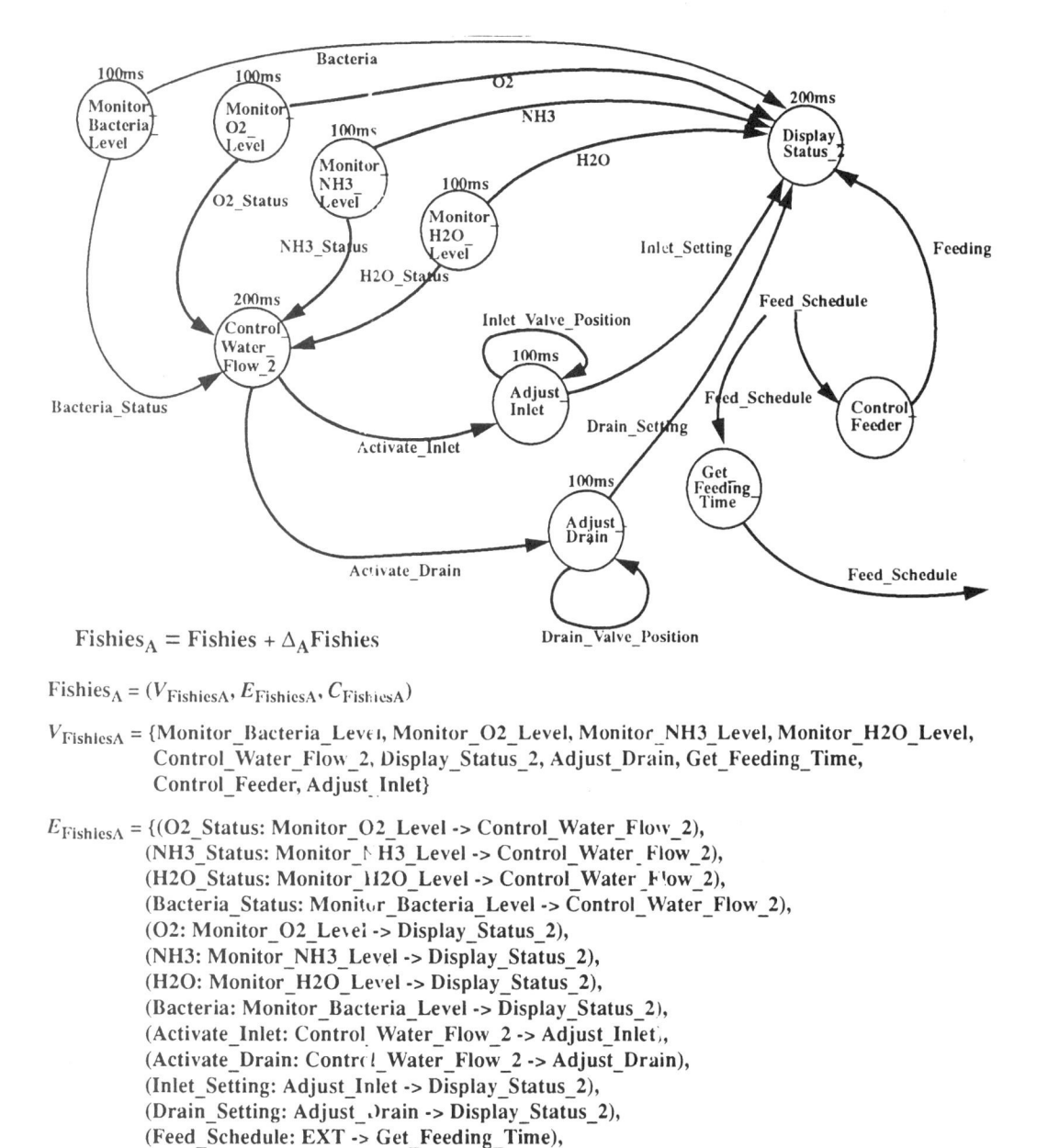

$\text{Fishies}_A = \text{Fishies} + \Delta_A \text{Fishies}$

$\text{Fishies}_A = (V_{\text{FishiesA}}, E_{\text{FishiesA}}, C_{\text{FishiesA}})$

$V_{\text{FishiesA}} = \{$Monitor_Bacteria_Level, Monitor_O2_Level, Monitor_NH3_Level, Monitor_H2O_Level, Control_Water_Flow_2, Display_Status_2, Adjust_Drain, Get_Feeding_Time, Control_Feeder, Adjust_Inlet$\}$

$E_{\text{FishiesA}} = \{$(O2_Status: Monitor_O2_Level -> Control_Water_Flow_2),
(NH3_Status: Monitor_NH3_Level -> Control_Water_Flow_2),
(H2O_Status: Monitor_H2O_Level -> Control_Water_Flow_2),
(Bacteria_Status: Monitor_Bacteria_Level -> Control_Water_Flow_2),
(O2: Monitor_O2_Level -> Display_Status_2),
(NH3: Monitor_NH3_Level -> Display_Status_2),
(H2O: Monitor_H2O_Level -> Display_Status_2),
(Bacteria: Monitor_Bacteria_Level -> Display_Status_2),
(Activate_Inlet: Control_Water_Flow_2 -> Adjust_Inlet),
(Activate_Drain: Control_Water_Flow_2 -> Adjust_Drain),
(Inlet_Setting: Adjust_Inlet -> Display_Status_2),
(Drain_Setting: Adjust_Drain -> Display_Status_2),
(Feed_Schedule: EXT -> Get_Feeding_Time),
(Inlet_Valve_Position: Adjust_Inlet -> Adjust_Inlet),
(Drain_Valve_Position: Adjust_Drain -> Adjust_Drain),
(Feed_Schedule: EXT -> Control_Feeder), (Feed_Schedule: Get_Feeding_Time -> EXT),
(Feeding: Control_Feeder -> Display_Status_2)$\}$

$C_{\text{FishiesA}} = \{$max_exec_time(Monitor_O2_Level, 100ms), max_exec_time(Monitor_NH3_Level, 100ms), max_exec_time(Monitor_H2O_Level, 100ms), max_exec_time(Monitor_Bacteria_Level, 100ms), max_exec_time(Adjust_Inlet, 100ms), max_exec_time(Adjust_Drain, 100ms), max_exec_time(Control_Water_Flow_2, 200ms), max_exec_time(Display_Status_2, 200ms), period((Control_Water_Flow_2, 2000ms)$\}$

Figure 3. Example of the changed operator **Fishies$_A$**.

In this definition, the union, intersection, and difference operations are defined as normal operations on sets. The difference operation, (A − B) for example, yields the part of the function present in the modification, but not in the base version. The intersection operation yields the part of the function preserved from the base version in both modifications. This model preserves all changes made to the base version, whether extensions or retractions. In this model, two changes conflict if the construction produces a relation that is not a single valued function.

In this section, we outline an approximate method for merging prototypes using the change model described in the previous section and the above definition. This method is approximate in the sense that the change merging construction is applied to the structure of a PSDL program, rather than to the mathematical function it computes. This method is simple, corresponds to common programmer practice, and produces semantically correct results most of the time. We are working on methods to certify correctness of the results and to detect potential semantic problems.

The approximate method can be understood as follows. All PSDL implementations are graphs, whose structure roughly models their functionality. We have represented these graphs using sets. Different variations of a prototype are the result of different changes being applied to a common base version. We can merge the two new versions A and C together by applying the change that produced A from B to version C, or applying the change that produced C from B to version A. The result is the same in either case.

Earlier, we expressed the $(i + 1)$st iteration of a software prototype as $S_{i+1} = S_i + \Delta S_i$. Let us consider an ith version which has been changed in two different ways, via Δ_A and Δ_B. The results of these two changes are denoted as S_A and S_B respectively. Now let us consider a case where the $(i + 1)$st iteration is the result of merging these two changes:

$$S_{i+1} = S_A[S_i]S_B = (S_A - S_i) \cup (S_A \cap S_B) \cup (S_B - S_i)$$

The components of S_{i+1}; V_{i+1}, E_{i+1} and C_{i+1} can be defined similarly:

$$V_{i+1} = V_A[V_i]V_B = (V_A - V_i) \cup (V_A \cap V_B) \cup (V_B - V_i),$$
$$E_{i+1} = E_A[E_i]E_B = (E_A - E_i) \cup (E_A \cap E_B) \cup (E_B - E_i) \text{ and}$$
$$C_{i+1} = C_A[C_i]C_B = (C_A - C_i) \cup (C_A \cap C_B) \cup (C_B - C_i)$$

To demonstrate the concept of the merging operation, we provide the following example: The base prototype is as in Figure 1. Change A is outlined in Figure 2, with the result shown in Figure 3. Change B is outlined in Figures 4 and 5. The merging operation is

$\Delta_B \text{Fishies} = \{VR_B, VA_B, EA_B, ER_B, CA_B, CR_B\}$

$VA_B = \{\}$
$VR_B = \{\text{Get\_Feeding\_Time}\}$
$EA_B = \{\}$
$ER_B = \{(\text{Feed\_Schedule: EXT -> Get\_Feeding\_Time}),$
$\qquad (\text{Feed\_Schedule: Get\_Feeding\_Time -> EXT})\}$
$CA_B = \{\}$
$CR_B = \{\}$

Figure 4. Change B applied to Op1.

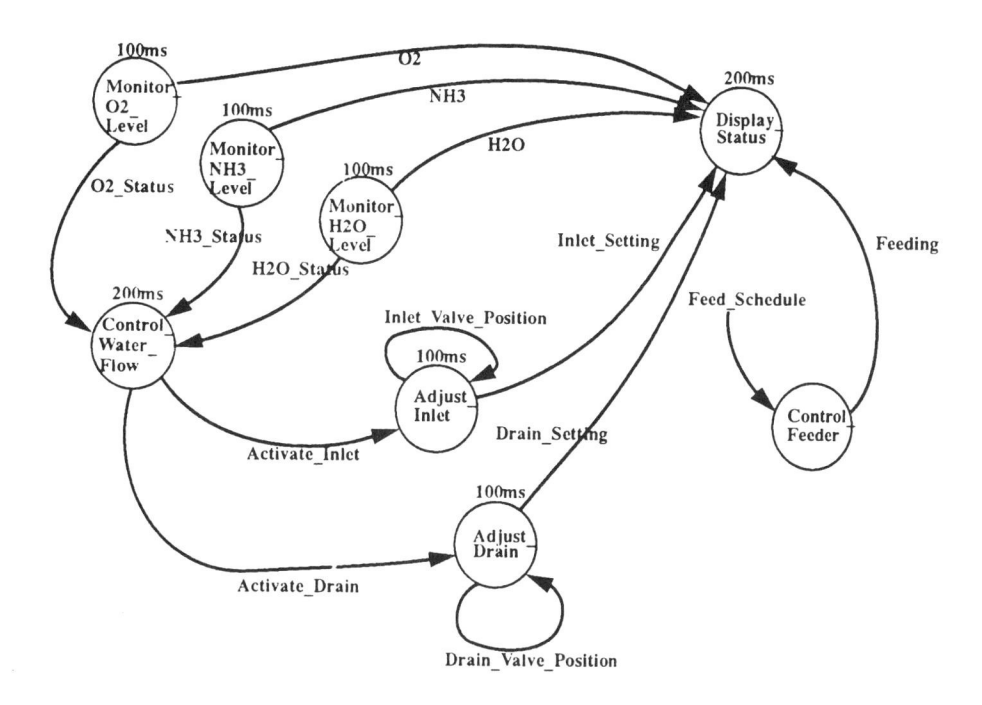

$Fishies_B = Fishies + \Delta_B Fishies$

$FishiesB = (V_{FishiesB}, E_{FishiesB}, C_{FishiesB})$

$V_{FishiesB}$ = {Monitor_O2_Level, Monitor_NH3_Level, Monitor_H2O_Level, Control_Water_Flow, Display_Status, Adjust_Drain, Control_Feeder, Adjust_Inlet}

$E_{FishiesB}$ = {(O2_Status: Monitor_O2_Level -> Control_Water_Flow),
(NH3_Status: Monitor_NH3_Level -> Control_Water_Flow),
(H2O_Status: Monitor_H2O_Level -> Control_Water_Flow),
(O2: Monitor_O2_Level -> Display_Status),
(NH3: Monitor_NH3_Level -> Display_Status),
(H2O: Monitor_H2O_Level -> Display_Status),
(Activate_Inlet: Control_Water_Flow -> Adjust_Inlet),
(Activate_Drain: Control_Water_Flow -> Adjust_Drain),
(Inlet_Setting: Adjust_Inlet -> Display_Status),
(Inlet_Valve_Position: Adjust_Inlet ->Adjust_Inlet),
(Drain_Valve_Position: Adjust_Drain ->Adjust_Drain),
(Drain_Setting: Adjust_Drain -> Display_Status),
(Feed_Schedule: EXT -> Control_Feeder),
(Feeding: Control_Feeder -> Display_Status)}

$C_{FishiesB}$ = {max_exec_time(Monitor_O2_Level, 100ms), max_exec_time(Monitor_NH3_Level, 100ms), max_exec_time(Monitor_H2O_Level, 100ms), max_exec_time(Adjust_Inlet, 100ms), max_exec_time(Adjust_Drain, 100ms), max_exec_time(Control_Water_Flow, 200ms), max_exec_time(Display_Status, 200ms), period((Control_Water_Flow, 2000ms)}

Figure 5. Results of applying change B to Op1.

performed in Figure 6 and the result is shown in Figure 7. The effect of change B is to remove the Get_Feeding_Time operator.

$$Fishies_M = Fishies_A[Fishies]Fishies_B =$$
$$(Fishies_A - Fishies) \cup (Fishies_A \cap Fishies_B) \cup (Fishies_B - Fishies),$$
$$V_{FishiesM} = V_{FishiesA}[V_{Fishies}]V_{FishiesB} =$$
$$(V_{FishiesA} - V_{Fishies}) \cup (V_{FishiesA} \cap V_{FishiesB}) \cup (V_{FishiesB} - V_{Fishies}),$$
$$E_{FishiesM} = E_{FishiesA}[E_{Fishies}]E_{FishiesB} =$$
$$(E_{FishiesA} - E_{Fishies}) \cup (E_{FishiesA} \cap E_{FishiesB}) \cup (E_{FishiesB} - E_{Fishies}) \text{ and}$$
$$C_{FishiesM} = C_{FishiesA}[C_{Fishies}]C_{FishiesB} =$$
$$(C_{FishiesA} - C_{Fishies}) \cup (C_{FishiesA} \cap C_{FishiesB}) \cup (C_{FishiesB} - C_{Fishies})$$

Figure 6. Performing the merge operation.

The merge operation outlined in Figure 6 involves determining the real effect of changes made to the base, and any conflict that may arise due to similar changes between the two variations.

This is a simple example illustrating the merging of two changed prototypes, which do not conflict with one another. In some cases, two changes to a prototype can conflict with one another, and the result of their merging can be an inconsistent program. In such cases, the engineer must resolve the conflict off-line. The following section describes some possible conflicts and possible methods for resolving those conflicts.

5. Conflict Resolution

There are a number of possible conflicts that can arise during the performance of the merging operation. Conflicts arise when different changes applied to the prototype affect the same portion of the prototype in different ways. Some examples of conflicts are as follows:

1. If one change adds an output edge to a vertex A, while another change removes vertex A from the prototype. In this case, automatic resolution of the conflict is not yet possible, so the system would have to notify the designer that a conflict has occurred and give him or her the opportunity to resolve it. In the case of such a conflict the construction produces a graph that is not well formed, in the sense that it has edges whose endpoints do not belong to the vertex set of the graph and are distinct from the artificial node EXT that serves as an endpoint for external flows.
2. If the two changes assign different timing constraint values to the same operator, i.e., (max_exec_time, F, 50ms) and (max_exec_time, F, 40ms). In this case, the conflict can be handled automatically, since any operator that executes in under 40ms must also execute in under 50ms. In situations in which different maximum execution times have been assigned, the minimum value can always be chosen. This is also true of two different values for latency, maximum response time, and finish within timing constraints.

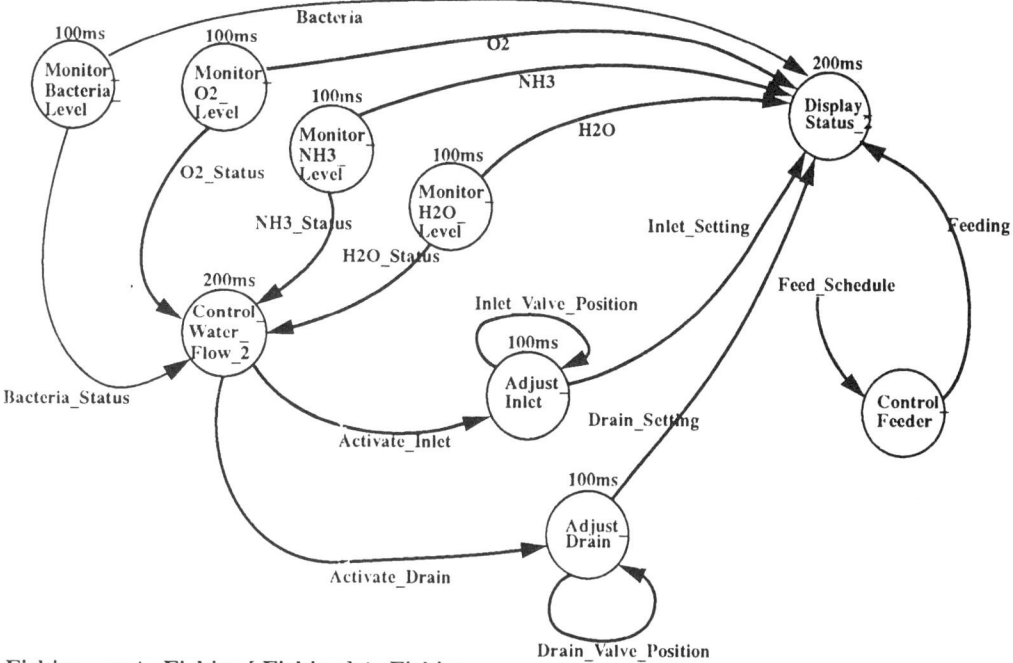

Fishies$_M$ = Δ_AFishies [Fishies] Δ_BFishies

V_{FishiesM} = {Monitor_Bacteria_Level, Monitor_O2_Level, Monitor_NH3_Level, Monitor_H2O_Level,
Control_Water_Flow_2, Display_Status_2, Adjust_Drain, Get_Feeding_Time,
Control_Feeder, Adjust_Inlet}

E_{FishiesM} = {(O2_Status: Monitor_O2_Level -> Control_Water_Flow_2),
(NH3_Status: Monitor_NH3_Level -> Control_Water_Flow_2),
(H2O_Status: Monitor_H2O_Level -> Control_Water_Flow_2),
(Bacteria_Status: Monitor_Bacteria_Level -> Control_Water_Flow_2),
(O2: Monitor_O2_Level -> Display_Status_2),
(NH3: Monitor_NH3_Level -> Display_Status_2),
(H2O: Monitor_H2O_Level -> Display_Status_2),
(Bacteria: Monitor_Bacteria_Level -> Display_Status_2),
(Activate_Inlet: Control_Water_Flow_2 -> Adjust_Inlet ,
(Activate_Drain: Control_Water_Flow_2 -> Adjust_Drain),
(Inlet_Setting: Adjust_Inlet -> Display_Status_2),
(Inlet_Valve_Position: Adjust_Inlet ->Adjust_Inlet),
(Drain_Valve_Position: Adjust_Drain ->Adjust_Drain),
(Drain_Setting: Adjust_Drain -> Display_Status_2),
(Feed_Schedule: EXT -> Control_Feeder),
(Feeding: Control_Feeder -> Display_Status_2)}

C_{FishiesM} = {max_exec_time(Monitor_O2_Level, 100ms), max_exec_time(Monitor_NH3_Level, 100ms),
max_exec_time(Monitor_H2O_Level, 100ms),
max_exec_time(Monitor_Bacteria_Level, 100ms), max_exec_time(Adjust_Inlet, 100ms),
max_exec_time(Adjust_Drain, 100ms), max_exec_time(Control_Water_Flow_2, 200ms),
max_exec_time(Display_Status_2, 200ms), period((Control_Water_Flow_2, 2000ms)}

Figure 7. Result of the merge operation.

The minimum calling period timing constraint would have to be merged using the maximum of the different values. Different period values for the same operator in different changes result in a conflict that would have to be be resolved by the designer. Different control constraints for the same part of the prototype in different changes can also result in a conflict. Some of these conflicts can be resolved automatically. Current work is addressing methods for automatic resolution of conflicts.

6. Slicing of Prototypes

Another method we have been exploring to automatically capture changes made to a prototype is that of *prototype slicing*, analogous to the program slicing introduced in [21]. To do the slicing, we have to embed the graph defined in Section 3 in a new graph called a *Prototype Dependence Graph* (**PDG**).

A **PDG** for a prototype P is an augmented, fully expanded PSDL implementation graph $G_P = (V, E, C)$, where the set of edges, E has been augmented with a *timer dependency edge* from v_i to v_j, when $v_i, v_j \in V$ and v_i contains timer operations that affect the state of a PSDL timer read by v_j.

A slice of a PSDL prototype P with respect to a set of streams X, $S_P(X) = (V, E, C)$ is a subgraph of the (**PDG**), G_P, and includes that portion of P that affects the values written to that set of data streams. A slice is constructed as follows:

1. V is the smallest set that contains all vertices $v_i \in G_P$ that satisfy at least one of the following conditions:
   v_i writes to one of the data streams in X.
   v_i precedes v_j in G_P, and $v_j \in V$.

2. E is the set that contains all of the data streams $x_k \in G_P$ that satisfy one of the following conditions:
   $x_k \in X$.
   x_k is directed to some $v_i \in V$.

3. C is the set that contains all of the timing and control constraints associated with each operator in V and each data stream in E.

An example of a prototype slice is provided in Figure 8. This is a slice of the prototype **Fishies** introduced in Figure 1 and is taken with respect to the stream **Activate_Drain**. In this example, only the operators and data streams that affect the values written to the stream **Activate_Drain** are included in the slice.

One of the possible uses of slicing in our work is analogous to that used the *Integrate Algorithm* developed for merging while-programs in [9]. Using prototype slicing, we can determine automatically which parts of the prototype have been affected by a change and which parts have been preserved. For example, consider the slice of **Fishies$_A$** taken with respect to **Activate_Drain**, illustrated in Figure 9. It is easy to see the effect of change A on the base prototype, **Fishies**.

[Figure: diagram showing Monitor_O2_Level (100ms), Monitor_NH3_Level (100ms), Monitor_H2O_Level (100ms) all feeding into Control_Water_Flow (200ms) via O2_Status, NH3_Status, H2O_Status respectively, with Activate_Drain output]

$S_{Fishies}(\{Activate\_Drain\}) = (V, E, C)$

V = {Monitor_O2_Level, Monitor_NH3_Level, Monitor_H2O_Level, Control_Water_Flow}

E = {(O2_Status: Monitor_O2_Level -> Control_Water_Flow),
(NH3_Status: Monitor_NH3_Level -> Control_Water_Flow),
(H2O_Status: Monitor_H2O_Level -> Control_Water_Flow),
(Activate_Drain: Control_Water_Flow -> Adjust_Drain)}

C = {max_exec_time(Monitor_O2_Level, 100ms), max_exec_time(Monitor_NH3_Level, 100ms), max_exec_time(Monitor_H2O_Level, 100ms), max_exec_time(Control_Water_Flow, 200ms), period((Control_Water_Flow, 2000ms)}

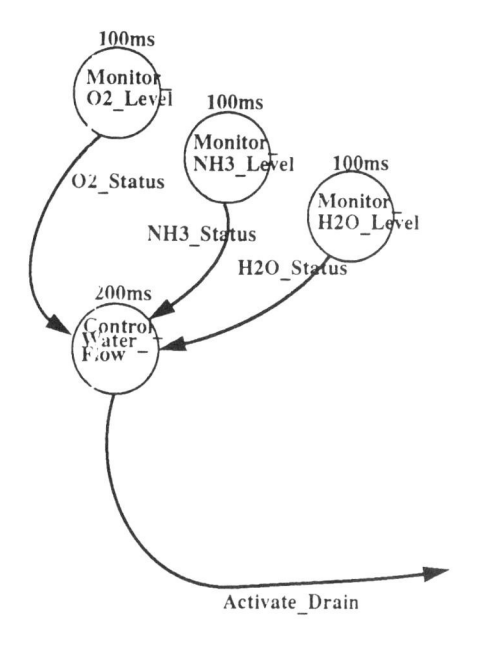

Figure 8. $S_{Fishies}(\{Drain\_Setting\})$.

If we were to take the same slice of **Fishies$_B$**, we would discover that it is identical to the slice in Figure 8. This shows us that this part of the Fishies prototype is not affected by Change B. One of the differences between slicing for PSDL prototypes and slicing for while-programs is that PSDL programs are inherently concurrent and nondeterministic and while-programs represent individual deterministic sequential processes. Slices are important because they capture all of the parts of a program that can affect the behavior visible in a set of data streams, so that if two different programs have the same slice on a set of streams, they will also have the same behavior on that set of streams. The preserved part of a prototype is then the largest set of streams that have the same slice in all three versions, and the affected streams of each modification are those not contained in the preserved part. The merge is formed by taking the union of the preserved part of all three versions and the affected parts of the two modified versions. If the slice of the merged version with respect to the streams affected by each modification is the same as the corresponding slice of the modified version, and if the slice of the merged version with respect

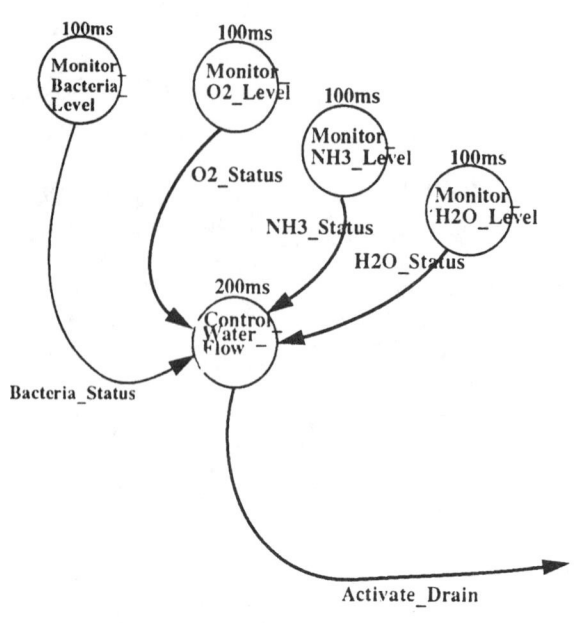

$S_{\text{FishiesA}}(\{\text{Activate\_Drain}\}) = (V, E, C)$

$V = \{\text{Monitor\_Bacteria\_Level, Monitor\_O2\_Level, Monitor\_NH3\_Level, Monitor\_H2O\_Level,}$
$\text{Control\_Water\_Flow}\}$

$E = \{(\text{O2\_Status: Monitor\_O2\_Level -> Control\_Water\_Flow}),$
$(\text{NH3\_Status: Monitor\_NH3\_Level -> Control\_Water\_Flow}),$
$(\text{H2O\_Status: Monitor\_H2O\_Level -> Control\_Water\_Flow}),$
$(\text{Bacteria\_Status: Monitor\_Bacteria\_Level -> Control\_Water\_Flow}),$
$(\text{Activate\_Drain: Control\_Water\_Flow -> Adjust\_Drain})\}$

$C = \{\text{max\_exec\_time(Monitor\_O2\_Level, 100ms), max\_exec\_time(Monitor\_NH3\_Level, 100ms),}$
$\text{max\_exec\_time(Monitor\_H2O\_Level, 100ms), max\_exec\_time(Control\_Water\_Flow, 200ms),}$
$\text{max\_exec\_time(Monitor\_Bacteria\_Level, 100ms), period((Control\_Water\_Flow, 2000ms)}\}$

Figure 9. $S_{\text{FishiesA}}(\{\text{Activate\_Drain}\})$.

to the preserved streams is the same as the corresponding slice of the base version, then semantic correctness of the merged version with respect to the modifications is established.

When applied to the example used earlier in this article, the slicing method for merging produces exactly the same results as the approximate method. The preserved part of the base is shown in Figure 10. The affected part of each modification is shown in Figure 11. When the union of all three is constructed, the result is the same graph as seen in Figure 7. One possible use for the slicing method would be to verify semantic correctness of a merge constructed using the approximate method. This could be done by taking the slice of the merged prototype with respect to the affected parts of both modifications. If the slices are preserved in the merged version, then semantic correctness can be established.

The slicing method has the advantage of a clear-cut semantic criterion of correctness, and the disadvantage of reporting conflicts whenever two changes can affect the same output stream, regardless of whether there exists any computation history in which the two changes actually interact or conflict with each other. These advantages and disadvantages

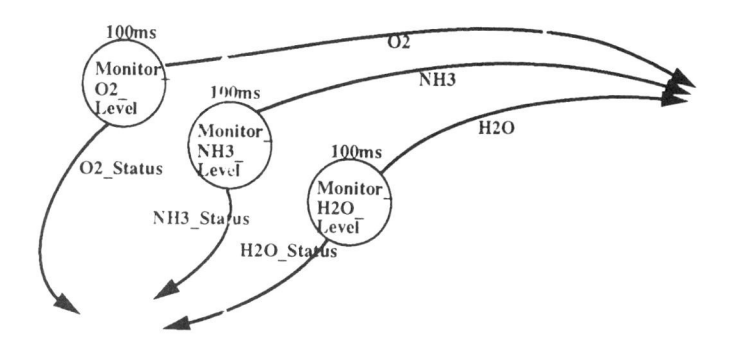

Figure 10. Preserved parts of base in both modifications.

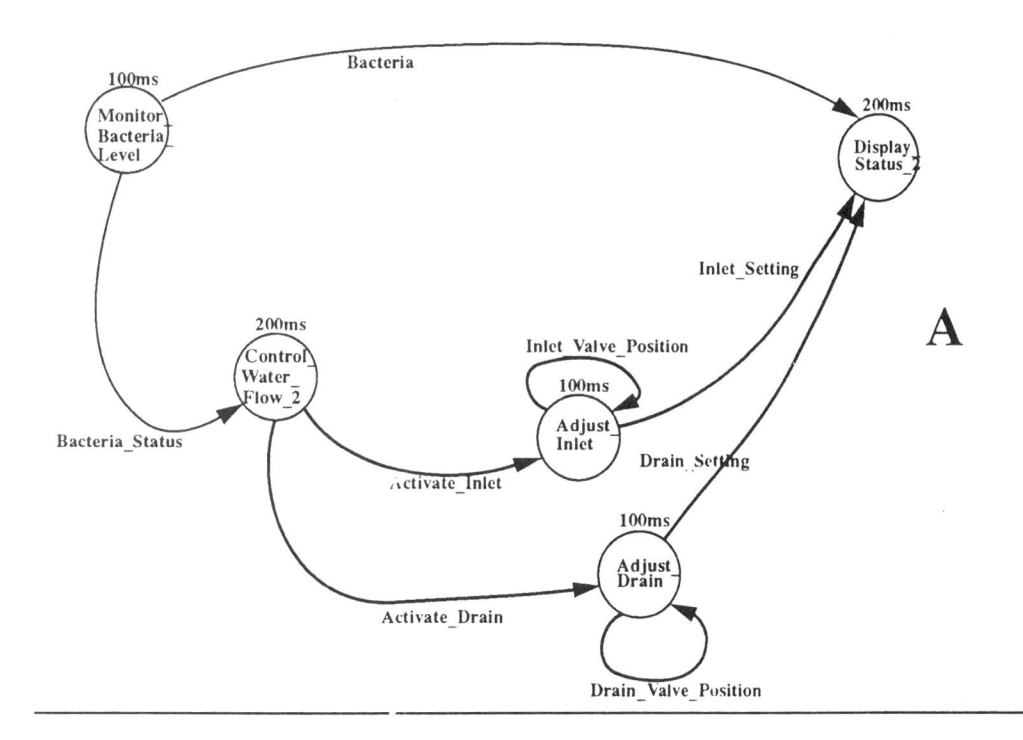

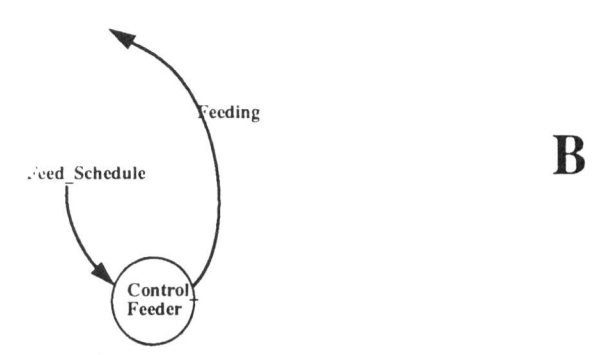

Figure 11. Affected parts of both modifications.

are analogous to those of the original integration algorithm [9]. The advantages of the approximate method are that it is simple and fast and can perform correct and successful merges in cases where the slicing method produces conflicts, and a disadvantage is that the approximate method can sometimes produce results that are not completely correct. We note that the parts of the input space for which the behavior of a prototype produced by the approximate merging method are often sparse, so that the approximate method may be useful in the context of prototyping even if it does not always produce exactly the right result. The approximate method produces exact results whenever the functions computed by the operators are one to one, and we are working on tighter characterizations of the cases where the method produces exact results, so that the merging tool can check for possible semantic interference after the approximate merge has been constructed.

7. Conclusions

Tool support for manipulating and combining specifications is especially important for computer-aided prototyping. We are currently working to improve the resolution and accuracy of the methods presented here to increase their effectiveness in practical contexts. The approximate method described here works correctly whenever the functions computed by the operators are one to one. As has been pointed out in [3], a global analysis of the system may be necessary to ensure that the functions computed by the operators do not interfere in the general case. For a more detailed discussion of the reasons for this, see [3].

Related work on configuration management and version control is also being performed [1] to integrate the methods presented here with comprehensive support for maintaining the global consistency of a large system that is undergoing multiple, concurrent modifications. Some issues to be considered in future work are treatment of change merging for data types and component specifications, finding semantically safe methods with better resolution (fewer spurious conflict reports), and detection and diagnosis of semantic interference between modifications.

Acknowledgment

This research was supported in part by the National Science Foundation under grant number CCR-9058453 and in part by the Army Research Office under grant number ARO-145-91.

References

1. S. Badr and V. Berzins, "A design management and job assignment system," *Technical Report* NPS CS-92-020, Computer Science Department, Naval Postgraduate School, 1992.
2. V. Berzins, "On merging software extensions," *Acta Informatica*, Springer-Verlag, pp. 607–619, 1986.
3. V. Berzins, "Software merge: Semantics of combining changes to programs," *Technical Report* NPS 52-91-5, Computer Science Department, Naval Postgraduate School, 1990.
4. V. Berzins, "Software merge: Models and methods for combining changes to programs," *Journal of Systems Integration*, vol. 1, no. 2, pp. 121–141, August 1990.

5. V. Berzins and Luqi, *Software Engineering with Abstractions*. Addison-Wesley: Reading, MA, 1991.
6. V. Berzins, Luqi, and A. Yehudai, "Using transformations in specification-based prototyping," IEEE Transactions on Software Engineering, vol. 19, no. 5, pp. 436–452, May 1993.
7. N. Boudriga, F. Elloumi, and A. Mili, "On the lattice of specifications: Applications to a specification methodology," *Formal Aspects of Computing*, Springer-Verlag, vol. 4, pp.. 544-571, 1992.
8. D. Dampier, *A Model for Merging Different Versions of a PSDL Program*. Master's Thesis, Naval Postgraduate School, Monterey, California, June 1990.
9. S. Horwitz, J. Prins, and T. Reps, "Integrating non-interfering versions of programs," Conference Record of the Fifteenth ACM Symposium on Principles of Programming Languages, Association for Computing Machinery, New York, New York, pp. 133-145, 13-15 January 1988.
10. S. Horwitz, T. Reps, and D. Binkley, "Interprocedural Slicing Using Dependence Graphs," *ACM Transactions on Programming Languages and Systems*, pp. 26–60, January 1990.
11. Luqi, V. Berzins, and R. Yeh, "A Prototyping Language for Real Time Software," *IEEE Transactions on Software Engineering*, pp. 1409-1423, October 1988.
12. Luqi, "Software Evolution Through Rapid Prototyping," *IEEE Computer*, pp. 13-25, May 1989.
13. Luqi, "A Graph Model for Software Evolution," *IEEE Transaction on Software Engineering*, vol. 16, no. 8, pp. 917-927, August 1990.
14. Luqi, "Computer-Aided Prototyping for a Command-And-Control System Using CAPS," *IEEE Software*, pp. 56-67, January 1992.
15. R. Longer, H. Mill, B. Witt, Structured Programming: Theory and Practice, Addison-Wesley: Reading, MA, 1979.
16. T. Reps, and W. Yang, "The semantics of program slicing," *Computer Science Technical Report #777*, University of Wisconsin-Madison, 1988.
17. T. Reps, "On the algebraic properties of program integration," *Computer Sciences Technical Report #856*, University of Wisconsin at Madison, June 1989.
18. I. Silverberg, *Source File Management with SCCS*. Prentice Hall: Englewood Cliffs, NJ, 1992.
19. M. Tanik, and R. Yeh, "Rapid Prototyping in Software Development," *Computer*, vol. 22, pp. 9-10, May 1989.
20. W. Tichy, "Design, Implementation, and Evaluation of a Revision Control System," in *Proceedings of the 6th International Conference on Software Engineering*, IEEE, Tokyo, September 1982, pp. 58-67.
21. M. Weiser, "Program Slicing," *IEEE Transactions on Software Engineering*, vol. 10, no. 4, pp. 352-357, July 1984.

Bibliography

Recent developments and directions

Proc. ARO/AFOSR/ONR Workshop on Increasing the Practical Impact of Formal Methods for Computer-Aided Software Development: Software Slicing, Merging, and Integration, 1993, U.S. Naval Postgraduate School, Monterey, Calif.

Merging guarded fragments of while-programs

Huang, J., "State Constraints and Pathwise Decomposition of Programs," *IEEE Trans. Software Eng.,* Vol. 16, No. 8, Aug. 1990, pp. 880–896.

An improvement to (Horwitz 89) for merging changes to while-programs

Yang, W., S. Horwitz, and T. Reps, "A Program Integration Algorithm that Accommodates Semantics-Preserving Transformations," *Proc. 4th ACM SIGSOFT Symp. Software Development Environments,* ACM Press, New York, N.Y., 1990, pp. 133–143.

Merging for real-time prototypes

Dampier, D., "A Formal Method for Semantics-Based Change-Merging of Software Prototypes," PhD Thesis, Naval Postgraduate School, June 1994.

Merging for Prolog

Sterling, L., and A. Lakhotia, "Composing Prolog Meta-Interpreters," *Proc. Logic Programming 5th Int'l Conf. and Symp.,* MIT Press, Cambridge, Mass.,1988, pp. 386–403.

Mathematical merging models: Browerian algebra

Reps, T., "Algebraic Properties of Program Integration," *Science of Computer Programming,* Vol. 17, Nos. 1–3, Dec. 1991, pp. 139–215.

Aspects of software specifications related to merging

Berzins, V., and Luqi, *Software Engineering with Abstractions,* Addison-Wesley, Reading, Mass., 1991, pp. 182-188.

Berzins, V., Luqi, and A. Yehudai, "Using Transformations in Specification-Based Prototyping," *IEEE Trans. Software Eng.,* Vol. 19, No. 5, May 1993, pp. 436–452.

Bourdriga, N., F. Elloumi, and A. Mili, "On The Lattice of Specifications: Applications to a Specification Methodology," in *Formal Aspects of Computing,* Springer, New York, N.Y., 1992, pp. 544–571.

Other applications of slicing

Gallager, K., and J. Lyle, "Using Program Slicing in Software Maintenance," *IEEE Trans. Software Eng.,* Vol. 17, No. 8, Aug. 1991, pp. 751–761.

Griswold, W., "Direct Update of Data Flow Representations for a Meaning-Preserving Program Restructuring Tool," *Proc. First ACM SIGSOFT Symp. Foundations of Software Eng.,* Software Eng. Notes, Vol. 18, No. 5, ACM Press, New York, N.Y., Dec. 1993, pp. 42–55.

Gupta, R., M. Harrold, and M. Soffa, "An Approach to Regression Testing Using Slicing," *Proc. 1992 IEEE Conf. Software Maintenance,* IEEE CS Press, Los Alamitos, Calif., 1992, pp. 299–308.

Weiser, M., "Programmers Use Slices When Debugging," *Comm. ACM,* Vol. 25, No. 7, July 1982, pp. 446–452.

Slicing for specifications

Oda, T., and K. Araki, "Specification Slicing in Formal Methods of Software Development," *Proc. 17th Ann. Int'l Computer Software and Applications Conf.,* IEEE CS Press, Los Alamitos, Calif., 1993, pp. 313–319.

Experimental evaluation of dynamic slicing

Venkatesh, G., "Experimental Results from Slicing C Programs," to appear in *ACM Trans. Programming Languages and Systems,* Vol. 17, No. 2, Mar. 1995.

Optimizations for dynamic slicing

Ball, T., and J. Larus, "Optimally profiling and Tracing Programs," *Proc. Conf. Record 19th ACM Symp. Principles of Programming Languages,* ACM Press, New York, N.Y., 1992, pp. 59–70.

Choi, J., B. Miller, and R. Netzer, "Techniques for Debugging Parallel Programs with Flowback Analysis," *ACM Trans. Programming Languages and Systems,* Vol. 13, No. 4, Oct. 1991, pp. 491–530.

General background and context: software evolution and maintenance

Longstreet, D., *Software Maintenance and Computers*, IEEE CS Press, Los Alamitos, Calif., 1990.

Relation to automated configuration management

Badr, S., and Luqi, "Design Management and Job Assignment System," *Proc. 5th Int'l Conf. Software Eng. and Knowledge Eng.*, IEEE CS Press, Los Alamitos, Calif., 1993, pp. 225–227.

Badr, S., "A Model and Algorithms for a Software Evolution Control System," PhD Thesis, Computer Science Department, Naval Postgraduate School, Monterey, Calif., Dec. 1993.

Theoretical background

Linger, R.C., H.D. Mills, and B.I. Witt, *Structured Programming: Theory and Practice,* Addison-Wesley, Reading, Mass., 1979.

Scott, D., "Data Types as Lattices," *SIAM J. Computing*, Vol. 5, 1979, pp. 522–587.

About the Author

Valdis Berzins received the BS degree in physics in 1975, MS degree in electrical engineering in 1975, EE degree in electrical engineering in 1975, and PhD degree in computer science in 1979, all from MIT. Currently a Professor of Computer Science at the Naval Postgraduate School in Monterey, California, he has taught at the University of Texas and the University of Minnesota. He has developed several specification languages, software tools for computer-aided software design, and fundamental theory of software merging. He is the author of over 50 technical papers in journals and conferences, more than 70 technical reports, and many other publications, including a book on software engineering and an article in the *Encyclopedia of Computer Science and Engineering*. He is a member of the IEEE and ACM.

IEEE Computer Society Press

Press Activities Board

Vice President: Joseph Boykin, GTE Laboratories
Jon T. Butler, Naval Postgraduate School
Elliot J. Chikofsky, Northeastern University
James J. Farrell III, Motorola Corp.
I. Mark Haas, Bell Northern Research, Inc.
Ronald G. Hoelzeman, University of Pittsburgh
Gene F. Hoffnagle, IBM Corporation
John R. Nicol, GTE Laboratories
Yale N. Patt, University of Michigan
Benjamin W. Wah, University of Illinois

Press Editorial Board

Advances in Computer Science and Engineering

Editor-in-Chief: Jon T. Butler, Naval Postgraduate School
Assoc. EIC/Acquisitions: Pradip K. Srimani, Colorado State University
Dharma P. Agrawal, North Carolina State University
Ruud Bolle, IBM T.J. Watson Research Center
Vijay K. Jain, University of South Florida
Yutaka Kanayama, Naval Postgraduate School
Gerald M. Masson, The Johns Hopkins University
Sudha Ram, University of Arizona
David C. Rine, George Mason University
A.R.K. Sastry, Rockwell International Science Center
Abhijit Sengupta, University of South Carolina
Mukesh Singhal, Ohio State University
Scott M. Stevens, Carnegie Mellon University
Michael Roy Williams, The University of Calgary
Ronald D. Williams, University of Virginia
Lotfi Zadeh, University of California, Berkeley

Press Staff

T. Michael Elliott, Executive Director
H. True Seaborn, Publisher
Matthew S. Loeb, Assistant Publisher
Catherine Harris, Manager, Press Product Development
Edna Straub, Lead Production Editor
Mary E. Kavanaugh, Production Editor
Lisa O'Conner, Production Editor
Regina Spencer Sipple, Production Editor
Penny Storms, Production Editor
Robert Werner, Production Editor
Perri Cline, Electronic Publishing Manager
Frieda Koester, Marketing/Sales Manager
Thomas Fink, Advertising/Promotions Manager

Offices of the IEEE Computer Society

Headquarters Office
1730 Massachusetts Avenue, N.W.
Washington, DC 20036-1903
Phone: (202) 371-0101 — Fax: (202) 728-9614
E-mail: hq.ofc@computer.org

Publications Office
P.O. Box 3014
10662 Los Vaqueros Circle
Los Alamitos, CA 90720-1264
Membership and General Information: (714) 821-8380
Publication Orders: (800) 272-6657 — Fax: (714) 821-4010
E-mail: cs.books@computer.org

European Office
13, avenue de l'Aquilon
B-1200 Brussels, BELGIUM
Phone: 32-2-770-21-98 — Fax: 32-2-770-85-05
E-mail: euro.ofc@computer.org

Asian Office
Ooshima Building
2-19-1 Minami-Aoyama, Minato-ku
Tokyo 107, JAPAN
Phone: 81-3-408-3118 — Fax: 81-3-408-3553
E-mail: tokyo.ofc@computer.org

IEEE Computer Society

IEEE Computer Society Press Publications

CS Press publishes, promotes, and distributes over 20 original and reprint computer science and engineering texts annually. Original books consist of 100 percent original material; reprint books contain a carefully selected group of previously published papers with accompanying original introductory and explanatory text.

Submission of proposals: For guidelines on preparing CS Press books, write to Manager, Press Product Development, IEEE Computer Society Press, P.O. Box 3014, 10662 Los Vaqueros Circle, Los Alamitos, CA 90720-1264, or telephone (714) 821-8380.

Purpose

The IEEE Computer Society advances the theory and practice of computer science and engineering, promotes the exchange of technical information among 100,000 members worldwide, and provides a wide range of services to members and nonmembers.

Membership

All members receive the monthly magazine *Computer*, discounts, and opportunities to serve (all activities are led by volunteer members). Membership is open to all IEEE members, affiliate society members, and others interested in the computer field.

Publications and Activities

Computer Society On-Line: Provides electronic access to abstracts and tables of contents from society periodicals and conference proceedings, plus information on membership and volunteer activities. To access, telnet to the Internet address info.computer.org (user i.d.: guest).

***Computer* magazine:** An authoritative, easy-to-read magazine containing tutorial and in-depth articles on topics across the computer field, plus news, conferences, calendar, interviews, and product reviews.

Periodicals: The society publishes 10 magazines and seven research transactions.

Conference proceedings, tutorial texts, and standards documents: The Computer Society Press publishes more than 100 titles every year.

Standards working groups: Over 200 of these groups produce IEEE standards used throughout the industrial world.

Technical committees: Over 29 TCs publish newsletters, provide interaction with peers in specialty areas, and directly influence standards, conferences, and education.

Conferences/Education: The society holds about 100 conferences each year and sponsors many educational activities, including computing science accreditation.

Chapters: Regular and student chapters worldwide provide the opportunity to interact with colleagues, hear technical experts, and serve the local professional community.